MW01639841

Black Women Theorizing Curriculum Studies in Colour and Curves

This book explores the curriculum theorizing of Black women, as well as their historical and contemporary contributions to the always-evolving *complicated conversation* that is Curriculum Studies. It serves as an opportunity to begin a dialogue of revision and reconciliation and offers a vision for the transformation of academia's relationship with Black women as students, teachers, and theorizers.

Taking the perennial silencing of Black women's voices in academia as its impetus, the book explains how even fields like Curriculum Studies – where scholars have worked to challenge hegemony, injustice, and silence within the larger discipline of education – have struggled to identify an intellectual tradition marked by the Black, female subjectivity. This epistemic amnesia is an ongoing reminder of the strength of what bell hooks calls "imperialist white supremacist capitalist patriarchy", and the ways in which even the most critical spaces fail to recognize the contributions and even the very existence of Black women. Seeking to redress this balance, this book engages the curricular lives of Black women and girls epistemologically, bodily, experientially, and publicly.

Providing a clarion call for fellow educators to remain reflexive and committed to emancipatory aims, this book will be of interest to researchers seeking an exploration of critical voices from nondominant identities, perspectives, and concerns.

This book was originally published as a special issue of *Gender and Education*.

Kirsten T. Edwards Williams is Associate Professor and Associate Chair of Educational Leadership & Policy Studies at the University of Oklahoma, Norman, USA, where she is also Core Affiliate Faculty for Women's & Gender Studies and the Center for Social Justice.

Denise Taliaferro Baszile is Associate Professor in the Department of Educational Leadership and Associate Dean of Diversity and Student Experience for the College of Education, Health, and Society at Miami University, Ohio, USA.

Nichole A. Guillory is Professor of Curriculum & Instruction in the Department of Secondary & Middle Grades Education at Kennesaw State University, USA, where she is also Affiliate Faculty in the African and African Diaspora Studies program.

Black Women Theorizing Curriculum Studies in Colour and Curves

Edited by
Kirsten T. Edwards Williams, Denise Taliaferro Baszile and Nichole A. Guillory

LONDON AND NEW YORK

First published 2019
by Routledge
2 Park Square, Milton Park, Abingdon, Oxon OX14 4RN

and by Routledge
52 Vanderbilt Avenue, New York, NY 10017

Routledge is an imprint of the Taylor & Francis Group, an informa business

British Library Cataloguing-in-Publication Data
A catalogue record for this book is available from the British Library

ISBN13: 978-0-367-13577-5

Typeset in Myriad Pro
by codeMantra

Publisher's Note
The publisher accepts responsibility for any inconsistencies that may have arisen during the conversion of this book from journal articles to book chapters, namely the possible inclusion of journal terminology.

Disclaimer
Every effort has been made to contact copyright holders for their permission to reprint material in this book. The publishers would be grateful to hear from any copyright holder who is not here acknowledged and will undertake to rectify any errors or omissions in future editions of this book.

Contents

Citation Information

The following chapters were originally published in the journal *Gender and Education*, volume 28, issue 6 (October 2016). When citing this material, please use the original page numbering for each article, as follows:

Introduction
When, where, and why *we enter: Black women's curriculum theorising*
Kirsten T. Edwards, Denise Taliaferro Baszile and Nichole A. Guillory
Gender and Education, volume 28, issue 6 (October 2016) pp. 707–709

Chapter 1
Towards decolonial praxis: reconfiguring the human and the curriculum
Karishma Desai and Brenda Nyandiko Sanya
Gender and Education, volume 28, issue 6 (October 2016) pp. 710–724

Chapter 2
'I know what you are about to enter': lived experiences as the curricular foundation for teaching citizenship
Amanda E. Vickery
Gender and Education, volume 28, issue 6 (October 2016) pp. 725–741

Chapter 3
'You can't see for lookin'': how southern womanism informs perspectives of work and curriculum theory
Berlisha Morton
Gender and Education, volume 28, issue 6 (October 2016) pp. 742–755

Chapter 4
The Black Women's Gathering Place*: reconceptualising a curriculum of place/space*
Arianna Howard, Ashley Patterson, Valerie Kinloch, Tanja Burkhard and Ryann Randall
Gender and Education, volume 28, issue 6 (October 2016) pp. 756–768

Chapter 5
Curriculum homeplacing as complicated conversation: (re)narrating the mentoring of Black women doctoral students
Ebony C. Pope and Kirsten T. Edwards
Gender and Education, volume 28, issue 6 (October 2016) pp. 769–785

Chapter 6

Complicated contradictions amid Black feminism and millennial Black women teachers creating curriculum for Black girls
Tiffany M. Nyachae
Gender and Education, volume 28, issue 6 (October 2016) pp. 786–806

Chapter 7

Talking back in cyberspace: self-love, hair care, and counter narratives in Black adolescent girls' YouTube vlogs
Robin J. Phelps-Ward and Crystal T. Laura
Gender and Education, volume 28, issue 6 (October 2016) pp. 807–820

The following chapters were originally published in the journal *Gender and Education*, volume 30, issue 2 (March 2018). When citing this material, please use the original page numbering for each article, as follows:

Chapter 8

Super-Girl: strength and sadness in Black girlhood
Nia Michelle Nunn
Gender and Education, volume 30, issue 2 (March 2018) pp. 239–258

Chapter 12

Curriculum as colour and curves: a synthesis of Black theory, design and creativity realised as critical curriculum writing
Lucinda McKnight
Gender and Education, volume 30, issue 2 (March 2018) pp. 222–238

The following chapters were originally published in the journal *Gender and Education*, volume 30, issue 3 (April 2018). When citing this material, please use the original page numbering for each article, as follows:

Chapter 9

Reparative readings: re-claiming black feminised bodies as sites of somatic pleasures and possibilities
Esther O. Ohito and Shenila Khoja-Moolji
Gender and Education, volume 30, issue 3 (April 2018) pp. 277–294

Chapter 10

Mapping the margins and searching for higher ground: examining the marginalisation of black female graduate students at PWIs
Dari Green, Tifanie Pulley, Melinda Jackson, Lori Latrice Martin and Kenneth J. Fasching-Varner
Gender and Education, volume 30, issue 3 (April 2018) pp. 295–309

Chapter 13

Black women's bodies, ideology, and the public curriculum of the pro- and anti-choice movements in the US
Maria del Guadalupe Davidson
Gender and Education, volume 30, issue 3 (April 2018) pp. 310–321

The following chapter was originally published in the journal *Gender and Education*, volume 29, issue 3 (2017). When citing this material, please use the original page numbering for the article, as follows:

Chapter 11

Revealing a hidden curriculum of Black women's erasure in sexual violence prevention policy
Sara Carrigan Wooten
Gender and Education, volume 29, issue 3 (2017) pp. 405–417

For any permission-related enquiries please visit:
http://www.tandfonline.com/page/help/permissions

Notes on Contributors

Denise Taliaferro Baszile's research focuses on understanding curriculum as racial/gendered text with an emphasis on disrupting traditional modes of knowledge production, validation, and representation. Her scholarship draws on curriculum theory, critical race theory, and Black feminist theory.

Tanja Burkhard's research centers on the intersections of race, gender, and migration, particularly from a women-of-color feminist and anti-colonial perspective.

Maria del Guadalupe Davidson's research interests include rhetorical theory, Black feminist subjectivity, and women and gender studies.

Karishma Desai's research interests include the politics of education, the practice and politics of teachers, and curriculum theory.

Kirsten T. Edwards Williams' research merges philosophies of higher education, college curriculum, and pedagogy. She is interested in the ways that sociocultural identity and context influence teaching and learning in postsecondary education.

Kenneth J. Fasching-Varner is Research Associate at Louisiana State University, Baton Rouge, USA, and is a critical race and sociocultural foundations scholar whose focus is on equity and social justice in (inter)national and institutional contexts.

Dari Green's research focuses on issues of equity, which, broadly defined, includes issues of social justice, fairness, and equality of access and opportunity, race and ethnicity, social inequality, community, and culture.

Nichole A. Guillory's research interests include curriculum and education, hip-hop theory, hip-hop feminism, and Curriculum Theory and Teacher Education.

Arianna Howard is Founder and Principal Consultant of Plant-A-Seed Educational Consulting. She coaches urban high school teachers, encouraging them to explore implicit biases and the ways these biases influence interactions with and expectations of urban youth.

Melinda Jackson is Research Associate at Louisiana State University, Baton Rouge, USA. Her research interests include race theory, sociology, and race and ethnicity within education.

Shenila Khoja-Moolji's work examines the interplay of gender, race, religion, and power in transnational contexts, particularly in relation to Muslim populations, and combines historical and cultural studies with ethnographic work to examine the construction of the figure of the 'educated girl' in colonial India and postcolonial Pakistan.

Valerie Kinloch's scholarship examines the literacies of youth and adults inside and outside schools, with attention placed on race, place, literacy, and equity. She is a past recipient of the Outstanding Book of the Year Award from the American Educational Research Association and the Rewey Belle Inglis Award for Outstanding Women in English Education from the National Council of Teachers of English.

Crystal T. Laura's work has focused on the social foundations of education, diversity, and equity in schools, and building the capacity of educational leaders to address the school-to-prison pipeline.

Lori Latrice Martin's research interests include race and ethnicity, demography, Black ethnicity, wealth inequality and asset poverty, race and sports, school-to-prison pipeline, and race and education.

Lucinda McKnight's research interests are in the intersections of gender, race, neoliberal policy, and education, and how these are enacted in curriculum design.

Berlisha Morton is an intellectual activist, performance artist, and afro-futurista who studies and performs Blackness. Her scholarship and art are driven by a desire to communicate the contributions of women to discourse on art and education.

Nia Michelle Nunn is committed to learning and engaging audiences creatively and intensely through music, education, scholarship, and activism. Her research focuses on anti-racist feminist pedagogy, Black girl empowerment/emancipatory learning, and performing arts/human rights curriculum development.

Tiffany M. Nyachae's current research interests include supporting the ideological becoming, racial literacy, and social justice teaching of urban teachers committed to social justice and educating students of color for liberation.

Esther O. Ohito is an interdisciplinary Black feminist scholar concerned chiefly with race and gender issues that reside at the nexus of curriculum, pedagogy, embodiment, and emotion. Her publications have appeared in journals such as *Gender and Education*.

Ashley Patterson has experience teaching a variety of courses addressing literacy issues through a social justice lens. Her research focuses on the intersection of identity and educational experiences as she considers the influence of race and other identity markers on both learners and learning spaces.

Robin J. Phelps-Ward's research focuses specifically on mentoring and formal mentoring programs to support students of color, Black faculty and staff belonging, Black women and girls' natural hair and identity development, and pedagogical practices for critical consciousness and social justice.

Ebony C. Pope is Instructor of Expository Writing and teaches argumentative writing to first-year students through the interrogation of race and power through higher education schooling. Her work is centered on multiple critical approaches to exploring Black women and girls' experiences in education and communal spaces.

Tifanie Pulley's primary research interest involves examining the intersectionality of race, gender, and class in the academy. Her publications include "Death by Residential Segregation and the Post Racial Myth", with Lori Martin and Kenneth Fasching-Varner in *Violence Against Black Bodies* with Routledge.

Ryann Randall shares her passion for issues related to diversity, equity, inclusion, and social justice with faculty, staff, and students, and is Research Associate of the Multicultural and Equity Studies in Education program in the Department of Teaching and Learning.

Brenda Nyandiko Sanya's research interests concern transnational perspectives on Black subjectivity, the function of education in determining citizenship and immigration rights, and feminist/queer epistemologies.

Amanda E. Vickery's research interests include utilizing experiential and community knowledge to reconceptualize the construct of citizenship, social and urban education, and social studies and practice.

Sara Carrigan Wooten's research interests include the intersections of higher education policy, campus rape culture, feminist post-structuralism, queer theory, and critical race theory.

INTRODUCTION

When, where, and *why* we enter: Black women's curriculum theorising

Kirsten T. Edwards, Denise Taliaferro Baszile and Nichole A. Guillory

> For people of color have always theorized – but in forms quite different from the Western form of abstract logic. And I am inclined to say that our theorizing (and I intentionally use the verb and not the noun) is often in narrative forms, in the stories we create, in the riddles and proverbs, in the play with language because dynamic rather than fixed ideas seem more to our liking. How else have we managed to survive with such spiritedness the assault on our bodies, social institutions, countries and our humanity? – Christian (1996)

From the slave woman quoted in Gerda Lerner's *Black Women in White America* to the likes of Anna Julia Cooper, Ida B. Wells, Barbara Christian, bell hooks, Angela Davis, and Patricia Hill Collins among others, Black women's theorising has contributed in significant ways to thinking through the dilemmas of education, liberation, and democracy. And although their voices are sometimes whispered into academic conversations, the depth and breadth of Black women's contributions has yet to be represented as a significant and collective body of work. Furthermore, the models of recognition, the ways in which the academy defines theory, research, and practice rarely allow for the boundary-crossing practices of Black women scholars. The counterhegemonic and counter-intellectual spaces that Black women are compelled to produce continue to exist as illegible.

While the academy has maintained a habitus of erasure in relation to the dispossessed (Franco 1994), particularly as it concerns Black women, resistant spaces have emerged. Curriculum Studies has for several decades worked to challenge hegemony, injustice, and silence within the larger discipline of education. Borrowing from sociological, philosophical, cultural, theological, and historical criticism, the field has positioned itself as an ever-present clarion call for fellow educators to remain reflexive and committed to the emancipatory aims of our vocation (Pinar et al. 2008). Nevertheless, while occupying a critical and sometimes marginal space, Curriculum Studies, like other fields, struggles to identify an intellectual tradition marked by Black female subjectivity. Our field's epistemic amnesia is an ongoing reminder of the strength of 'imperialist white supremacist capitalist patriarchy' (hooks 2015, 1), and the ways in which even the most critical spaces fail to recognise the contributions, and even the very existence, of Black women.

Even today as curriculum theorists frame curricular texts as racialised, gendered, sexualised, and classed, the canonical family tree continues to be centred primarily by dominant identities, perspectives, and concerns. These perennial silences mark the impetus for this special issue. We, the special issue editors, are primarily concerned with representing the curriculum theorising of Black women; with mining their historical and contemporary contributions to the always evolving *complicated conversation* that is curriculum studies. We have attempted to craft this platform as an opportunity to begin/continue a dialogue of revision and reconciliation. While we focus on Curriculum Studies, challenging the field to rise to its highest ideals, there is an explicit vision for transforming the discipline of education and the academy writ large in regards to its relationship with Black women students, teachers, and theorisers.

To this end, this special issue of 'Curriculum in Colour and Curves' and further articles in up-coming issues of *Gender and Education*, addresses five primary themes that engage the curricular lives of Black women and girls epistemologically, bodily, experientially, and publicly. The special issue begins with Desai and Sanya, and Vickery *troubling foundational notions* of the human and citizenship. By applying the theoretical offerings and experiential realities of Black women scholars, they call attention to the ways dominant frames write out the lives of Black women. They also offer 'reconfigur[ations]' (Desai & Sanya, *this issue*) rooted in Black feminised (re)conceptualizations that promote the formation of a more humane citizenry.

Morton; Howard, Patterson, Kinloch, Burkhard, and Randall; and Pope and Edwards extend Pinar (1991) and Ng-A-Fook's (2007) work by theorising Black feminised *curricula of place*. Morton roots her analysis in the physical space Black women occupy in the US Deep South. Howard et al. consider the supportive cultural and epistemic space Black women create in community. Pope and Edwards similarly take up these considerations as they emerge in the context of Black women's mentoring relationships. Both Howard et al. and Pope and Edwards' articles excavate the challenges to and necessity of doing this work within an academic context of oppression.

Pope and Edwards' attention to the development of the next generation of healthy, whole, resistant Black women theorists sets the stage for Phelps-Ward and Laura and Nyachae's respective articles exploring the beauty and tragedy of *Black girlhood*. Phelps-Ward and Laura's study reveals the innovative ways Black girls carve out space for themselves in cyber-space. Nyachae makes transparent the contradictory messages that are often embedded in curriculum designed for Black girls by millennial Black women teachers. She suggests that the lack of exposure to Black feminism and Black women's theorizations in their own curriculum studies can impede their efforts to cultivate counter-curricular spaces for their Black girl students.

Subsequent articles will continue the curriculum theorising of Black girlhood. In addition, the remaining themes will be addressed: *Black women collegians* and *public discourse as public curriculum about Black women*. We look forward to continuing this complicated conversation in colour and curves.

Disclosure statement

No potential conflict of interest was reported by the authors.

References

Christian, B. 1996. "The Race for Theory." In *Radically Speaking: Feminism Reclaimed*, edited by D. Bell and Re. Klein, 311–320. North Melbourne: Spinifex Press.

Franco, J. 1994. "Beyond Ethnocentrism: Gender, Power and the Third-world Intelligentsia." In *Marxism and the Interpretation of Culture*, edited by C. Nelson and L. Grossberg, 503–509. Urbana, IL: University of Illinois Press.

hooks, b. 2015. *Understanding Patriarchy*. No Borders: Louisville's Radical Lending Library. http://imaginenoborders.org/pdf/zines/UnderstandingPatriarchy.pdf.

Pinar, W. F., W. M. Reynolds, P. Slattery, and P. M. Taubman 2008. *Understanding Curriculum*. New York: Peter Lang.

Ng-A-Fook, N. 2007. *An Indigenous Curriculum of Place: The United Houma Nation's Contentious Relationship with Louisiana's Educational Institutions* (Vol. 25). New York: Peter Lang.

Pinar, W. F. 1991. "Curriculum As Social Psychoanalysis: On the Significance of Place." In *Curriculum as Social Psychoanalysis: The Significance of Place*, edited by J. L. Kincheloe and W. F. Pinar, 165–186. Albany: State University of New York Press.

Towards decolonial praxis: reconfiguring the human and the curriculum

Karishma Desai and Brenda Nyandiko Sanya

ABSTRACT
This theoretical inquiry applies threads of Sylvia Wynter's intellectual project to scholarship in curriculum studies to consider how Wynter's insights might urge new potential in educational theorising and practice. The central concern driving Wynter's intellectual project is that our present understanding about what it means to be human is entrenched in epistemological legacies of colonialism that preserve a Western bourgeois genre of Man. This essay begins by detailing Sylvia Wynter's rigorous and innovative intellectual project that reworks the category of the human. We argue that contemporary curriculum is based upon this Western genre of the human and explore the limits of multicultural curricula. Synthesising Wynter's interrelated lines of thought – how the notion of being hybridly human calls forth a conceptualisation of humanness as a collective act – we argue that her revised category of the human is a necessary means to radically reimagine and decolonise curriculum.

> … to give humanness a different future, itself historically chartered by that past. (Sylvia Wynter; quoted in Wynter and McKittrick 2015, 73)

Sylvia Wynter's dense, lush intellectual, and creative corpus spans a range of disciplinary perspectives and topics. A focal node that cuts across this body of work is her concerted labour to rethink the ontology of the human by unsettling the epistemological assumptions embedded in our current definitions of Man. She does this by unearthing the knowledge(s) buried in the histories of the ex-slave archipelago in the tradition of Caribbean diasporic scholars.[1] Sylvia Wynter is a Cuban-born Jamaican scholar who began her professional life in the performing arts as a dancer, actress, and playwright. Wynter, who is a highly esteemed professor and critical theorist, stepped into academia through her creative writing and political engagements, and has since contributed tremendously to antiracist and decolonial thought. As a preeminent scholar on theories of the human, Wynter's scholarship stretches outside of the Caribbean, the Americas and has global resonance in anticolonial discourses. Wynter's insistence that the colonisation of the field of knowledge is enmeshed with the long history of Western imperialism provides an opening to explore what Joyce E. King has described as 'social contradictions involved in education under conditions of racial domination' (1992, 320). The recent turn to Sylvia Wynter, Frantz Fanon, and Hortense Spillers by scholars in the humanities and interpretive social sciences[2] has revived 'the interrogation of the "human" as a technology of racialization' (Luciano and Chen 2015, 187). These scholars address questions of the human, what it means to be (non)human, and the significance of a humanistic turn. In contrast to anti-humanist theorists who wish to discard notions of the human because of its located-ness within racial colonial structures and liberal humanism, Wynter insists rather, that the category should be revised (Scott 2000; Weheliye 2014).

Consistent with the invaluable traditions of Black women's intellectual labour and its influence on education, this essay engages Sylvia Wynter's theorisation of the human to illustrate how her scholarship forwards a necessary means to radically reimagine curriculum. Wynter's unsettling of the category of the human elicits

> a sense that in every form that is being inscripted, each of us is also in that form, even though we do not experience it. So the human story/history becomes the collective story/history of these multiple forms of self-inscription or self-instituted genres, with each form/genre being adaptive to its situation, ecological, geopolitical. (Scott 2000; as cited in McKittrick 2015, 3)

Engaging in a reparative reading (Sedgwick 1997), Wynter simultaneously historicises how our contemporary view of being human has gained prominence, and recovers Black embodied knowledge that has been pushed to the margins. In doing so, she forwards humanness as a collective body as opposed to an individual autonomous entity, and firmly claims that *being human is praxis* (McKittrick 2015). She argues that specifically located narratives, origin myths, and constructed cosmogonies connect particular human beings with one another and these stories are employed to associate as members of a specific group (class, ethnicity, clan, etc.) or what she calls genre-specific modes of being human. Wynter reminds us even as race is a social construct, it is also 'lodged in the body' (Marriott 2015, 1). Underscoring the significance of Fanon's (2008) revolutionary insights of skin/masks, she insists that Black embodied knowledge, that is, the experiential knowledge that an individual derives as a raced and gendered body has been undervalued though essential. She thereby 'disentangles Man from the human in order to use the space of those subjects placed beyond the grasp of this domain as a vital point from which to invent hitherto unavailable genres of the human' (Weheliye 2008, 323). She contends that while individuals may not explicitly experience other genres of the human, each individual is interwoven in and with the other. This reparative reading compels new ways of imagining curriculum that educates towards deep and active interconnectivity.

Our paper, therefore, is a theoretical inquiry that applies threads of Sylvia Wynter's intellectual project to scholarship in curriculum studies to consider how these insights might urge new potential in educational theorising and practice. Specifically, our analysis lifts themes derived from her revisioning of the human that we find productive for reimagining possibilities in and through curriculum. We begin by discussing how Sylvia Wynter's scholarship is situated within the legacies of anticolonial movements, and a decolonial paradigm. The next section details Wynter's interrogation of the Western genre of man and her reconceptualisation of the human. We consider what Wynter means by 'hybridly human' and how this leads to imagining new ways of relating to our social and natural world. Next, we consider the current neoliberal context of education, and argue that what is deemed worthwhile curricular knowledge, and attempts to diversify curriculum, are based upon the Western genre of Man. Following this, we synthesise Wynter's interrelated lines of thought – how the notion of hybridly human calls forth a conceptualisation of humanness as a collective act – and apply this to curriculum to consider the potential for decolonised curriculum when thinking with a new genre of human. We engage these decolonial arguments to consider the radical possibilities for curricula if the hegemonic genre of human is unsettled and rearticulated.

A decolonial intervention

Sylvia Wynter's work is situated within a tradition of anticolonial and decolonial thought. Along the lines of Franz Fanon, CLR James, Aime Cesaire, and Antonio Cabral, Wynter's epistemological concerns and contributions are significantly shaped by her deep involvement in anticolonial struggles. Whereas postcolonial and decolonial theoretical paradigms both draw on anticolonial movements, they diverge, and we maintain that Wynter's work is a decolonial intervention. Sylvia Wynter has often called postcolonialism into question suggesting that the space for imagining otherwise is missing; she also probes postcolonial scholarship's heavy reliance on European scholars such as Lacan, Foucault, and Derrida. Or as noted by Scott (1999), in postcolonial critique's attempt to maintain antiessentialist orientation, it has in fact, essentialised the colonial/anticolonial historical moment by highlighting how this moment answered questions about colonialism, decolonisation, and emancipation.

While anticolonial movements informed postcolonial and decolonial paradigms, the project of decoloniality involves a double gesture. First, it calls for the re-embodiment and relocation of thought in order to unmask the limited situation of modern epistemologies and their linkages with coloniality. Second, it demands delinking oneself from these knowledge systems and reimagining present-futures (Mignolo 2007). The decolonial orientation counters the Cartesian paradigm that assumes thinking comes before being and argues that 'it is a racially marked body in a geo-historical marked space that feels the urge or get the call to speak, to articulate, in whatever semiotic system, the urge that makes of living organisms "human" beings' (Mignolo 2009, 2). Accordingly, the decolonial framework engenders 'epistemic disobedience' (Mignolo 2009). Epistemic disobedience calls for careful attention to the silences of Western epistemologies, the excavation of those silences, and affirms the epistemic rights of the margins.

Re-visioning the genre of human

Wynter's intellectual labour has been centred on unpacking and theorising what it means to be human. She illustrates how notions of the human are entrenched in epistemological legacies of colonialism that preserve a Western bourgeois genre of Man (Scott 2000; Weheliye 2014; McKittrick 2015). These epistemological legacies are consequence of the processes of coloniality, a concept that Mignolo (2007) suggests moves beyond the historical project of colonialism and imperialism. Rather, coloniality is an epistemological frame that binds these historical projects to contemporary times in an integral way. Coloniality recognises how colonial power relations left lasting marks in the areas of authority, sexuality, knowledge, economy, and in our naturalised understanding of what it means to be human. Decoloniality, then, requires delinking from coloniality and modernity, which is Wynter's fierce endeavour in her retheorisation of the human.

In her foundational text *Unsettling the Coloniality of Being/Power/Truth/Freedom: Towards the Human, After Man, Its Overrepresentation – An Argument*, Wynter posits that the modern conception of Man is overrepresented as *the* way of being human, and thereby maintains a hierarchical ordering of humanness. Specifically, the construction of Man, derived from Christian theology, secular philosophy, and Western sciences, is equated to and normalised as the correct and only way of being human. By synthesising the development of the natural sciences, history, and theological thought, Wynter illustrates how our present-day understanding of the human is based on the Western genres of human which she conceptualises as Man 1 and Man 2, constructs that have developed in tandem with theology, science, and the formation of the modern nation state. She traces the development of Man 1 by noting how Copernicus' declaration that the Earth moves countered the Christian theological premise that the Earth was fixed at the centre of the Universe as the location of the fallen Adam. This declaration that occurred during the Renaissance revalorised the Latin- Christian *homo religiousus* into *homo politicus,* a figure of Man governed by science, reason, and the state which also opened up space for Darwinian origin stories and categorisations (Wynter 1995). The enacting of a secular liberal conception of human that was developed in the latter half of the nineteenth century, Man 2 or *homo oeconomicus*, largely based on the idea that humanness is based on accumulation.

She destabilises the genre of Man by examining epistemological shifts in modern thought and analyses colonialism as economic, cultural, and symbolic assemblages of power that have produced and naturalised unequal racialised categories distinguishing the rational/irrational; haves/have-nots; and human/sub-human (Wynter 2003; da Silva 2015). The colonial project partakes in the sedimentation of racial difference as a signification of humanness, and therein, Wynter perceives 'coloniality as the juridical-economic referent of racial difference' (da Silva 2015, 91). The two descriptive statements of the human generated from the colonial project that, as detailed above marks the significance of the state and the law in contemporary times in upholding racial categories.

In her quest to revise the genre of Man and therefore, the practice of being human, Wynter draws on the concept of hybridity specifically theorised by Franz Fanon to pose possible *ways out* of the Western conception of Man. That is, Wynter posits that what is at stake in her theoretical investments is not the inclusion of

> the oppressed within the already existing strictures of liberal humanism, or conversely, to abolish humanism because of its racio-colonial baggage; instead Wynter insists on reinventing the foundational building blocks of the human at the juncture of the culture and biology feedback loop. (Weheliye 2008, 323).

Specifically, she expands Fanon's notion of sociogeny articulating what semiotician Walter Mignolo calls a 'decolonial scientia' (2015, 116), or theoretical ways of knowing about existence that are lodged in the experiences of the imperial Other. It is 'the project of decolonial scientia … recontextualizes our global nodes of space, time, and subjectivity' (117). Accordingly, it reimagines the links between geo-political histories and knowledge production. Decolonial scientia examines the embodied consequences of Western expansion, and urges the creation of communities in which life as opposed to economic profit prevails.

In contrast to the biocentric scientific frame that defines the order of knowledge governing our understanding of the human, Fanon (1952) theorises that, skins (pylogeny, ontogeny) and masks (sociogeny), or redefined by Wynter as *bios* and *mythios*, together constitute our humanness. This in turn marks our hybridness as beings. Sociogeny, according to Wynter is linked with the neuro-biological processes of evolutionary development (phylogeny) and ontogeny (Wynter 1995, 2003). Accordingly, there is an active relationship between our genetic and non-genetic codes informing our subjective self-understanding and our understanding of a shared group identity, which provides a sense of belonging to a specific place and community. This interaction is one in which bios or genetic codes neurochemically inscribes what Wynter calls the 'second set of instructions' or the creation stories and myths for particular humans.

Therefore, the bio-origin narrative (*mythios*) guides post-Enlightenment Westernized liberalism, and now a neoliberal economically driven genre of human which Wynter terms *homo oeconomicus.* This genre of the human has naturalised micro and macro injustices. Micro injustices are seen in assumptions about what is knowledge, who can and does produce knowledge, and who is disenfranchised through micro-aggressions and hidden curriculums. On the macro level, violences enacted by the state are individually and communally debilitating, yet they remain, as they are economically generative for private enterprise and national economies. These injustices are as prevalent as the school-to-prison pipeline, prison-industrial complex, and the ever-shrinking labour protections for workers. Those who are considered outside the realm of the 'human' as designated by the Western liberal human are perceived as and perceive themselves to be sub-human. In these debates, Wynter refuses to entirely deny or erase with the category of the human; rather, she calls for a transformation of the category away from Western universalising humanism.

The unconscious act of perceiving oneself as Other based upon the experiential knowledge that one is seen as sub-human by imperial eyes causes dissonance that generates the diasporic subject's (in this case, Fanon's) subjective experience. Yet, this very awareness of the sociogenic principle has potential to generate decolonial personhoods. This decolonial scientia then synthesises and necessitates the dismembering of naturalised spatial, chronological, and subjective nodes as it exposes global linkages across history, the centring of life over economic gain, and therefore the recognition that local responses to a global order are insufficient.

The ontological stance of being 'hybridly human' centres blackness as the subjective, embodied, and symbolic site from which the human can be rearticulated through 'relationality and interhuman narratives' (McKittrick 2015, 2). This ontological orientation enables communal and interrelated ways of understanding life and addressing urgent global concerns. Wynter posits that anticolonial and antiapartheid resistance to the hierarchical world system institutionalised by the ex-slave archipelago were not solely economic struggles. Rather, these movements perhaps marked a desire to overhaul the *homo oeconomicus* genre of the human altogether (Scott 2000).

Divesting man: beyond multicultural curriculum

What is deemed worthwhile curricular knowledge is rooted in how the human is conceptualised. This normalised notion of the human rooted in legacies of colonialism has shaped curricula and the study of curriculum for the last century, informing what knowledge is considered valuable, this teaching us what we should strive for. Neoliberalism has saturated the world since 1970s, as a discourse, and practice, not only in economics, but in almost every aspect of social life (Ong 2006). Neoliberalism, takes in the forms of 'deregulation, privatization, and withdrawal of the state from many aspects of social provision' (Harvey 2005, 3) to enhance competition and innovation in service of economic growth. According to neoliberal reasoning, markets must be created in areas that 'markets do not exist,' including education (Harvey 2005, 2).

Dominant curriculum is derived from, normalises, and preserves *homo oeconomicus,* an individualised, accumulation-oriented Western genre of human based on free-market capitalism. As Popkewitz and Brennan note, it is essential to consider how power/knowledge dynamics inform educational spaces because 'knowledge [defined by power relationships] has a material element in social life' (1997, 288). Specifically, Popkewitz emphasises that curriculum is 'particular, *historically* formed knowledge that inscribes rules and standards by which we "reason" about the world and our "self" as a productive member of that world' (1997, 132, *emphasis added*). Thereby curricula are technologies of social regulation that discipline our ontological understandings of the Self and Other.

The reasoning that directs the differential distribution of knowledge and how value is ascribed to different knowledges, Wynter would argue, is rooted in the epistemological order produced by colonialism and sustained in its legacies. The *homo oeconomicus* genre is preserved by high-stakes testing and technically oriented pedagogy (Pinar 2004). Educational philosopher Lewis (2009) names these educative practices 'necropedagogy,' pedagogical processes governed by neoliberal human capital logics based on cost-benefit analysis regarding the payoffs of educating certain bodies over others, and thereby excluding and neglecting certain bodies. Necropedagogy, then, has the tendency to instrumentalise students.

Even efforts to represent and engage knowledge systems outside of the Western cultural model, such as multicultural education, have perpetuated racism and orientalism (McCarthy 1994). While educational scholarship has attended to colonial influences on ways of knowing and on school curriculum (Willinsky 1998; Andreotti 2006), Wynter's intervention that considers *how* genres of human were developed and sustained adds an essential dimension to deconstructing and revisioning curriculum.

Wynter's anticolonial analyses, which offer a fundamental revision of the category of 'race' in the construction of the human, illustrate and extend possibilities for liberatory learning through the quest for ontological sovereignty. Her scholarship offers invaluable resources to trouble efforts of inclusion, suggesting that they often produce exclusion. For example, in *Do Not Call Us Negros* (1992), Wynter questions the efficacy of commonplace multicultural curricula, raising questions about representation versus historical excavations that provide historical realities that create 'a total abjection of being' (Scott 2000, 188) among minoritised students. She states,

> I knew nothing about my own historical reality, except in negative terms that would have made it normal for me, as Fanon points out, both to want to be a British subject and, in so

> wanting, to be anti-black, anti-everything I existentially was. I knew what it was to experience a total abjection of being. (Scott 2000, 188)

Wynter pushes us to re-construct curricula, holding in tension our knowledge of how education curricula construct subjects and shapes their differential relationships to the state based upon assumptions about their relative humanness.

Multicultural curricula that fail to unsettle Eurocentricism centre the Western idea of Man and construct the 'Other' in contrast. Often, multicultural curricula are what Ahmed (2012) has called 'a nonperformative commitment to diversity.' That is, they have an impression of commitment to diversity without action. Citing Judith Butler, 'performativity must be understood not as a singular or deliberate "act," but, rather, as the reiterative and citational practice by which discourse produces *the effects that it names*' (1993, 2, *Ahmed's emphasis*), Ahmed argues that those who work toward institutional (we read curricular) diversity, are practitioners working '*with* as well as *in* the gap between words and deeds' (Ahmed 2012, 116). However, the curriculum becomes a site that naturalises Eurocentric ontology. Multicultural curricula often work to reinvest learners in liberal humanism by including violent colonial histories merely as symbolic representation, as opposed to encouraging inquiries that distill consequences of colonialism and imperialism (Wynter 1992). Therein, Wynter's decolonial ontology unsettles the multicultural call to solely integrate students lived realities into the curriculum or to examine the histories of pre-colonial societies in the global South.

A multicultural curricular approach framed by Eurocentrism fails to acknowledge the insidious presence of global capitalism. Eurocentrism is ingrained in the European colonial project in Africa, Asia, the Caribbean, and the Americas, and is part of larger interrelated global processes, two of which are important for our argument: first the establishment of capitalist accumulation through enslaved, free or cheap labour, leading to the control of economic markets; and second, the control of knowledge centres based on the 'Western Idea of Man' (Wynter 2003), by ascribing rationality/humanity to Westerners and irrationality/savagery to non-Westerners. Consequently, Eurocentrism (implicitly read as superiority) is not simply historical, but rather a sustained racial-economic ideology reinforced in modern and contemporary configurations of race and racism. Wynter pushes for a humanism that is critically aware of these difficult histories, and centres Black ontologies. Wynter reminds us, that it is not that curriculum completely ignores colonialism and racial enslavement; rather the inclusion interprets colonialism and slavery as processes that were left in a dark chapter. The persistent violences and reverberations of these processes that were not shaken off with emancipation, or political independence are occluded. When Native American dispossession or enslavement of Africans is treated as a dark moment that ends with the obtainment of legal citizenship, continued structural violences are often obscured. Furthermore, textbooks confine these histories into small sections that fulfil the 'multicultural lesson.' Multicultural curriculum, in this form, conceals the knowledges, ideologies, and privileges that abide. These forms of 'multicultural inclusion' are treated as a solution to critiques of Eurocentric curriculum.

This kind of multicultural approach distracts from the more important conversation, one that moves from history depicted as marginalised groups demanding representation (Wynter 1992), towards clearer rubrics to understand globalisation when manifested in the imprisonment, suffering, and death of migrants at the hands of nation-states, and the internal strife witnessed in state force used against marginalised populations. For instance, Wynter describes how the Civil Rights Movement[3] was an example of a sustained push for reorganisation of systems of knowledge (Wynter 1992, 11). However, this restructuring can be re-interrogated through the lens of the much-publicised state violence. While the Civil Rights Movement successfully demanded political rights (e.g. voting rights), and brought some reprieve from state violence, it also led to the rise of ideas about cultural difference. Also elided in most curricula on 'civil rights' is that the limited conception of 'rights' fails to address: what are these rights? What epistemic foundation are these rights based on? who has these rights and who should be afforded them? What tension exists between the de facto and *de jure* allocation of these rights? These questions provide gaps that limit the significance of the movement and its representation in curriculum.

During the 1930s and 1940s, African-American leaders collaborated with anticolonial allies in Africa, Asia, the Caribbean, and Latin America to pursue an expansive set of human rights.[4] This turn to human rights provided a collaborative groundwork for the resistance to complex 'global *intimacies*' (Lowe 2006, 192) seen in the 'sometimes overlapping, struggles for freedom, full citizenship, and self-determination' that were galvanised at the 1955 Asian-African Conference of Nonaligned Nations held in Bandung, Indonesia. The 1950s saw a rise in transnational collaborations located at the interstices of political struggle articulated at Bandung, where 'the so-called darker races of the world sought to attain juridical independence' (Kelley 2002; Wilkins 2006, 192–193; Iton 2008). These actions had reverberating implications on the African and Asian continents. And as Lorraine Hansberry argued, 'the sweep of national independence movements globally was inextricably linked to the political initiatives of Black Americans engaged in similar, and sometimes overlapping, struggles for freedom, full citizenship, and self-determination' (Wilkins 2006, 192). The documented histories in textbooks and the mediated historical memories of the Civil Rights Movement represent a fraction of the broad organising principles that took decades to build, and were global in their reach. As such, the *broader* conception of global 'human rights' was replaced by a *limited* conception of 'civil rights,' which we read as a turning away from 'the human' in favour of an even more limited category: 'American' or the national citizen. Furthermore, the political solidarities cultivated between African-Americans and anticolonial struggles in the global South are hardly explored in curriculum about the Civil Rights Movement.

This perspective represents an example of how 'major conflicts and compromises among groups with competing visions of "legitimate" knowledge and what is a "just" society inform curriculum'. Curriculum theorist Apple continues, noting '... such conflicts have deep roots in conflicting views of racial, class, and gender justice in education and the larger society ... ' (2000, 230). These debates persist and are part of the whitewashed, inclusive, multicultural histories that pick and choose aspects of the Civil Rights Movements as tools to dismantle present movements for liberation that are of the same historical trajectory. Aspects of historical liberation movements (such as what means and processes led to certain outcomes) get elided in these selective 'civil rights' curricula, and these histories are then deployed in the service of either erasing or actually demonising contemporary movements. One can only imagine how different civil rights curricula would if they started out with questions about what it means to be human and not as a moment in history, with a movement whose work is complete. However, multi-culturalism became the response and as Wynter explains,

> Multiculturalism can seem to be an attractive answer to the particularism of the Euro-Immigrant perspective from which the present textbooks are written ... Rather than seeking to reinvent our present cultural native model, the multi-culturalism alternative seeks to 'save' the nation model by multiculturalizing it. It does not move outside the conceptual field of our present EuroAmerican cultural model. (Wynter 1992, 16)

Scholars like Weheliye, following Wynter, see the reimagining of the terms of the human as a struggle against the way in which 'structures, discourses, and institutions ... detain black life and thought within the strictures of particularity' (2008, 332). This revisioning is neither a call not to include the excluded other from traditional universalising concepts of humanism nor is it a call to dismantle humanism.

Curricular futurities

> In every human order there are always going to be some groups for whom knowledge of the totality is necessary, seeing that it is only with knowledge of the totality that their dispossession can be brought to an end.
> – Sylvia Wynter. (Scott 2000, 188)

Curriculum is informed by how we understand what it means to be human and what we hope for our collective future. Therefore, employing Sylvia Wynter's anticolonial theorising of the human also decolonises what counts as valuable and desirable knowledge. Therein, her intellectual project powerfully imagines new knowledge mappings that can imagine and sustain decolonial personhoods. In what follows, we provide examples of this etched in her work.

In addition to Fanon, Wynter draws on Aimé Césaire, to propose that we are hybrdily human as explicated in the previous section. She contends that this is empirically illustrated in the Blombos Cave in South Africa where archaeologists found ochre engravings made in what seems to be an art workshop and shells that evidence communal cooking, what she marks is the Third Event. Wynter suggests that the ochre symbolises menstrual blood; therefore, in this ritual, the first form, or biological life is translated into symbolic life, which she calls *homo narrans*, the human being as mythmaker or storyteller, and therefore the significance of telling our worlds. Through this example, what Wynter proposes, then, is that individually born biological life is transformed into the 'genre specific communal referent-we of symbolic life' (Wynter and McKittrick 2015, 68). And, therefore the archaeological remains evoke the truth of solidarity, considering this initiation ritual illustrates that 'we are reborn of the same origin story rather than of the womb ... therefore, each such genre-specific displacement/replacement origin narrative would have imperatively functioned ... against their individual subjects, giving priority instead to the genetically encoded innate interests of one's kin ... ' (Wynter and McKittrick 2015, 68). This offering centres the truth of deep solidarity, one that recognises that human beings are inextricably bound to one another, to all planetary life, and to the cosmos.

Revisioning curriculum drawing on Wynter engenders a pedagogy of solidarity that can disturb and reject static cultural essentialisms and confront how White supremacy continues to informs what is worthwhile knowledge (Gaztambide-Fernández 2012). We are reminded by the rendering of the Blombos Cave that European cosmogony that has been overly represented, and infused in curriculum around the world, is only *one* of a multitude of human cosmogonies. As Tuck (2011) reflects in respect to Indigenous epistemologies, non-Western cosmologies that have more interlinked explanations of human–human and human–Nature relationships as they depart from Darwinistic models of relational life based on fictions of natural scarcity that have shaped intimate and systemic dynamics, and thereby have the potential to dramatically redistribute power and knowledge. That is, our current mode of understanding relationships within our social and natural world is anthropocentric, is based on the assumption that the human is an autonomous individual, and supposes that only the fittest survive because there are scarce resources. In contrast to this, many Indigenous and global South cosmologies have embedded within them the notion that we exist in deeply interrelated cosmic circles. Several epistemological threads from the global South further assert that the notion of an autonomous being and human agency itself is a fallacy. Rather, we exist in and through what new materialists now call 'intra-actions' (Barad 2007) or the mutual constitution of entangled agencies amongst human and non-human worlds. Bodies intra-act in co-constitutive ways, and the ability to act, or agency, occurs from *within* the assemblages of these bodies. This ontological orientation presents *new* ways of seeing our relationships with each other, nature, and the material world. Wynter's rendering compels understandings of solidarity at the inter-species level and in relation to our natural world. This act of rewriting what humanness means by deliberating attending to the Third Event that marked the recognition/formation of the human species as hybridly human has the potential to enable what Wynter calls the production of 'self knowing subjects' (Wynter 1992). This occurs through the act of what Joyce E. King (1992) calls repossessing 'our story,' and what is meant by human consciousness.

This act of repossession is evident in *Maskarade*: *a Jonkonnu Musical Play*, where Wynter provides a linguistically complex assault on chauvinism and coloniality that is culturally relevant and at the same time provides epistemologically alternative understandings of how to be human. *Maskarade* was written by Wynter in 1973 and deals with the Jamaican performative form called *jonkonnu* that integrated rites from Yoruba and Igbo festivals, English morris dancing, and French carnival customs. The play is linked to an essay written by Wynter in which she underscores the significance of cultural resistance to colonisation, and thereby draws on the performative form of *jonkonnu* to illustrate an example of how local populations created indigenous cultural practices and modes through the integration of African, Amerindian, and European traditions. She suggests that cultural resistance- reviving and reinhabiting cultural forms considered to be backwards were serious acts of decolonisation.

As such, *Maskarade*

> creatively conveys the ways in which economies of transatlantic slavery and its colonizing twin – processes meant to comprehensively dispossess and thrive on land exploitation – produced the conditions through which black subjects developed alternative ways of human being and a sense of belonging nor based on territorialisation but through acts of localized/grounded (translocal) cultural production. (Boyce Davies 2015, 220)

By exploring how carnival can be liberating, unifying, and governed by the democratic laws of community freedom, Wynter provides a theatrical text instructive in understanding, and re-imagining the ways in which curriculum constructs the subject. In the play, Wynter does not shy away from colonial histories where Black people are marginalised. Comparably, Morrison (1992), in *Playing in the Dark*, challenges the language of self-referentiality that has been used to support the idea of a free-standing, self-forming white male identity and authority. Both Morrison and Wynter, emerge with characters which are 'overturning oppressive monolithic representations of black people … and enable an ancestral anamnesis that forages in a collective cultural memory for the material that would inform the interiority of the collective identity to be constructed' (McCarthy, Patel, and Sanya, forthcoming). In addition to being educative, Wynter points out that Jonkonnu is an emblem of self-definition, resistance in the face of colonial history as seen in Césaire's négritude.

Wynter (1970) describes the significance of the Jonkonnu festival in Jamaica and its history relating to imperialism; she argues that the incorporation of traditional performance elements to contemporary theatre can shift the overall meaning. When this happens, an indigenisation occurs, where 'the more secretive process by which the dominated culture survives' and stretches existing colonial definitions and thereby shifts how we value various modes of representation (Wynter 1970, 39). Jonkonnu characters are a product of African culture in Jamaica, and although European elements are present, they participate in gender identities that are not defined by European ideas. For example, males played all gender roles in Jonkonnu characters, and as Wynter explains 'this spirit is known as Ara-Orun, a citizen of heaven. The Mask, that is, the costume, must entirely cover the dancer. He carries a whip and speaks in a ventriloquial voice' (Wynter 1970, 37). As such counter-hegemonic gender identities and performances have had room in Jonkonnu processions, which do not confine gender to masculinity and femininity ascribed by Western hegemonic models.

Queer theorist, José Muñoz explains the breadth of this argument by describing the challenges in minoritised and marginalised peoples attempting to 'enact counter-publics through alternative modes of culture-making and intellectual work,' for example, he argues for the importance of including archives that are ephemeral, to broaden what is considered evidence with a focus on '*"decipherment" as opposed to interpretation*' (Muñoz 1996, 11, *emphasis added*). Citing Wynter, Muñoz explains that 'ephemera includes traces of lived experience and performances of lived experience, maintaining experiential politics and urgencies long after these structures of feeling have been lived' (Muñoz 1996, 10–11). This is key, because Wynter situates performance and theatre as a 'cultural guerrilla resistance against the market economy' (Wynter 1970, 36).

The production and enactment of artistic performances work as a form of curricula, steeped with knowledges and teachings that have potential, as depicted in Wynter's play, to call forth active resistance to/reimaginings of neoliberal logics that govern contemporary social worlds. The result is that there is more prominence of the dynamism of local community experiences that offer culturally specific, but non-essentialist snapshots of cultural life, which disrupt deeply lodged and naturalised structures. Wynter explains that prescriptive rules which regulate thought and scholarship are part of a system that need to have order, an order that relies upon distorting those who are not considered to be human.

> The system-conserving mainstream perspectives of each order (or well-established scholarship) therefore clash with the challenges made from the perspectives of alterity … For, it is the task of established scholarship to rigorously maintain those prescriptions, which are critical to the order's existence. (Wynter 1992, 27)

This productive liminal space of alterity 'offers us the possibility of thinking differently about what is at stake in refashioning what it means to be human ... [and] ... Wynter sees minority discourses as being capable of creating "new forms of human life"' (Walcott 2009, 57). Keeping in mind that 'history has mainly been about the European super structure of civilisation,' Wynter directs us to 'the interstices of history [where] we see, in glimpses, evidences of a powerful and pervasive cultural process which has largely determined the unconscious springs of our being' (Wynter 1970, 35). These interstices are sites where alternative intellectual works, such as women of colour feminisms and queer of colour critiques, have flourished.

The transnational solidarities possible in these interstices offer the enactment of 'being human as praxis' as humanness is performed collectively, or as Wynter calls through the referent we. Here, we ask: How might curriculum foster solidarity as a performance of the collective humanness Wynter forwards? Wynter posits that the active transnational engagements that build anticolonial movements in the 1960s proposed alternatives to the Western genre of the human. Shared oppressions and exploitations, albeit experienced differently, led to shared resistance, and a desire for common emancipation. Drawing on this inspiration, and the current networks of solidarity as reflected upon by feminist scholars such as Alexander (2005), Mohanty (2003, 2014), and Kaplan and Grewal (1994), Wynter calls upon us to enact the human differently. Curriculum that fosters an understanding of the geo-political linkages and illuminating current engagements of solidarity may cultivate 'alternative collective futures' (Nandy 2000). Spivak contends that education should be an 'noncoercive re-arrangement of desires' (2004, 526) oriented towards an 'ethical relationship to the Other, before will' (535). Wynter illustrates that this is possible if we dramatically revision and reteach what being human means. Sharma proposes that if we make new social bodies by rethinking the geographies of our selves in a way that imagines a 'new social body' (2015, 180), we can come to act and be what is in existence. This recognition may provoke our abilities to expand and reconsider our affective ties with(in) the world in which we live.

Conclusion

Wynter's work is emblematic of Black women's labour in both formal and informal educative spaces. The intellectual, physical, and emotional labour of Black women has been vital in generating theories and advancing practice at the nexus of education, justice, and the quest for liberation. This is evident from accounts of enslaved women, formerly enslaved women, bondswomen, and children of freed men and women, like Sojourner Truth, Phillis Wheatley, and Lucy Craft Laney, and domestic worker activists like Esther Cooper Jackson, and Claudia Jones, in Black Arts movement as seen in Audre Lorde, Nina Simone, Toni Morrison, and Lorraine Hansberry, to prominent Black educators and activists who fuse all these traditions together, like Anna Julia Cooper, Marva Collins, Theresa A. Perry, and Vanessa Siddle Walker. Scores of unnamed Black women have engaged the relationship between Black embodied knowledge, cultural experiences, practices, and curriculum to influence education within and outside schools and have challenged taken-for-granted understandings of Black culture in and beyond the United States.

Black women are simultaneously producers and subjects of empirical and theoretical knowledge. In this essay we focused on Sylvia Wynter's rich, life-long contributions to critical theory, antiracism, and anticolonialism and the lessons this vast body of work provides for curriculum development and studies. Her theorising on the category of the human is integral to critical questions about who is educated, how are certain populations educated, and what knowledge is to be preserved or valorised. We argue that her scholarship has critical significance in the field of education particularly with regards to the relationships between knowledge, curricula, and personhood. By giving 'humanness a new future' (Wynter and McKittrick 2015, 73), Wynter opens up radical possibilities for centring relational ways of being and knowing, and thereby reconfigures the knowledge landscape of educational sites. In the end, Wynter, we argue, pushes us to develop curricula committed to disrupting forgone conclusions about social relations, the central figures in history, the assumed heartbeat of knowledge production. Wynter critically calls us towards a curriculum that is nimble and hybrid. At the centre of such curricula is not merely a representation and reproduction of caricatures of those who embody cultural difference but rather, it is a push for a curricular space in which the human and the non-human thrive.

Notes

1. The authors would like to thank the issue's editors for such a timely special issue. This essay has been part of an ongoing conversation we have been having about new materialisms and Black/Queer ontologies, which crystalised during and after the 'Sylvia Wynter: On Being Human Panel' at the 2015 meeting of the American Educational Research Association, where Joyce E. King, Katherine McKittrick, Sandra Richards, Rinaldo Walcott, and Alexander Weheliye, held a panel discussion on the transformative possibilites of Wynter's work in the field of education, and the relevance of Wynter at this historical juncture. We would like to acknowledge them, the fruitful conversation and productive ideas that have been generated by Sylvia Wynter's life work. And finally, we would like to thank Warren Crichlow, Durell Callier, and Malathi Iyengar, for sustained conversation, critical reading and invaluable comments.
2. Largely influenced by women of colour feminisms and queer of colour critique, scholars have recently returned us to Wynter's questions of the human. See most recently, Zakiyyah Iman Jackson's *Animal: New Directions in the Theorization of Race and Posthumanism* (2013), Weheliye's *Habeas Viscus* (2014), McKittrick's *On Being Human as Praxis* (2015), and Luciano and Chen's (2015) GLQ Special Issue titled, *Queer Inhumanisms.*
3. Civil Rights Movement, which is understood as the rights of citizens to political and social freedom and equality, is often understood in relation to the U.S. Black liberation struggles' achievements in the 1950s and 1960s. Therefore, even though the *Civil Rights Act* of 1964 was a momentous decision, as it marked the end of legal discrimination, the Black liberation has a long trajectory that can be traced back to the first enslaved people in the Americas. The act, which outlawed discrimination based on race, color, religion, sex, or national origin, had outlawed racial segregation in schools, at work, and in access to public facilities. The passing of this act also ended the unequal application of voter registration requirements.
4. The turn to human rights was not towards human rights as is presently described by the United Nations. Universal human rights that are circulated presently have been highly critiqued for their Western universal liberal orientation. However, human rights advanced by the cadre of transnational anticolonial leaders and the Civil Rights Movement included Afro-Asiatic and Latin American tenets, and were not steeped solely in Western humanism.

Disclosure statement

No potential conflict of interest was reported by the authors.

References

Ahmed, Sara. 2012. *On Being Included: Racism and Diversity in Institutional Life*. Durham, NC: Duke University Press.

Alexander, M. Jacqui. 2005. *Pedagogies of Crossing: Meditations on Feminism, Sexual Politics, Memory, and the Sacred*. Durham, NC: Duke University Press.

Andreotti, Vanessa. 2006. "Soft Versus Critical Global Citizenship Education." *Development Education: Policy and Practice* 3: 83–96.

Apple, Michael W. 2000. "Can Critical Pedagogies Interrupt Rightist Policies?" *Educational Theory* 50 (2): 229–254.

Barad, Karen. 2007. *Meeting the Universe Halfway: Quantum Physics and the Entanglement of Matter and Meaning*. Durham, NC: Duke Univeristy Press.

Boyce Davies, Carole. 2015. "From Masquerade to Maskarade: Caribbean Cultural Resistance and the Rehumanizing Project." In *Sylvia Wynter: On Being Human as Praxis*, edited by Katherine McKittrick, 203–225. Durham, NC: Duke Univeristy Press.

Butler, Judith. 1993. *Bodies That Matter: On the Discursive Limits of Sex*. New York: Routledge.

Fanon, Frantz. 1952. *Black Skin, White Masks*. Translated by Charles Lamm Markman. New York: Grove Press.

Fanon, Frantz. 2008. *Black Skin, White Masks*. London: Pluto Press.

Gaztambide-Fernández, Rubén A. 2012. "Decolonization and the Pedagogy of Solidarity." *Decolonization: Indigeneity, Education and Society* 1 (1): 41–67.

Harvey, David. 2005. *A Brief History of Neoliberalism*. New York: Oxford University Press.

Iton, Richard. 2008. *In Search of the Black Fantastic: Politics and Popular Culture in the Post-civil Rights Era*. New York: Oxford University Press.

Jackson, Zakiyyah Iman. 2013. "Animal: New Directions in the Theorization of Race and Posthumanism." *Feminist Studies* 39 (3): 669–685.

Kaplan, Caren, and Inderpal Grewal. 1994. *Scattered Hegemonies: Postmodernity and Transnational Feminist Practices*. Minneapolis: University of Minnesota Press.

Kelley, Robin D. G. 2002. *Freedom Dreams: The Black Radical Imagination*. Boston, MA: Beacon Press.

King, Joyce E. 1992. "Diaspora Literacy and Consciousness in the Struggle Against Miseducation in the Black Community." *Journal of Negro Education* 61: 317–340.

Lewis, Tyson. 2009. "Biopower, Play, and Experience in Education." In *Marcuse's Challenge to Education*, edited by D. Kellner, T. Lewis, C. Pierce, and K. D. Cho, 45–57. Lanham: Rowman and Littlefield.

Lowe, Lisa. 2006. "The Intimacies of Four Continents." In *Haunted by Empire: Geographies of Intimacy in North American History*, edited by Ann Lauria Stoler, 191–212. Durham, NC: Duke University Press.

Luciano, Dana, and Mel Y. Chen. 2015. "Has the Queer Ever Been Human?" *GLQ: A Journal of Lesbian and Gay Studies* 21 (2–3): 183–207.

Marriott, David. 2015. "The Racialized Body." In *The Cambridge Companion to the Body in Literature*, edited by David Hillman and Ulrika Maude, 163–176. Cambridge: Cambridge University Press.

McCarthy, Cameron. 1994. "Multicultural Discourses and Curriculum Reform: A Critical Perspective." *Educational Theory* 44 (1): 81–98.

McCarthy, Cameron, Rushika Patel, and Brenda N. Sanya. Forthcoming. "Toni Morrison and the Discourse of the Other: Against the Hypocrisy of Completeness." In *Beyond Abyssal Curriculum*, edited by Joao M. Paraskeva. New York: Routledge.

McKittrick, Katherine. 2015. "Yours in the Intellectual Struggle: Sylvia Wynter and the Realization of the Living." In *Sylvia Wynter: On Being Human as Praxis*, edited by Katherine McKittrick, 1–8. Durham, NC: Duke Univeristy Press.

Mignolo, Walter D. 2007. "Delinking: The Rhetoric of Modernity, the Logic of Coloniality and the Grammar of Decoloniality." *Cultural Studies* 21 (2–3): 449–514.

Mignolo, Walter D. 2009. "Epistemic Disobedience, Independent Thought and Decolonial Freedom." *Theory, Culture & Society* 26 (7–8): 159–181.

Mignolo, Walter D. 2015. "Sylvia Wynter: What Does It Mean to Be Human." In *Sylvia Wynter: On Being Human as Praxis*, edited by Katherine McKittrick, 106–123. Durham, NC: Duke Univeristy Press.

Mohanty, Chandra Talpade. 2003. "'Under Western Eyes' Revisited: Feminist Solidarity Through Anticapitalist Struggles." *Signs: Journal of Women in Culture and Society* 28 (2): 499–535.

Mohanty, Chandra Talpade. 2014. "'Under Western Eyes' Revisited: Feminist Solidarity Through Anticapitalist Struggles." *Signs* 40 (1): 499–535.

Morrison, Toni. 1992. *Playing in the Dark: Whiteness and the Literary Imagination*. Cambridge, MA: Harvard University Press.

Muñoz, José Esteban. 1996. "Ephemera as Evidence: Introductory Notes to Queer Acts." *Women & Performance: A Journal of Feminist Theory* 8 (2): 5–16.

Nandy, Ashis. 2000. "Time Travel to a Possible Self: Searching for the Alternative Cosmopolitanism of Cochin." *Japanese Journal of Political Science* 1 (2): 295–327.

Ong, Aihwa. 2006. *Neoliberalism as Exception: Mutations in Citizenship and Sovereignty*. Durham, NC: Duke University Press.

Pinar, William F. 2004. *What Is Curriculum Theory?* Mahwah: Lawrence Erlbaum Associates.

Popkewitz, Thomas S. 1997. "The Production of Reason and Power: Curriculum History and Intellectual Traditions." *Journal of Curriculum Studies* 29 (2): 131–164.

Popkewitz, Thomas S., and Marie Brennan. 1997. "Restructuring of Social and Political Theory in Education: Foucault and a Social Epistemology of School Practices." *Educational Theory* 47 (3): 287–313.

Scott, David. 1999. *Refashioning Futures: Criticism after Postcoloniality*. Princeton, NJ: Princeton University Press.

Scott, David. 2000. "The Re-enchantment of Humanism: An Interview with Sylvia Wynter." *Small Axe* 8 (120): 173–211.

Sedgwick, Eve Kosofsky. 1997. "Paranoid Reading and Reparative Reading, or, You're So Paranoid, You Probably Think This Introduction Is about You." In *Novel Gazing: Queer Readings in Fiction*, edited by Eve Kosofsky Sedgwick, 1–37. Durham, NC: Duke University Press.

Sharma, Nandita. 2015. "Strategic Essentialism: Decolonizing Decolonization." In *Sylvia Wynter: On Being Human as Praxis*, edited by Katherine McKittrick, 164–182. Durham, NC: Duke Univeristy Press.

da Silva, Denise Ferreira. 2015. "Before Man: Sylvia Wynter's Rewriting of the Modern Episteme." In *Sylvia Wynter: On Being Human as Praxis*, edited by Katherine McKittrick, 90–106. Durham, NC: Duke University Press.

Spivak, Gayatri Chakravorty. 2004. "Righting Wrongs." *The South Atlantic Quarterly* 103 (2): 523–581.

Tuck, Eve. 2011. "Rematriating Curriculum Studies." *Journal of Curriculum and Pedagogy* 8 (1): 34–37.

Walcott, Rinaldo. 2009. *Black Like Who? Writing Black Canada*. Toronto: Insomniac Press.

Weheliye, Alexander G. 2008. "After Man." *American Literary History* 20 (1–2): 321–336.

Weheliye, Alexander G. 2014. *Habeas Viscus: Racializing Assemblages, Biopolitics, and Black Feminist Theories of the Human*. Durham, NC: Duke University Press.

Wilkins, Fanon Che. 2006. "Beyond Bandung: The Critical Nationalism of Lorraine Hansberry, 1950–1965." *Radical History Review* 2006 (95): 191–210.

Willinsky, John. 1998. *Learning to Divide the World: Education at Empire's End*. Minneapolis: University of Minnesota Press.

Wynter, Sylvia. 1970. "Jonkonnu in Jamaica: Towards the Interpretation of Folk Dance as a Cultural Process." *Jamaica Journal* 4 (2): 34–48.

Wynter, Sylvia. 1992. *Do Not Call Us Negros: How 'Multicultural' Textbooks Perpetuate Racism*. San Francisco, CA: Aspire.

Wynter, Sylvia. 1995. "1492: A New World View." In *Race, Discourse, and the Origin of the Americas: A New World View*, edited by V. L. Hyatt and R. Nettleford, 5–57. Washington, DC: Smithsonian.

Wynter, Sylvia. 2003. "Unsettling the Coloniality of Being/Power/Truth/Freedom: Towards the Human, After Man, Its Overrepresentation – An Argument." *CR: The New Centennial Review* 3 (3): 257–337.

Wynter, Sylvia, and Katherine McKittrick. 2015. *Unparalleled Catastrophe for Our Species? Or, to Give Humanness a Different Future: Conversations*, edited by Katherine McKittrick. Durham, NC: Duke Univeristy Press.

'I know what you are about to enter': lived experiences as the curricular foundation for teaching citizenship

Amanda E. Vickery

ABSTRACT

This qualitative multiple case study documents how two African American women social studies teachers utilise their lived experiences as the curricular foundation for teaching differing notions of citizenship to African-American students. Particular events, experiences, and relationships helped shape their perception of their roles as teachers and how they approached crafting a curriculum that was representative of their lived experiences as well as those of their students and community. This study hopes to shed light on how experiences may be used as valuable sources of knowledge in creating a more inclusive curriculum that mirrors the diversity seen in classrooms.

Education has been an enduring and consistent theme in the life, struggle, and resistance of African-American women (Collier-Thomas 1982). Collier-Thomas once wrote:

> This history of black women in education offers valuable insights into the larger role played by women and blacks in the struggle for racial and sexual equality. It illuminates the extent to which the black community was involved in the struggle to improve and "uplift" the masses. (178)

Education has been used as the vehicle to 'uplift' African-American communities and to achieve first-class citizenship. For centuries African-American women, in particular, have played a significant role working to liberate their community. Yet, political scientist Harris-Perry (2011) argued that because of the misrecognition of Black women in the larger society, their work in educating and uplifting the community has been ignored and under-recognised as valid forms of citizenship. The work of Black feminists (e.g. Collins 2009; Giddings 1984; Guy-Sheftall 1995; Harris-Perry 2011; Hooks 1999) have attempted to correct this omission by illuminating the many ways in which for centuries Black women have actively engaged in the work of resisting oppression, community uplift, and demanding public recognition of Black women as citizens (i.e. Anna Julia Cooper, Mary Church Terrell, Ida B. Wells- Barnett, Amy Jacques-Garvey, Pauli Murray, Ella Baker, Jo Ann Robinson, Septima Clark, Angela Davis). With that said how can we expect students, in particular African-American students, to become active and justice-oriented citizens when they are prevented from seeing examples of fearless African-American women throughout the past and present engaging in the fight for equality and citizenship?

While the construct of citizenship and its qualifications have changed over the course of U.S. history to include more people, it is most commonly recognised as a signifier of a legal status that ties an individual to a particular country (Knight Abowitz and Harnish 2006; Marshall [1950] 1998). Several scholars have argued the importance of citizenship education being a primary purpose of teaching social studies (Barton and Levstik 2013; Parker 1996, 2003; Westheimer and Kahne 2004). However, the standard model of citizenship education is aimed at teaching a singular civic identity rooted in individualism, a common body of civic and historical knowledge, and blind patriotism (Hahn 2008). This traditional, and frankly Whitestream and patriarchal, definition of citizenship has been criticised for its failure to include the voices and experiences of non-Whites and women (Ladson-Billings 2004; Lomawaima and McCarty 2002; Rosaldo 1997; Yuval-Davis 1997). For example, Spinner (1984) argued that traditional liberal citizenship had failed African Americans because it is premised on individual rights (which had been denied to African Americans), ignores histories of oppression, and does not recognise communal membership as citizenship. Therefore, it is no surprise that Ladson (1984) found that African-American students' loyalty was to their cultural community first and to the nation-state second. These are all factors in how and why a *double consciousness* (DuBois [1903] 1994), or dual sense of citizenship, and feelings of *civic estrangement* (Tillet 2012) persists among many African Americans.

Tillet (2012) used the concept of *civic estrangement* to describe the ways in which African-Americans possess full legal citizenship yet continue to be marginalised in how they are represented in the American citizenship narrative and memory that promotes a national identity. She wrote,

> In the case of African Americans, civic estrangement occurs because they have been marginalized or underrepresented in the civic myths, monuments, narratives, icons, creeds, and images of the past that constitute, reproduce, and promote an American national identity. Civic estrangement is both ascriptive and affective. As a form of an ongoing racial inequality, civic estrangement describes the paradox post-civil rights African Americans experience as simultaneous citizens and "non-citizens," who experience the feeling of disillusionment and melancholia of non-belonging and a yearning for civic membership. (Tillet 2012, 3)

Civic estrangement is rooted in the work of W.E.B. DuBois and the notion that African-Americans have struggled with being able to see their true selves as human beings because of the White supremacist structure that has denied them that realization. But for African-American women they exist by being seen through a racialised *and* gendered veil that positions them differently than Black men in terms of their identities as citizens. Civic estrangement leads to not only the development of a 'double consciousness' in terms of a citizen identity, but also a search for a new site of citizenship. In fact, we have seen Communities of Colour taking it upon themselves to reconceptualise citizenship frameworks that are more inclusive and representative of their own history and experiences (Bondy 2015; Castro 2013; Dilworth 2004, 2008; Lomawaima and McCarty 2002; Rosaldo 1997). This would include adopting a culturally sustaining (Paris 2012) and revitalizing (McCarty and Lee 2014) pedagogies in their classrooms.

Historically, African-American women educators have been known to utilise culturally relevant curriculum and pedagogy and go above and beyond to educate African-American citizens in their communities (Collier-Thomas 1982; Harley 1996;

King 2014; Murray 2012; Walker 1996). To some African-American women, teaching is more than a job; it is a spiritual calling and a way to serve and uplift their communities (Dixson and Dingus 2008; Gordon 1985; Walker 1996). Teaching is perceived as a form of activism and a way to resist the oppressive structures that continue to marginalise African-American citizens and communities. These teachers prepared their students to one day take their place as citizens in a world where they continued to be positioned outside the realm of citizenship. For that reason, they chose not to teach a traditional understanding of citizenship. Instead, they taught a conceptualization rooted in the specific knowledge passed down by generations of African Americans that mirrors their experiences, communal values, and history of civic engagement (Harley 1996; Murray 2012). Because African-American women in the present day continue to express feelings of estrangement as citizens on account of the intersections of their race and gender (see Vickery 2015, 2016), it is important for us to examine how these teachers teach the construct of citizenship. Furthermore, how do they draw on their experiential knowledge as African-American women to craft a curriculum that is representative of their reality?

Teacher identity

There has been an emergence of literature exploring how a teacher's identity influences their practice. A teacher brings with her/him a unique identity as a teacher, but as more time is spent in the field, that identity is renegotiated (Agee 2004). For African-American women, the *double consciousness* (DuBois [1903] 1994) – or, as King (1988) suggested, 'double jeopardy' – of their intersecting identities as being both African-American and women has given them a distinctive perspective (Collins 2009; Crenshaw 1989, 1991) and is bound to influence their teacher identity. Dixson and Dingus (2008) found a recurring view among African-American women teachers – namely, that they drew on the legacies of African-American women, families, and communities as reasons why they entered the profession. Teaching was perceived as community work and an opportunity to uplift and empower African Americans. Collins (2009) argued that for Black women, 'empowerment involves rejecting the dimensions of knowledge, whether personal, cultural, or institutional, that perpetuates objectification and dehumanization ... and views the skills gained in schools as part of a focused education for Black community development' (230). In order to empower students and the community, a number of African-American teachers will use their personal experiences and make purposeful curricular and pedagogical decisions to reject oppressive knowledge structures and replace it with an affirmative representation of African-American history and self (Dixson 2003).

Gordon (1985) believed a teacher's decision to privilege the cultural knowledge of students to be a emancipatory because it is 'born out of the African-American community's historic common struggle and resistance against the various oppressive effects of capitalism and racism' (7). Researchers have documented how teachers of colour legitimise the cultural knowledge and experiences of their students in addition to making connections between students' home lives and the school culture/community (e.g. Howard 2002, 2010; Salinas and Castro 2010; Salinas, Vickery, and Franquiz 2016; Vickery 2016). This practice of teachers using their cultural and community knowledge to challenge the official curriculum is not only a form of resistance, but an act of caring and a way to show students that their lives matter and that their cultural and experiential knowledge has an important place in schools.

Feminist frameworks of caring

While caring is traditionally seen as 'women's work' in the private sphere, there have been attempts to reconceptualise feminine notion of caring in society – particularly within the context of schooling. Noddings (1988) used the term *authentic caring* as a way to describe the necessity of sustaining reciprocal relationships between teachers and students for learning to occur. However, scholars such as Thompson (1998) and Valenzuela (1999) have critiqued the notion of caring in teaching because it operates from a colour-blind perspective that fails to account for the intersections of race, gender, and class and how they can influence notions of caring. According to Black feminist and womanist scholars (Beauboeuf-Lafontant 2002; Collins 2009; Dillard 2000, 2012; Walker 1983), African-American women have been known to draw from their concrete experiences that reinforces the notion of caring in the Black community. A Black feminist ethic of caring represents an epistemology that is premised on teachers bringing to the classroom specific ways of knowing that are unique to their experiences and reflective of their community (Thompson 1998). This view of the world is grounded in African-American women's sensibilities and communal knowledge that is rooted in the need to uplift and sustain the community. This knowledge can be described as 'honest, but not innocent' (Thompson 1998, 16) and taught to ensure the survival of African-American students. The teaching of this type of knowledge, which to some might appear harsh, is done out of love to prepare African-American students for the harsh realities of civic estrangement and racism. This form of caring emphasises the teaching of integrity and the will needed to endure a possible reality plagued by inequality. It is a recognition of Black women's contributions to the survival and transformation of their communities and validates the collective wisdom that originates from the lived experiences of African-American women.

Research context and methodology

This study used a qualitative multiple case study methodology. Merriam (2009) defined case study research as 'an in-depth description and analysis of a bounded system' (40). Data were collected and analysed for two African-American women social studies teachers. Each case was analysed separately to determine the emerging themes. Then, the themes were compared across cases as a way to provide insight into my research question (Miles, Huberman, and Saldaña 2013). The question that framed this study explored how do the intersections of identity, and the lived experiences that arise from those identities, influence the curricular and pedagogical decisions of African-American women teachers when teaching citizenship to their African-American students? By studying African-American women, this study seeks to illuminate how these teachers are drawing on multiple sources of knowledge and ways of knowing in how they enact a citizenship education curriculum that is more inclusive of different experiences than the traditional curriculum.

This research study occurred in the spring of 2014. The teachers highlighted both taught in a suburban school district, located in a large state in the southwest United

States. This study was conducted in the suburb of Dayton (pseudonym). This community was purposely selected because it is a majority African-American community with an administrative and teaching force that is reflective of the community. I located two secondary African-American women social studies teachers who agreed to participate and serve as my cases. Zoe Eaton (pseudonym) was in her tenth year of teaching United States history at Dayton High School (DHS). Ms Eaton lived in the Dayton community with her three children, all of whom attended Dayton schools. Rhegan Byrd (pseudonym) was an educator with nearly thirty years of public school teaching experience. At the time of the study she was in her fifth year teaching ninth grade world geography at DHS. While Mrs Byrd had only been a teacher at DHS for a short amount of time, she had been a member of the Dayton community for over 20 years. Both women were purposely selected to participate in this study because they self-identified as African-American women who had lived and served the Dayton community for a number of years.

The data collected from this study included classroom and school observations, observation and interview notes, interview transcripts, and artefacts from the participants' classrooms. During the four semi-structured interviews we spoke about a variety of topics such as why each woman wanted to become teachers, what they considered the purpose of social studies, the concept of citizenship, and how they designed their curriculum. After the interviews, I manually coded the interview transcripts and analysed them as Miles, Huberman, and Saldaña (2013) suggest by noting patterns and themes, arriving at comparisons and contrasts, and determining conceptual explanations of the study. This process not only allowed me to organise the data, but also perform a cross-case analysis. I have member checked and conducted follow-up interviews with my participants as Merriam (2009) suggest confirming the emerging themes. The patterns, themes, and comparisons of the data led me to the findings included in this paper.

Findings

After spending time with each teacher and her students, it was quite clear that the participants' backgrounds and experiences as African-American women significantly impacted how they taught citizenship to their students. Two findings emerged from the data that spoke to this phenomenon. First, the teachers' prior experiences heavily shaped their teacher identity and how they approached teaching conceptions of citizenship. The second finding demonstrated that both teachers felt the urgency, the *necessity*, of teaching students about the realities of experiencing civic estrangement (Tillet 2012) and how to successfully navigate those waters. Their curricular and pedagogical decisions were rooted in a Black feminist ethic of caring (Collins 2009; Thompson 1998) in which Black women's cultural knowledge was privileged and utilised in the classroom as legitimate sources of knowledge.

Ms. Eaton

Eleventh grade American history teacher Zoe Eaton sat quietly thinking. She opened her mouth to speak, but then suddenly changed her mind. After a few brief moments, she smiled and then responded,

> Many of them say ... well, I think they would say that I am stern, but flexible. I do have expectations, and I keep my expectations ... So yeah, I think the students would say that Ms. Eaton is very stern. That she is going to keep her expectations, but at the same time, Ms. Eaton is approachable as well. (Eaton interview, 05/16/14)

Ms Eaton was responding to a question I had asked about how she thought her students viewed her as a teacher. Ms Eaton's classroom was a space of rigorous learning, reflection and application, with the occasional life lesson. Throughout my observations I noted that her curriculum was rooted in notions of leadership, 'real life,' and the students' roles as citizens.

> I just want my students to understand that they have a responsibility as students now and in the future to be productive citizens, and that takes leadership and all the things I try to implement in the classroom is what I want you to get out of social studies class. So I mean, honestly, maybe five or six years down the line, you may not remember the content, but hopefully you do remember some of those life lessons that I have taught you about leadership. (Eaton interview, 05/16/14)

Life lessons of struggle and resilience

When asked how she developed her curricular framework and approach to teaching citizenship, Ms Eaton noted that the women in her family were strong influences in her life and teaching.

> I guess my mother, and all of my aunts — I have 5 aunts, they're all single, they're all strong ladies. So I saw a lot of leadership from a woman's perspective and a lot of goal setting that my aunts did. I could remember hearing them talk about what they wanted to do and I believe they really influenced how I am in the classroom as far as making sure they [students] have leadership skills, as far as letting the girls or boys these days really know that you don't have to depend on other people. I mean, I put all of that into the curriculum. And so I would just say just the influence of my mother and my aunts ... just seeing how they went through it all: raising children on their own, no men involved, and just to see them earn their master's degree and see them going through college and so to me it was just ... like it is understood I am going to college. My mom and my aunts did this before — it is just a matter of how can I do it successfully on my own. (Eaton interview, 05/16/14)

According to Ms Eaton, her aunts and mother were examples of strong women who exhibited leadership in their personal and professional lives. More importantly, they embodied the image of successful African-American women who, despite adversity and experiencing 'life,' set goals and worked hard to achieve those goals.

Although her statements above, suggesting that 'you don't have to depend on other people', appears to negate the notion of communal citizenship, it instead refers to her sentiments regarding the reality of struggle in her own life and that of the women in her family. Ms Eaton recounted her own difficulties not only in balancing life as a teacher, single mother of three children, and doctoral student, but also in dealing with the reality of oppression and how others view her as a citizen. While discussing the obstacles she faced in her daily life, she stated the biggest one she had to negotiate was her perceived position in society as an African-American woman. She stated, 'The world is full of people who do not see me as an equal. I have to work extra hard and stay focused on my goals' (Eaton interview, 05/16/14). The feeling of subjugation or being seen as an outsider is not uncommon among African-American women (Collins 2009; Harris-Perry

2011). The silence and exclusion of African-American women in public intellectual spaces are attempts to negate the reality and experiences of Black womanhood (Collins 2009). Nevertheless, instead of accepting this reality Ms Eaton implied that it motivated her to continue on her chosen path and to teach her students to do the same.

This acknowledgement and experience of struggle in her own life and the lessons it had taught her was purposely embedded into a leadership unit she designed and taught in May of 2014. She used the unit as an opportunity for students to become aware of their future roles as citizens. Ms Eaton designed the leadership unit using her own life experiences as well as material from a graduate course she took on leadership. She was purposeful in the fact that she wanted to make the curriculum relevant to the lives of students and create a space where students, whose voices are typically silenced, had the opportunity to be heard. For instance, in one class session Ms Eaton had her students reflect on different quotations and poems associated with leadership skills and how they could relate the material to their own lives. One such writing assignment stated, 'If the leader can't navigate the rough waters he is liable to sink. Explain that concept and how it applies to your life' (Eaton classroom artefact, 05/14/14). Analysis and application of class content was a fundamental premise throughout her leadership unit. Several times I witnessed Ms Eaton referring back to the reality of experiencing 'rough waters' and how students should not let it deter them from their goals and dreams. She normalised the existence of struggle and treated it as something that was a common occurrence in life for African Americans but reiterated that leaders/citizens needed to learn how to navigate the 'rough waters' and stay on course.

Another assignment asked students to read the poem 'What Life Is All About' (Author unknown n.d.) and make text-to-self connections. The poem attempted to move away from an individualistic and materialistic mindset towards what is important in life.

> Life isn't about keeping score ...
> But, life is about who you love and who you hurt. It's about who you make happy or unhappy purposefully ...
> It's about who you've ignored with full control and intention ...
> But most of all, it's about using your life to touch or poison other people's hearts in such a way that could have never occurred alone ... (Eaton classroom arte fact, 05/14/14)

The poem sought to have the reader adopt an outlook on life concerned with a person's relationship to others and contributions to society. By completing the written reflection and analysis of the poem, the students were sent the message that while struggle is a normal part of life, they need to be concerned with how their actions affect others and dedicate their lives to the betterment of others. She reiterated to her students a communal perspective of citizenship and the necessity of students being concerned with how their actions affect and attend to the needs of others and the community (Avoseh 2001).

I asked Ms Eaton why she thought it was important to include lessons on struggle in her leadership unit. She stated that as African-American citizens, struggle would be part of their lives and she wanted the unit and lessons to be relevant to the experiences that lay ahead for her students.

> Well, it is the reality ..., it is what I have learned and observed. It is almost summertime, so many of them are going to be seeking employment. And they need to know that the world may not always pacify them, the world is not going to be nice to you, and so I

> wanted them to know that. And another reason why I want them to know that is because they declared that I am so mean, that I'm so — *cold hearted* is what they say — but what I wanted them to know is that that's by far the opposite. I do these things because I know what you are about to enter: A world that is competitive, a world that will spit in your face and stab you in the back, and so I wanted to just bring that lesson in. (Eaton interview, 05/16/14)

Life lessons of struggle and resilience were prominent in the leadership unit. One class session focused on perseverance and how to change society. Ms. Eaton began the lesson by asking,

> Remember, we've talked about those rough waters, how we are going to encounter them in life no matter what because they are a part of life. So we have to stay focused and stay set on what we want to accomplish .... I know I said it plenty of times, but there will be challenges that you will have, and so it will be up to you to make the right decision to stay on the path that you have for yourself. Today we are going to watch a movie about the Tuskegee Airmen, a group of African American pilots who despite racism were able to make a mark on society ... You already know that you will encounter several challenges, but how do you still persevere and how do you leave a contributing mark in society? (Eaton classroom observation, 05/22/14)

Through writing reflections and class discussions, the students were tasked with finding connections between the leadership themes in the movie and their lives. This reflective practice was done so that students could use examples of historical figures demonstrating perseverance and apply it to their own lives.

Ms Eaton added another layer to the importance of this activity by choosing to use the example of the Tuskegee Airmen. Ms Eaton later stated that the decision to feature African Americans was intentional 'to show students it is not impossible for them to accomplish their goals or be leaders in a global society' (Eaton interview, 08/18/14). In a number of her lessons she prominently featured African-American historical figures as a way for her students (who were African American) to see themselves reflected in the curriculum. In an earlier lesson the students watched a movie about Ruby Bridges and her efforts to integrate New Orleans public schools in the 1960s. Ms Eaton later stated that she used a variety of African-American historical figures and examples to show that people of all ages, genders, and races can endure hardships or trauma to change society. By choosing to feature these particular African Americans she demonstrated to students the reality of institutional racism, segregation, and second-class citizenship. But despite these barriers, students learned a more valuable lesson in ordinary citizens fighting oppression, uplifting the community, and working towards the public recognition of African Americans as citizens.

Thompson (1998) noted the significance of utilising African-American narratives in an effort to reclaim the past in order to known oneself. She argues the necessity of not only reasserting and reclaiming Black narratives, but that remembering the past can be empowering by helping inform the present. By drawing on historical examples of African Americans, Ms Eaton used the past to teach her students lessons about the reality of struggle in the present day and how, despite the hardships they may endure, one must succeed and help change society for the better.

Mrs Byrd

The bell rings as the last few students rush through the door and take a seat in their ninth grade world geography classroom. Mrs Rhegan Byrd walks into the classroom, seemingly exuding the nearly thirty years of education experience, wearing heels, a dark brown suit, and bright gold jewellery. She had an impressive presence as she took her place at the front of *her* classroom. She greeted the students with a simple, 'Good afternoon,' and on cue, 32 students replied, 'Good afternoon, Mrs Byrd' (Byrd classroom observation, 05/13/14). She gave her class instructions for their bell ringer activity and the students went right to work. Not long afterwards Mrs Byrd noticed two young men who were, as Mrs Byrd remarked, 'making bad decisions' (Byrd classroom observation, 05/13/14). She frowned at the students and stared at them with her penetrating brown eyes and a look of disappointment. One of the young men caught her gaze and defensively told Mrs Byrd, 'Miss, I don't know the answer.' Her eyes widened, as if shocked by his response and fired back,

> Don't just sit there and wait. You have the same resources this young man has. The only thing that varies in this classroom is your motivation and your determination. And no one can give that to you. Now we can try to motivate ya, but if you don't make the decision to do it, it won't happen. (Byrd classroom observation, 05/13/14)

The young men responded to Mrs Byrd's reprimand by quickly getting to work. A few minutes later, a young woman publicly complained to the class about the amount of work they had to do. Mrs Byrd paused, peered at the young woman, and then turned to address the entire class:

Mrs. Byrd:	Education do not harm children. Now it might challenge you, it may even force you to challenge that comfort zone a little bit, and make you a little angry, and give you a little anxiety, but last time I checked it does not harm.
Titus (pseudonym):	Taking in too much information does your brain harm.
Mrs. Byrd:	Uh ... no. Son, there have been millions upon millions upon millions of children who have taken classes and who have lived to tell the tale.
Seth (pseudonym):	You jokin', right?
Mrs. Byrd:	No son, when have you ever known me to joke about work?

This exchange allows us a snapshot into a typical day in the classroom of Mrs Byrd, a veteran social studies teacher with experience in school leadership and counselling. As this glimpse shows, Mrs Byrd integrated life lessons, or as her students affectionately referred to them as *sermons*, in her teaching as a way to teach students about the importance of education for African-American citizens.

By any means necessary: using sermons to disrupt the pipeline

Mrs Byrd has held a variety of positions and roles in her 30 years educating future citizens. But she credited her time as a high school lead counsellor and middle school teacher in a large urban district ten miles north of Dayton for dramatically impacting her view on the importance of her work as a teacher.

In her role as lead counsellor, she was responsible for identifying and placing all of the repeat ninth graders in the district in alternative education programmes that would place them on a path to graduate from high school. She remembered during a particularly tumultuous year for the district, the largely poor and minority community was furious with the district's decision to shut down one of the high schools because of years of poor standardised test scores. The decision to close the school would scatter the students to other low performing schools outside of their immediate community. After several heated protests by community members, tensions were high as the new school year was about to commence. Mrs Byrd was especially worried because she had not yet been able to locate and place dozens of students who needed to be registered at their new schools. And so she made a decision: 'We go to their houses. They won't come here; we got to go to their houses because we provide an important service and that's just what we gotta do' (Byrd interview, 05/16/14). District officials attempted to deter her from pursuing this course of action because of the tension between the community and school district. But Mrs Byrd would not be swayed and she went door-to-door, registering and placing dozens of students in school and community programmes that would set them on a path to graduate from high school.

> So I told them, at that point I realized, okay this is more than just about working: This is about saving lives ... So I developed a different perspective of the classroom. And I always knew the role that I play, even more so then, was so important. But I was missing the children and I was in the administration still working with children but not directly on a day-to-day basis. I was still missing that camaraderie and so I told my coworkers that before I retired I would go back and teach a few more years and be with the children. And here I am. (Byrd interview, 05/16/14)

This anecdote illustrates Mrs Byrd's approach to teaching: a teacher must do whatever is necessary to provide students an education. Mrs Byrd's words and actions reflect a historic tradition within the African-American community and the significant role African-American women teachers have played in the uplift of future citizens. Scholars have documented the rich history of African-American teachers engaging in notions of racial and community uplift because they understood that an education was an important way to empower communities (Irvine 1986; Walker 1996).

Mrs Byrd began to see her role as an educator was not only to teach students the assigned curriculum that would pass them to the next grade level, but also to provide an education that included the knowledge about life needed to be successful citizens in an unequal world.

> Well, I know each day I have a responsibility and if I don't take that responsibility seriously for the sake of the children, it will cause grave harm for them. ... I once met a lady, I guess it was my second or third year of teaching, she came in to have lunch. She came sat over by me, and seemed to have a pleasant face and we just sat and talked and I happened to ask her what was her job and she said, 'I am a juvenile probation officer.' So to hear that she said, 'Well, I get them when you all have failed.' And that stuck with me. Because if I can say and do something that makes a difference in a child's life, that keeps them from doing bad, then I think I've done a good job. And having dealt with so many 'at-risk' students, that makes my fight even greater. (Byrd interview, 05/16/14)

The probation officer's presence in the school surprised Mrs Byrd and demonstrated the existence of a direct pipeline from schools to prisons. While this realization was shocking to Mrs Byrd, the officer's comment that 'I get them when you all have failed' was both disheartening yet hopeful in that she recognised that teachers can play a significant role in helping students and families successfully navigate the murky waters of the structure of school and away from the criminal justice system. Her awareness of the interconnectedness of schools and prisons led to a realization of the position teachers play in deciding whether students receive an education or sent down the pipeline.

Mrs Byrd's interaction with the probation officer served as a call to action, and thus began her fight for her students:

> So when a child refuses to do what is necessary or don't want to learn then I know where they can end up very easily without them knowing they made that decision. So it's not just about the lesson. That's why lot of them say, "Oh! She is going to preach to us again," because I want them to understand it's never about me, everything I do is about them. So when I come in here and I am fussing and I am not fighting you ... I am fighting *you* about *you*. I am fighting for you, and hopefully one day we can fight together. (Byrd interview, 05/16/14)

Even after three decades in public education, Mrs Byrd continued to fight daily on behalf of her students. Mrs Byrd viewed her role as a fighter, an advocate for students. She understood the importance of students' receiving an education that consisted of both social studies content with the inclusion of life lessons in the form of 'sermons' meant to share her own perceptions of the world based on her experiences as an African-American woman working in the community.

One day Mrs Byrd witnessed a student cheating on her homework, and that signalled the necessity of a sermon.

> Mrs Byrd: Do not compromise yourself. ... It's time for a sermon. Y'all are LONG overdue for a story.
> Students: Uh hum. Preach it!
> Mrs Byrd: This young student was very promising.
> Students: Very promising!
> Mrs Byrd: And he had a full ride to college ... His second year he joined this fraternity, became the chairperson for that fraternity. And because of a little power he took liberty of their money and stole. Right now that man can't get a job anywhere. They put him in jail, and it was only a thousand dollars. But this young man, because he stole something that did not belong to him ... They put him out of college. He can't even find a job to do his community service, cuz you wanna know why? No business will deal with a person who will steal something or cheat ... So you've got to be very careful when you think you are helping your friends. It's all about choices people ... And I know you been taught, see that's what angers me, because you didn't reach this age and no one has said this to you all. You just still make the decisions not to have any regard for what's right. (Byrd classroom observation, 05/23/14)

Mrs Byrd was speaking to a sad and all too common narrative of poor decision-making resulting in a drastically changed reality. She was attempting to show students that minor decisions, such as cheating, could lead to a lifetime habit of poor choices with serious consequences later on down the road. This was especially true for young men and women of colour who are frequently reprimanded by law enforcement officials because of their hypervisibility and the harmful stereotypes attached to their raced and gendered bodies (Noguera 2003).

Mrs Byrd utilised the tradition of 'communal truth telling' that describes communal shared knowledge of reality and the way things are. Thompson (1998) described this form of storytelling as 'authors calling out recognition and empathy when the stories that are told resonate with others' experience' (14). I had witnessed several 'truth telling' moments aimed at urging students to consider their own decisions and how it could impact their futures. 'Truth telling' moments could occur as a whole class, with an individual student, or even on graded papers (Byrd classroom artefact, 05/29/14). One such conversation occurred when Mrs Byrd taught a lesson on the push and pull factors of the spread of the English language during colonization and she noticed a young woman copying another student's map. Mrs Byrd expressed her disappointment in both students for their poor judgment and used it as an opportunity to teach the class a valuable lesson on self-reliance:

> If I don't break that habit from you, I have not done my job. When you sit there and copy, you do not learn. It is easier, because someone else did the work. But you aren't learning. (Byrd classroom observation, 05/27/14)

She then turned to the student who allowed the young woman to copy her map and gave her a 'talkin' to':

> You gon teach her how to fish or teach them self-reliance? It's okay to help them immediately, but you got to teach her how to sustain for the rest of her life. You can do this. You are not quite hungry but, you can do this. (Byrd classroom observation, 05/27/14)

Mrs Byrd used life lessons and storytelling as vehicles to teach notions of personal ethics and morality, which represents important skills needed to thrive as future citizens in their community (Thompson 1998). Many have used the term 'warm demanders' (Vasquez 1988) to encapsulate a teaching style that is 'tough-minded, no-nonsense, structured and disciplined classroom environment for kids whom society has psychologically and physically abandoned' (Irvine 1998, 1). This style of teaching is premised on the belief not only that these children can learn but that they *must* learn; their very survival depends on it. To outsiders, Mrs Byrd's style of teaching could be misunderstood as harsh or cold, but that assessment would be far from accurate. Mrs Byrd's approach to teaching was premised on students acquiring the knowledge and skills needed to succeed as citizens in both the Dayton community and the larger society. A great deal of love, support, and resilience went into each one of her lessons and sermons. Mrs Byrd's sermons, lectures, and battles with students taught students how to keep their heads high with pride as they go out into the world as citizens. It was not only about avoiding the prison pipeline, but also about learning how to become decent human beings with a sense of pride and self-worth.

At the end of each class, Mrs Byrd appeared visibly exhausted in waging her daily war on behalf of her students. Nevertheless, she refused to give up and cited the little victories that kept her going:

> I don't know how they see me, but I would like for them to see that I do care although I won't give up, although I am firm with them, although I just ride them to a point and then I back off, and sometimes I don't back off. I want them to become angry because I need you to get mad at yourself. ... So a hundred children will be on this floor and I made a difference in one, that's okay. There have been days like, I don't want to be here, the children are choking me, the children they draining me. And one kid comes and says something to me, and let me know okay, I need to be here. Forget it, Rhegan; it's not about you. Let it go, and deal with the children. (Byrd interview, 5/16/14)

The school bell rang and the students rushed out of the classroom. The door finally closed and Mrs Byrd walked slowly towards her desk. She sat down, rested her head on top of her hands, and let out a slow exhale. She slowly shook her head and confided to the nearly empty room, 'I feel like I need more time with the children. There is so much more that I need them to learn' (Byrd classroom observation, 05/27/14). Her admission remained saturated in the quiet classroom. Moments later, students began to trickle in, excitedly discussing their projects. Mrs Byrd smiled, stood up, and was ready to welcome her students.

Discussion

This paper highlights the connections between African-American women teachers lived experiences, how they made sense of those experiences, and how it leads to acts of resistance in the ways they craft a curriculum to teach alternative notions of citizenship. The participants in this study drew on the collective history and experiential knowledge of African-American women possessing a double consciousness (DuBois [1903] 1994) and civic estrangement (Tillet 2012) in order to teach a construct of citizenship that was relevant to their lives and particular community. African-American women teachers recognise that part of this dual consciousness of citizenship is teaching students the knowledge and skills needed to succeed in a society that continues to marginalise non-White bodies.

Because of their experiential knowledge, a number of African-American women teachers are aware of the schooling and societal structures that continue to harm students and Communities of Colour. Burdened but armed with this awareness, 'teaching provided the opportunity to heal souls, imparting encouraging words for spirits wounded by racial discrimination, poverty, and miseducation across generations' (Dixson and Dingus 2008, 827). Teaching is political and African-American teachers in the research literature do not limit themselves to the assigned curriculum (Dixson and Dingus 2008; Gordon 1985; Ladson-Billings 2009). They often find ways to teach lessons that fosters the development of an intelligent and critical citizenry. It is important to note that their citizenship work of racial uplift has changed throughout history and looks differently based on each teachers' own knowledge, experiences, and the unique needs of their community. Because of the political consciousness and activism of African-American women teachers, their students develop an awareness of the structural inequities that aligns with their complicated experiences as dual citizens. This new way of seeing the world is taught in conjunction with lessons of struggle and perseverance rooted in lived experiences.

Collins (2009) wrote, 'survival is a form of resistance ... and represents the foundation of Black women's activism' (216). Part of a Black teacher's activism is passing on to her students' lessons of perseverance in a society where they continue to experience both racism and civic estrangement (Tillet 2012). This is often done by utilizing 'sermons,' life lessons, or stories as ways of teaching students how to navigate the duality of citizenship. Thompson (1998) noted that a Black feminist ethic of caring

> ... have paid close attention to the issue of race ... and emphasize knowledge. Indeed, an almost defining feature of Black feminist theory is that, characteristically, it is referenced to Black culture as experienced, interpreted, and reproduced by Black women and "womanish" girls. (9)

The stories that African-American women teachers tell their students originates from their own experiences as women of colour who are conscious of the duality – or, as King (1988) suggested, 'double jeopardy' – of citizenship their students (will) face. Teachers share the honest knowledge with their students about the reality of struggle in an effort for students to reflect upon and extrapolate meaning from these stories about what it means to be a racialised and gendered citizen. While this knowledge is honest and not innocent, it is taught in order to ensure the future resilience of the community. African-American teachers are frank in teaching students about struggle and discrimination while calling on the historic narratives of African Americans whose legacies continues to promote racial uplift towards full citizenship.

While these life lessons are taught as an effort to uplift the community, they also demonstrate to students that African-American women's cultural and experiential knowledge are powerful and legitimate sources of knowledge. African-American women teachers rooting their understandings of citizenship in their own lived experiences are not merely critiquing the dominant knowledge structure of the citizenship curriculum but more importantly, asserting an African-American woman's standpoint has a legitimate place in the teaching of future citizens. The teachers not only use their positions to teach notions of citizenship that is meaningful and reflective of their reality, but simultaneously empowering African-American women, thus continuing the legacy of 'lifting as we climb.'[1]

Conclusion

The findings from this study allow further reflection on how African-American women teachers infuse their experiential knowledge into their curriculum. The literature on teacher identity suggests that their sense of self, prior experiences, cultural knowledge, and beliefs are relevant to how they approach teaching and impacts their curricular and pedagogical decision-making (Agee 2004). An implication from this study reveals that we must begin to examine how to best prepare teachers to critically reflect on the complexity of their intersecting identities and how it will influence their teacher identity and curricular decision-making. Teacher educators are most often focused on White teacher identity and teachers of colour are ignored, or it is assumed that because they are from that community they do not need to reflect on the tenets of their identities. This is a faulty assumption, and oftentimes teachers of colour have different needs and areas of growth that are neglected in teacher education and in-service programmes.

We know that epistemology is fundamental in teaching, yet we continue to ignore how teachers construct knowledge and what they choose to privilege or reject and why. We never ask teachers how and why they want to construct narratives in particular ways. From a Black feminist perspective, Black women teachers draw on a sociohistorical lens and ways of knowing (i.e., uplifting) in how they make curricular and pedagogical decisions. We can still see it today, but its roots are in the distant past. Teachers come into teaching with a wealth of knowledge and experiences that they accumulate from their various spatial and social locations. Because the structure of knowledge production and validation is controlled by elite White men, their knowledge is deemed as the universal truth, and the experiences and knowledge of women of colour are distorted and excluded from what counts as legitimate forms/sources of knowledge (Collins 2009).

Experience is a valid source of knowledge, and teacher education programmes and ongoing professional development must empower teachers to challenge dominant bodies of knowledge so that traditionally subjugated knowledge is taught and legitimised.

While there are teacher education programmes and professional development courses that push teachers to present critical and diverse narratives of the past, the result is that subjugated knowledge (of women of colour in particular) is taught using an 'additive' approach and not as part of the dominant historical narrative. A recommendation would be that teachers must be encouraged by teacher educators and practitioners to challenge the prevailing knowledge validation structure and work to transform the curriculum to represent diverse voices and perspectives.

Note

1. "Lifting as we climb" was the motto of National Association of Coloured Women.

Disclosure statement

No potential conflict of interest was reported by the author.

References

Agee, J. 2004. "Negotiating a Teaching Identity: An African American Teacher's Struggle to Teach in Test-Driven Contexts." *Teachers College Record* 106 (4): 747–774.

Avoseh, M. B. M. 2001. "Learning to be Active Citizens: Lessons of Traditional Africa for lifelong learning." *International Journal of Lifelong Education* 20 (5): 479–486.

Barton, K. C., and L. S. Levstik. 2013. *Teaching History for the Common Good*. Mahwah, NJ: Routledge.

Beauboeuf-Lafontant, T. 2002. "A Womanist Experience of Caring: Understanding the Pedagogy of Exemplary Black Women Teachers." *The Urban Review* 34 (1): 71–86.

Bondy, J. M. 2015. "Hybrid Citizenship: Latina Youth and the Politics of Belonging." *The High School Journal* 98 (4): 353–373.

Castro, A. J. 2013. "What Makes a Citizen? Critical and Multicultural Citizenship and Preservice Teachers' Understanding of Citizenship Skills." *Theory & Research in Social Education* 41 (2): 219–246.

Collier-Thomas, B. 1982. "Guest Editorial: The Impact of Black Women in Education: An Historical Overview." *The Journal of Negro Education* 51 (3): 173–180.

Collins, P. H. 2009. *Black Feminist Thought: Knowledge, Consciousness, and the Politics of Empowerment*. New York, NY: Routledge.

Crenshaw, K. 1989. "Demarginalizing the Intersection of Race and Sex: A Black Feminist Critique of Antidiscrimination Doctrine, Feminist Theory and Antiracist Politics." *The University of Chicago Legal Forum* 139–167.

Crenshaw, K. 1991. "Mapping the Margins: Intersectionality, Identity Politics, and Violence against Women of Color." *Stanford Law Review* 43: 1241–1299.

Dillard, C. B. 2000. "The Substance of Things Hoped for, the Evidence of Things Not: Examining an Endarkened Feminist Epistemology in Educational Research and Leadership." *International Journal of Qualitative Research in Education* 13 (6): 661–681.

Dillard, C. B. 2012. *Learning to (Re)member the Things We've Learned to Forget: Endarkened Feminisms, Spirituality, and the Sacred Nature of Research and Teaching*. New York: Peter Lang.

Dilworth, P. P. 2004. "Multicultural Citizenship Education: Case Studies from Social Studies Classrooms." *Theory and Research in Social Education* 32 (2): 153–186.

Dilworth, P. 2008. "Multicultural Citizenship Education." In *The Sage Handbook of Education for Citizenship and Democracy*, edited by J. Arthur, I. Davies, and C. Hahn, 424–437. Los Angeles, CA: Sage Publications.

Dixson, A. D. 2003. "'Let's Do This!' Black Women Teachers' Politics and Pedagogy." *Urban Education* 38 (2): 217–235.

Dixson, A., and J. Dingus. 2008. "In Search of Our Mothers' Gardens: Black Women Teachers and Professional Socialization." *The Teachers College Record* 110 (4): 805–837.

DuBois, W. E. B. [1903] 1994. *The Souls of Black Folk*. New York: Dover Thrift Editions.

Giddings, P. 1984. *When and Where I Enter: The Impact of Black Women on Race and Sex in America*. New York: William Morrow.

Gordon, B. M. 1985. "Toward Emancipation in Citizenship Education: The Case of African American Cultural Knowledge." *Theory & Research in Social Education* 12 (4): 1–23.

Hahn, C. 2008. "Education for Citizenship and Democracy in the United States." In *The Sage Handbook of Education for Citizenship and Democracy*, edited by J. Arthur, I. Davies, and C. Hahn, 263–278. Los Angeles, CA: Sage.

Harley, S. 1996. "Nannie Helen Burroughs: 'The Black Goddess of Liberty'." *Journal of Negro History*, 81: 62–71.

Harris-Perry, M. 2011. *Sister Citizen: Shame, Stereotypes, and Black Women in America*. New Haven, CT: Yale University Press.

Hooks, B. 1999. *Ain't I a Woman: Black Women and Feminism*. New York: South End Press.

Howard, T. C. 2002. "Hearing Footsteps in the Dark: African American Students' Descriptions of Effective Teachers." *Journal of Education for Students Placed at Risk (JESPAR)* 7 (4): 425–444.

Howard, T. C. 2010. *Why Race and Culture Matter in Schools: Closing the Achievement Gap in America's Classrooms*. New York, NY: Teachers College Press.

Irvine, J. J. 1986. "An Analysis of the Problem of Disappearing Black Educators." *The Elementary School Journal* 88 (5): 503–515.

Irvine, J. J. 1998. "Warm Demanders." *Education Week*, May 13. www.edweek.org/ew/articles/1998/05/13/35irvine.h17.ht.html?override=web.

King, D. K. 1988. "Multiple Jeopardy, Multiple Consciousness: The Context of a Black Feminist Ideology." In *Words of Fire: An Anthology of African-American Feminist Thought*, edited by B. Guy-Sheftall (1995), 294–317. New York: The New Press.

King, L. G. 2014. "When Lions Write History." *Multicultural Education* 22 (1): 2–11.

Knight Abowitz, K., and J. Harnish. 2006. "Contemporary Discourses of Citizenship." *Review of Educational Research* 76 (4): 653–690.

Ladson, G. 1984. "Citizenship and Values: An Ethnographic Study in a Black School Setting." Unpublished dissertation, Stanford University, Palo Alto, CA.

Ladson-Billings, G. 2004. "Culture Versus Citizenship: The Challenge of Racialized Citizenship in the United States." In *Diversity and Citizenship Education: Global Perspectives*, edited by J. A. Banks, 99–126. San Francisco, CA: Josey-Bass.

Ladson-Billings, G. 2009. *The Dream Keepers Successful Teachers of African American Children*. San Francisco, CA: Jossey-Bass.

Lomawaima, K. T., and T. L. McCarty. 2002. "When Tribal Sovereignty Challenges Democracy: American Indian Education and the Democratic Ideal." *American Educational Research Journal* 39 (2): 279–305.

Marshall, T. H. [1950] 1998. "Citizenship and Social Class." In *The Citizenship Debates*, edited by G. Shafir, 93–111. Minneapolis: University of Minnesota Press.

McCarty, T., and T. Lee. 2014. "Critical Culturally Sustaining/Revitalizing Pedagogy and Indigenous Education Sovereignty." *Harvard Educational Review* 84 (1): 101–124.

Merriam, S. B. 2009. *Qualitative Research and Case Study Applications in Education*. San Francisco, CA: Jossey-Bass.

Miles, M. B., M. A. Huberman, and J. Saldaña. 2013. *Qualitative Data Analysis: A Methods Sourcebook*. Los Angeles, CA: Sage.

Murray, A. D. 2012. "Countering the Master Narrative in U.S. Social Studies: Nannie Helen Burroughs and New Narratives in History Education." In *Histories of Social Studies and Race: 1865–2000*, edited by C. Woyshner, and C. H. Bohan, 99–114. New York: Palgrave Macmillian.

Noddings, N. 1988. *Caring: A Feminine Approach to Ethics and Moral Education*. Berkeley: University of California Press.

Noguera, P. A. 2003. "Schools, Prisons, and Social Implications of Punishment: Rethinking Disciplinary Practices." *Theory into Practice* 42 (4): 341–350.

Paris, D. 2012. "Culturally Sustaining Pedagogy a Needed Change in Stance, Terminology, and Practice." *Educational Researcher* 41 (3): 93–97.

Parker, W. 1996. "'Advanced' Ideas about Democracy: Toward a Pluralist Conception of Citizenship Education." *The Teachers College Record* 98 (1): 104–125.

Parker, W. C. 2003. *Teaching Democracy: Unity and Diversity in Public Life*. New York: Teachers College Press.

Rosaldo, R. 1997. "Cultural Citizenship, Inequality, and Multiculturalism." In *Latino Cultural Citizenship: Claiming Identity, Space, and Rights*, edited by W. V. Flores, and R. Benmayor, 27–38. Boston, MA: Beacon Press.

Salinas, C., and A. J. Castro. 2010. "Disrupting the Official Curriculum: Cultural Biography and the Curriculum Decision Making of Latino Preservice Teachers." *Theory & Research in Social Education* 38 (3): 428–463.

Salinas, C., A. E. Vickery, and M. Franquiz. 2016. "Advancing Border Pedagogies: Understandings of Citizenship Through Comparisons of Home to School Contexts." *The High School Journal* 99 (4): 322–336.

Spinner, J. 1984. *The Boundaries of Citizenship: Race, Ethnicity, and Nationalist in the Liberal State*. Baltimore, MD: John Hopkins University Press.

Thompson, A. 1998. "Not the Color Purple: Black Feminist Lessons for Educational Caring." *Harvard Educational Review* 68 (4): 522–555.

Tillet, S. 2012. *Sites of Slavery: Citizenship and Racial Democracy in the Post-Civil Rights Imagination*. Durham, NC: Duke University Press.

Valenzuela, A. 1999. *Subtractive Schooling U.S. Mexican Youth and the Politics of Caring*. Albany: State University of New York Press.

Vasquez, J. A. 1988. "Contexts of Learning for Minority Students." In *The Educational Forum* (Vol. 52, No. 3, pp. 243–253). Taylor & Francis Group.

Vickery, A. E. 2015. "It was Never Meant for Us: Towards a Black Feminist Construct of Citizenship in Social Studies." *The Journal of Social Studies Research* 39 (3): 163–172.

Vickery, A. E. 2016. "'I Worry about My Community': African American Women Utilizing Communal Notions of Citizenship in the Social Studies Classroom." *International Journal of Multicultural Education* 18 (1): 28–44.

Walker, A. 1983. *In Search of our Mother's Gardens: Womanist Prose*. San Diego, CA: Harcourt Brace Jovanovich.

Walker, V. S. 1996. *Their Highest Potential: An African American School Community in the Segregated South*. Chapel Hill: University of North Carolina Press.

Westheimer, J., and J. Kahne. 2004. "What Kind of Citizen? The Politics of Educating for Democracy." *American Educational Research Journal* 41 (2): 237–269.

Yuval-Davis, N. 1997. "Women, Citizenship and Difference." *Feminist Review* 57: 4–27.

'You can't see for lookin'': how southern womanism informs perspectives of work and curriculum theory

Berlisha Morton

ABSTRACT
Southern womanism is the theory that evokes a self-reflexive process to challenge scholars, teachers, and activists to reconceptualise the agency of 'workers.' Southern womanism claims that theoretical knowledge resides within the histories of southern Black women workers which developed as they transitioned from enslavement to domestic work to birthing a generation of African ascendant scholars and artists. Within their work is the theoretical possibility of exploring these women as agential subjects whose intellectual history is found in the intersections of region, regional identity, race, gender, sexuality, nature, art, food, and spirituality.

I was halfway through my first year as a visiting professor at a small, elite liberal arts university in the northeastern portion of the United States when I encountered the dilemma of whether or not to overenrol my race and education course for the spring semester. The prospect of a class of potentially 40 students would not have raised eyebrows at the research one institution where I had just received my doctorate a year prior. But at my institution of employment, my decision to drastically overenrol the course would be considered antithetical to the pedagogical philosophy of my department, and in complete opposition to the University's student–teacher ratios which are part of complex algorithms used to determine national rankings. With this knowledge, a decision to not overenrol the course was the best option for my career in addition to the fact that more students equal more work, so not having a small class would make my life easier. But for some reason, this line of thinking was not resting well within my spirit.

I went home to Louisiana for my winter break, and I was visiting with my mother's sister, Aunt Hazel, when my mother mentioned my dilemma. Aunt Hazel asked me what I was going to do, and I told her that I decided to not overenrol the course. Her eyes widened with shock and disbelief, and she looked at me right in the eye, and in her deep south Louisiana accent, she said, 'Baaaybee, you turning people away!' And with a scolding tone she added, 'That's not what we do.' Aunt Hazel's *we* did not refer to people with doctorates, philosophers, historians, or even people with bachelor's degrees. Aunt Hazel's *we* did, however, refer to those of us who were raised on Warren Street in Kenner, Louisiana by Black women such as Bertha Harbor, Lillian White, Carrie

Henderson, Edna Harper, Annie Bell Payton, Mamie Montgomery, Carrie Franklin, Lelia Thompson, Rebecca Nelson, and Ernestine Davis.

These women worked hard to keep their own homes just as immaculate as the homes of the white people they maintained a few miles up the road in New Orleans. These women gave to others when they themselves had little to survive on; but they gave because they knew that God always provided. Women who had enough love to care for the children in the houses they cleaned, the children they gave birth to, and the children of their friends on Warren Street. These women were not perfect – they worked too hard, ate too much of the wrong things, yelled too loud, coddled the boys and whipped the girls, and loved the wrong men too hard. But they lived these lives of too much work, too much food, and too much love with grace and elegance. As members of the exploited domestic class, they rode busses into the heavy fog of racism, sexism, and classism every day. They were not mere witnesses of inequality; they dusted the cabinets, shined the crystal, washed the china, combed the hair, and ironed the shirts of capitalistic patriarchy. But somehow, they made sure that girl-children like me never saw them crumble. They made sure to show us that work might be hard, unfair, and demeaning, but if you could make it back home, if you could make it to church on Sunday, and if could you make it to your friend's porch for a fresh glass of lemonade and a good laugh, everything would be alright. My Aunt Hazel was also one of these girl-children, therefore, she had to let me know that turning away people is not what *we* do; *we* work, even when work is hard.

In spite of the literature I had read over the years about how the women I just described are broken and damaged by the strong Black woman archetype, and in spite of my understanding of the importance of self-care, I decided to overenrol the course. And it was hard work. I had to create a hybrid lecture/seminar course in which I lectured for the first half of the 120-minute class and divided the class into small groups for discussion during the second half. My decision was not well received. My radical students of all colours were angry because they perceived that I had reduced the integrity of the course because I did not weed out the students they thought created inhospitable learning environments – white male athletes, conservative students of colour, and conservative white women. They thought the class should have been more closely guarded, and that I should have created a space for *them*. My department chair was angry with me because I committed several violations from throwing off the department's and the University's student–professor ratios, to violating the building's fire codes, to giving the appearance that I was being abused by the department. After a hard day of reprimands from students and administrators, I sought out the closest thing to southern comfort food I could find and trudged home. My mind wandered as I ate my chicken Dilbar creamy masala with garlic naan while pretending that it was bowl of steaming hot chicken and sausage gumbo with a fresh yeast roll. I realised that Professor Morton was not a real person. She was an amalgamation of other people's projected fetishes and fantasies. To my radical students, I was a fetishised object that had the magical powers to erase racism from the classroom, serve as judge and jury for the racist students, and open their hearts and minds to the mystical powers of the Universe. To my sheltered, conservative students, I was a living fantasy – an oversexed, angry Black sister *gurl* sent from the bowels of the inner-city who used all my affirmative action benefits to make them feel bad about themselves and their mamas and their cousins too. To my senior colleagues who had dedicated their lives to studying and eradicating racism and sexism, I was a dream of fantasy and fetish – a poor, oppressed little Black girl who internalised racist stereotypes and as such, needed saving from herself. As flawed as a human as I was/am, I did not recognise this fetishised and fantasised *Professor*. But somehow, this person called Professor Morton had to show up to work the next day and be the *Professor* that each individual she encountered expected her to be; I had to go to *work*. Heeding James Baldwin's warning, I knew that Berlisha would become schizophrenic if she tried to live up the expectations of the fetishes, and she would become bitter and tired if she tried to fight against the fantasies.

Instead of choosing a side, I decided to teach from this site of unrest and confusion. Berlisha would remain open and vulnerable while the *Professor* would take the hits. When the *Professor's* nose was too bloodied to teach, Berlisha would take over for a little while until the *Professor* was healed. And most importantly, Berlisha always made sure to be leery and distrustful of the *Professor*.

My decision to teach from this site of chaos and confusion created a pedagogical moment where the *Professor* could be fearless in the classroom while I would be protected. The Professor had nothing to lose; I, however, risked losing my family, my identity, my culture, my spirituality, and my very life. Professor Morton was a fantasy the world could afford to lose, but Berlisha had to survive.

I did survive, and the class turned out to be successful according to my standards because the work that the *Professor* did in that space managed to change some minds and move some consciences. During my end of the year performance review with my department chair, the issue of my decision to overenrol race and education was revisited. I recounted my Aunt Hazel's admonition to not turn people away to my department chair, but I did not adequately explain who the *we* were that she was talking about. Upon hearing the abbreviated version of my Aunt Hazel story, my department chair, a sympathetic and knowledgeable man of colour, proceeded to tell me in a highly respectful, extremely politically correct, loving way that I would not survive in the elite liberal arts college world much less academia if I based my decision-making based on cute sayings from my poor old auntie in the South. As he continued to talk, my mind wandered to all of the educational theories and philosophies I had been exposed to, and I realised that Dewey, Foucault, Derrida, and Eurocentric understandings of epistemology, could not explain my Aunt Hazel's understanding of pedagogy and how her understanding influenced my pedagogical practices. They had never been to Warren Street, and they did not understand what it meant to be raised by Black working women. These women constructed and tested theories of universal truth from ontological realisations that have not been valued in the traditional epistemological frame of intelligence. In that moment, southern womanism had never been more real. It was time to write about how southern womanism both *interrupts* curriculum theory and *is* curriculum theory.

The need for southern womanism

This work defines southern Black women workers as the enslaved and domestic workers whose bodies were used and abused for the advancement of US capitalistic patriarchal culture (Fox-Genovese 1988; Harley and The Black Women and Work Collective 2002; Hunter 1997; Jones 2009; Rollins 1985). African ascendant (Dillard 2012) people in the South locked in the grips of chattel slavery were systematically and brutally denied access to educational systems that would have allowed them advanced mastery of the

Western system of letters. While the primary intention of these laws were to limit the communication capabilities of African and African ascendant people to deter slave rebellions, these laws also inhibited their abilities to record their histories and stories via the most privileged medium in Western culture – the written word. To be sure, when America grew as a nation, the systematic denial of educational access coupled with the rise of scientific racism allowed for the erasure of the lived histories of African and African ascendant people from the traditional historical data sources – books, diaries, journals, etc. This erasure results in an 'out of sight, out of mind, does not exist' mentality in historiographical research. As such, the intellectual histories of African and African ascendant women were not passed through privileged renderings of history. Instead, their intellectual history was passed down through their work – cooking, ironing, planting, growing, harvesting, cleaning, and caretaking. This intellectual history transcends genre, and therefore manifested in the work of the ascendants as literature, poetry, song, dance, recipes, pedagogy, activism, and academic scholarship.

While these women have been historicised as tragic yet quaint, folk-like objects, southern womanism argues that these women are pedagogues whose pedagogy relied upon a prophetic vision of the future rooted in spirituality. Within the experiences of the women who picked the fruits and bore the children of capitalistic patriarchy resides important information about how to work, how to survive, and how to teach survival within the most egregious circumstances of society. The experiences of southern Black women workers are critical to the field of curriculum studies and educational history because these women and their experiences are part and parcel to the birthing of a generation of African ascendant (Dillard 2012) scholars and artists. Within their work is the theoretical possibility of seeing these women as agential subjects whose intellectual history is found in the intersections of region, regional identity, race, gender, sexuality, nature, art, food, and spirituality. I humbly name their work *southern womanism* to evoke the spirits and blessings of the Black women who worked and worked themselves to death to ensure the survival of their people and liberation of working women.

Southern womanism challenges scholars to centre the subjectivity of southern Black women workers as an onto-epistemological space to reconceptualise how we think about our work as scholars, teachers, and activists. African ascendant women understand that our histories and identities cannot be constructed from dominant historical narratives that have intentionally erased, fragmented, and romanticised the histories of our foremothers. Therefore in our research and teaching, we constantly pull from multiple sites of understanding – theoretical, historical, personal, spiritual, sexual, poetical, and cultural – to construct our truths in the process of constructing the truths of other unheard voices. For African ascendant women who identify as scholar-activists, this is not a new process; however, southern womanism seeks to move this process one step further with this question: what would our work look like if we theorised *through* the experiences of southern Black women workers instead of theorising their lives *from* our current positionality? In other words, how can we see these women beyond the painful and tragic stereotypes of the mammy/matriarch and begin to understand that within their experiences is knowledge that can be mined for valuable insight about pedagogy, theory, and research?

Southern womanism does not present static definitions of identity, race, gender, religion, and space to which experience can be compared; however, the focus is on within. It embraces the rich, mystical, and tragic tradition in the space *called* the US South and combines it with the theoretical call for universality and inclusion associated with womanism. It has an emphasis on listening; history becomes an active and universal process where all voices and expressions are heard, whether they are spoken or unspoken or *supernatural* or *natural*. Southern womanism is also concerned with journey and asks readers to travel down roads both seen and unseen. Therefore, southern womanism is purposeful in its terminology. It does not seek to define a 'southern woman,' yet uses the terms southern and womanism to evoke an interdisciplinary space that merges history, discourse analysis, narrative inquiry, and Black female subjectivity in an effort to transcend the boundaries of methodological genre. On the methodological level, the southern piece draws on historiographical research methods and sources used in Southern Studies and literary analyses of Southern literature; the womanism piece evokes a theoretical space that draws on womanist theories, Black feminist thought, and discourse analysis. The possibility for using southern womanism as a theory that can inform curriculum history and research is posited in other works (Morton forthcoming); however, what follows is an explanation of how southern womanism can inform the pedagogical praxis of scholar-activists.

Working through the South

If we are to recognise southern Black women workers as pedagogues, we must first disrupt the epistemological tradition that consistently centres the concept of mothering as the primary site for interrogating the experiences of women in the classroom (Grumet 1988; Noddings 1984). In recognising the existence of Black female subjectivity, curriculum scholars have carefully documented how mammy/matriarch/angry Black woman stereotypes manifest in academia, and the physiological and spiritual impact these manifestations have on the Black female body (Berry 2006; Collins 2000; Dillard 2012; Edwards 2010; Guillory 2011; Hooks 1994; Taliaferro Baszille 2004). However, within the field of curriculum theory, there is a gap between the work of African ascendant women who have documented the lives of southern Black women workers and how Black Feminist Thought is conceptualised for pedagogical praxis. To be sure, these important, yet also epistemologically dominant, feminist post-structural analyses of the female body being tied to problematic societal images of the mother are essential within the field of curriculum studies. Southern womanism does not reject this tradition; however, southern womanism argues that within this tradition is a pattern of pathological whiteness which binds southern Black women workers within mammy/matriarch stereotypes which, in turn, does not consider Black women's unique relationship with work. Black women scholars have acknowledged that the schisms in how white women have conceptualised their relation to work and how Black women have conceptualised their relationship to work (Jones 2009). While the mammy/Black matriarch is attached to societal fantasies and fetishes of Black femininity and sexuality, these stereotypes are also heavily tied to the socio-historical consciousness of the Black woman worker.

Feminist post-structural discourse has correctly challenged scholars think about how the silent image is often more powerful the spoken word. Images of June Cleaver vacuuming in heals on the 1950s sitcom *Leave it to Beaver* and Juanita Moore's performance of Annie Johnson in the 1959 film *Imitation of Life* burned images of white motherhood and Black motherhood into the collective consciousness of generations of Americans. June's life was ideal. Her immaculate home and clothes reflected her immaculate life style. Annie's life was to be avoided; who wanted to be a life-long domestic who was rejected by her own child – even if the reward was to have Mahalia Jackson sing at your funeral. Eventually, Bill Cosby gave the post-civil rights generation (and beyond) our own June Cleaver – Claire Huxtable. Unlike Florida Evans from Good Times, Mabel Thomas from *What's Happening!!* and even Diahann Carroll as Julia in the sitcom *Julia*, we never saw Claire unkempt, frustrated, or angry. Her uniform was sleek silk blouses and satin dresses. In scenes where she was the disciplinarian, she wielded her punishments by use of wit and charm; she never yelled or screamed, or even frowned for extended periods of time. Black art adorned the Huxtable household and Bill Cosby's character Cliff Huxtable frequently wore Historically Black College and University paraphernalia. However, the message was clear, the new Black Mother was a caramel complexioned June Cleaver; but she was also a worker. Her work as lawyer was not demeaning or tiresome. Her work allowed her the time to take care of five children without a nanny. Her work fulfilled her and allowed her to maintain a slim figure. Her work allowed her plenty of rest so that she never took her anger out on her children and loved ones. She was the ideal mother, but she was also the *ideal worker*.

The whitewashing of the Black women worker is a similar phenomenon that happens in the fields of curriculum studies and educational history. While we are quick to dissect and reject the June Cleaver image, theories of mothering are still rooted Eurocentric conceptualisations of femininity and womanhood which place all women on progressive track toward the idea of a deconstructed feminine ideal. On this progressive track, the kind mammy and the overbearing Black matriarch are images that are thrown away into the world of feminist post-structural analysis, and justly so. In spite of Claire Huxtable's pristine hair and dry cleaned suits, the image of the benevolent mammy and the angry Black matriarch dominate students' images of what the Black female professor *should be*. However, in our efforts to disrupt the stereotypes of the Black Mammy and the Black Matriarch, we have learned to forget (Dillard 2012) that behind these stereotypes are real women who have something to teach us about how we teach and why we teach. Essentially, this emphasis on mothering produces a racist and paternalistic discourse that sees Black women in the professoriate as objects to be taken care of or protected from damage of stereotypes. In that vein, these schisms directly relate to one of the colloquial reasons as to why Black women were (and still are) reluctant to join any type of feminist movement due the perception that feminism is concerned with white women's 'right to work' vs. the idea that Black women have always worked – by their men's side. In recognising this caveat, southern womanism is not looking for place within the mothering tradition in curriculum studies. Instead, southern womanism is taking the work that Black scholars have performed with regard to Black southern subjectivity and is merging it with the work of Black women curriculum theorists such as Lisa Delpit, Denise Taliaferro Baszille, Kirsten T. Edwards, Nichole Guillory, Theordora R. Berry, LaVada Taylor-Brandon, and Sabrina Ross. The synergy from this merging rescues the mammy/matriarch from the binary of the tragic stereotype/bad mother, and positions them as southern Black women workers. From this position, they are agential subjects within the onto-epistemological in-between (Barad 2003; Taliaferro-Baszille 2006), and their work can become a *pedagogy of work*. This pedagogy of work is found in their cooking, cleaning, ironing, and gardening. But it is also found in their bodies, their bones, and their words. In this sense, southern womanism posits that this pedagogy of work has two traits – action and utterance.

In this pedagogy of work, the theoretical underpinnings of action and utterance can be traced throughout the periods of enslavement, Reconstruction, Post-Reconstruction, the Jim Crow Era, Post-Civil Rights, and the Black Lives Matter movement. As southern womanism is concerned with the travel through time and space, the US South becomes critical spatially as the site where action and utterance was born and nurtured. In popular culture, southern identity is constricted to the angry, violent white male, and his foil, the docile southern belle sitting on the porch in a hoop skirt drinking sweet iced tea. While all southerners, in general, must confront stereotypes of being 'slow,' 'shiftless,' and 'ignorant,' the Black southerner is often feminised as a victimised servant or as the fat and sassy servant. These images serve two purposes. Images of happy-go-lucky mammies appeared after the US Civil War to clean up the US South's image and to solidify the narrative that the enslaved people were well taken care of and happy (Wallace-Sanders 2008). The second image of the victimised servant is part of a larger socio-historical project to pathologise racism in the South as opposed to or outside of traditional American values (Cobb 2005). However, the work of Black scholars such as Robinson (2014) and Laymon (2013) are speaking back against perceptions of southern identity as wholly white, male, docile, and tragic. When southern identity ceases to be white and male, and instead focuses on southernism as subjectivity, the South becomes a work site with a wealth of information about how Black women workers navigated a racist terrain while creating a knowledge base from their understandings of race, gender, religion, and sexuality. In this sense, the South cannot be solely historicised as a problem space, but is also a place of work in which Black women survived through action and utterance.

Action – I ain't whistlin' Dixie

Southern womanism defines action as the physical act of work, but also the connection of the physical act of work to a higher purpose. In this sense, work becomes more than the process to gain capital for survival. Work becomes necessary for the survival of the African ascendants. In the introduction to her 2008 text, *Making a Way of Out of No Way,* Coleman defines the concept of 'making a way out of no way' as a 'central theme in black women's struggles and God's assistance in helping them to overcome oppression' (9). As a womanist theologian, Coleman defines and applies this concept in relation to the socio-religious experiences of Black women. In previous work, this concept of 'making a way out of no way' was utilised to express African ascendant people's mystic connection to educational opportunity (Morton and Hart 2015). However, I found that this concept is also a pathway to learning from the past and highly useful in understanding the pedagogy of Black women workers. Coleman uses postmodernist womanist theology to define the past as a 'critical dimension in "making a way out of no way"' (122). She informs readers that in order to learn from the past, we must acknowledge that 'those who have died have never left' and that

> We *learn* from the past and then use what we have learned, what we have experienced, toward God's ideals of truth, beauty, adventure, art, peace, justice, and quality of life. Creative transformation remains the process, goal, and measure for 'making a way out of no way.' (122)

'Making a way out of no way' is an onto-epistemology embedded in the collective consciousness of Black women workers and can be used in the classrooms and scholarship of curriculum scholars to better understand the concept of action. Whether the work was forced upon them by enslavement or necessary for the survival of their families when they became freedwoman, the work that Black women domestics faced was harrowing, demeaning, and often times physically and sexually violent (Jones 2009). Westernised understandings of ontology and epistemology would posit that these women and their descendants are bound to a traumatic and tragic existence, if they survived at all. However, these women made meaning out of demeaning work. This meaning contained a metaphysical understanding that the Higher Power will take from our bodies what is needed for the survival of our ascendants. In this sense, work became a social, economic, and spiritual process for the survival of Black people in the United States. But more importantly, imbedded in this meaning are the possibilities of a boundless Black womanhood. Black southern women workers found their worth in their work. As scholar-activists, if we were to look for our worth in our work, what would our work be worth?

The very nature of collegiate teaching is elite. And although scholars might be committed to working for social justice, the universities can in many ways separate us from the community. Now, I am not suggesting that teacher-scholar-activists *need* to identify with marginalised communities in order to be effective. I am suggesting that sometimes we might have to be resourceful and creative when our attempts to enact an anti-oppressive curriculum fall on deaf ears. For example, how can our work change if we are creative and resourceful like the Black woman activist Bree Newsome?

During the early morning hours of 27 June 2015, Brittany 'Bree' Newsome scaled a 30 foot flag pole in front of the South Carolina State House to remove the confederate flag that had been flying there for 53 years. Newsome, a Black woman activist and filmmaker from North Carolina, removed the flag in an act of protest and healing in response to Dylann Roof's massacre of nine members of Charleston, South Carolina's historically Black church, Emmanuel A.M.E. (Mother Emmanuel). Roof, a self-proclaimed white supremacist, was photographed with the confederate flag to symbolise his white supremacist ideology. When these photos surfaced in the media, they reignited debates about whether the flag is a symbol of hate or heritage, and if the flag should continue to fly in memorial at the South Carolina State House. While the media, lawmakers, and general public talked about their positions on the true meaning of the flag, Bree Newsome went to work.

With professional climbing equipment, she scaled the flag pole, removed the flag, hoisted it in the air and proclaimed, 'You come against me with hatred, and oppression, and violence; I come against you in the name of God. This flag comes down today.' Bree continued to hold the flag as she made her descent, and as she got closer to the police officers waiting at the bottom of the pole to arrest her, she recited the Psalm, 'The Lord is my light and my salvation, whom shall I fear … The Lord is a stronghold in my life, of whom shall I be afraid.' While it is possible to read her act as a part of the melee within the aftermath of the Mother Emmanuel massacre, Bree's work exemplifies the pedagogy of work through action that is southern womanism. She sacrificed her body in a space that is both home and hostile in an act of mental acumen rooted in her spirituality.

Utterance – ain't I a theorist?

Utterance is a complex intersection of art, spirituality, and pedagogy. It can be understood as an intense epistemological process in which spiritual wisdom morphed into self-protective utterances that spoke to a specific need for self-preservation from the egregious racism and sexism that southern Black working women experienced in their work and home environments (Morton forthcoming). As such, southern womanism argues that when southern Black women domestics are acknowledged as agential subjects, their utterances, or phrases, such as 'feed him with a long handled spoon' and 'a bad start makes a good ending' become more than quaint colloquialisms. They contain valuable information about how to relay complex life lessons in a manner that causes a reluctant listener to reflect on her actions. Utterance follows the Black oral/aural tradition of using riddles and rhymes to confuse or trick outsiders of plans for escape, riot, or revolt. Utterance can be likened to riddles, or one-line parables.

The most critical aspect of utterance is that it usually happens in close or closed spaces among women. In these spaces, utterances are spoken to teach a valuable life lesson, or to prevent a young woman from making a detrimental mistake. Because time is truly of the essence for southern Black working women, utterances had to be spoken quickly and forcibly. But although utterances are short in words, they carry deep meanings that forced the listener to sit and reflect on (1) the answer to the riddle and (2) the relevance of the riddle to her life. Essentially, utterance is a complex pedagogical dance between the utterer and the listener. Once the listener has unveiled the meaning of the utterance and realised the application of the utterance to her life, the listener becomes the utterer, and then proceeds to pass the knowledge of the utterance to the next ascendant. What follows are some examples of utterances, their hidden meanings, and their possibilities within the field of curriculum theory:

I ain't whistlin' Dixie

Dixie is a colloquial name for the South and the shortened name of the song, 'I wish I was in Dixie.' Dixie, the song, was performed in Black-face minstrel shows during the 1850s, and eventually became the infamous anthem of the Old South after the US Civil War. Because Dixie is a song of longing to be 'In the Land of Cotton' where 'Old Times There are Not Forgotten,' anyone caught 'whistlin' Dixie' was thought be lounging in a lazy state of reminiscence. However, when Black women utter, 'I ain't whistlin' Dixie,' there is a deeper meaning. First, there is a rejection of the racist overtones of the song. Second, there is a rejection of the laziness and wistfulness associated with having the time to whistle. Finally, the utterance is intended to let the listener know that they are they serious – they are not lounging, whistling, or reminiscing – they are ready for action.

I'm gonna tell you in the front so you don't stick out behind

The use of this utterance is twofold because it is used to preface information but also serves as a warning. Due to the intimacy of domestic work which oftentimes found Black women in the homes of whites, Black women gained valuable insider knowledge about the 'ways of white folks.' These 'ways' were the idiosyncrasies that manifested into the culture of power with hidden rules and curriculums to enforce systems of white supremacy (Delpit 2006). Black women who did not live with their employer made daily travels between two worlds of privilege and oppression. On a day-to-day basis, these women resided within an onto-epistemological in-between in places where they did not quite belong (Taliaferro-Baszile 2006), but these spaces allowed them to gain insight into how whiteness not only worked, but thrived. Although they were trapped in the servant class, they saw knowledge and education as the path to a better life for their ascendants. But, they were also aware that book knowledge was not the only knowledge or language of whiteness. There were social cues and idiosyncrasies that could cause you 'stick out behind' meaning that there is an embarrassment associated with not knowing, but more importantly, there is physical danger in not knowing. Hunter (1997) explains this phenomenon when she writes,

> Most household workers were hired by word of mouth, some by newspaper advertisements or employment agencies. Workers exchanged information among themselves about the availability of jobs and the reputations of those seeking help. Women leaving good situations took special care to pass on the jobs to younger relatives or friends. (52)

These referrals were critical for the safety of Black women workers because their bodies were in constant danger. McGuire (2010) explains,

> White men lured black women and girls away from home with promises of steady work and better wages: attacked them on the job; abducted them at gunpoint while traveling to or from work or church; raped them as a form of retribution or to enforce rules of racial and economic hierarchy; sexually humiliated and assaulted them on street cars and buses; in taxi cabs and trains, and in other public spaces. (xviii)

The meaning of this utterance is critical to southern womanism and a pedagogy of work because it acknowledges that Black women workers were aware of hidden rules and hidden curriculums. Black women workers parlayed this awareness into a pedagogy that relied upon an honest and forthright exchange of information.

Don't bite off more than you can chew

On the surface, this utterance appears to be a warning against gluttony, but it is actually a warning about knowing and appreciating your limits. Although this concept may seem contradictory to southern womanism's vision of a boundless Black womanhood, this concept is central to the survival of not only Black women in the professoriate, but all curriculum scholars. At this point, I must return to a series of questions posed at the beginning of this work – what can women who found meaning in their work tell us about our work; if our work was our worth, what would our work be worth? In the efficiency and accountability age of higher education, our worth is often found in our productivity and the length of our CVs. In an attempt to fill our CVs with conference papers and journal articles, we sometimes 'bite off more than we chew.' In other words, we're working, but are we able to fully digest what we're doing? While the professoriate places demands on our time in regard to the holy trifecta of teaching, research, and service which leads us to live lives of perpetual busyness, southern womanism forces us to pause and ask ourselves if we are chewing and digesting or wallowing and swallowing. These questions are critical for scholar-activists dedicated to creating curriculums that reject sexism, racism, homophobia, transphobia, and ableism. And herein lays the beauty of utterance. Utterances are not intended to make the listener feel good; they are meant to disrupt the listener's worldview and create discomfort. This disruption and discomfort was critical to the survival of southern Black women workers and is equally critical in the evaluation of our work as scholar-activists because sometimes, *we can't see for lookin'.*

You can't see for lookin'

My grandmother would tell her children that 'you can't see for looking,' whenever we could not find something that was in plain sight. 'It's right here in front of your face,' she would tell us whenever she had to stop what she was doing to show us that the pot, comb, or towel was directly in our sight, but somehow we could not see it. When we would sass back that 'we couldn't see it,' she would reply, 'You didn't wanna see it.' The phrase 'you can't see for lookin'' has three theoretical elements. The first element is in regard to how we often do not pay attention to the world around us. The second element attacks the laziness and carelessness found within the act of not paying attention to the world around us. The last element addresses the people and things we disturb when we have to call someone else in to find an object for us.

For example, after a particularly challenging day that ended with a late afternoon class, a young woman approached me after the class for a private conversation. From the look on her face, I could tell that this was going to be a serious talk, and I was not sure if I had the strength to be who she needed me to be in the moment. But somehow, I found the energy to listen to her story. To be clear, this story does not end with me being an engaged pedagogical super hero. The woman confided in me that she could not attend a required film screening about sexual violence because of her personal history. She did not go into details, but from her body language I could tell that the trauma was severe. However, my mind was so busy running through my knowledge of engaged pedagogy that did not *see* her guarded stance. I looked at her, and thought she just needed a hug. I was so busy *looking that I did not see* – I did not see her struggle, and therefore, I did not adequately hear the implications of her sexual trauma. When I reached out to hug her, she recoiled, and profusely apologised and went on to explain that she has problems with physical contact. With tears in her eyes, she said, 'I really want to hug you, but I can't … I just can't.' Now, I could be lazy and blame my inability to see her guarded stance on the fact that I am not a professional counsellor and therefore cannot expected to be recognise the signs, symptoms of severe sexual trauma. However, as a scholar-activist who made a commitment to creating an anti-oppressive, liberatory classroom where individuals can let their pain breathe so that it can heal, I have to work harder to see because sometimes *sight beats the word.*

Sight beats the word

The meaning behind the utterance, sight beats the word, can be difficult for scholar-activists to digest because our survival in the academy depends on our mastery of the written word. However, this utterance tells us that sometimes we have to see things to believe them; but unfortunately, this gift of sight only comes after our mistakes force us to actually see the error of our ways. As curriculum scholars, we revel in complexity, problematising, and troubling conceptualisations of people, places, and ideas. We are always looking for something, and we believe the answer in the complex philosophies of Foucault, Derrida, de Certeau, and Deleuze. We are so busy looking for the answers in these works that we cannot see what is right in front of us. Maybe if we stopped looking, perhaps, we might see that all our work is not *working* for *who it needs to work for the most*. However, seeing is dangerous because if we stopped looking to see, we might see that we are not that good at working. Seeing can take multiple forms. Sometimes, the act of seeing means making a way out of no way. Sometimes the act of seeing means leaning how to scale a flag pole. Sometimes seeing means taking the risk of overenroling a class because one of the students you overenroled left with a greater understanding of racial injustice.

And therein lays the pedagogical wisdom of southern Black women workers. The work of southern Black women workers extended beyond the tasks of their employment. They continued to work hard in their homes, in their neighbourhoods, and in their communities because they knew that there was always more work to be done. While the girl-children like me look back on this work with a critical eye and admonish them for not practicing more self-love and self-care, I also have to realise that they taught me how to work. These women worked hard because they had to let girl-children like me know that there is always more work to be done, and no – we cannot get tired. And this work was not and is not in vain. Girl-children like me know that survival is possible, but sometimes it means taking the time to *see*. Seeing is hard work, but southern womanism can help us learn to *see* well and therefore *work* well.

Possibilities for curriculum theory

Southern womanism argues that scholars who are committed to creating and advocating for anti-oppressive curriculums should look to the intellectual histories of southern Black women workers. When workers are seen as agents, their wisdom not only feeds our spirits, but provides an intellectual guide on our work of researching, teaching, reading, and being activists. To be clear, I am not glorifying or romanticising the work of our Black foremothers. I am not excusing the emotional labour that is placed upon Black women in the professoriate. In my work, I am often angry, bitter, and emotionally exhausted. These feelings are often coupled with the guilt that my life resembles Claire Huxtable's and not Florida Evans. I do not sweat on my job, lift heavy objects, or utter the words 'yes ma'am and no sir.' My over enrolment of the course I mentioned at the beginning of the course did not cause me any physical pain or stress beyond the initial negative reactions of my department chair and students. However, what causes me pain is that work that I did in that space will not ever be recognised as valuable within the holy trifecta of teaching, service, and research. For example, how can I adequately relay the contents of a final paper in which a white male student painstakingly documented his emotional connection with Adichie's Americanah? This student wrote in great detail that he believed that he understood the opening scene of the novel in which Ifemelu is traveling by train from Princeton, New Jersey, to Trenton, New Jersey, to get her hair braided. He wrote that he comprehended the racist undertones of going to school in a place that does not adequately provide for all of the physical and social needs of people of colour. However, he did not understand how this pain manifests in the lives of people of colour until he witnessed this pain during a weekend visit home. His best friend, a Black male student also enrolled in the course, needed a haircut, but he had to drive 30 minutes outside his hometown to find a barbershop because they were turned away from the local barbershops. While his friend remained calm and explained that not all white barbers know-how (or want to know-how) to cut Black hair, he was infuriated. This moment was special for me as a teacher not only because these two students were part of the group that I over-enroled (i.e. personal validation that I made the right choice). But more so because the Black male student approached me about four classes into the course and said, 'I'm really enjoying this class. It's really great and eye opening for me, but I really hope my best friend *gets it*.' I am not sure if these friends shared these moments with each other, and I will not receive institutional credit for this moment. But these are the moments that sustain me as I carry on the work of my foremothers. Therefore, whenever I am tired and frustrated. Whenever I am in my office long after others have gone home because I have to finish the work I could not complete during normal work hours because I had to mentor a child through a crisis, I pause and give thanks. I remember that once upon a time, I was the work of Bertha Harbor, Lillian White, Carrie Henderson, Edna Harper, Annie Bell Payton, Mamie Montgomery, Carrie Franklin, Lelia Thompson, Rebecca Nelson, and Ernestine Davis and countless other Black women who possibly missed some 'me time' to 'take up time' with me. These women were also tired, but they worked to make sure that one day I could work in place where my body was safe, and that my worst day consisted of having too many students to mentor and too many books to read. My department chair is right; the path that I have placed myself on will probably not put me on the fast track to win any early career awards for research production. But when my students of colour and white students come into my office sad and broken, I give the gift of action and utterance. And as a southern womanist, I know that worthwhile work is being done.

Disclosure statement

No potential conflict of interest was reported by the authors.

References

Barad, K. 2003. "Posthumanist Performativity: Toward an Understanding of How Matter Comes to Matter." *Signs: Journal of Women in Culture and Society* 28: 801–831.

Berry, T. R. 2006. "What the Fuck, Now What? The Social and Psychological Dilemmas of Multidimensional being as Woman of Color in the Academy." In *From Oppression to Grace: Women of Color and Their Dilemmas*, edited by T. R. Berry and N. D. Mizelle, xi–xix. Sterling, VA: Stylus Publishing.

Cobb, J. 2005. *Away Down South: A History of Southern Identity*. New York: Oxford University Press.

Coleman, M. 2008. *Making a Way Out of No Way: A Womanist Theology*. Minneapolis, MN: Fortress Press.

Collins, P. H. 2000. *Black Feminist Thought: Knowledge, Consciousness, and the Politics of Empowerment*. 2nd ed. New York: Routledge.

Delpit, L. D. 2006. *Other People's Children: Cultural Conflict in the Classroom*. New York: New Press.

Dillard, C. B. 2012. *Learning to (Re)member the Things We've Learned to Forget: Endarkened Feminisms, Spirituality, and the Sacred Nature of (Re)search and Teaching*. New York: Peter Lang.

Edwards, K. T. 2010. "Incidents in the Life of Kirsten T. Edwards: A Personal Examination of the Academic In-between Space." *Journal of Curriculum Theorizing* 26 (1): 113–128.

Fox-Genovese, E. 1988. *Within the Plantation Household: Black and White Women of the Old South*. Chapel Hill: University of North Carolina Press.

Grumet, M. R. 1988. *Bitter Milk: Women and Teaching*. Amherst: University of Massachusetts Press.

Guillory, N. A. 2011. "What's a Hip Hop Feminist Doing in Teacher Education? A Journey Back to Curriculum Theory in Three Acts." *Journal of Curriculum Theorizing* 27 (3): 20–32.

Harley, S. 2002. *Sister Circle: Black Women and Work*. New Brunswick, NJ: Rutgers University Press.

Hooks, B. 1994. *Teaching to Transgress: Education as the Practice of Freedom*. New York: Routledge.

Hunter, T. W. 1997. *To 'Joy My Freedom: Southern Black Women's Lives and Labors after the Civil War*. Cambridge, MA: Harvard University Press.

Jones, J. 2009. *Labor of Love, Labor of Sorrow: Black Women, Work, and the Family, from Slavery to the Present*. New York: Basic Books.

Laymon, K. 2013. *How to Slowly Kill Yourself and Others in America: Essays*. Chicago, IL: Bolden.

McGuire, D. L. 2010. *At the Dark End of the Street: Black Women, Rape, and Resistance – A New History of the Civil Rights Movement from Rosa Parks to the Rise of Black Power*. New York: Alfred A. Knopf.

Morton, B. Forthcoming. "Ain't Nothin' Wrong With Cleanin' Houses: Utterances on Southern Womanism and the Search for Our Mothers' Gardens." In *Womanish Ways: Renderings at the Intersections of Race, Gender, and Curriculum Theorizing*, edited by D. Taliaferro-Baszile, K. Edwards, and N. Guillory. New York: Lexington Books (Rowman & Littlefield Publishing).

Morton, B., and D. Hart. 2015. "Making a Way Out of No Way: A Contextualized History of African Americans in Higher Education." In *African American Students' Career and College Readiness: The Journey Unraveled*, edited by J. R. Curry and M. A. Shillingford, 39–54. Washington, DC: Lexington Books.

Noddings, N. 1984. *Caring: A Feminine Approach to Ethics & Moral Education*. Berkely: University of California Press.

Robinson, Z. 2014. *This Ain't Chicago: Race, Class, and Regional Identity in the Post-Soul South*. Chapel Hill: University of North Carolina Press.

Rollins, J. 1985. *Between Women: Domestics and Their Employers*. Philadelphia, PA: Temple University Press.

Taliaferro Baszille, D. M. 2004. "'Who Does She Think She Is?' Growing Up Nationalist and Ending Up Teaching Race in White Space." In *Broken Silence: Conversations about Race by African American Faculty and Graduate Students*, edited by D. Cleveland, 158–170. New York, NY: Peter Lang.

Taliaferro-Baszile, D. M. 2006. "In this Place Where I don't Quite Belong: Claiming the Ontoepistemological In-between." In *From Oppression to Grace: Women of Color and Their Dilemmas*, edited by T. R. Berry and N. D. Mizelle, 195–208. Sterling, VA: Stylus Publishing.

Wallace-Sanders, K. 2008. *Mammy: A Century of Race, Gender, and Southern Memory*. Ann Arbor: University of Michigan Press.

The *Black Women's Gathering Place*: reconceptualising a curriculum of place/space

Arianna Howard, Ashley Patterson, Valerie Kinloch, Tanja Burkhard and Ryann Randall

ABSTRACT

This article de-centres imperialist, capitalist, patriarchal traditions of critical approaches in Curriculum Studies via an examination of experiences shared at The *Black Women's Gathering Place* (*BWGP*), a non-traditional space where a diverse, intergenerational group of Black women engage with each other through the sharing of stories. In the *BWGP*, we enact components of Pinar's [2004. *What is Curriculum Theory*? Mahwah, NJ: Lawrence Erlbaum] concept of currere, simultaneously re-entering our collective and individual pasts and re-imagining our futures in an effort to reconcile our public and private selves. Taking up tenets of Black feminist theory, theoretical framings of hidden curriculum, and components of Ng-A-Fook's [2007. *An Indigenous Curriculum of Place: The United Houma Nation's Contentious Relationship with Louisiana's Educational Institutions*. New York, NY: Peter Lang] 'Curriculum of Place,' we reconceptualise a curriculum of place/space that negotiates dominant norms expressed in social environments. In this space, we validate traditional knowledges upheld in communities of Black women across the Diaspora. The *BWGP* allows us to argue for a re-presentation of extant knowledge by and about Black women.

Where we enter

Despite the efforts of scholars in education and curriculum studies to challenge hegemonic practices that silence and perpetuate injustices towards people of colour, the historical foundations of these fields reflect the identities and perspectives of dominant groups (Joseph 2000; Ladson-Billings and Tate 2006; McKnight 2003; Winfield 2007). These ontological and epistemological perspectives are often highly regulated and formalised, promoting a single, absolute, and final truth; they circulate specific discourses about historically marginalised groups and the justification of the 'white supremacist project' (Tuck and Gaztambide-Fernández 2013, 75). Classrooms and the curricula forwarded within them reproduce particular codes of power (Delpit 2006) that exclude many people who do not fit into mainstream ways of being. Given the hegemony associated with power and privilege, curriculum – if not looked upon with a critical eye towards the adoption of postcolonial and decolonial conceptualisations and re-imaginings – becomes a function of hegemonic practice and perspective.

This article de-centres imperialist, white supremacist, capitalist, and patriarchal traditions of critical approaches in Curriculum Studies via an examination of the ways in which standpoints of Black women support and depart from these approaches. We draw attention to the experiences shared at the *Black Women's Gathering Place* (*BWGP*), a non-traditional, real *and* imagined space where a diverse, intergenerational group of Black women engage with each other through the sharing of stories. In the *BWGP*, we enact elements of currere (Pinar 2004), simultaneously re-entering our collective and individual pasts and re-imagining our futures in an effort to reconcile our public and private selves. Via the enactment of components of currere and the taking up of tenets of Black feminist theory, theoretical framings of hidden curriculum, and components of Ng-A-Fook's (2007) 'Curriculum of Place,' we reconceptualise a curriculum of place/space that negotiates the dominant norms, values, and beliefs expressed in social environments. In this space, we validate traditional knowledges and practices, both historical and contemporary, upheld in communities of Black women across the Diaspora. The *BWGP* allows us to argue for a re-presentation of extant knowledge by and about Black women while simultaneously moving towards reconceptualising twenty-first century curricula – curricula that acknowledges and appreciates the ways in which students view, understand, and interact with the world and draws from the long, rich histories of different sources of knowledge.

In moving towards a reconceptualisation of curricula, we are well aware that history and literature books used in today's public school classrooms often neglect the experiences of people of colour. Texts that do incorporate the histories, knowledges, perspectives, and reflections of non-dominant groups often take up 'spectator-like structures of epistemology and knowledge' while failing to incorporate the in-depth examinations of the experiences of historically marginalised groups (Pinar 2004, 38). As Pinar (2004) suggests, and we, too, believe, centring the 'autobiographical histories and reflections' of historically marginalised groups is an important and critical first step towards challenging hegemonic practices and reconceptualising twenty-first century curricula (38).

Pinar (2004) identifies the African-American autobiographical practice as an example to which educational and curriculum scholars should turn. He states:

> African-American autobiographical practices racialize, politicize, and historicize self-narration … African-American autobiographies fill in many of the blanks of the nation's self-knowledge. They document what has been ignored in American life by many white writers and critics. Further, they show how white critical judgment has been limited, indeed deformed, by racial blind spots … From slave narratives to contemporary writing, African-American autobiography has functioned as a powerful means of addressing and contesting social, political, and cultural realities in the United States. (40–42)

We agree with Pinar's assertion, realising the significance of moving towards a more expansive understanding of curricula that includes storytelling, non-traditional learning spaces, and a discourse of care that embraces and respects the positionalities of Black women in and across the United States. Additionally, we believe that Pinar's movement towards the recognition and centring of the narratives and educational practices of non-white people can only materialise through the explicit naming and rejection of colonialist agendas that are largely promulgated within academic disciplines and adopted school curricula.

Towards a black woman's curriculum of place/space

Storytelling and black feminist thought

The *female* African-American autobiographical practice of storytelling (Collins 2000; Dillard 2000; Royster 2000) provides critical insights into how women in *The BWGP* share their perspectives on encounters with various forms of oppressions in schools and throughout society. We contend that our storytelling practices reveal a Black womans' *curriculum of place/space* that recognises and negotiates the dominant norms, values, and beliefs expressed in 'mainstream' social environments (e.g. classrooms, society, etc.). Collins' (2000) and Royster's (2000) use of Black feminist theory, Ng-A-Fook's (2007) idea of a 'Curriculum of Place,' and components of Pinar's (2004) concept of currere provide strong theoretical bases for challenging the (un)-intended consequences of the hidden curriculum of everyday experience. They provide insights into ways of theorising our collective and individual pasts and re-imagining our futures in an effort to reconcile our public and private selves.

For many Black people, storytelling provides opportunities to disrupt and reconstruct existing knowledge. Stories – in the forms of narratives, parables, stories, vignettes, and extended conversations – can make visible how particular discourses function to both privilege and silence the multiple ways of understanding and interacting in the world as Black women. Reflecting on the history of pre-colonial West African culture, Royster (2000) details the historical significance of storytelling:

> Storytelling served as the primary medium for cultural preservation and for the transmission of beliefs. Through a variety of communicative practices – stories, metaphors, wise sayings, proverbs, and so forth – [African-American] women used language to 'instruct' their listeners in ways of believing and ways of doing. Constructing meaning through accessible symbols, images and thought patterns, African American women could sustain perhaps their most important traditional role – as the interpreters and reinterpreters of the world. (112)

According to Royster, Black women have long been the symbolic keepers and champions of (and within) Black communities, and this work shows up in tangible ways. Storytelling, for Black women across the Diaspora, disrupts the ongoing struggle to create spaces that acknowledge and affirm the intellectual contributions of Black female subjectivities and the ways these contributions have shaped theoretical and epistemological framings of education, liberation, and democracy. According to Davies (1994), Black female subjectivity 'asserts agency as it crosses the borders, journeys, migrates and so re-claims as it re-asserts' (37), which ultimately requires a consistent re-negotiation of identities as migration happens and borders are crossed. Storytelling and writing, then, become ways to construct new subjectivities that do not result in the creation of an essential Black female subject. Instead, storytelling and writing allow for deeper understandings to be generated about people's experiences with racism and sexism across different contexts. This writing and telling of one's own stories, the practice of autobiography, is a conduit for embodied knowing to become legible for others who may or may not share the same experiences.

Insofar as racism and sexism are concerned, Pinar (2004) notes that 'many black women [writers] understood the symbiotic relationship between' the two (43). Specifically, Black feminist scholars understand this relationship as more complexly involving added dimensions even beyond these two identity markers alone. For Collins, Black women's daily experiences are situated within three mutually influencing oppressions[1]: economic exploitation, political marginalisation, and ideological manipulation via the use of controlling images. She (2000) writes:

> Taken together, the supposedly seamless web of economy, polity, and ideology function as a highly effective system of social control designed to keep African American women in an assigned, subordinate place. This larger system of oppression works to suppress the ideas of Black women intellectuals and to protect elite White male interests and worldviews. (5)

This 'seamless web' of marginalisation is the way of life for many Black women. Collins (2000) underscores the importance of intersectional paradigms to 'understanding the connections between knowledge and empowerment [as] they stimulate new interpretations of African-American women's experiences' (227; see also Beaubeouf-Lafontant 2002).

The ideological dimension of oppression that Black women navigate is perhaps the most pervasive and the hardest to counteract. Negative stereotypes about Black women pervade the American cultural and social fabric. The qualities and characteristics of these images (e.g. mammy, matriarch, welfare queen) are linked to the Black female body and used to unfairly justify marginalisation. Controlling images distort those facets of Black female behaviour that dominant groups believe threaten hierarchies of power and control (Collins 2000). An unchallenged acceptance of these stereotypes serves to naturalise forms of social injustice. Collectively, the network of economic exploitation, political marginalisation, and ideological manipulation operates in the interests of white male elites. These discursive tools of oppression serve as filters through which many Black women's ways of knowing, being, and doing get misunderstood and even re-appropriated.

Black women have consistently and courageously engaged in literary practices that have 'yielded remarkable rewards for themselves and for others' (Royster 2000, 4). Tracing the rich literate traditions of nineteenth and twentieth centuries African-American women trailblazers, Royster (2000) disrupts discourses that fail to acknowledge these historical contributions. These literary trailblazers (e.g. Clara Howard, Anna Julia Cooper, Maria W. Stewart) focused on sociopolitical issues, 'deliberately engaging in the social and political conversations around them' (Royster 2000, 21) and 'focusing readers' attention instructively on dimensions of [their] experience that establish the unique viewpoints of African-American women as a gendered, racialized, and economically defined group' (Royster 2000, 20).

For us, Black feminist thought provides an alternative, self-defined lens through which Black women can be seen and their experiences understood in relation to themselves. This utilisation of Black feminist thought disrupts the dominantly accepted image of 'normal' (as white, as privileged). It neither seeks to flatten the experiences of individual Black women into one monolithic description nor imply that such a standpoint in itself will create consciousness. Rather, by offering a vehicle for making the consciousness that already exists legible to Black women themselves and to others alike, Black feminist thought opens possibilities for Black women to push back against oppressive forces that seek to limit their forms of agency and self-empowerment.

A black woman's curriculum of place/space

Theorisations of space and place have gained importance in numerous approaches to feminist scholarship. These efforts have ranged from re-defining the very notion of 'space' from feminist perspectives on cultural and human geography (Bondi 2005; Day 1999; Koskela 1997), to explorations of what makes spaces safe or unsafe (Kenney 2001; The Roestone Collective 2014), and diasporic 'moving spaces' navigated by Black women in various contexts (Ahmed 1996). Bondi (2005) notes that 'space is continuously "produced" through the dynamic interconnections between and among places and social relations' (142; see also Lefebvre 1991). Based on this materialist rearticulation, spaces are relational, fluid, and directly shaped by the experiences of race, class, gender, and sexual orientation within social contexts. In our particular gathering space, we both contextualise our varied personal understandings of Black womanhood by sharing stories of the past and narratively illustrating our everyday experiences by eliciting commentary and feedback from fellow sharers of the space. What matters to our discussion, then, is both the space as we create it, as well as the place in which it occurs. It is noteworthy that despite our differences in nationality, place of birth, class, and religion, the individual members of the group decide to repeatedly gather in one place due to our shared identities as Black women. Arguably, part of this experience has been our ongoing grappling with racism and sexism inside and outside academic spaces.

Ng-A-Fook's (2007) notion of a 'Curriculum of Place' allows for the appropriation of the academic education promoted in schooling as well as the resistance to 'systemic cultural assimilation' (176). Resisting this assimilation provides the space for students (and, we add, Black women) to validate the knowledges of their cultures and communities. This act is bi-directional as students (Black women) influence and are influenced by experiences within (and outside) the classroom. Ng-A-Fook (2007) argues that a curriculum of place grants students access to 'write, rewrite, and reeducate the public at large about the historical representations of their past' (200). The *BWGP* affords its members opportunities to 'write, rewrite, and reeducate the public at large' in relation to extant knowledge by and about Black women; an added dimension of the Black woman's curriculum of place. Ng-A-Fook (2007) identifies three sources of knowledge acquisition that students who belong to indigenous and historically marginalised communities should exploit: 'traditional knowledge (from generation to generation), empirical knowledge (gained from observation), and revealed knowledge (acquired through spiritual origins and recognised as a gift)' (Ng-A-Fook 2007, 175; see also Castellano 2000). We agree that these sources of knowledge should be taken up by students of colour. We wish to add to this list two additional sources of knowledge acquisition that emanate from the histories and practices of Black women across the Diaspora: embodied knowing and historical consciousness. These sources of knowledge should be embraced by teachers and taken up by students belonging to historically marginalised groups, particularly Black female students.

According to scholars of Black feminist thought, a Black woman's knowledge is acquired through experience, through living and surviving within multiple forms of oppression. It is a self-defined, embodied way of knowing; a standpoint epistemology (Beaubeouf-Lafontant 2002; Collins 2000; Cooper 2003; Dillard 2000; Few 2007) and provides the foundation for the Black woman's curriculum of place/space. In an article examining the womanist caring practices of Black teachers, Beaubeouf-Lafontant (2002) writes, 'because so many black women have experienced the convergence of racism, sexism, and classism, they often have a particular vantage point on what constitutes evidence ... valid action ... and morality' (72). Collins (2000) identifies this type of embodied knowing as a form of wisdom, and it is this wisdom that derives from multiple places: from a West African system of belief and action (Royster 2000) and from Black women's ongoing forms of survival against and resistance to systemic oppression.

The many and varied experiences of individual Black women contribute to a collective understanding that is larger than any single woman herself. Our collective understanding is deeper than the histories we have been told about ourselves, the stories shared by the dominant curriculum. Evoking the spiritual and psychological power of African and African-American storytelling, Royster (2000) asks that we acknowledge our historical consciousness, which includes those stories we do not know to be able to put into words, but that we know in that they are an integral part of us:

> We can set aside for a moment what we cannot easily know ... and proceed instead to look more carefully at evidence, even trace evidence, from 'collective' experiences, from the 'facts' and artifacts that whisper rather than scream, in order to see how else we might still come to historical consciousness and thereby to other renderings of this collective body of lived experiences. (Royster 2000, 80)

Royster (2000) encourages contemporary Black women to call upon the ancestral spirit of our cultural knowledges to help us understand 'who we are, how we should see the world, how we should perceive ourselves in it, and also how we might assume the authority to speak and to act as thinkers, writers, and leaders' (89).

Currere and the **BWGP**

Pinar (2004) puts forth the concept *currere*, repositioning an understanding of curriculum as a passive entity with a consideration of curriculum as a verb, a conversation. Before we highlight those components of currere germane to our discussion of BWGP, we interrogate the ontological underpinnings of Pinar's (2004) work. As mentioned earlier, Pinar fails to fully recognise the roles curriculum studies plays in the maintenance of what Tuck and Gaztambide-Fernández (2013) call 'settler colonialism' or the elimination of Indigenous epistemologies through the normalisation of whiteness and white subjectivity (73; see also Patel 2015). This curricular practice is ongoing; it continues to justify the 'theft and occupation of Indigenous land' through the construction of particular narratives that continue to reiterate white supremacist ideologies (Tuck and Gaztambide-Fernández 2013, 75; see also Patel 2015; Smith 2003; Tuck 2009).

A critical interrogation of this ontological and epistemological orientation can extend Pinar's (2004) concept of currere. According to Pinar, much of the conversation occurs between components of academic knowledge and personal aspects of life history. The conversation must also include interrogations of the origins and histories of academic knowledge. In addition, a developed self-understanding is required in order to understand traditional academic curricula – to come to understanding the interrogation and critique. This self-understanding must be contextualised in terms of culture, society, politics, and time. Ultimately, 'the student of *currere*' as Pinar (2004) describes her, uses her lived experiences as informative points of reference that help to make the future legible (36). These lived experiences (particularly of those lives and histories located in the USA) are contextualised within a legacy of white supremacy via practices of silencing and replacement (McKnight 2003; Tuck and Gaztambide-Fernández 2013; Winfield 2007). Through analysis of this temporal data, experiences of the past and present combined with imaginations of future experiences, the student of *currere* – for us, participants of the *BWGP* – are able to 'regulate information signaled to others and to interrupt signals received' (Pinar 2004, 37). This process of analysis allows for and encourages the critical consumption of curricular points that can, and do, come in the form of everyday experiences.

We take up Pinar's concept as a means for understanding the work taking place in the *BWGP*. In the space, the participants are engaged in the exchange of stories that chronicle past lived experiences. In the present, participants contemplate, deconstruct and reflect upon those past experiences both collectively and as individuals. Data pulled from these lived experiences also serve to project understandings of the future – yet unknown in specificity, but clear in inductive formation terms. What is taking place is Pinar's (2004) explanation of the method of *currere*, or a 'complicated conversation with oneself… an ongoing project for self-understanding in which one becomes mobilised for engaged pedagogical action … with others in the social reconstruction of the public sphere' (37). As a collective of individuals, members of the *BWGP* engage in interactions that disrupt White supremacist, capitalist, patriarchal traditions of curriculum. Much like the understandings achieved within the group, its inception and formation were organic, yet purposeful.

How the *BWGP* came to be

In the spring of 2014, nearly one hundred teachers, students, and community members gathered to celebrate the success of a three year critical service-learning initiative. The initiative, led by Kinloch, supported public school teachers and support staff in developing more than 80 critical service-learning projects that broke down barriers between classrooms and community spaces across a Midwestern urban school district. Once again redefining the spaces that are typically understood by K-12 students and teachers as spaces of learning, the work of participants in the initiative was showcased at the celebration event. Second graders spoke of their collaboration with a Tanzanian sculptor, a group of middle and high school students discussed how they worked to bring awareness of human trafficking issues to members of the local community, and high school students recounted their experiences attending national educational conferences where they talked with educators and policymakers about the importance of community-engaged forms of critical service-learning.

The students and teachers sharing their experiences on stage were not the only ones sharing novel perspectives on the possibilities of curriculum while reflecting on learning in this out-of-school space. Near the back of the room, a Black woman quietly moved about as she set up and maintained the food display. As she moved from the preparation room to the display table, she listened to each presentation and story being shared; becoming a learner in a space she had only intended to be a service provider. Near the end of the event, Kinloch approached the woman to thank her for her service. The woman replied,[2]

> I just have to say, I have thoroughly enjoyed this program. The work that you are doing is just great … .I mean, these kids! We need this. Our community needs this. It is just making me so proud to see you up there doing all of this. You da bomb, girl. You gotta keep doing what you doing.

Weeks after the service-learning celebration Howard, Patterson, and Kinloch met and discussed memories of the event, making note of the importance of explicitly recognising the many spaces primed for continued learning and for encouraging self-understanding. In the weeks since the event, each of us had reflected on the input of the catering woman and had imagined what prompted the woman to share her thoughts. We realised that in her willingness to expose her vulnerable side, the woman had inspired us to acknowledge and reconnect to our own vulnerabilities as Black women. In sharing with us her lived experiences, the woman had invoked a curriculum none of us necessarily planned to take part in on that day, but that was positively influential none-the-less. We wanted to pass on to other Black women this opportunity for reflection, for learning from the lived experiences of others, for openly engaging in the work that Black women have been called upon to do for generations. And so the idea of the *BWGP* came to be.

We wanted the *BWGP* to be intentionally centred on Black women: our issues, our concerns, our voices, our way. We generated some guiding questions, and decided on a time and location for the first meeting. We sent invitations to twelve other Black women, all in the field of education to some degree, but each having different perspectives, life paths and experiences. We showed up to the first meeting and excitedly waited to see how a Black woman's curriculum would begin to show itself.

Vignettes of disruption from within *the BWGP*

From the very first session, we shared stories of oppression, of negative portrayals of Black women in the media, and how these portrayals influenced the ways we loved on ourselves and the degree of safety we felt in public spaces. Two participants' words[3] hung heavily in the air that evening.

> Katrina[4]: I went to an all Black high school … I've always had Black friends … but I also try to be friends of people that are other ethnicities … one thing I've noticed about white women in general is this stereotype … sometimes there's a stereotype that they're all really nice and sweet [laughs] … I just find that they're so passive aggressive … people frame Black women to be angry [group members chime in in agreement] … and bitter … and then a lot times when there are situations involving a white woman and a Black woman, Black women are framed as being crazy … I'm generalizing so much and it probably sounds a little cliché, but I've noticed even at College University[5] I'm around more white people than I've ever been around and a lot of times white women can be very passive aggressive … but it's never really spoken about, you know … that's never a stereotype that's publicized in the media, but angry Black woman is …

Throughout her commentary, Katrina recognises the pervasive use of the controlling image of the matriarch by others ('people frame Black women to be angry … and bitter'). One of the most pervasive controlling images used to characterise African-American women; the matriarch represents the antithesis of the mammy image, and expectedly in keeping with the other controlling images of Black women, fails to model 'appropriate' Black female behaviour. She is loud, bossy, demanding, and emasculating towards her African-American male partners. The Sapphire image is a contemporary translation of the matriarch stereotype, which Austin (2003) defines as the 'stereotypical black bitch – tough, domineering, emasculating, strident, and shrill' (301). Controlling images distort those facets of African-American female behaviour that dominant groups believe threaten hierarchies of power and control (Collins 2000). These stereotypes serve to naturalise forms of social injustice.

The historical legacy of this controlling image can encourage others to view the behaviours and speech patterns of Black women unfairly. Katrina keenly recognises what she sees as negative stereotypical behaviours in white women that go unrecognised and are not attributed to the entire group in the way controlling images are applied to Black women. Katrina states, '... white women can be very passive aggressive ... but it's never really spoken about, you know ... that's never a stereotype that's publicized in the media, but angry Black woman is ... ' In the *BWGP*, the lived experiences of the Black women in attendance serve as the content that makes up the curriculum. The sharing of these experiences brings elements of the hidden curriculum into light. By putting her observations on the table, Katrina took the opportunity to recognise and interrogate what may have been considered standard, unspoken knowledge in other settings. Her making legible the hidden curriculum allowed other *BWGP* members to digest these thoughts and to contemplate them in terms of their own experiences. Once Katrina called out and named these characteristics ('passive aggressive'), Ryann took a turn detailing the ways she resisted this behaviour exhibited by one of her previous supervisors.

> Ryann: ... they will try you ... you [generalized other] can't try this one [referring to herself] ... but that's why ... you have to tell them off with a smile ... never raise your voice cause what can they say? No. I'm not gonna do what you want me to do cause right now you're trying to make me upset you're trying to make me go off ... [begins reminiscing about a particular event] ... so, my former supervisor was a white woman and she was very passive aggressive and I'm sitting at the computer, I sit up front and the coffee machine was right across from my desk ... So the assumption was 'Ryann's gonna fill the coffee'. Well, I don't drink coffee ... so I would do it every now and then. First thing in the morning I'll do it. Well one day I'm doing my work. My supervisor walks past and she has her coffee mug [in her hand and says to me] 'Ryyyaaann ... Ryyyaaann ... we're out of coffee.' And I looked at her and I said [to myself], 'She wants me to go off on her right now.' I looked at her ... I had nothing to say cause if I say something it's gonna be bad news ... [speaking subconsciously to her boss] 'Don't you ever sit there and disrespect me like I'm your servant to fix your-I don't even drink the coffee. You drink the coffee!' She knew my look at her and I turned my head. She knew not to talk to me for the rest of the day ... she already knew ... don't disrespect me.

Ryann's vignette showcases the use of two particular speech patterns, collectively referred to as talking with attitude (TWA) (Fordham 1993; Koonce 2012; Troutman 2010). TWA is a Black women's speech practice comprised of expressive language and non-verbal acts (e.g. silence, neck-rolling, finger popping, smart talk) exercised to maintain cultural integrity, form camaraderie, exude confidence and show resistance in oppressive spaces and situations (Koonce 2012; Troutman 2010). It combines characteristics of polite behaviour with assertiveness. In the above vignette, Ryann employs the use of two TWA practices: silence and smart talk. Silence, as it used in this case and in other situations by Black women, is not to be mistaken for compliance. It is an act of boldness, a refusal on behalf of herself, the Black woman, to accept the attempts of those who wish to position her or control her behaviour and speech (Fordham 1993).

Ryann begins her speaking turn by describing a particular type of silence: 'tell[ing] them off with a smile.' Ryann recognises how the use of silence can successfully overcome attempts of others (in this case, white women) to affect her disposition. She narrates an interesting type of silence: subconscious speech. To her supervisor, Ryann says nothing.

She stays quiet, but uses a look to express her frustration. She lets us know that there is, indeed, something going on behind this look. She says, '... I looked at her and I said [to myself], she wants me to go off on her right now ... I looked at her ... I had nothing to say cause if I say something it's gonna be bad news.' Ryann knows that speaking up, at this moment, could result in a heated exchange between her and her supervisor. So, she remains quiet. This act of silence, combined with a look of attitude communicates, in Ryann's mind, that she is not to be messed with, not to be disrespected.

Smart talk, a second TWA speech practice, is employed by Black women when we need to speak our mind, to rebel against an unjust act (Koonce 2012). Ryann begins her utterance with a declaration: 'you can't try this one'. Responding in part to Katrina's naming of perceived passive aggressive behaviour in white women, Ryann lets her listeners know she is not one who tolerates this type of behaviour. Ryann continues with the narration of several instances of the use of smart talk, albeit subconscious smart talk, to respond to what she perceives as an abusive use of power wielded through passive aggression on behalf of her supervisor. Ryann illustrates one such example: 'So the assumption was "Ryann's gonna fill the coffee"'. Even though she does not drink coffee, Ryann tells her listeners she would refill the pot 'every now and then ... first thing in the morning.' Her supervisor came to expect Ryann to fill the coffee pot each time it ran empty. As Ryann explains, 'one day I'm doing my work my supervisor walks past and she has her coffee mug [in her hand and says to me] Ryann ... Ryann ... we're out of coffee.' Instead of asking Ryann to fill the coffee pot, her supervisor presents the empty coffee pot as a problem Ryann is expected to remedy. Ryann responds, subconsciously, to the attempts of her supervisor to position her as a servant. She narrates: '... don't you ever sit there and disrespect me like I'm your servant to fix your-I don't even drink the coffee. You drink the coffee!' Ryann recognises her supervisor's words and behaviour as disrespectful, as unjust, and the manner of her response worked against the angry Black woman controlling image.

A Black woman's curriculum of place is embodied. It travels with her, in and out of various spaces, and it influences and is influenced by her experiences within those spaces. One of the group members is a veteran high school teacher who works in the local public school district. At our third gathering, she shared the impact of the *BWGP* beyond the few hours each month that we had spent together.

> Liz: I really find myself reflecting on the things we share here all the time. Like the discussion we had about the fact that there's this angry Black woman stereotype but no one is talking about the archetype passive aggressive white woman ... I had never thought of that, but now I'm thinking about interactions I have at work through that lens. It doesn't really change what's happening, but it has changed the way I view certain situations and I feel like I can see them better.

Liz's time spent at the *BWGP* influences the way that she views interactions, circumstances, and situations at her workplace. As a result, we can imagine that Liz's interactions with others in her workplace are shaped and are being shaped by the curriculum in the *BWGP*. The Black woman's curriculum of place travels with her, becomes the lens through which she assesses the actions and words of co-workers. Through participation in collective recollections of past lived experiences, Liz has the opportunity to consider new experiences she has as an individual outside the space in a novel way. This new mode of consideration has provided Liz with analytical tools for interrogating and rethinking her interpretation of the interactions she has with white female co-workers in particular. She has also developed skills for pushing back against negative ideological imagery in place about herself as an individual within the collective of Black women in society at-large. She is not compelled to buy into, subconsciously endorse, or be limited by the angry Black woman stereotype, presented as some anomaly of social misbehaviour that applies solely to the idea that there are socially deviant Black women.

The *BWGP* provides a safe space for us to talk about the web of oppressions we encounter daily. We each share our strategies of resistance, encouraging fellow members to hone her own techniques, to be bold in ways the she may have felt timid, to speak up in instances where she may have wanted to remain silent, to remain silent during occasions where words were insufficient to convey her message. This embodiment of the Black woman's curriculum of place/space is currere in action, which, for Pinar (2004), represents

> an autobiographical method [that] asks us to slow down, to remember even re-enter the past, and to meditatively reimagine the future. Then slowly and in one's own terms, one analyzes one's experience of the past and fantasies of the future in order to understand more fully, with more complexity and subtlety, one's submergence in the present … the achievement of self-hood and society. (4)

This act of re-entering and reimagining through the practice of storytelling helps us, as Black women, to hone our resistance strategies to the web of oppressions we encounter daily. These intellectual navigations are not traditional components of education and curriculum studies. They are, however, vital aspects of our need to exist as healthy, whole, and intellectual beings within a society that actively oppresses our self-knowledge and self-worth. In these ways, then, it becomes important for everyone, and especially Black women, to see themselves reflected in the fields of education and curriculum studies as well as within and across various disciplinary areas. Current conceptions of curricula often fail to incorporate critical perspectives from non-dominant groups, perspectives that explore their histories, validate their knowledges, and centre their concerns. Moving beyond current conceptions of curriculum and outside traditional schooling spaces, the *BWGP* provides a concrete example of new possibilities for the lives, histories, knowledges, cultural practices, struggles, and concerns of Black women to be safely and authentically explored.

The work accomplished in/at the *BWGP* answers Pinar's (2004) calls for a reconceptualisation of twenty-first century curricula, curricula that centres the knowledges of historically marginalised groups. This article showcases Black women's knowledge and ways of interacting with/in the world, and especially in out-of-school spaces. We argue that these sources and strategies can be incorporated into classrooms in ways that can help teachers: (1) understand the ontological orientations of students – how they view, understand, and interact with the world – and the ways in which these may differ from traditional curricular ontological orientations, and (2) recognise, value, and explore the long, rich histories of different sources of knowledge. In other words, 'our professional obligation,' according to Pinar (2004), 'is the reconstruction of the public sphere in education.' In this way, we cannot do this work if we are not refiguring

> the *private sphere* in education … where teachers and students connect academic knowledge to their self-formation, a connection made in historical time, embedded in regional, national,

> and diasporic cultures ... The reconstruction of the public sphere cannot proceed without the reconstruction of the private sphere. (21)

The pedagogical, theoretical, and epistemological contributions of historical and contemporary Black women are wide and deep (Collins 2000; Dillard 2000; Fisher 2008; Guy-Sheftall 1995; Royster 2000). These contributions build a foundation upon which current work such as the *BWGP* is imagined and actualised. Relying on the scholarship of Black Feminist and curriculum scholars to closely examine the lived experiences and shared stories of participants in the *BWGP* allows us to argue for a re-presentation of extant knowledge by and about Black women. In so doing, we argue that the lives, identities, and perspectives of Black women can advance the fields of education and curriculum studies, on the one hand, and can create a deeper stream of possibility and consciousness for centring Black women's intellectual traditions in theory and practice.

Notes

1. Collins' (2000) defines oppression as 'any unjust situation where, systematically and over a long period of time, one group denies another group access to the resources of society' (4).
2. Each story, unless otherwise noted, is a re-presentation of a speaker's utterances. We aim to disrupt practices of presenting the recollected experiences of others as their own, deleting any trace of the voice of the researcher. We evoke, instead, the practice of re-storying (see Connelley and Clandinin 1990; Kinloch and San Pedro 2014; McCormack 2002). In re-storying, we evoke the essence of a speaker's experience, as the exact words and nonverbal interactions have since faded from memory.
3. These vignettes were transcribed from an audio-recording of this meeting.
4. Pseudonym, as are all other names of *BWGP* participants whose commentary is shared here.
5. Pseudonym.

Disclosure statement

No potential conflict of interest was reported by the authors.

Funding

This work was supported by Corporation of National and Community Service: Learn and Serve Program.

References

Ahmed, S. 1996. "Moving Spaces: Black Feminism and Post-Colonial Theory." *Theory, Culture & Society* 13 (1): 139–146.

Austin, R. 2003. "Sapphire Bound!." In *Critical Race Feminism: A Reader*, edited by A. Wing, 301–308. New York: New York University Press.

Beaubeouf-Lafontant, T. 2002. "A Womanist Experience of Caring: Understanding the Pedagogy of Exemplary Black Women Teachers." *The Urban Review* 34 (1): 71–86.

Bondi, L. 2005. "Troubling Space, Making Space, Doing Space." *Group Analysis* 38 (1): 137–149.

Castellano, M. B. 2000. "Updating Aboriginal Traditions of Knowledge." In *Indigenous Knowledges in Global Contexts*, edited by G. Sefa Dei, B. L. Hall, and D. G. Rosenberg, 21–36. Toronto: University of Toronto Press.

Collins, P. H. 2000. *Black Feminist thought: Knowledge, Consciousness, and the Politics of Empowerment.* New York: Routledge.

Connelley, F. M., and D. J. Clandinin. 1990. "Stories of Experience and Narrative Inquiry." *Educational Researcher* 19 (5): 2–14.

Cooper, C. 2003. "The Detrimental Impact of Teacher Bias: Lessons Learned from the Standpoint of African American Mothers." *Teacher Education Quarterly* 30 (2): 101–116.

Davies, C. B. 1994. *Black Women, Writing and Identity: Migrations of the Subject*. New York: Routledge.

Day, K. 1999. "Embassies and Sanctuaries: Women's Experiences of Race and Fear in Public Space." *Environment and Planning D: Society and Space* 17 (3): 307–328.

Delpit, L. 2006. *Other People's Children: Cultural Conflict in the Classroom*. New York: New Press.

Dillard, C. 2000. "The Substance of Things Hoped for, the Evidence of Things not Seen: Examining an Endarkened Feminist Epistemology in Educational Research and Scholarship." *International Journal of Qualitative Studies in Education* 13 (6): 661–681.

Few, A. 2007. "Integrating Black Consciousness and Critical Race Feminism Into Family Studies Research." *Journal of Family Issues* 28 (4): 452–473.

Fisher, M. 2008. *Black Literate Lives: Historical and Contemporary Perspectives*. New York: Routledge.

Fordham, S. 1993. "'Those Loud Black Girls': (Black) Women, Silence, and Gender 'Passing' in the Academy." *Anthropology and Education Quarterly* 24 (1): 3–32.

Guy-Sheftall, B. 1995. *Words of Fire: An Anthology of African-American Feminist thought*. New York: New Press.

Joseph, P. ed. 2000. *Cultures of Curriculum*. Mahwah, NJ: Lawrence Erlbaum.

Kenney, M. R. 2001. *Mapping gay L.A.: The Intersection of Place and Politics*. Philadelphia, PA: Temple University Press.

Kinloch, V., and T. San Pedro. 2014. "The Space between Listening and Storying: Foundations for Projects in Humanization." In *Humanizing Research: Decolonizing Qualitative Research with Youth and Communities*, edited by D. Paris, and M. Winn, 21–42. Los Angeles, CA: Sage.

Koonce, J. 2012. "'Oh, Those Loud Black Girls!': A Phenomenological Study of Black Girls Talking with an Attitude." *Journal of Language and Literacy Education* 8 (2): 27–46.

Koskela, H. 1997. "'Bold Walk and Breakings': Women's Spatial Confidence Versus Fear of Violence." *Gender, Place & Culture* 4 (3): 301–320.

Ladson-Billings, G., and Tate, W. F. eds. (2006). *Education Research in the Public Interest: Social Justice, Action, and Policy*. New York: Teachers College Press.

Lefebvre, H. 1991. *The Production of Space*. Malden, MA: Blackwell.

McCormack, C. 2002. "Storying Stories: A Narrative Approach to in-Depth Interview Conversations." *International Journal of Social Research Methodology* 7 (3): 219–236.

McKnight, D. E. 2003. *Schooling, The Puritan Imperative, and the Molding of an American National Identity: Education's "Errand Into the Wilderness"*. Mahwah, NJ: Lawrence Erlbaum.

Ng-A-Fook, N. 2007. *An Indigenous Curriculum of Place: The United Houma Nation's Contentious Relationship with Louisiana's Educational Institutions*. New York: Peter Lang.

Patel, L. 2015. *Decolonizing Educational Research: From Ownership to Answerability*. New York: Routledge.

Pinar, W. 2004. *What is Curriculum Theory?* Mahwah, NJ: Lawrence Erlbaum.

Roestone Collective. 2014. "Safe Space: Towards a Reconceptualization." *Antipode* 46 (5): 1346–1365.

Royster, J. J. 2000. *Traces of a Stream: Literacy and Social Change among African American Women*. Pittsburgh, PA: University of Pittsburgh.

Smith, G. 2003. "Indigenous struggle for the transformation of education and schooling." Accessed May 23, 2015. http://ankn.uaf.edu/Curriculum/Speeches/Graham_Smith.

Troutman, D. 2010. "Attitude and its Situatedness in Linguistic Politeness." *Poznań Studies in Contemporary Linguistics* 46 (1): 85–109.

Tuck, E. 2009. "Suspending Damage: A Letter to Communities." *Harvard Educational Review* 79 (3): 409–428.

Tuck, E., and R. Gaztambide-Fernández. 2013. "Curriculum, Replacement, and Settler Futurity." *Journal of Curriculum Theorizing* 29 (1): 72–89.

Winfield, A. G. 2007. *Eugenics and Education in America: Institutionalized Racism and the Implications of History, Ideology, and Memory*. New York: Peter Lang.

Curriculum homeplacing as complicated conversation: (re) narrating the mentoring of Black women doctoral students

Ebony C. Pope and Kirsten T. Edwards

ABSTRACT

Through personal and dialogical narratives, we explore the ways Black women mentors (do not) reveal to their mentees their lived-experiences and the personal pain associated with the pursuit of careers in higher education; how and why their narratives of pain and pursuit are negotiated, sanctioned, and/or strategically altered; and the impact these decisions have on the development of Black women graduate students. Drawing on hooks' notions of 'imperialist white supremacist capitalist patriarchy' (2015), 'radical honesty' (2004), and 'homeplace' (1990), we deploy the concept of curriculum homeplacing to more critically examine Black women's mentoring relationships.

There is a compelling need for doctoral students to engage in meaningful mentoring relationships throughout the degree-seeking process. Research identifies mentorship as the single-most important factor in graduate student success, providing career/professional preparation and psychosocial support (Crawford and Smith 2005; Fedynich and Bain 2011; Kram 1985; Lechuga 2011; Patton 2009; Patton and Harper 2003). This is crucial for Black women doctoral students, particularly in regards to the guidance received within same race-gender mentoring relationships (Grant 2012). Black women doctoral students are often the most vulnerable to systemic inequality maintained within colleges and universities (Humble et al. 2006). This is exacerbated at historically white institutions due to the paucity of Black women faculty.

When available, same race-gender mentoring relationships diminish feelings of being the 'onliest one' (Gregory 1999). Those fortunate enough to form these types of connections ideally benefit from engaging a mentor who has lived the struggle of navigating intersectional injustice within post-secondary education. As Crenshaw (1991) notes, living at the intersections of race and gender marginalisation relegates Black women 'to a location that resists telling' and camouflages the 'dimensions of violence' that infiltrate their lives (1242). She challenges the conflation of single identity dimensionality, positing that violence to women is bound to the intermingling multiple dimensions of one's social location. The awareness of the aforementioned location is particularly evident in the lack of Black women faculty and doctoral students available to engage in mentoring relationships.

Even when these relationships are available, they are not immune to the ubiquity of systemic injustice (hooks 2015). Black women faculty often willingly accept the responsibility of mentoring Black women doctoral students within an institutional context that simultaneously burdens them with and punishes them for increased service labour (Baez 2000). They are also intimately acquainted with the academic landscape that assaults their Black women doctoral students with self-doubt, frustration, and isolation.

Black women faculty mentors and student mentees are often caught in a web that necessitates, while also hinders, truth-telling and transparent narration in academic preparation. We argue, when Black women mentors conceal the injuries of racism and sexism in dialogue with their same race-gender mentees, they potentially participate in mentoring practices that unconsciously support the very systems that continue to damage Black women academics.

Defining curriculum homeplacing

In the present article we ask, 'In what ways does imperialist white supremacist capitalist patriarchy impact Black women's same race-gender mentorships?' (hooks 2015). Relatedly, how can Black women faculty and doctoral students effectively respond to this interlocking system of oppression in their academic interactions? To answer these questions, we draw on hooks' notion of the 'homeplace' (1990). As hooks notes, the homeplace is 'the one site where one could freely confront the issue of humanization, where one could resist … where all black people could strive to be subjects, not objects' (hooks 1990, 42). Our understanding of *curriculum homeplacing* is a deliberate response to hooks call for Black people to create homeplaces within white supremacist capitalist patriarchy. For us, *curriculum homeplacing* is the creation of a particular 'curriculum of place' (Ng-a-Fook 2007; Pinar 1991) developed by Black women engaged in mentoring relationships that are informed by Black feminised cultural practices and communal commitments. Curriculum homeplacing places Black women and Black women's ways of knowing at the centre. It is first and foremost about asserting the humanity of Black women and consciously resisting institutional frames that would seek to invalidate their position as knowers, theorists, and scholars. We argue in this study that the on-going experience of ontoepistemological injury (Baszile 2006), as well as the hierarchal, detached demands placed on mentoring by a Euro-masculinist academy impacts the ways mentoring is narrated by and between Black women faculty and students. In light of these struggles, we suggest that curriculum homeplacing should be the response to the perennial challenges faced by Black women.

There is an abundance of literature referring to *advising* and *mentoring* interchangeably (Bertrand Jones, Wilder, and Osborne-Lampkin 2013). However, there are distinctions that set them apart. Mentoring provides career/professional preparation and psychosocial support (Crawford and Smith 2005; Fedynich and Bain 2011; Kram 1985). Advising focuses on academic program progression (Bertrand Jones, Wilder, and Osborne-Lampkin 2013). By focusing on mentoring, we are indicating a movement beyond advising, highlighting those relationships that possess the potential to be rooted in the cultural narratives of Black women (Dillard 2012; Edwards and Baszile 2016), and support curriculum homeplacing.

We also recognise the ways disciplining forces inhibit Black women's ability to transition from institutionally acceptable forms of mentorship to the more powerful work of curriculum homeplacing. Black women faculty not only live with unseen damage, but because vulnerability is a privilege available only to those afforded humanity, they also potentially participate in the damaging of their Black women doctoral students by not engaging in the practice of truth-telling or what hooks describes as 'radical honesty' (hooks 2004, 68). We contend that vulnerable truth-telling is necessary for Black women's mentorships to grow into curriculum homeplacing. We envision this treatise serving as not only an accounting, but also a reckoning and a model of relationship as resistance. Our hope is that the present work will compel Black women faculty and students, as well as other marginalised peoples, to more deliberately develop mentoring relationships that unabashedly resist dehumanisation and purposefully centre communal love-practices.

Current state of affairs

Faculty

The literature is clear: Black women faculty do not receive the same level of support as their white and/or male counterparts (Thomas and Hollenshead 2001). They are often the recipients of institutionally sanctioned harassment (Burgess 1997; Gregory 1999). Black women confront daily messages that they do not fit the prototype of the successful, tenured faculty member (Taylor-Brandon 2006). These messages appear in the form of exclusion from institutional networks such as mentoring, experiences of silencing and stereotyping, and the assumption of incompetence, which often exacerbates feelings of impostorship (Brown 2012; Dancy and Jean-Marie 2014; Everett, Hall, and Hamilton-Mason 2010; Gutierrez y Muhs et al. 2012). These are just a few of the challenges faced.

These difficulties affect hiring processes, retention, and probability of tenure and promotion. On the road to success, Black women are also subjected to unwritten rules and expectations related to the focus and quantity of their work, as well as their service to the institution (Patitu and Hinton 2003). These pressures often create a climate of exclusion and invalidation, requiring Black to women bear the difficult responsibility of creating change for one another (Pittman 2012).

All of these realities produce robust amounts of stress for Black women as they labour extensively to serve the institution and their students (Harley 2007; Wallace et al. 2012). Undoubtedly, multiple aspects of the Black woman academic's professional life are not immune to the compounded result of *gendered* and racial battle fatigue (Smith, Yosso, and Solórzano 2006), including their mentoring practices.

Graduate students

Research on the experiences of Black women collegians is sparse (Patton 2009; Watt 2006). Of the literature present, the vast majority underscores the difficulties this population faces and the ever-present barriers to their success (Berkel and Constantine 2005; Henry 2008; Johnson-Bailey 2004). Many have thought deeply about the work necessary to thwart systemic injustice and promote success in the lives of Black women collegians (Grant 2012; Watt 2006). Of these considerations, the benefits of same race-gender mentorship, particularly for Black women graduate students, have come to the fore (Grant 2012). Still, several complications impact its formation.

Similar to faculty, doctoral students often experience underrepresentation, racially motivated victimisation, and isolation as a result of being one of a few (Crawford and Smith 2005; Gregory 1999). They, too, experience an intersecting form of racialised fatigue. Black women's collegiate experiences are also often marked by pressure to conform, as well as, hostility (Ancis, Sedlacek, and Mohr 2000; Schwartz et al. 2003). The onslaught of psycosocial trauma often produces internalised impostorship (Brookfield 2005; Dancy and Brown 2011; Tyler 2008).

The purpose of mentorship in the lives of minoritised students is to subside those feelings (Bertrand Jones, Wilder, and Osborne-Lampkin 2013; Crawford and Smith 2005; Dancy and Brown 2011; Fedynich and Bain 2011; Grant 2012; Humble et al. 2006; Johnson-Bailey 2004; Lechuga 2011; Patton 2009; Patton and Harper 2003; Tillman 2001). Same race-gender mentoring further affirms Black women in ways that are often absent in other mentoring models. As Holmes and associates suggest, same race-gender mentorships teach this population how to 'navigate a [w]hite environment as a Black woman' (Holmes, Danley Land and Hinton-Hudson 2007, 111). Black women represent approximately 2–3% of post-secondary faculty in the US (U.S. Department of Education 2014), which means many Black women graduate students will not have the opportunity to form these types of mentoring relationships.

An area that has not received as much attention is the factors that influence the character of mentoring after the relationship is established. In this article we explore the ways Black women mentors (do not) reveal to their mentees their lived-experiences and the personal pain associated with the pursuit of careers in higher education; how and why their narratives are negotiated, sanctioned, and/or strategically altered; and the impact these decisions have on the development of Black women doctoral students and the work of curriculum homeplacing.

Resistant theoretical framing

We situate the present study within hooks' notion of 'imperialist white supremacist capitalist patriarchy' as a theoretical lens to critically analyse the complexities of Black women's mentoring relationships and the ways in which they develop in academic settings (hooks 2015). hooks describes imperialist white supremacist capitalist patriarchy as 'the interlocking ... systems [of oppression] that are the foundation of our nation' (1). As such, the policies and directives that shape human experience emerge from multiple systems of inequality working in concert to produce a socio-political landscape that necessitates the devaluing of some in order to affirm the value of others. These interlocking systems also work to maintain the perceived veracity of the social order. More than simply affecting policy, imperialist white supremacist capitalist patriarchy influences the hearts and minds of those who produce, enforce, and enact expectations for human interaction in public and private settings. The impact of imperialist white supremacist capitalist patriarchy creates a web in which certain bodies are not understood as fully human. Dehumanisation of the oppressed impedes equitable relationships with others, protection from harmful environments, and freedom of self-representation, among other toxic consequences.

The effects are not isolated to the relationships between oppressed and oppressors. The robustness and absolution of the system is seen in its ability to inform all aspects of our lives, including relationships among the oppressed. Several scholars have thought deeply about the challenges experienced between disenfranchised communities. Longstanding struggles in feminist communities reflect a sordid history of racist complicity by white women to the detriment of women of colour (Collins 1990; Hawkesworth 2006; hooks 1981; Hull, Scott, and Smith 1982). Patriarchy and misogyny have plagued US Black communities and, save a few notable figures, erased the legacies of Black women, despite the fact that they have been at the centre of racial uplift (Brooks and Houck 2011; Higginbotham 1993; Lorde 1984). These are just two examples of the ways systems of power affect individuals living at the intersections of multiple identities (Crenshaw 1991). Same race-gender mentoring relationships among Black women academics is no exception. We explore here the ways the violence of imperialist white supremacist capitalist patriarchy infiltrates the love-labour of Black women faculty in mentorships, specifically in regards to dialogue and truth-telling. Through this work of uncovering and testifying (Baszile 2008; Edwards and Baszile 2016) we critically assess these radical relationships to ultimately support the work of curriculum homeplacing.

Putting down methodological roots

The current study seeks to better understand the characteristics of academe that influence mentoring relationships between Black women, particularly in regards to the ways these relationships emerge and are negotiated with/in dialogue. As such, we situate this study within the narrative research tradition. Narrative researchers have long attended to the significance of relationship and subjectivity in intellectual work, deliberately resisting positivist assumptions about valid scholarship that silence the voices of individuals and communities living through/in the research (Barone 2007; Clandinin and Murphy 2009).

We employ Scholarly Personal Narrative (SPN) as it centres and values the scholar's experiences in research (Nash 2004). Nash (2004) describes SPN as 'the unabashed, upfront admission that ... your own life has meaning, both for you and for others' (24). Not only does SPN recognise the importance of experience in research, but it recognises that researchers as human beings have valuable and meaningful subjectivities worthy of analysis. We employ this methodological tradition as it allows (1) realities and validations to emerge within our own experiences in the ways that we understand them to be true, and (2) intentional opportunity to centre ourselves and our experienced relationship as well as explore the meaning of it as constructed on our own terms (Nash 2004). SPN pays particular attention to issues of systemic injustice and the ways narratives can disrupt silenc(ing)e and incite personal and communal liberation (Nash 2004). By connecting SPN with an explicit analysis of raced-gender experience, we hope to push narrative research beyond conventional boundaries.

Through a transcribed conversation between the authors, as well as individual personal narratives, we explore emerging themes as well as points of convergence and divergence. It is our own attempt at vulnerable truth-telling in an effort to more deliberately excavate the challenges and complications that shape academic mentorships between Black women, and the barriers to curriculum homeplacing. There are two simple questions that birthed this dialogical project: For Ebony, 'What is informing my expectations of mentorship?' and for Kirsten, 'What is informing my mentoring practices?'

Throughout the analysis, we pay particular attention to the ways we, as mentor and mentee, negotiate dialogue and information-sharing. As an analytical strategy, SPN assisted us in clarifying the interpretative frames we used to understand our mentoring relationship. These frames eventually serve as emerging themes and findings. Taken together, our SPNs offer a rich analysis of the life and breathe of a Black feminised mentorship that is growing, developing, and resisting towards curriculum homeplacing within a context of imperialist white supremacist capitalist patriarchy.

In our own words

An honest conversation

Kirsten: The argument that we are essentially trying to make is that you come … seeking advisement and mentorship, and whatever questions you are asking me, because of the world that I'm functioning in, my responses … are being adapted … And … are causing you to think certain things … So it would make sense that [this project] would be in a conversational mode … and maybe those starting questions are the questions that you've had that have led you [here]. What were the questions you were asking that got you these responses … that led to a misconception of the academy. Maybe it could be a … 'what do you think as a student you need to be successful?' And I could ask, 'what do I think you need to be successful?' (Ebony laughs)

Ebony: I was at the same time thinking, 'Without prompt, what would you give me?' I mean if I just came in and was like, 'I don't know what to do. I'm just here.', and you just [begin advising] … And so when you started saying, 'What do I need?', I'm thinking, 'What would you give me without me saying what I need, and then would what you give me be the same as what I think I need?' *That's* what prompts me to think about if you're just [formally advising me]. Because … I'm really looking for more of a connection to you than that. [I'm looking] for you to give me the real deal opposed to what everybody is telling *their* advisees and mentees, but I'm looking for you to tell me as a Black woman, 'This is what you gotta do[, and this is why].' … 'This is what I still experience, period.' 'I know what you goin' through … ' [pause]. So … the questions I was thinking [were,] 'What could you give me without me seeking?' 'What would you think I would need?' [pause] … And they're different … they CAN be different things. I don't know if that makes sense.

Kirsten: It does! But I'm thinking that it doesn't have to be so separate … what I'M asking and what YOU'RE asking actually are woven into … the same fabric … We can start with … 'My questions were this, but then her questions for me were this.' And then do an analysis of how those things are actually interwoven in really kind of intricate ways. Because I'm thinking, when you say what would I give you without prompting, I would give you things that I think would give you resilience. But that would mean that I would also not initiate [personal] vulnerability. So I would give you things like, 'You need to hustle.' 'I need you to write this amount of time … There's a special issue coming out, I need you to do this.' 'I need you to write this.' And so I'm giving you things that I feel are gonna … inoculate … well not inoculate you, but well maybe that's what I'm thinking in my brain … in my mind, 'What can I do to inoculate her from what she's going to experience as a Black woman? So I know if she has lots of publications, I know if she has teaching experience, I know if she goes to conferences,' and all of that stuff … I would give you preemptive strategies without telling you WHY you need these strategies. And I think that is what ... gets at the heart of this paper, is that ... you would walk in here, and you're like you want to be successful, and I would just give you ALL the strategies that ... I think would protect you, would protect your success. But it would take time before I told you the *why* behind that. It'll take time to tell you that I['ve] been damaged by this institution, and maybe if I would've had more publications from the gate, then they wouldn't have been able to come for me like they did. Maybe if I had studied more bell hooks and Afrocentric/Afro-womanism, then when I went to that conference that [white] woman wouldn't have told me ... 'Do you feel like you're alienating *yourself*?' You know? So when I tell you I want you to write a [annotated bibliography] of all these various kinds of Black, Black, Black feminized theoretical frames, I think it comes off as 'You just need to know this to write your dissertation,' but what I'm thinking, preemptively, is that when you get into that conference room with that [white] woman that you met in London, I want you to be able to pull out of your bag without hesitation.

Ebony: Which was so wonderful - to be able to name things to her [pause]. To say 'What about Audre Lorde; and this ... ; oh, well, you forget about ... ?' So to be able to say those things it did [pause]. And I did think [pause] and I was thinking in line [pause] into that annotated bibliography you had me do .... You know what I mean?

Kirsten: But it still didn't protect you, because you still walked out feeling like ... You know? So, it's like I gave you the tools that I thought would've protected you, and you STILL came out feeling like I feel when I'm in white academia.

Ebony: But, see, for me though, that's the important part of it. So we're talking about me, but then when I ask you how your presentation went and then you say to me that even with the preparation and what you know you feel like [I do]. I wouldn't have known that. I wouldn't have known that ... she knows what that feeling is, and, even though she may not have felt exactly like I felt when she walked outta her presentation, she had *some* feeling that was similar just by the responses ... the non-verbal responses of other people.

Kirsten: ... Ah ... I wish we were recording this conversation because it's so *good*! (lots of laughter)

Ebony: I been recording.

Kirsten: You know you suppose to tell people when you recording stuff. (still laughing)

Ebony: I know. I didn't. I forgot I was recording, because I was only planning to record when you was telling me exactly what I needed to do, so I would know, or so I would remember [pause]. MY BAD [pause]. Then I forgot ...

Kirsten: But it's good. It's good.

Ebony: Hopefully I can hear it.

Kirsten: I KNOW! ... so even though I told you what I experienced ... I also didn't tell you that I walked out feeling the same way you do, and every time I go to those conferences and I get treated like that, I walk out feeling like I'm not good enough ... But I'm not gonna tell you that. I'm just gonna tell you what happens and this is how they act ... so that you just [are] strong enough. You know? I just want you to be strong enough ... And is that antithetical to womanist practice? To not be able to be human enough to be vulnerable? You know? ... I was just thinking this ... actually this morning, maybe I'm just not good enough to do this work ... Maybe I thought I was smart, but I'm just not that smart. But I don't tell you that. All I tell you is that they act up in those rooms and you need to ...

Ebony: Ummm-hmmm, and [I think that] but about myself. So, when I hear you say that you have the same feelings and thoughts about the degree of your intelligence and belonging ... which I haven't heard until just now, then I start breathing. It's like I feel like I'm not breathing this whole time, and then when I hear *that*, I'm like [big exhale], 'Okay. I'm okay.' Then I start breathing because ... When I look at you, when I look at [another Black woman professor], I don't see [your struggle and injury]. [I think] maybe if they did ever feel like this, it was during THIS [doctoral] process, and once they were done they just got it and knew how to do it all. All I see is y'all got it goin' on. Y'all know what y'all doin' ... I'm trying to be like that ... but I ain't got it in me. I'm not smart enough ... .So, as this moment [of vulnerability] just happens, I'm thinkin', 'She been lyin' to me ... Even if she *never* lied, it's almost like an omission thing.' ... You never said that you didn't feel like that, but ... you never said you did [pause], but, as a student, is it okay for me to feel like you should tell me that? Telling me [those truths] is what I feel like I need ... because not only do I not feel like I'm good enough for the academy ... but I also feel I'm not good enough [for you] ... That's what I'm looking for, but ... then I [wonder if I'm] wrong as a student to really want that. And I don't ask for it because I didn't think you had the feelings that you just expressed to me. I didn't think that you made it to the point that you're at by feeling like [I do]. But when you do tell me, I feel closer to you. And then I feel like I can say ... 'I don't feel like I can write ... they don't know how long it took for me to come up with, hell, just that title, or just that abstract. Now I'm stressing about how Imma come up with a whole paper' ... Like when I sent you the abstract for [a conference], I literally said, 'I'm really scared for you to read this' (Kirsten laughs). I really didn't want you to read it ... for you to be like ... 'How did this get accepted? This is ... ' And then when you ... said that it read brilliantly, I was like 'Oh shit! *I can breathe*'. Maybe it was ... I don't feel like that about my work, and I'm always thinking [pause] ... 'I don't want to be failing Kirsten ... ' so it's not just everybody else [pause], but it's you too. So then, when I hear that from you, then I feel like 'Okay, now I'm connected to her more.' ... I'm not thinking, 'Maybe it's gonna just happen for me one day. I'm going to see myself in her [or her in me].' That's how I feel.

Kirsten: What is it that you would have similar feelings of fear around me that you feel around the academy? Like, there's something really disturbing about that. That ... we're so enmeshed in this ... fabric of ... imperialist which supremacist capitalist patriarchy that your support system ... the person who was supposed to be the lifeline ... those same feelings are directed toward that person as to the academy? ... It's like it gets so in ... into us, like IN.

Ebony: I don't know.

Dialogical self-reflection

Ebony

'What informs my expectation of mentorship?'. I have had amazing experiences with Black women faculty throughout my collegiate career. These relationships just formed organically. There was nothing forced or even anticipated about them, as there were no assigned titles given to those relationships. They were beautiful and protective; my heart's sisters. I did not see myself in this world of academia before them. They showed me how to *do* education and live in it as they shielded me as best they could from the fire and dangers of being a Black woman in the academy. They were the cushions that surrounded me as I walked in this white man's world so that I would not fall as I was kicked, punched, and shoved by the institution. They were not only physical beings but spiritual figures that held and kept me. And in that sense, they made university 'home' for me.

This is what mentoring *felt* like for me, so I did not expect any difference between me and Kirsten besides the formal, university-assigned roles of 'advisor' and 'advisee' that was the catalyst for our relationship. Walking into my interview, there SHE was, and I instantly saw a reflection when I looked at HER. Looking at her almost affirmed my walking into that room that day. I belonged there, as I was looking at myself watch as I walked into the room and sat across the table with myself. After seeing her name official printed as my advisor on my acceptance letter took me for a look, and I immediately began almost dreaming about this perfect experience that I was going to have with her. In my mind, she was going to advise me through kinship. She was going to be another other-mother/auntie/cousin/sister to me. I was going to get a real sense of what I'm getting myself into.

The others before her helped guide me to this path (doctoral work), and she was assigned as a guide *through* my doctoral work. But I expected the same spiritual guidance from her in protection and honesty. In my mind, there was a literal depiction of her having big beautiful wings and scooping my physical self into those wings to guide me; to nurture me. It was a real protection from all the shit; all the uncertainty; and all the former negative experiences that were following. This is what I expected of her because this is what I felt that I had in Black women before her. That is how I imagined the relationship with my advisor to be. I was following her, just as I followed those before her. I was trying to figure out how to be like her – like the rest of them – knowing, confident, strong, etc., but in a different way. They were all of these intimidating things that I was not. I was unsure of my belonging here.

Then, I was hit hard, and felt like I'd been lied to; like I had been deceived for so long. As I'm questioning myself and my whole purpose of being here, it was revealed to me that one of the first Black women who mentored me, who I am still so close to and trust so much had never let me in on something I interpreted as a secret. She told me of her struggles and injuries in traveling this road to academe and feeling like she belonged. After nine years, she opened up to me with a level of honesty about her experience in the academy that she had not displayed before. And she was not the only one. When I ran to Kirsten about the important and life-changing thing that I just found out, she seemed tight-lipped about it. It was like she knew something; like she could testify to something, but stayed professional in her demeanor. It's almost as though she was saying, 'It's not proper to talk about that in our relationship.' I was pissed! There is a system in this environment that prohibits the relationship that I expect from her, and I'm not sure how to function in it. It's killing me! She wouldn't tell me. She wouldn't be *family* with me and tell me what was up. Until now …

Kirsten

'What informs my mentoring practices?'

This was Ebony's question for me. And it was a surprisingly difficult question; difficult because there are a lot of unacknowledged and interrelated emotions that impact how I approach our mentoring relationship. The three that come to the surface most prominently are Love, Fear, and culturally *irrelevant* Institutional Expectations.

I am fiercely committed to Ebony's success. FIERCELY. I'm almost taken aback by how much I want this girl to *make it*! In a lot of ways, she is the reason why I am here. She represents for me the next generation of conscious Black woman brilliance. And if she fails, what the hell am I doing here! I mean, really? If all the work and bullshit I had to put up with to earn this damn degree doesn't result in getting my sister across the finish line – and not just across, but whole and empowered, and better – then I have fundamentally failed. Ebony is not simply my university-assigned student. She's the little sister/niece/daughter that the ancestors have entrusted to my care. And hot damn, I will not fail her!

This Black woman communal Love for Ebony also produces a certain level of Fear. I worry so very much. I'm constantly concerned about her success, because I know how crazy the academy can be. And how it can *seem as if* it is deliberately trying to destroy Black women on every turn. When I look at her, I see the same fire in her eyes, the same intensity, inquisitiveness, passion that I used to have as a young doc student, before the academy beat it out of me. And I just want to protect that Black Girl fierceness in her. That conscious unruliness. I find myself trying to shield her from the disciplining forces that work to contain Black women. 'Yes, that idea's brilliant!' 'Absolutely, that's a valid contribution.' 'Now let's figure out how to frame it for publication.' All the while, I'm thinking, 'These white folks are going to crucify her for coming for them!' So I try to give her all the tools she needs to fight the special brand of white supremacy reserved for Black women academics who don't follow the rules, and who state the obvious in order to disrupt racist (ir)rationality.

All of these emotions are hemmed in by Institutional Expectations for the formal advisor/advisee relationship; expectations that enforce a certain level of sterility and a particular kind of hierarchy. Institutional models of mentorship, complicit in white male patriarchal norms that work to make me feel like an idiot for caring so much; that convince me that if I get too close she won't respect me, she'll get too familiar and subsequently won't get what she needs from my guidance. As if familiarity somehow automatically prevents a student from receiving direction. And so I find myself constantly balancing these competing ideals when it comes to Ebony. I want her to maintain a womanist/Black feminist ethic of consciousness, care, and community, but I have to equip her with the dispositional astuteness to survive in a cut-throat, competitive, callous racist-sexist academy where relational investment is considered a liability. So I battle insomnia, I travail in my prayer closet, I challenge my colleagues, I do all these things hoping that maybe she won't have to, or at least she'll get a few extra hours of sleep at night.

Findings and analysis

A critical analysis of our conversation and narratives reveals potent moments of revelation rife with scholarly application and significance. Here we discuss three resonant ways in which our words illuminate the often unseen and under-theorised complications inherent within Black women's same race-gender mentorships. Through our *messy* (Mottern 2013) endeavour to 'work the hyphens' (Fine 1994), these findings support the development and nurture of Black women's mentoring relationships, and more importantly, the radical and resistant practice of curriculum homeplacing. Specifically, we discuss the (1) unspoken conversation between the literature on impostorship and same race-gender mentorships, (2) desire for kinship, and (3) reflections of self-in-other.

Impostorship within same race-gender mentorships

Stephen Brookfield's (1994) research on the experiences of adult educators and learners and his subsequent exploration into what he calls the *phenomenon of impostorship* has become a bedrock for scholarly discussions related to the experiences of traditionally underrepresented populations in post-secondary education. Brookfield describes impostorship as 'the sense ... that at some deeply embedded level [traditionally underrepresented individuals] possess neither the talent nor the right to become' successful students or academic professionals (Brookfield 1999, 11). Put differently, impostorship is the ever-present feeling of *not belonging* and un-deservedness that plague the lives of underrepresented populations within academe. In regards to the student–professor relationship, Brookfield admonishes professors to be honest about their own experiences with impostorship and to provide space for dialogue in the classroom to address these feelings. His reflection on the importance of vulnerability and honesty echoes our own theorisation in regards to truth-telling as fundamental to curriculum homeplacing. While the extant research does expose the detrimental impact impostorship can have on both students and mentors independently, there is a paucity of discussion on the ways it influences the mentoring relationship *between* the traditionally underrepresented (see Dancy and Brown 2011). Discouraged students are prompted to look to those who have 'made it' as evidence of their own potential, while struggling professors are expected to develop pedagogical practices of vulnerability, despite actively contending with their own questions of professional viability.

Similarly, the literature on same race-gender mentorship for Black women underscores the importance of doctoral students seeing possibilities for success that mirror them (Grant 2012; Tillman 2001). The literature also emphasises the importance of 'natural mentors' for Black women doctoral students' successful matriculation (Grant 2012). Inherent in these claims is the recognition that mentors that share similar socio-cultural experiences are not only better able to assist students in navigating the uniquely treacherous academic terrain they will encounter, but will also be most likely to identify these students as capable and worthy of success. The relevant scholarship rarely engages the professional challenges experienced by mentors. Understandably, the literature focuses primarily on the needs of the students, and instead provides cursory reflection on the struggles of Black women faculty mentors, inasmuch as these reflections add credence to this population's ability to develop relevant navigational strategies for their mentees.

Within the impostorship literature, there is an absence of socio-communal connection with mentors. Conversely, within same race-gender literature is an absence of the persistence and influence of impostorship among faculty when mentoring. The present study addresses the lacunae between these two literature bases. This disconnect is evidenced in our narratives as we both struggle with and against feelings of academic fraudulence while contending with imperialist white supremacist capitalist patriarchy. This struggle takes place within a context of cultural and professional expectations of sameness that frame, while not always informing, our mentoring relationship. While the literature and our own experiences with Black women's community apart from the academy, tell us that our relationship should be powerful and subversive, these ideals rarely take into consideration the contaminating influence of systemic injustice. Somehow same race-gender mentorship for Black women is assumed to be a quasi-pure space that defies epistemic violencing (Spivak 1988). And while we agree it does carry such potential, this project compels us to critically assess its limits.

Desire for kinship

Our narratives reveal longings for kinship as we walk *through the fire* of the academy. Our narratives reveal a search for home, or at least a semblance of it, in one another. This feeling of *home* is displayed in the terms that we use in describing our mentoring expectations. Whether we describe it as mother/sister/aunt/niece/cousin/daughter, it supersedes the normative expectations of university-sanctioned mentorships. The relevant literature does suggest that Black women seek same race-gender mentoring relationships as a means of connecting to someone who they can 'relate to and understand their struggles, both personally and professionally' (Patton and Harper 2003, 69). However, often these relational descriptions do not attend to the more familial characteristics revealed in our narratives. What is also often overlooked is the desire for kinship and communal connection on the part of the faculty mentor. This article offers an insertion of the faculty mentor perspective and acknowledges that there are aspects of the desire for kinship that are reciprocal between Black women faculty and doctoral students.

The level of care attached to Black women's mentoring relationships supports greater attention to communal bonding and personal connection, which has the potential to develop into curriculum homeplacing. However, these potent relationships are also regulated by the constraints embedded in institutionalised norms. This communal and spiritual desire for kinship finds its origins beyond the academy; in Black communities that model invested cross-generational, extended-kin relationships between Black women. As our narratives reveal, we see ourselves in relation to one another in the familial sense, and that feeling of *kinship* is not necessarily translated and communicated to one another in the formal processes of doctoral mentoring. It manifests more as a serendipitous, but unstated, need and expectation. We both describe it as a longing to be something more meaningful and subversive than *mentor* or *mentee.*

We ask, 'What does it mean that we are both looking for something that we appear unable to name in community with one another?' What does it mean to have a desire for kinship but deliberately resist communicating said desire to those most familiar with your needs and cultural practices? More specifically, how can Black women faculty and students become more intentional about exposing hegemonic institutional practices in an effort to infuse culturally specific practices into their mentoring relationships? How can they enact curriculum homeplacing?

Again, this desire for kinship is reflective of Black women's communities. It is connected to a womanist/Black feminist ethic of care that acknowledges the significance of connection for survival and collective humanisation. This is a deeper level of care that is not only unrequired, but in some respects disallowed in the university-sanctioned mentor/mentee relationship created and dictated by white supremacist patriarchal models of instruction and guidance. We contend this insistent desire/expectation for more, even if unnamed and unacknowledged, is fundamentally an act of resistance and subversion. The desire for kinship presented in both of our narratives resists academic models of sterility, while simultaneously succumbing to its forces by often rendering us silent in regards to our hopes and pain.

Reflections of self-in-other

We recognise another sentiment that arises beyond kinship. We believe it is what keeps us both ardently committed to one another despite the academic constraints endured by our mentoring relationship. We not only see ourselves as in-community or kin with one another, but also *as* one another. Although from different perspectives and vantage points, we see each other as reflections of our individual selves. Not only is she my kin, but *she* is also *me*. We find value and purpose in this non-binary reflection of self-in-other, or the 'other-self' (Schalk 2011).

We understand our responsibilities to one another as not only communal care, but also self-care. Understanding this causes us to individually prioritise not failing one another, whether that be in terms of our ability to do the work expected of an academic or the ability to model survival despite working within a system of oppression. This is a heavy burden, but the constant act of translating that need for one another to persist into one that is unselfish, intensifies the commitment to survival. The self-in-other episteme that foregrounds our engagement is also reflective of prominent Black faith practices rooted in the US Black Church tradition. These practices make sacred the self as in community and the importance of self-sacrifice for community uplift (Edwards 2013; Lincoln and Mamiya 1990). In our mentor/mentee relationship, we are operating in ways that are informed by our home communities, and while not always articulated, we are inciting a paradigmatic and methodological shift for mentoring in the academy.

In our narratives we reveal that Ebony sees the possibilities of who she wants to be in Kirsten. Subsequently, the ways that she conceptualises the relationship are informed by the reflection of self that emerges when she meets Kirsten. Relatedly, when Kirsten reflects on the academic journey that Ebony is currently enduring, she connects with the self as doctoral student and remembers the injury that characterises that process. Her intense commitment to Ebony is predicated on the other-self or self-in-other positionality. This is valuable as Kirsten feels a transcendent sense of familiarity with Ebony's journey, which compels her to engage in the act of radical honesty through vulnerable truth-telling.

The radical potential of other-self work as a part of curriculum homeplacing is constrained by the hierarchical structure of the university-sanctioned advisor/advisee relationship. Yet, we begin to experience a shift in our relationship as we reveal and reflect on the sameness of our experiences. In those kindred moments we begin to honestly see ourselves.

Conclusions: the struggle for love continues …

While the literature is clear that same race-gender representation in the professoriate positively influences minoritised graduate student matriculation, this must be understood as only a preliminary analysis. These relationships continue to develop within an epistemically violent context (Spivak 1988). Based on an analysis of our narratives, we identify three touchstones that characterise the praxis of curriculum homeplacing. They are (1) vulnerable truth-telling as resistance to impostorship, (2) attention to culturally informed kinship, and 3) self-in-other reflection. Curriculum homeplacing is relevant to the work of two scholarly communities. First, we see the discussion of love and labour in academic kinship relationships as a contribution to the ongoing 'complicated conversation' within curriculum studies. Second, we believe our subjectively nuanced reflection attending to the more intimate dimensions of Black women's academic lives has much to contribute to the literature on mentoring and minoritised communities in the field of higher education. We are not only affording due attention to the importance of mentoring relationships, but we are also observing more deeply the meaning-making process by and between mentor and mentee. In this way, we do not give focus to any one dimension, but explore those expectations and needs rarely verbalised.

By interrogating the complications inherent in mentoring relationships, the present study hopes to support endeavours within Black women's academic communities that more deliberately support curriculum homeplacing for the next generation of Black women scholars. Our hope is that this article will provide Black women with the opportunity to further explore how they might engage with one another in ways that acknowledge their cultural and communal subjectivities.

Although mentoring serves as important tool, attempts at academic relationship building in the traditional sense did not afford us the space to engage in vulnerable truth-telling. This is the type of radical vulnerability and honesty we found necessary to establish a form of academic engagement that honoured our subjective her stories and cultural memories (Dillard 2012). Within this departure from traditional mentoring practices, we crafted curriculum homeplacing. Our hope is that it will incite an exploration of mentoring practices that assert Black women's subjectivities in loving, revolutionary, and healing ways.

Disclosure statement

No potential conflict of interest was reported by the authors.

References

Ancis, J. R., W. E. Sedlacek, and J. J. Mohr. 2000. "Student Perceptions of Campus Culture and Climate by Race." *Journal of Counseling & Development* 78 (2): 180–185.

Baez, B. 2000. "Race-related Service and Faculty of Color: Conceptualizing Critical Agency in Academe." *Higher Education* 39: 363–391.

Barone, T. 2007. "A Return to the Gold Standard? Questioning the Future of Narrative Construction as Educational Research." *Qualitative Inquiry* 13 (4): 454–470.

Baszile, D. T. 2006. "In this Place Where I Don't Quite Belong: Claiming the Ontoepistemological in-between." In *From Oppression to Grace: Women of Color and their Dilemmas within the Academy*, edited by T. R. Berry and N. D. Mizelle, 195–208. Sterling, VA: Stylus Publishing.

Baszile, D. T. 2008. "Beyond All Reason: The Pedagogical Promise of Critical Race Testimony." *Race, Ethnicity and Education* 11 (3): 251–265.

Berkel, L. A., and M. G. Constantine. 2005. "Relational Variables and life Satisfaction in African American and Asian American College Women." *Journal of College Counseling* 8 (1): 5–13.

Bertrand Jones, T., J. Wilder, and L. Osborne-Lampkin. 2013. "Employing a Black Feminist Approach to Doctoral Advising: Preparing Black Women for the Professoriate." *The Journal of Negro Education* 82 (3): 326–338.

Brookfield, S. 1994. "Tales from the Dark Side: A Phenomenography of Adult Critical Reflection." *International Journal of Lifelong Education* 13 (3): 203–216.

Brookfield, S. 1999. What is College Really Like for Adult Students? *About Campus*, January-February, 10–15.

Brookfield, S. 2005. "Overcoming Impostorship, Cultural Suicide, and Lost Innocence: Implications for Teaching Critical Thinking in the Community College." *New Directions for Community Colleges* 2005: 49–57.

Brooks, M. P., and Houck, D. W., eds. 2011. *The Speeches of Fannie Lou Hamer: To Tell it Like it is.* Jackson: University Press of Mississippi.

Brown, A. J. B. 2012. "Black Women Faculty in Predominantly White Space: Negotiating Discourses of Diversity." In *Integrated but Unequal: Black Faculty in Predominately White Space*, edited by M. Christian, X–X. Trenton, NJ: Africa World Press.

Burgess, N. J. 1997. "Tenure and Promotion Among African American Women in the Academy: Issues and Strategies." In *Black Women in the Academy: Promises and Perils*, edited by L. Benjamin, 227–235. Gainesville: University Press of Florida.

Clandinin, D. J., and M. S. Murphy. 2009. "Relational Ontological Commitments in Narrative Research." *Educational Researcher* 38 (8): 598–602.

Collins, P. H. 1990. *Black Feminist Thought: Knowledge, Consciousness, and the Politics of Empowerment.* Boston, MA: Unwin Hyman.

Crawford, K., and D. Smith. 2005. "The we and the us: Mentoring African American Women." *Journal of Black Studies* 36 (1): 52–67.

Crenshaw, K. 1991. "Mapping the Margins: Intersectionality, Identity Politics, and Violence against Women of Color." *Stanford Law Review* 43 (6): 1241–1299.

Dancy II, T. E., and M. C. Brown II. 2011. "The Mentoring and Induction of Educators of Color: Addressing the Impostor Syndrome in Academe." *Journal of School Leadership* 21 (4): 607–634.

Dancy II, T. E., and G. Jean-Marie. 2014. "Faculty of Color in Higher Education: Exploring the Intersections of Identity, Impostorship, and Internalized Racism." *Mentoring & Tutoring: Partnership in Learning* 22 (4): 354–372.

Dillard, C. 2012. *Learning to (Re)member the Things we've Learned to Forget.* New York: Peter Lang.

Edwards, K. T. 2013. "Christianity as Anti-colonial Resistance? Womanist Theology, Black Liberation Theology, and the Black Church as Sites for Pedagogical Decolonization." *Souls: A Critical Journal of Black Politics, Culture, and Society* 15 (1–2): 146–162.

Edwards, K. T., and D. T. Baszile. 2016. "Scholarly Rearing in three Acts: Black Women's Testimonial Scholarship and the Cultivation of Radical Black Female Inter-Subjectivity." *Knowledge Cultures* 4 (1): 85–99.

Everett, J. E., J. C. Hall, and J. Hamilton-Mason. 2010. "Everyday Conflict and Daily Stressors: Coping Responses of Black Women." *Affilia* 25 (1): 30–42.

Fedynich, L., and S. F. Bain. 2011. "Mentoring the Successful Graduate Student of Tomorrow." *Research in Higher Education Journal* 12: 1–7.

Fine, M. 1994. "Working the Hyphens: Reinventing Self and other in Qualitative Research." In *Handbook of Qualitative Research*, edited by N. Denzin and Y. Lincoln, 130–155. Newbury Park, CA: Sage.

Grant, C. M. 2012. "Advancing Our Legacy: A Black Feminist Perspective on the Significance of Mentoring for African American Women in Educational Leadership." *International Journal of Qualitative Studies in Education* 25 (1): 101–117.

Gregory, S. T. 1999. *Black Women in the Academy: The Secrets to Success and Achievement.* Lanham, MD: University Press of America.

Gutierrez y Muhs, G., Y. F. Niemann, C. G. Gonzalez, and A. P. Harris. 2012. *Presumed Incompetent: The Intersections of Race and Class for Women in Academia.* Boulder: University Press of Colorado.

Harley, D. A. 2007. "Maids of Academe: African American Women Faculty at Predominately White Institutions." *Journal of African American Studies* 12 (1): 19–36.

Hawkesworth, M. E. 2006. *Globalization and Feminist Activism.* Lanham, MD: Rowman & Littlefield Publishers.

Henry, W. J. 2008. "Black Female Millennial College Students: Dating Dilemmas and Identity Development." *Multicultural Education* 16 (2): 17–21.

Higginbotham, E. B. 1993. *Righteous Discontent: The Women's Movement in the Black Baptist Church, 1880–1920.* Cambridge: Harvard University Press.

Holmes, S. L., L. Danley Land, and V. D. Hinton-Hudson. 2007. "Race Still Matters: Considerations for Mentoring Black Women in Academe." *The Negro Educational Review* 58 (1–2): 105–131.
hooks, bell. 1981. *Ain't I a Woman: Black Women and Feminism*. Boston, MA: South End Press.
hooks, bell. 1990. *Yearning: Race, Gender, and Cultural Politics*. Boston, MA: South End Press.
hooks, bell. 2004. *The will to Change: Men, Masculinity, and Love*. New York: Atria Books.
hooks, bell. 2015. *Understanding Patriarchy*. No Borders: Louisville's Radical Lending Library.
Hull, G. T., P. B. Scott, and B. Smith. 1982. *All the Women are White, all the Blacks are Men, but Some of us Are Brave*. New York: The Feminist Press at The City University of New York.
Humble, A. M., C. R. Solomon, K. R. Allen, K. R. Blaisure, and M. P. Johnson. 2006. "Feminism and Mentoring of Graduate Students." *Family Relations* 55: 2–15.
Johnson-Bailey, J. 2004. "Hitting and Climbing the Proverbial Wall: Participation and Retention Issues for Black Graduate Women." *Race Ethnicity and Education* 7 (4): 331–349.
Kram, K. E. 1985. *Mentoring at Work: Developmental Relationships in Organizational Life*. Glenview, IL: Scott, Foresman, and Company.
Lechuga, V. 2011. "Faculty-Graduate Student Mentoring Relationships: Mentors' Perceived Roles and Responsibilities." *Higher Education* 62 (6): 757–771.
Lincoln, C. E., and L. H. Mamiya. 1990. *The Black Church in the African American Experience*. Durham, NC: Duke University Press.
Lorde, A. 1984. *Sister Outsider*. Freedom, CA: Crossing Press.
Mottern, R. 2013. "The Messy World of Reflexivity: Qualitative Journeys." *The Qualitative Report* 18 (16): 1–2.
Nash, R. J. 2004. *Liberating Scholarly Writing: The Power of Personal Narrative*. New York: Teachers College Press.
Ng-A-Fook, N. 2007. *An Indigenous Curriculum of Place: The United Houma Nation's Contentious Relationship with Louisiana's Educational Institutions*. New York: Peter Lang.
Patitu, C. L., and K. G. Hinton. 2003. "The Experiences of African American Women Faculty and Administrators in Higher Education: Has Anything Changed?" *New Directions for Student Services* 2003: 79–93.
Patton, L. D. 2009. "My Sister's Keeper: A Qualitative Examination of Mentoring Experiences Among African American Women in Graduate and Professional Schools." *The Journal of Higher Education* 80 (5): 510–537.
Patton, L. D., and S. R. Harper. 2003. "Mentoring Relationships Among African American Women in Graduate and Professional Schools." *New Directions for Student Services* 2003: 67–78.
Pinar, W. F. 1991. "Curriculum as Social Psychoanalysis: On the Significance of Place." In *Curriculum as Social Psychoanalysis: The Significance of Place*, edited by J. L. Kincheloe and W. F. Pinar, 165–186. Albany: State University of New York Press.
Pittman, C. T. 2012. "Racial Microaggressions: The Narratives of African American Faculty at a Predominantly White University." *The Journal of Negro Education* 81 (1): 82–92.
Schalk, S. 2011. "Self, Other and Other-Self: Going Beyond the Self/Other Binary in Contemporary Consciousness." *Journal of Comparative Research in Anthropology and Sociology* 2 (1): 197–210.
Schwartz, R. A., B. L. Bower, D. C. Rice, and C. M. Washington. 2003. ""Ain't I a Woman, too?": Tracing the Experiences of African American Women in Graduate School." *Journal of Nigro Educaton* 72 (3): 252–268.
Smith, W. A., T. J. Yosso, and D. G. Solórzano. 2006. "Challenging Racial Battle Fatigue on Historically White Campuses: A Critical Race Examination of Race-Related Stress." In *Faculty of Color: Teaching in Predominately White Colleges and Universities*, edited by C. A. Stanley, 299–327. Boston, MA: Anker Publishing.
Spivak, G. C. 1988. "Can the Subaltern Speak?" In *Marxism and the Interpretation of Culture*, edited by C. Nelson, and L. Grossbeg, 271–316. Urbana: University of Illinois Press.
Taylor-Brandon, L. 2006. "Seen, Not Heard: A Conversation on what it Means to be Black and Female in the Academy." In *From Oppression to Grace: Women of Color and Their Dilemmas within the Academy*, edited by T. Berry and N. Mizelle, 168–194. Sterling: Stylus Publishing, LLC.

Thomas, G. D., and C. Hollenshead. 2001. "Resisting from the Margins: The Coping Strategies of Black Women and other Women of Color Faculty Members at a Research University." *The Journal of Negro Education* 70 (3): 166–175.

Tillman, L. 2001. "Mentoring African American Faculty in Predominantly White Institutions." *Research in Higher Education* 42 (3): 295–325.

Tyler, M. A. 2008. "The Whisperings of a Doctor of Philosophy Student's Phenomenography." *International Journal of Pedagogies & Learning* 4 (2): 6–14.

U.S. Department of Education, National Center for Education Statistics. 2014. The Condition of Education 2014 (NCES 2014-083), Characteristics of Postsecondary Faculty.

Wallace, S. L., S. E. Moore, L. L. Wilson, and B. G. Hart. 2012. "African American Women in the Academy: Quelling the Myth of Presumed Incompetence." In *Presumed Incompetent: The Intersections of Race and Class for Women in Academia*, edited by G. Gutiérrez y Muhs, Y. Flores Niemann, C. G. González, and A. P. Harris, 421–438. Boulder: University Press of Colorado.

Watt, S. K. 2006. "Racial Identity Attitudes, Womanist Identity Attitudes, and Self-Esteem in African American College Women Attending Historically Black Single-Sex and Coeducational Institutions." *Journal of College Student Development* 47 (3): 319–334.

Complicated contradictions amid Black feminism and millennial Black women teachers creating curriculum for Black girls

Tiffany M. Nyachae

ABSTRACT

Millennial Black women teachers wrestle with two simultaneous burdens: disrupting the racist and sexist status quo of schooling through curriculum, and employing tactics to survive school politics among their majority White women colleagues. This article describes how the *Sisters of Promise* (SOP) curriculum aligned with Black feminism and Black feminist pedagogy, and how it did not. This curriculum was created for Black girls within the margins of school by a millennial Black woman teacher and other Black women teachers. Analysis of the SOP curriculum revealed that even with the best of intentions, and even for relatively self-aware millennial Black women teachers, it is possible to present Black girl students with contradictory messages, due to a lack of exposure to Black feminism, Black feminist pedagogy, and the work of Black women educational scholars, in their curriculum studies. Included are implications and recommendations for millennial Black women teachers creating curriculum for Black girls.

The dilemma

Millennial Black[1] women teachers wrestle with two simultaneous burdens: disrupting the racist and sexist status quo of schooling through curriculum (hooks 1994), and employing tactics to survive school politics among their majority White women colleagues (Kohli 2016). This dilemma is the complicated product of school desegregation (Foster 1997), colour blindness rhetoric (King 1991), neo-liberal ideals (Taliaferro-Baszile 2005), and limited exposure to Black women educational scholarship in teacher education programmes (Taliaferro-Baszile 2006; Evans-Winters and Esposito 2010). In 2006, I was a millennial Black woman beginning teacher committed to the dissemination of Black history, believing all children could succeed, while tiptoeing around covert institutionalised racism in an effort to 'get along' with my White colleagues. At the time, I wondered why the veteran Black teachers, many of them mentors of mine, were so visibly frustrated. I was like so many Black women novice teachers, 'unprepared to engage in serious intellectual discourse within the complex and combative environment of the public schools' (Omolade 1994, 147). As a middle school Social Studies teacher of primarily African-American students, I found myself involved in a balancing act, espousing race consciousness while helping my students navigate mainstream school culture.

I argue that, although millennial Black women teachers may embody a Black consciousness, and may use this consciousness as a guide for teaching, their childhood schooling experiences, teacher preparation programmes, the school climate in which they teach, and competing neo-liberal educational agendas effect *what* curriculum they create for Black girls in contradictory ways. Considering the conflation of Black people and Black males that often happens in educational discourse (Blake et al. 2011; Brown 2011), curriculum created by millennial Black women teachers for Black girls may not recognise the nuances of how schools oppress Black girls as compared to Black boys. This shortcoming is partly due to the absence of Black feminism, by means of Black women educational scholarship, in curriculum studies. An inclusion of Black feminism and Black women education scholarship in curriculum studies would help to prepare teachers to fight against the racist and sexist tides of standardisation and conformity endemic in public school education. I also contend that, while many intervention programmes for Black girls are well-intended, it is important to consider whether their curriculum empowers Black girls and embodies Black feminism and Black feminist pedagogy, or simply maintains a racialised gendered status quo against the backdrop of teacher context.

The purpose of this article is to explore how the *Sisters of Promise* (SOP) curriculum, created by Black women teachers for Black girls within the margins of school, aligned with Black feminism and Black feminist pedagogy, and how it did not. In her critical autobiography, Taliaferro-Baszile (2006) reflected on her mis-education and her journey back to Black history and Black intellectual thought via curriculum theorising. This article illuminates what Taliaferro-Baszile described as 'the irony of continued "complicated contradictions" within its scope' (90), and for this reason, Black feminist qualitative research practices are employed. Black feminist researchers begin by reflecting on their own lived experiences (Evans-Winters 2015). Therefore, while this article is about my analysis of the SOP curriculum, I begin by situating this study within my own narrative.

Millennial Black girl's education, in school and with grandma

Born in the 1980s, I am considered a millennial. Millennials, also known as Generation Me or Generation Y (e.g. Twenge 2013), are individuals born between 1981 and 1997 (e.g. Lapidos 2015). According to some modern demographers and magazine editors (e.g. Twenge 2013; Lapidos 2015), a focus on equality and self-expression are cultural distinctions of Generation Y. These distinctions make sense, as Black millennials are beneficiaries of the Civil Rights Movement without directly having experienced the movement and its struggle. Instead, Black millennials experienced a different struggle – desegregated schools, de facto segregation in urban areas, and for some, integration in the suburbs (Evans-Winters and Love 2015) with an increasingly neo-liberal federal education agenda (Dumas and ross 2016). During the 1990s, I attended an urban public school from the third through the eighth grade with a Black, Latinx, and White student population, a large percentage of which was experiencing poverty or the working-class. Indeed, racial and cultural tensions were present at times and a few incidents erupted, but for the most part, we managed. The teachers and students rarely talked about race, let how alone how other identities complicated race – colour blindness was ever-present.

As an adolescent, I remember having many conversations with my paternal grandmother about 'the good ole days'. Grandma would talk about her little Black town in Alabama where everyone knew and looked out for each other. All of her teachers were Black and they loved her. She told me 'they gave us the best they had, you know'. I had only four Black women teachers from pre-K through the 12th grade. Although I was fortunate, I listened to Grandma talk about her Black teachers with envy. I will never forget the day I probed her thoughts about segregation. Grandma looked over my head, stared off into space, as we sat at her kitchen table and with a faint smile confessed 'I think it was better that way'. According to Foster (1997), desegregation came with the following liabilities: a drastic decrease in Black teachers due to the questioning of their intellectual competence, loss of community due to bussing, loss of high-quality education for Black students due to institutionalised racism, and loss of access to Black history in schools. Grandma had said enough; I knew exactly what she meant.

Grandma learned Black history from her Black teachers and she taught that history and personal oral histories to me. While I knew *herstories*[2] (Lewis 1988; Henry 2005; Alston and McClellan 2011) existed, I never asked how Grandma's Black woman-ness meshed with Black men, White women, White men, or even other women and men of colour. I guess I just meshed all Black people and Black experiences together somehow, and in other contexts I grouped all women struggles together. One night during a college course I took in my junior year of high school, a Black woman student in her early 20s passionately proclaimed that the Women's Rights Movement was never intended for Black women, that it was only intended for rich White women. As an intense lover of history and a millennial, who at the time advocated for all fights for equality, I was stunned. I believed that if Black women were women, and the movement was aimed at helping liberate women, giving them rights equal to those of men, then it could not have possibly excluded Black women. I was so wrong. This experience prompted my vow to teach my future students various standpoints and nuances within oppressed groups. The inclusion of Black feminism and Black feminist pedagogy in my undergraduate teacher education programme would have prepared me to do so. Unfortunately, my first time hearing 'Black feminism' was during my fourth semester as a doctoral student.

Millennial Black woman teacher creating curriculum

One of the greatest joys of my adult life was teaching Black students at a school in my childhood zip code. Instead of teaching in an urban public school like the one I attended, I taught in an urban public conversion charter school. One day, after about five years of teaching, my Black women colleagues and I had a conversation about the drastic change in our Black girls from the third through the eighth grade. Tacara was a third-grade teacher, Valerie, a fifth-grade teacher, and I taught the seventh and eighth grades.[3] Tacara asked me 'How's Deja doing? She was such a sweetheart when I had her'. I responded hesitantly, 'Deja ... well, she's very smart ... but she ain't so sweet anymore. I try to talk to her though'. Valerie chimed in 'You know, I noticed a shift beginning to happen when I had her in fifth grade'. The discussion went on about how we noticed this pattern happening to a lot of our girls – a pattern of Black girls being constantly disciplined and pushed out from school and learning (Morris 2016). We observed girls with whom we had good working relationships sitting in the office for disciplinary problems or even getting into gratuitous physical fights. We also noticed that some of our Black girls were declining in their academic achievement, engagement, and overall enjoyment of school. We wondered what caused our Black girls to change so drastically from the third through the eighth grade.

The phenomenon we were witnessing represented a microcosm of the criminalisation and pushing out of Black girls nationally, both in and out of school (Crenshaw 2015; Morris 2016). For example, Shakara, a 16-year-old Black girl student at Spring Valley High School in South Carolina, was violently flipped out of her chair and placed in a chokehold by a police officer for refusing to surrender her cell phone (Craven 2015). Even with the absence of a visible police presence, our Black girls were reacting to being overpoliced in school. As a result of our observations, we started an intervention programme called SOP that targeted fifth- through eighth-grade girls at our school and created the SOP curriculum. In the next section, I discuss the silences and contradictions with/in Black girlhood and Black womanhood in the academy and curriculum studies. In addition, I discuss how the absence of Black women educational scholarship in curriculum studies, specifically in the area of Black feminism, contributes to these silences and contradictions.

Silences and contradictions from Black girlhood to Black womanhood

Black girls and Black women who refuse to conform, choosing instead to enact their full cultural identities, are often pushed out of academic spaces (Morris 2016), while those who are silent and conforming are welcomed, and even thrive. This exclusion is due to notorious social constructions of Black girls in comparison to men and White women. Evans-Winters and Esposito (2010) claimed that Black girls are 'socially constructed as the epitome of exactly what whiteness (as maleness) and femininity (as whiteness) is not: dark, sinister, raunchy, belligerent, burly, and licentious' (18). To counter these negative characterisations, some Black girls conform to manifestations of a White womanhood normative by being silent and engaging in gender 'passing' through the outright exclusion of their culture, due to their desire for academic success (Fordham 1993). Other Black girls reveal their inner struggle to both 'pass' and enact their cultural identities in their inability to be silent (Fordham 1993). Tallaferro-Baszile (2006) reflected on her own battle between the 'real me' that was rooted in Black culture and consciousness, and the 'good school girl' who did what she had to in order to succeed. Similarly, Haddix (2012) found that two Black women preservice teachers faced a crossroad, between displaying their cultural knowledge and concealing their Blackness in order to navigate mainstream teacher education culture. Taken together, Black girl students and Black women students experience the burden of reconciling the complicated contradictions of being Black, woman, and successful in the academy.

For Black women teachers, silences and contradictions are further complicated when teaching Black girls and women. Although Dixson and Dingus (2008) found that Black women often enter teaching as a form of community work, I argue that sometimes their roles as community workers are not fully realised. Omolade (1987) reminisced on her teaching during the late 1970s of a course on the histories and experiences of Black women to a room full of Black women college students. She confessed that she failed to tap into the sisterhood that existed among them. Omolade's students mirrored her own complex and contradictory marginality within the White-male-dominated academy.

Often times, in order to support Black women and girl students, Black women teachers have had to collaborate with colleagues who question their intellectual competence (Omolade 1987). Despite these working conditions, educational scholar Cynthia Dillard insisted that Black women teachers must struggle for curricular and pedagogical power, especially during these neo-liberal times (Love and Evans-Winters 2015). Of course once this power is gained, *what* we create and employ is just as important. The full realisation of teaching as a form of community work for Black women teachers means creating curriculum for Black girls that centres Black girls, that is connected to the legacy of Black women who have come before them, and that is liberating.

With the absence of Black feminism, Black feminist pedagogy, and Black women educational scholarship within curriculum studies, it is easy not to (re)member our legacy (Dillard 2012). As does Taliaferro-Baszile (2006), I critique teacher education programmes for their 'lack of attention to Black voices' (97), exemplified by my limited exposure to Black scholars until graduate school. Moreover, Black women educational scholars are constantly overlooked in how their work challenges the status quo through curriculum. The underutilisation of Black woman educational scholarship (Evans-Winters 2015) is detrimental to *all* teachers. Their scholarship, specifically in the areas of Black feminism and Black feminist pedagogy, also affords students opportunities to examine the interworkings of society and to challenge neo-liberal ideology in an effort to transform society and education (King 1991; hooks 1994). Ultimately, Black women scholarship is critical to understanding the multiple identities and standpoints of Black women, and their intersections (Crenshaw 1989, 1991).

In the following section, I will describe Black feminism and Black feminist pedagogy in order to respond to the following research questions:

(1) To what extent did the SOP curriculum reflect Black feminism and Black feminist pedagogy?
(2) To what extent did this curriculum reinforce a racist and sexist status quo?

Theoretical framework

Black feminism

Black feminism centres on the standpoints and subjectivities of Black women (Lorde 1984; Collins 2000), thus legitimising the daily experiences and identities of Black women (Collins 1990). Critical race theorist Crenshaw (1991) coined the term 'intersectionality' to describe Black women's 'intersectional identity as both women *and* of color … [claiming that] women of color are marginalized within both' (1244). Although 'being Black' is shared among Black people, antiracist movements alone, focused only on racial relations, are insufficient for meeting the complex needs of Black women (Crenshaw 1991). Likewise, antisexism movements fail to address the racial oppression experienced by Black women (Crenshaw 1991). Crenshaw does not limit intersectionality to racial and gender identities, however. An understanding of intersectionality allows Black women standpoints to emerge by revealing the interplay of their various identities (i.e. ethnicity, nationality, culture, sexuality, class, etc.), which result in specific locations in our stratified society. Intersectionality empowers Black women by giving them new interpretations of familiar realities (Collins 2000).

Through the lens of Black feminism, Black women can articulate their realities in ways that allow them to simultaneously name and resist their oppressions (Dillard 2000). Explicitly, Black feminism is a self-conscious and active struggle for liberation (Joseph 1988; Collins 1990), and this struggle is evident in its 'humanist visions of community' (Collins 1990, 11). Community is accomplished through the valuing, liberation, consciousness-raising, and intellectual growth of Black women and Black men. Black feminism in the classroom is Black feminist pedagogy, or intentionally promoting activism from, by, with, and for Black women and girls.

Black feminist pedagogy

Black feminist pedagogy is centred on the research, study, and development of Black women and girls (Omolade 1987) as opposed to Eurocentric patriarchal curriculum (Henry 2005). According to Henry (2005), Black feminist pedagogy critiques the patriarchal structure of traditional education that is meant to serve the White elite and instead aims to create educational experiences that respect and utilise the standpoints of Black women. Although gendered, White feminist pedagogy's analysis of class and gender is insufficient for an examination of the intersectionality of the Black woman's experience (hooks 1981). Although raced, Black educational thought tends to privilege the interests of Black men, leaving amiss the educational concerns of Black women and girls (Omolade 1994). Black feminist pedagogy understands patriarchy through an examination of the social constructions of race, nationality, culture, gender, sexuality, and class (Henry 2005). This examination informs curriculum decisions in meaningful ways (hooks 1994).

Black feminism in education means activism for social change and community building (Henry 2005). Therefore, this pedagogy leads with a political commitment that goes beyond classroom walls (Henry 2005), working towards liberation (Omolade 1987). It is also a pedagogy of connection between students and teachers, academic rigour, and intellectual sharing (Omolade 1987; Ladson-Billings 1995, 2009; Henry 2005), with the power to transform consciousness (hooks 1994). In essence, this pedagogy is one that informs and empowers Black girls about social structures for the purpose of social change. While learning the *herstories* of Black women is crucial, Black feminist pedagogy encourages students to develop new interpretations of traditional curriculum in order to enhance their consciousness through a critical societal analysis (Henry 2005). Keeping in mind the conceptions of Black feminism and Black feminist pedagogy discussed, what follows is the study's context, a description of the SOP curriculum as focal data, and data analysis.

Methods

Context

Valerie, Tacara, and I collaborated to develop the SOP curriculum for the second year of the programme during the summer of 2012. This programme, with its new curriculum, was to be implemented the following fall at our school located in the northeastern region of the USA. During SOP's first year of operation, we partnered with a non-profit organisation for girls called *Eniola Sisters*. They provided the curriculum and the staff to teach, while we ran the programme. Once our partnership ended, we needed to create our own curriculum, teach it, and run the programme while working as full-time teachers.

In general, we received schoolwide support for the programme. Quite a few teachers signed up to volunteer. In reality, however, only three staff members followed through – three other Black women: a reading specialist, our special education director, and our building substitute teacher. When the programme was in full swing, several teachers, by way of showing their support, took it upon themselves to periodically tell us how some of our Black girl participants were 'misbehaving' because 'they thought we should know'.

Valerie, Tacara, and I started our K-12 teaching careers at this school. Valerie was in her late 40s at the time we were planning the SOP curriculum, with eight years of teaching experience at the fifth-grade level. Valerie was a career changer, moving from the government sector to teaching. Tacara, a few years older than me, was in her early 30s, with six years of teaching experience at the third-grade level. Prior to coming to our school, Tacara worked as a preschool and daycare teacher. I was in my late 20s with six years teaching experience at the seventh- and eighth-grade levels.

Our goal was to recruit at least 80 girls in grades 5 through 8. We knew this would not be hard, because 70 girls had participated the year prior. We presented our proposal to our principal and the organisation and corporation involved with our school. Once we had their support, we passed out flyers to fifth- through eighth-grade teachers to be sent home to parents, emailed school staff, and made announcements at staff meetings. As a result, over 80 girls signed up. Over 95% of the girls attending our school were African American and qualified for reduced or free lunch. All of the girls involved in the programme were Black girls.

The SOP included weekly afterschool classes, one-on-one academic reflection and planning meetings, parent involvement initiatives, one camping trip, an end-of-the-year gala, an annual trip to a tech-savvy event for girls, and other purposeful events. Our mission was to empower the girls – academically, intellectually, socially, emotionally, and physically – to embrace sisterhood, so as to move towards becoming future leaders in their communities. During our first-year planning, Valerie felt spiritually led to write a creed (see Appendix 1). We analysed the creed to discover the core values it represented. We did this by ascribing one of the following core values to each stanza of the creed: sisterhood, leadership, self-awareness, health awareness, financial literacy, effective communication, and womanly character. After many meetings, much dialogue, and emails about what these core values meant to us, we wrote the SOP curriculum (see Table 1 for our interpretations of

Table 1. Interpretations of *SOP* core values.

Core value	Interpretations
Sisterhood	Developing a strong bond with other girls in order to support each other in achieving similar goals
Leadership	Possessing the ability to set high standards and act positively so that others will want to follow
Self-awareness	Having a consciousness of self in terms of who you are and your purpose in terms of the rest of the world
Financial literacy	An education in budgeting, making wise monetary decisions, securing a promising future through a solid financial plan for today as well as the future
Health awareness	Knowing the general condition of your body, working towards being in the best condition, and being balanced in mind, body, and soul
Effective communication	Speaking in a manner that exhibits respect for yourself and others along with listening to others
Womanly character	Embodying the poise, grace, and dignity of a sophisticated young lady

these core values). The curriculum explained the meaning and scope of each core value. The curriculum also included lesson outlines.

Data analysis

The focal data for my analysis are eight texts from the SOP curriculum. Each text is based on one of the following core values listed in Table 1. Each text includes the meaning and scope of one core value, transferable learning goals, and a lesson outline (see Appendix 2 for the self-awareness section of the curriculum).

Through the theoretical lens of Black feminism and Black feminist pedagogy, I employed a qualitative content analysis method, specifically a directed content analysis of each text. I wanted to grasp the extent to which the SOP curriculum reflected Black feminism and Black feminist pedagogy, or reinforced a racist and sexist status quo. Qualitative content analysis involves systematic coding of themes and patterns within text content for the purpose of subjective interpretation (Hsieh and Shannon 2005). Directed content analysis is one approach that starts with a theory or perspective (Seker and Guney 2012). Hence, directed content analysis allowed me to begin my analysis of the SOP curriculum through the subjectivities of Black feminism and Black feminist pedagogy.

First, I engaged in quick line-by-line coding (Charmaz 2014), highlighting all text that appeared to represent aspects of Black feminism and Black feminist pedagogy. Simultaneously, I highlighted text that seemed to represent the exact opposite of Black feminism and Black feminist pedagogy. Next, I coded the highlighted text using predetermined codes (e.g. liberation, connection, self-conscious struggle, individualism, assimilation, and conformity). For example, the *effective communication* goal of being 'able to communicate, impart their ideas, thoughts, and concepts to others' (SOP Curriculum 2012, 17) was coded as Black feminism because it promotes the many standpoints and voices of Black women being brought to the fore. Another example is the *self-awareness* goal of 'love and respect themselves and others' (SOP Curriculum 2012, 14), which was coded as Black feminist pedagogy because it promotes connecting Black girls to each other. For a final example, the description of *self-awareness* as 'noticing behaviors that are undesirable and making a conscience effort to correct them or modify them' (SOP Curriculum 2012, 14) was coded as opposite to Black feminism, and labelled as conformity. Any aspects of text that could not be coded using the predetermined codes were given new codes. Lastly, I wrote several big ideas with explanations about what the data were showing (Saldaña 2013).

In the following sections, I present findings on the extent to which the SOP curriculum reflected Black feminism, Black feminist pedagogy, or a racist and sexist status quo; a discussion of my interpretation of the findings; and implications and recommendations for millennial Black women teachers, teacher education programs, and curriculum studies.

Findings

Traces of Black feminism

As indicated in Figure 1, data analysis suggests that there are traces of Black feminism throughout the SOP curriculum. Figure 1 shows how the curriculum encourages a

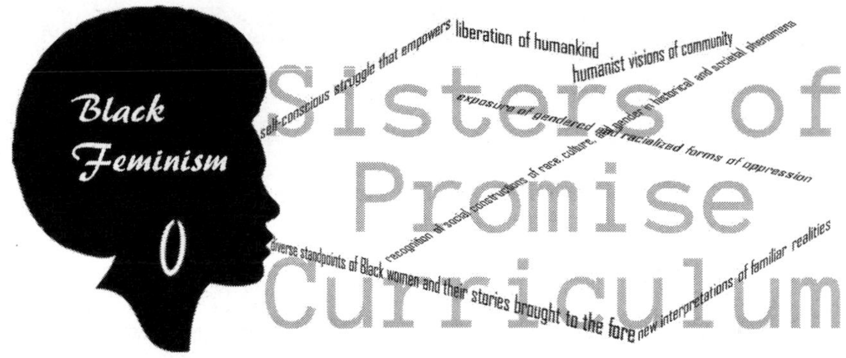

Figure 1. Black feminism in SOP curriculum.

self-conscious struggle within the mind, which ultimately empowers and leads to liberation and humanist visions of community. The SOP curriculum, according to Figure 1, also provides space for the voices of Black women and their diverse standpoints, allowing for new interpretations of familiar realities through intersectionality. Recognising and exposing the social constructions of raced, cultured, and gendered oppressions are in the shape of an X in Figure 1, representing their centrality to the curriculum. In this section, I will describe the extent to which the SOP curriculum revealed Black feminism, including (a) self-conscious struggle, oppression, and intersectionality; (b) recognition of social constructions; (c) liberation through realities and stories; and (d) humanist visions of community. While other aspects of Black feminism were evident, these four were the most prominent.

Self-conscious struggle, oppression, and intersectionality

The SOP curriculum reflects Black feminism's self-conscious struggle that empowers Black girls, exposes the oppression of Black women in contemporary American society, and critically examines the world as it relates to each Black girl's intersectionality. For example, *self-awareness* (see Table 1) is described as '… maneuvering through the process of life with a clear and concise understanding of who you are, your limitations, boundaries, and the way you interact with the world around you … ' (SOP Curriculum 2012, 14). In other words, while there is a shared consciousness of Black girlhood, each girl will experience it differently based on the intersections of her various identities, and this is why an awareness of self is so important.

Recognition of social constructions

Womanly character (see Table 1) in the SOP curriculum reveals social constructions of race, culture, and gender in historical and societal phenomena. The curriculum states that Black girls are 'inundated with negative ideas and images' (SOP Curriculum 2012, 26). In this sense, the SOP curriculum recognises the ways in which Black girls are socially constructed in the world. Black girls must first name the fallacy of these constructions in order to resist them, and work towards liberation.

Liberation through realities and stories

The SOP curriculum also expresses Black feminism's conceptions of liberation of humankind, new interpretations of familiar realities, the notion of coexistence, and personal stories. For instance, the curriculum states the following:

> Sisters of Promise will have the opportunity to explore themselves inside and out in order to initiate the process of self-awareness as young ladies being given an early start at getting to know themselves and how they co exist with parents, peers, teachers, and siblings. (14)

This passage suggests that by searching for their self-hood, Black girls are free to simply 'be'. Through exploration, the curriculum provides space for Black girls to not only be comfortable in their own skins, but also to reinterpret their realities. This permission, and the freedom to coexist, results in an unapologetic awareness of self that encourages Black girls to be *loud Black girls*[4] and refreshingly confident in their identities. Their identities are voiced through the sharing of personal stories in the lesson outlines. The curriculum also states that *effective communication* (see Table 1) is important because it allows girls 'to communicate, impart, their ideas, thoughts, and concepts to others ... ' (17). Sharing personal stories and dialogue brings the many standpoints and stories of Black women to the centre.

Humanist vision of community

Black feminism's humanist vision of community is also reflected in the SOP curriculum. This vision is about 'getting involved with something that goes beyond yourself and your daily situations' (SOP Curriculum 2012, 26). Those who are concerned with the well-being of others embody *sisterhood*. According to the SOP curriculum, sisterhood (see Table 1) is 'having love and support for one another and being there for each other when no one else is there' (26). Although self-awareness is emphasised, social responsibility and a concern for humanity are also promoted. Similarly, connection among Black women, and the fortification of healthy strong relationships between Black girls and their families are recommended throughout the curriculum.

A signature of Black feminist pedagogy

According to Figure 2, curriculum analysis suggests that there is also a signature of Black feminist pedagogy in the SOP curriculum. Figure 2 displays how Black feminist pedagogy operationalises Black feminism. Figure 2 suggests that, in order for liberation and empowerment to occur, education for liberation and social change must also occur. Moreover, according to Figure 2, once various forms of oppression are exposed in the curriculum, it is necessary to dissect the social constructions that create oppressions, so that they can be recognised and resisted. Finally, Figure 2 shows how the SOP curriculum connects Black women to each other through intellectual inclusion, partnership, and providing space for the questions and educational experiences of Black women. In this section, I will describe the extent to which the SOP curriculum reflected the following aspects of Black feminist pedagogy: (a) study of social constructions, (b) education for liberation, (c) political commitment via activism and social change, and (d) connecting Black women to each other. I will focus on these four components because they were the most outstanding.

Figure 2. Black feminist pedagogy in SOP curriculum.

Study of social constructions

The SOP curriculum reveals the study of social constructions of race, culture, and gender in historical and societal phenomena, a crucial component of Black feminist pedagogy. This aspect is promoted mostly in the *self-awareness* (see Table 1) core value. The SOP curriculum suggests that 'self-awareness allows you to understand others and how they perceive you' (14). In order to understand others and their perceptions of you, it is necessary to understand how perception is influenced by socially constructed notions of Blackness, being African American, and being Black girls who grow up to become Black women. This knowledge lends itself to 'knowing your limitations and boundaries' (SOP Curriculum 2012, 14) and being conscious of who you are around others.

Education for liberation

Encouraging girls to move through life with 'a clear and concise understanding of who [they] are' (SOP Curriculum 2012, 14) liberates Black girls from powerlessness. The curriculum's charge to girls to 'love and respect yourself and others' (SOP Curriculum 2012, 14) is liberating. Free people love others and are loved by others, allowing them to possess their humanity (Freire 1970). The very notion that a Black girl could live with a clear understanding of who she is, that she could have self-confidence, and retain her dreams, is in itself an act of empowerment and liberation. The notion of 'dreaming' that is advanced in the SOP curriculum conveys that, in spite of the social constructions that seek to limit Black girls, they too can (and should) cultivate their goals and ambitions. For Black girls to have the audacity to maintain high aspirations, and set lofty goals which they deem achievable, is revolutionary.

Political commitment via activism and social change

There is a theme of activism for social change throughout the curriculum. *Sisterhood* (see Table 1) is about 'getting involved with something that goes beyond yourself and your daily situation' (SOP Curriculum 2012, 26). In essence, Black girls should not only care about their personal situations, but also work towards social change through activism for the benefit of humanity. Embodying *sisterhood* is characterised as having 'impact on the world around you, because when women come together there is nothing they can't do' (SOP Curriculum 2012, 27). Working towards social change is best done when in collaboration with others; together, Black girls can change the world.

Connecting Black women to each other

The SOP curriculum reveals a signature of Black feminist pedagogy's emphasis on connecting Black girls to each other through *sisterhood*. The curriculum states:

> Sisterhood deals with the relationship between sisters and the feeling of kinship and closeness to a group of women … It is sharing all the good and the hard times with people who understand … Sisterhood also deals with friendship and unity. (26–27)

This passage suggests that the curriculum is intentional in connecting Black girls to one another because it 'promotes sisterhood and not dissention' (SOP Curriculum 2012, 17). The communal tradition of African-American culture, specifically among Black women, is emphasised here through fostering healthy and meaningful relationships with other women. Connection among Black girls is also emphasised through *effective communication*. Under this core value, the connection is made between active listening and girls uniting, promoting 'sisterhood not dissention' (SOP Curriculum 2012, 17). The curriculum suggests that Black women are powerful and unstoppable when they unite, and that 'there is nothing they can't do' (SOP Curriculum 2012, 27). This core value of effective communication contradicts the images often witnessed on television of Black women divided, bickering, and, occasionally, physically fighting (Love 2012).

Complicated contradictions with/in SOP curriculum

Although the intent of the SOP curriculum is to encourage and promote sisterhood, there are complicated contradictions present with/in it, with Black feminism and pedagogy coexisting with individualism and conformity. Figure 3 reveals the noticeable contradictions with/in SOP curriculum. In Figure 3, the word 'conformity' is written in all capital letters in a large-sized block font, suggesting its bold and alarming presence within the SOP curriculum, a finding that may cause Black feminist scholars to take issue with the curriculum. The word 'conformity' overlaps Black feminist pedagogy's education for liberation, activism, and social change and Black feminism's empowerment and liberation of humankind in Figure 3. It is extremely contradictory for liberation and empowerment to coexist with conformity. In addition, the middle circle in Figure 3 includes neo-liberalism; the centrality of recognising and exposing social constructions of raced, cultured, and gendered oppressions; and Black feminist pedagogy showing an even larger contradiction. Moreover, this middle circle, directly in the image of the Black woman's vantage point, suggests that she is constantly struggling with these contradictions. Finally, in Figure 3, American rugged individualism coexists with connection among Black women, partnership, and the varied stories of Black women. Is it possible to embody both individualism and sisterhood? In this section, I will describe the extent to which the SOP curriculum did not reflect Black feminism and Black feminist pedagogy, and the areas in which it reflected a racist and sexist status quo including (a) conformity, (b) individualism, and (c) the absence of 'Black' and *herstories*.

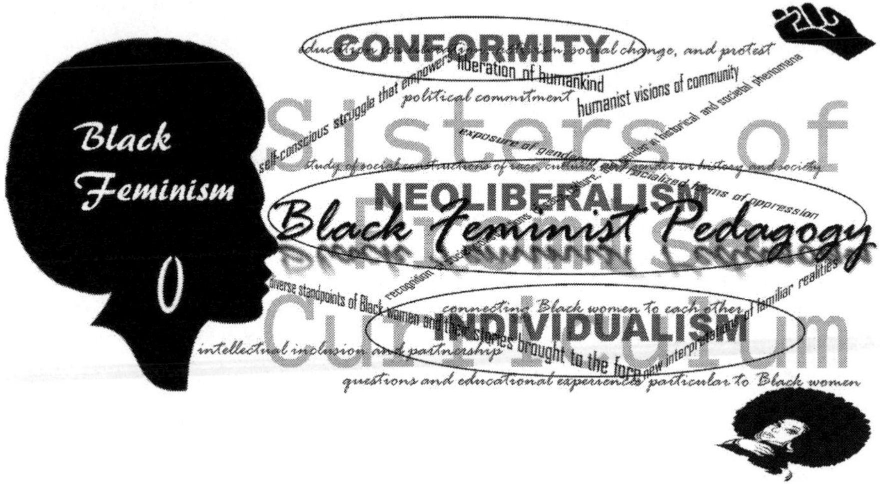

Figure 3. Complicated contradictions with/in SOP curriculum.

Conformity

Within the *self-awareness* and *womanly character* sections of the SOP curriculum, conformity is suggested in the following words: 'undesirable' (14), 'correct' (14), 'self-control' (14), 'moral correctness' (26), and 'refinement' (26). At the reading of such words, I am left to wonder the following: undesirable to whom? Correct to whom? Self-control for what purpose? Whose version of morality and refinement? One function of their growing self-awareness, as presented in the curriculum, is that girls are encouraged to notice which behaviours are undesirable to others, and to modify them. Classically, the suggestion that Black girls modify their behaviour has been in order to suppress their Blackness, not to understand why these behaviours are considered undesirable, and what social dynamics have created this racist and sexist status quo. Black feminist pedagogy is liberating and not conforming.

I am also left to wonder what exactly does it mean to 'be a lady' or 'be virtuous', according to our curriculum? The curriculum contends that these young women find it difficult to act like a 'lady', and be accepted by their peers because they are seen as acting 'funny' (26). A 'lady' is described as one who is educated, and carries herself with poise, grace, and dignity. One could argue that the curriculum promotes being virtuous in order to counter what society expects from Black women. However, I find this argument problematic, as it reflects misogynistic views towards Black women in its very assumption that Black girls are ontologically in need of virtue and poise. Moreover, what if a girl simply is not graceful, in the same way that Fordham's (1993) Rita could not be silent? Does this mean that she is not a woman or 'lady' … whatever that means? What if a student in our programme does not identify as a 'lady'? The notion of 'being a lady' enforces heteronormativity, which contradicts Black feminism's openness to various gendered and sexual identities.

At the same time, the SOP curriculum is telling Black girls that they are free to be; it also implicitly tells them that they need to meet a White middle-class normative of womanhood in calling them to be virtuous ladies. Virtuousness and moral correctness are complicated notions, and can be problematic when imposed on others, especially when White middle-class womanhood is taken as the standard. Therefore, in suggesting that Black girls be virtuous and ladies, the SOP curriculum reaffirms racist and sexist forms of oppression and maintains the status quo by positioning elite White women as superior. Black girls only need to be empowered to think critically, employing their agency in an effort to problematise decision-making in accordance with their multiple identities and the multiple contexts in which they engage.

The contradiction of the presence of neo-liberalism suggests that the SOP curriculum could be confused with behaviour modification programmes instead of transformative empowerment. While this was not our intention in creating this curriculum, the likelihood of this possibility remains. Through various aspects of this curriculum, we may have promoted survival tactics possibly at the expense of stirring up true activism and social change within Black girls. Moreover, the SOP curriculum does not ask Black girls what they need or want to know. The curriculum tells them what *they* need to, and what they *should*, know.

Individualism

The concept of self-awareness is advanced throughout the curriculum as an attempt to allow girls to understand how they interact with the world, and to help them to have a positive interaction with the world. In a way, this concept points to individualism without accounting for the institutions, systems, and structures that Black girls interact with as they navigate the world. Where is the critique of these systematic factors? I am not convinced that self-awareness alone (nor American rugged individualism, for that matter) will guarantee a positive interaction with the world.

The absence of 'Black' and herstories

The SOP curriculum is for Black girls, and yet there is an absence of Black women's history within it, or an explicit mention of 'Black' girls. I can attest that Valerie, Tacara, and I had issues specific to Black girls in mind when we created this curriculum, but we did not use the word 'Black' to describe the girls in the curriculum, when it was intended for Black girls. It would have been very powerful to begin teaching about self-awareness by uncovering the history of Black women and their legacy of activism. This is the heritage of Black girls. Connecting Black girls to each other without connecting them to their unique histories and their Blackness allows a considerable gap to remain present. Moreover, leadership, sisterhood, effective communication, and aspects of womanly character are evident in the histories, or rather, *herstories*. Connecting to one's history and culture brings understanding and foregrounds critical analysis.

Self-awareness is problematic in the absence of *herstories*, in that it entails Black girls knowing who they are outside of a historical context; considering their motivations out of context to their surroundings; and knowing their beliefs and emotions out of context to the world around them. While it is important and necessary for Black girls to get to know themselves, it is dangerous to do so out of context. Black girls rarely get an opportunity to get to know themselves and explore who they are and their interests, so I appreciate this part of the curriculum. I do, however, worry about the implications of self-discoveries that are disconnected from the unique history of African-American woman. A critical analysis of how structures, systems, and institutions interact with one's conception of the self is also necessary.

Discussion

Based on my analysis of the SOP curriculum, I argue that – even with the best of intentions, and even for relatively self-aware millennial Black women teachers – it is possible to present Black girl students with contradictory messages, due to the lack of exposure to Black feminism, Black feminist pedagogy, and the contributions of Black women scholars in their curriculum studies. One contradiction within the SOP curriculum is that Black girls are encouraged to name their oppression without resisting it. A second contradiction is that Black girls are to be self-aware for the benefit of others, more than for themselves. In reality, Black girls who are hard-working, self-aware, and conforming are not guaranteed the advantage of racist and sexist institutions, systems, and structures working on their behalf. A third contradiction is that the SOP curriculum supports the liberation of Black girls only so long as it fits within the White womanhood normative of what it means to be a 'lady'. If at the end of the day Black girls are advised to be silent and to conform, in order to 'pass' in the academy (Fordham 1993), then this curriculum is neither empowering nor liberating, despite our greatest intentions. Furthermore, the promotion of the White womanhood normative and heteronormative ultimately limits the stories and realities Black girls will share. If there is no explicit mention of 'Black' girls, and *herstories*, in the curriculum created by Black women teachers for Black girls, then this curriculum does not centre Black women. The SOP curriculum presents Black girls with a difficult decision: fully 'be' *loud Black girls*, or conform. Due to the unique culture-specific girlhood of Black girl students, the SOP curriculum needed to problematise conformity, individualism, and neo-liberalism's status quo.

As Black women teachers, our aim was to improve the schooling experiences of our Black girls and to empower them, but we were faced with the stark reality that these girls had to survive within an individualistic, disciplinary, White school culture, and so did we. This is one of the complicated contradictions of creating such programmes within the margins of school. We felt a call to respond to what we had observed happening to our Black girls, while our White colleagues had not; not in the same sense. Although our White colleagues expressed their support, the added burden of 'cultural taxation' that many teachers of colour carry deemed us solely responsible for the cultural work with Black girl students (Padilla 1994). The White teachers at my school believed this programme was a good endeavour for us, as Black teachers, to oversee. We did not receive any resistance towards the programme from our White women colleagues, but we did not experience much in terms of participation, even after some had agreed to do so. This is interesting, considering that in some ways the SOP curriculum could help them to maintain the status quo. As it was, the SOP programme, with its three Black women teacher leaders, was still too Black and too Black feminist. These Black girls were their students too, and yet many felt no calling or urge to involve themselves in their betterment. Still, had we understood Black feminism, Black feminist pedagogy, and our role as Black women pedagogues, we would have better understood how to disrupt the very system we were teaching our girls to conform to. In this sense, we did not fully realise our roles as community workers.

If the goal of education (Woodson, 1933/2015) is to liberate the minds of racialised and gendered youth, then it is crucial for teacher education programmes to include the educational scholarship of Black women. Black feminism and Black feminist pedagogy within curriculum studies will help teacher candidates to educate for social change, honour different stories and realities, and challenge the status quo through curriculum. Teachers and teacher educators of all backgrounds must continue to refuse traditional curriculum, with its focus on American individualism and tendency towards conformity. Lastly, in order to delineate the importance of Black women subjectivities, we must bring to the fore educational experiences, and the collective consciousness, particular to Black women.

Implications

This study informs the field of the importance of curriculum studies within intervention programming, or other grass-roots programming, which claims to liberate youth while maintaining a status quo. We cannot use these programmes as quick fixes, which primarily serve the needs of the White elite. This study also calls on teacher education programmes to include the rich contributions of Black women educational scholars. We cannot assume that Black preservice women teachers are aware of their unique roles in education. Even so, perhaps if my White women colleagues had more Black women educational scholarship in their teacher education programmes, our Black girl students would not have been targeted for disciplinary issues. Perhaps the inclusion of Black feminism and Black feminist pedagogy will help millennial Black teachers, like myself, engage fully in transformative education and programming, fully realising our roles as community workers, and resisting the status quo. Black feminist pedagogy frees the minds of Black women and Black girls, and the minds of others about Black women and Black girls. Teachers, teacher educators, administrators, and educational researchers must be informed, so they can enact curricular decisions that are in service of, and responsive to, Black girls.

The status of Black girls is increasingly receiving more attention. As is and was the case with Black boys, there will be many more intervention programmes created to 'improve' the state of Black girls. I conclude this article by offering the following curricular recommendations for millennial Black women teachers (and others), in order to avoid advancing curricular contradictions which can ultimately lead to the disempowering of Black girls:

(1) Engage in your own ongoing personal discovery, education, and deep study of the work of Black women educational scholars, Black feminism, Black feminist pedagogy, and *herstories*. This educational process will help you to process what is happening in school, to you and your students, and inspire you to use your curricular power to resist, as may be necessary. (This recommendation does not excuse teacher education programmes from their responsibilities to provide their students with such opportunities.)
(2) Problematise your own potentially narrow understandings of Black girlhood through critical self-reflection.
(3) Recall your (or others') stories, realities, and experiences as a Black girl, Black woman, and Black woman teacher, and use them to guide your curricular work with Black girls.
(4) Provide space in your curriculum for Black girls to tell you who they are and what they want to know.
(5) Seriously listen to the perspectives of Black girls on the type of education they desire on a regular basis, and use their perspectives to guide your curriculum.

(6) Ask yourself periodically: Does my curriculum empower and liberate Black girls, or does it impose *on* Black girls?
(7) Form community and engage in self-care and wellness as you do this work, in order to avoid burnout, because you may continue to do this important work as community work alone in your specific location, or with a limited few.
(8) If your curriculum is in fact for Black girls, do not be afraid to explicitly identify it as such, and include the legacy of Black women in your curriculum.
(9) Remember that Black girls are magic, and so are you.
(10) Remember that Black girls should not be silenced or forced to conform, and neither should you.

Notes

1. I use the identifiers Black and African American interchangeably throughout this article to mean individuals who are descendants of US slaves and socially constructed as Black based on an African phenotype. However, Black is usually used to identify people worldwide who are of African descent and phenotype, whereas African American refers to Black people born in the USA.
2. According to Black educational theorist and feminist-womanist Henry (2005), *herstories* tell how Black women educators fought to transform the social conditions of Black people. In other words, *herstories* centre the activist work of Black women teachers. Educational scholars Alston and McClellan (2011) described *herstories* as the history of Black women activists (e.g. Septima Clark, Fannie Lou Hamer, and Angela Davis). In contrast, freelance writer Lewis (1988) conceptualised *herstory* as Black girls' perceptions of their realities. Lewis promoted the use of *herstory* to inform Afrocentric work and programming with Black girls. Building on each of these understandings, I use *herstories* here to describe the relationship between one Black woman's reflection on her identity, activism, personal history, and interactions with others, as connected to the intergenerational history of Black women. *Herstory* is important in Black feminist pedagogy because it centres on the standpoints of Black women and helps us to (re)member our legacy (Dillard 2012).
3. Pseudonyms are used here.
4. *Loud Black girls* is used here to convey Fordham's (1993) notion of loudness to mean the insistence of Black girls to be seen in their full Black girlhood. Loud Black girls refuse to be considered powerless or viewed as 'nothingness' (Fordham 1993, 25). Therefore, they bear their culturally specific identities of womanhood as resistance and struggle.

Disclosure statement

No potential conflict of interest was reported by the author.

ORCiD

Tiffany M Nyachae http://orcid.org/0000-0001-8420-3638

References

Alston, J. A., and McClellan, P. A. 2011. *Herstories: Leading with the Lessons of the Lives of Black Women Activists*. New York, NY: Peter Lang.

Blake, J. J., B. R. Butler, C. W. Lewis, and A. Darensbourg. 2011. "Unmasking the Inequitable Discipline Experiences of Urban Black Girls: Implications for Urban Educational Stakeholders." *Urban Review* 43: 90–106. doi:10.1007/s11256-009-0148-8.

Brown, A. F. 2011. "Descendants of "Ruth:" Black Girls Coping Through the "Black Male Crisis"." *Urban Review* 43: 597–619. doi:10.1007/s11256-010-0162-x.

Charmaz, K. 2014. *Constructing Grounded Theory*. 2nd ed. Los Angeles, CA: Sage.

Collins, P. H. 1990. "Defining Black Feminist Thought." http://www.feministezine.com/feminist/modern/Defining-Black-Feminist-Thought.html.

Collins, P. H. 2000. *Black Feminist Thought: Knowledge, Consciousness, and the Politics of Empowerment*. 2nd ed. New York, NY: Routledge.

Craven, J. 2015. "The Girl Who Was Assaulted by a Cop on Camera at Spring Valley High is Now Facing Charges." *Huffpost Politics*. http://www.huffingtonpost.com/entry/charges-assault-spring-valley-high_us_56733c14e4b014efe0d4d59c.

Crenshaw, K. 1989. "Demarginalizing the Intersection of Race and Sex: A Black Feminist Critique of Antidiscrimination Doctrine, Feminist Theory and Antiracist Politics." *University of Chicago Legal Forum* 1 (8): 139–167.

Crenshaw, K. 1991. "Mapping the Margins: Intersectionality, Identity Politics, and Violence Against Women of Color." *Standford Law Review* 43 (6): 1241–1299.

Crenshaw, K. 2015. *Black Girls Matter: Pushed Out, Overpoliced and Underprotected*. New York, NY: African American Policy Forum.

Dillard, C. B. 2000. "The Substance of Things Hoped for, the Evidence of Things not Seen: Examining an Endarkened Feminist Epistemology in Educational Research and Leadership." *International Journal of Qualitative Studies in Education* 13 (6): 661–681. doi:10.1080/09518390050211565.

Dillard, C. B. 2012. *Learning to (re)Member the Things We've Learned to Forget*. New York, NY: Peter Lang.

Dixson, A. D., and J. E. Dingus. 2008. "In Search of our Mothers' Gardens: Black Women Teachers and Professional Socialization." *Teachers College Record* 110 (4): 805–837.

Dumas, M. J., and k. m. ross. 2016. ""Be Real Black for me": Imagining BlackCrit in Education." *Urban Education* 51 (4): 415–442. doi:10.1177/0042085916628611.

Evans-Winters, V. E. 2015. "Black Feminism in Qualitative Education Research: A Mosaic for Interpreting Race, Class, and Gender in Education." In *Black Feminism in Education: Black Women Speak Back, Up, and Out*, edited by V. E. Evans-Winters, and B. L. Love, 129–142. New York, NY: Peter Lang.

Evans-Winters, V. E., and J. Esposito. 2010. "Other People's Daughters: Critical Race Feminism and Black Girls' Education." *Educational Foundations* 24 (Winter/Spring): 11–24.

Evans-Winters, V. E., and B. L. Love. 2015. "Introduction." In *Black Feminism in Education: Black Women Speak Back, Up, and Out*, edited by V. E. Evans-Winters, and B. L. Love, 1–6. New York, NY: Peter Lang.

Fordham, S. 1993. ""Those Loud Black Girls": Women, Silence, and Gender "Passing" in the Academy." *Anthropology & Education Quarterly* 24 (1): 3–32.

Foster, M. 1997. *Black Teachers on Teaching*. New York, NY: The New Press.

Freire, P. 1970. *Pedagogy of the Oppressed*. New York, NY: Continuum.

Haddix, M. M. 2012. "Talkin' in the Company of My Sistas: The Counterlanguages and Deliberate Silences of Black Female Students in Teacher Education." *Linguistics and Education* 23: 169–181. doi:10.1016/j.linged.2012.01.003.

Henry, A. 2005. "Black Feminist Pedagogy: Critiques and Contributions." In *Black Protest Thought and Education*, edited by W. H. Watkins, 89–105. New York, NY: Peter Lang.

hooks, b. 1981. *Ain't I A Woman: Black Woman and Feminism*. London: Pluto Press.

hooks, b. 1994. *Teaching to Transgress: Education as the Practice of Freedom*. New York, NY: Routledge.

Hsieh, H., and S. E. Shannon. 2005. "Three Approaches to Qualitative Content Analysis." *Qualitative Health Research* 15 (9): 1277–1288. doi:10.1177/1049732305276687.

Joseph, G. 1988. "Black Feminist Pedagogy in Capitalist America." In *Bowles and Gintis Revisited: Correspondence and Contradiction in Educational Theory*, edited by M. Cole, 174–186. London: Falmer.

King, J. 1991. "Dysconscious Racisim: Ideology, Identity, and the Miseducation of Teachers." *The Journal of Negro Education* 60 (2): 133–146.

Kohli, R. 2016. " Behind School Doors: The Impact of Hostile Racial Climates on Urban Teachers of Color." *Urban Education*, 1–27. doi:10.1177/0042085916636653.

Ladson-Billings, G. 1995. "Toward A Theory of Culturally Relevant Pedagogy." *American Educational Research Journal* 32 (3): 465–491.

Ladson-Billings, G. 2009. *The Dreamkeepers: Successful Teachers of African American Children*. 2nd ed. San Fransciso, CA: Jossey-Bass.

Lapidos, J. 2015. "Wait, What, I'm A Millennial?" http://www.nytimes.com/2015/02/05/opinion/wait-what-im-a-millennial.html?_r = 0.

Lewis, M. C. 1988. *Herstory: Black Female Rites of Passage*. Chicago, IL: African American Images.

Lorde, A. 1984. *Sister Outsider*. New York, NY: Ten Speed Press.

Love, B. L. 2012. *Hip Hop's Li'l Sistas Speak: Negotiating Hip Hop Identities and Politics in the new South*. New York, NY: Peter Lang.

Love, B. L., and V. E. Evans-Winters. 2015. "Why we Matter: An Interview with Dr. Cynthia Dillard (Nana Mansa II of Mpeasem, Ghana, West Africa)." In *Black Feminism in Education: Black Women Speak Back, up, and out*, edited by V. E. Evans-Winters, and B. L. Love, 201–209. New York, NY: Peter Lang.

Morris, M. W. 2016. *Pushed Out: The Criminalization of Black Girls in School*. New York, NY: The New Press.

Omolade, B. 1987. "A Black Feminist Pedagogy." *Women's Studies Quarterly* 15 (3/4): 32–39.

Omolade, B. 1994. *The Rising Song of African American Women*. New York, NY: Routledge.

Padilla, A. M. 1994. "Ethnic Minority Scholars, Research, and Mentoring: Current and Future Issues." *Educational Researcher* 23 (4): 24–27.

Saldaña, J. 2013. *The Coding Manual for Qualitative Researchers*. 2nd ed. London: Sage.

Seker, H., and B. G. Guney. 2012. "History of Science in the Physics Curriculum: A Directed Content Analysis of Historical Sources." *Science and Education* 21: 683–703. doi:10.1007/s11191-011-9416-6.

SOP (Sisters of Promise). 2012. "Program Proposal. Education." U. S. Public Conversion Charter School NY.

Taliaferro-Baszile, D. 2005. "Criminal Acts Committed in the Name of Good Education." *Journal of Curriculum & Pedagogy* 2 (1): 20–23.

Taliaferro-Baszile, D. 2006. "Rage in the Interests of Black Self: Curriculum Theorizing as Dangerous Knowledge." *Journal of Curriculum Theorizing* 22 (1): 89–98.

Twenge, J. M. 2013. "Who Are The Millennials?: Generation Me and the Future." https://www.psychologytoday.com/blog/our-changing-culture/201305/who-are-the-millennials.

Woodson, C. G. 1933/2015. *The Mis-Education of the Negro*. Lexington, KY: Tribeca Books.

Appendix 1

SOP creed:

I am a Sister of Promise
I love and respect myself and others
I speak to be understood and
I listen to hear others
I promote sisterhood and not dissension
I lead through positive actions and words
I am balanced in mind, body, and soul
I am establishing a promising financial future
I embrace, encourage, and uplift my sisters
I carry myself with poise, grace, and dignity
I am a Sister of Promise

Appendix 2

Self-awareness

Self-awareness is having a clear perception of your personality including strengths, weaknesses, thoughts, beliefs, motivations, and emotions. Self-awareness allows you to understand others and how they perceive you.

Self-awareness is the first step in manoeuvring through the process of life with a clear and concise understanding of who you are, your limitations, boundaries, and the way you interact with the world around you in a positive way. Self-awareness is important in noticing behaviours that are admired in oneself and working at nurturing and cultivating those qualities and traits as well as noticing behaviours that are undesirable and making a conscience effort to correct them or modify them.

SOP will have the opportunity to explore themselves inside and out in order to initiate the process of self-awareness as young ladies being given an early start at getting to know themselves and how they coexist with parents, peers, teachers, and siblings.

What will participants of SOP who possess self-awareness be able to do?

- Understand what self-awareness is and how it relates to them.
- Get to know themselves (internal qualities, motivations, etc.).
- Understand the correlation between self-awareness and self-confidence.
- Use what they learn about themselves to build stronger personal relationships.
- Understand the correlation between self-awareness and self-control.
- Maintain a positive relationship with themselves (meditation, journaling, etc.).
- Love and respect themselves and others.

Lessons outline:

(I) Introduction of self-awareness (through read aloud, personal stories, media; video and Internet)

(II) Who am I?
- (A) What is my perception of myself?
- (B) Important events in my life that have made me who I am (grandma died, moved to a new neighbourhood, new school, etc.)
- (C) What/who motivates me to do well? What/who motivates me to be kind?
- (D) Who are the important people in my life? Why?

(III) Who am I when I'm around others?
- (A) My personality – am I outgoing or more reserved? (introvert vs. extrovert)
- (B) My friendships (Do I value friendships? How do I maintain them?)
- (C) How am I affected by peer pressure?
- (D) Maintaining my individuality within friendships
- (E) The importance of family relationships (parents, siblings, and extended family)

(IV) Self-awareness and self-confidence
- (A) Analysing myself from the inside out
- (B) What are my personal strengths? What are my personal weaknesses?
- (C) My black is beautiful (embracing physical appearances, shades of black, and physical features)
- (D) Taking care of myself (physical and emotion health and well-being, personal hygiene, and personal up-keep)
- (E) Do I exude self-confidence?

(V) Self-awareness and self-control
- (A) Dealing with negative emotions (anger, jealousy, embarrassment, and nervousness)
- (B) Recognising stress/anger triggers
- (C) Stress management: How to reduce, prevent and cope with stress
- (D) Avoiding negative factors (alcohol, drugs, tobacco, and sex)

(VI) Maintaining a positive relationship with ME
 (A) Meditation
 (B) Journaling
 (C) Rest and relaxation
 (D) Personal daily confirmations
(VII) Sharing ME with Others
 (A) Giving and showing the 'good' within myself (through actions and words)
 (B) Acts of kindness
 (C) Charity and volunteerism

Talking back in cyberspace: self-love, hair care, and counter narratives in Black adolescent girls' YouTube vlogs

Robin J. Phelps-Ward and Crystal T. Laura

ABSTRACT

While the 'natural hair movement' has grown in popularity and criticism, educational researchers have not attended to how Black adolescent girls with all textures of natural hair are navigating the implications of foregoing chemical alterations to their curl patterns. This article reports on an investigation of self-talk in 56 internet video logs constructed by Black adolescent girls with natural hair, describing the messages of self-love, hair care, and counter narratives to dominant discourse that emerged from an in-depth ethnographic content analysis. Hair politics may seem irrelevant to the field of education, but findings suggest that the topic should matter to anyone who cares deeply about the social and academic worlds of Black adolescent girls.

Black girls are faced with numerous troubling realities that are organised around negative stereotypes, societal pressures, and conflicting messages. Grounded in a troubling racialised history in the United States of measuring Black peoples' – particularly Black women's – appearances against Eurocentric standards of acceptability and decency (Crenshaw 1991; West 2002), characterisations of Black girls as 'angry' and 'loud', 'unintelligent' and 'ugly' abound. For example, long-held misperceptions of naturally curly Black hair as dirty, unclean, unkempt, and messy have been invoked in contemporary public dialogue about Black females in politics (e.g. First Lady Michelle Obama), sports (e.g. Rutgers women's basketball team, Gabby Douglas), the armed services (e.g. AR 670-1 grooming policy), the workplace (e.g. firing of employees for wearing dreadlocks, Glamour editor's slideshow presentation and comment that dreadlocks are dreadful), consumer preferences (QVC host's statement about Black female model's hair), popular culture (e.g. Zendaya and Blue Ivy), and even schools (e.g. sanctions on afros, mohawks, and other hairstyles typically worn by Black Americans) – discourse that has been disseminated en masse through mainstream and social media, and consumed by many, including young girls.

As two Black female educators with naturally curly hair, we worry about the cumulative impact of consistent messages regarding Black natural hair as 'bad' on the wellbeing of our youngest sisters. Black adolescent girls with naturally curly hair, or Black curly girls, are navigating issues of self-esteem, identity development, and valuations of beauty (Byrd and Tharps 2002; Robinson 2011) while growing up in social institutions that narrow the scope of how they might be seen by others and come to see themselves. To date, scholars have not yet attended to the meanings and implications of these specific issues for Black curly girls. Against this backdrop of hair politics, cultural hegemony, and symbolic violence – or the painful, damaging, wounds inflicted by the wielding of words, symbols, and standards (Bourdieu 1977; Ferguson 2001) – Black curly girls' self-definitions, as expressed in self-talk (Diller 1999) and the relationship of those self-definitions to dominant discourse about Black hair are the central subjects of this article.

Background

Coupled with the tumultuous period of adolescence, which has been characterised by scholars as a time of crisis and confusion (DeCuir-Gunby 2009), Black girls experience a unique challenge in their identity development. The intersection between race and gender adds complexity to the developing identities of Black girls influenced by numerous internal and external factors (Crenshaw 1991). Numerous scholar-activists have highlighted the voices of young, Black women located at the intersection of race, gender, and many other identities (Davis 2005; Evans-Winters 2011; Jacob 2002; Ladner 1995; Love 2012). Their work positions Black girls as knowers while addressing injustices in our society.

In 17-year-old Kiri Davis' (2005) documentary about Black girls' experiences and opinions of beauty, teenagers discussed the effect of others' perceptions about their hair, body, and skin type. One young woman addressed the complicated pressure of beauty standards on Black girls and its connection to ethnogenesis brought on by the slavery of African people in America.

> I feel like we're busy searching for [our culture] while everybody else in society is throwing their ideas and what they believe we should be at us.... Personally, we know that's not what we should be, but we're going to take it because we don't know exactly what it is that we should be because we don't really know where we came from.

Davis' documentary emphasised the importance of discovering answers to developmental questions of 'Who am I?' and 'Where do I come from?' Such questions are more difficult for Black girls to answer and can lead to a cycle of negative behaviours. This was evident in Jacob's (2002) work in which she collected hundreds of letters from girls of colour across the country who authored and told their own stories of empowerment, conceptions of race and ethnicity, relationships, and family. These stories served to centre the voices of Black girls – a practice that does not always occur within the literature.

While some have chosen to tell the stories of Black girls through a deficit lens, Evans-Winters (2011) chose to highlight the opposite. In her book *Teaching Black girls: Resiliency in urban classrooms*, Evans-Winters focused on the resiliency and achievement of African-American girls rather than social problems. Through her ethnographic work she shared the educational resilience stories of girls who had faced adversity in schools and advocated for more research that targets the role of social structures in society rather than victims. Ladner (1995) and Love (2012) addressed such structures of inequity in their work focused on the identity development of girls who grew up in urban communities. These texts and others emphasise the power and stories of Black girls who engage in creative expression and use their voices to talk back (Hooks 1989) and transform social systems like formal education.

Scholars in psychology, sociology, education, and other fields have discussed the developing identities of Black girls in several ways relative to influencing factors and the subsequent effects of such factors. With the exception of a relatively small group of scholars (Evans-Winters 2011; Green 2013; Jacob 2002; Ladner 1995; Love 2012; Muhammad 2012; Winn 2010), few have drawn their attention to the creative practice within the community of Black girls that has been sparked by a need and desire to counter narratives that do little to empower and uplift young, Black women. Further, a smaller number of scholars have combined notions of Black girls' identity development with theories of self-talk (Brinthaupt, Hein, and Kramer 2009; Brown 1973) and internal dialogue (Chohan 2010) to investigate the internal voices that mitigate and challenge negative societal views of Black curly girls.

In order to better understand the complexity of Black curly girls' experiences and how they cope with negative perceptions in society, manage dominant narratives of beauty, and grow into their unique identities, we review relevant scholarly literature. First, we discuss the constructs of identity and self-concept and the factors that influence Black girls' identity development. Next, we explain the research focused on creative expression and the art forms of writing and performance, which Black girls have used to grow in their identities and combat negative messages. Lastly, within this literature review we present the theories of self-talk and internal dialogue as part of the internal efforts that mobilise Black girls' identity development and their ability to 'talk back' against hegemonic, European standards (Patton 2006).

Black girls' identity and self-concept

Scholars have investigated multiple factors that influence the developing identities and self-concept of young, Black girls. Some have explained distal (e.g. media images) and proximal (e.g. peers and family members) factors that impact Black girls' identity development (Duke 2000; Gordon 2008; Thomas, Hoxha, and Hacker 2013), while other scholars have noted the role self-esteem, internalisation, and maternal support possess in girls' lives (Buckley and Carter 2005; Hesse-Biber et al. 2004). The phenomenon of racial identity development is commonly investigated and continues to be the focus of numerous studies concerned with understanding adolescents' experiences in education (DeCuir-Gunby 2009). More specifically, Black identity has been a prominent focus of racial identity development research and is defined as the 'attitudes and beliefs that an African American has about his or her belonging to the Black race individually, the Black race collectively, and their perceptions of other racial groups' (DeCuir-Gunby 2009, 103). Thus, an adolescent will have reached a level of identification with his or her Blackness when a strong association with a cultural group exists. Although conceptualisations of Black racial identity have been critiqued for viewing individuals in monolithic terms (DeCuir-Gunby 2009), Black racial identity has been a major focus of studies centred on the experiences of Black girls. For example, Buckley and Carter (2005) sought to investigate the intersection of racial identity and gender roles by surveying 200 Black girls between the ages of 14 and 18 years old and they found that girls who described themselves in both feminine and masculine ways (i.e. androgynous) had higher levels of self-esteem than those who only reported high racial identity perceptions. This study exists counter to other research from scholars, which explains the power of Black racial identification.

In their study, which employed focus group interviews with 78 African-American girls between the ages of 9 and 18 years old, Hesse-Biber et al. (2004) found that racial identity was highly linked to self-esteem (self-confidence derived from culture, society, others, and the self), non-internalisation (the ability to disregard others' negative comments), and maternal support. The authors wrote: 'A strong sense of group identification causes one to internalize the group's values, attitudes, and beliefs, while simultaneously rejecting those held by the larger society' (72). Thus, when girls reported strong identifications with their race that did not align with Eurocentric culture, they also reported increased levels of self-confidence, which served to promote positive body image.

Although research from Townsend et al. (2010) supported the protective functions of a strong racial identity within adolescent girls, their survey of 270 African-American girls' attitudes about stereotypical images, colourism, and risky sexual behaviour found that racial identification was not enough to shield girls from negative sexual risk outcomes. Instead, they found a greater protective function in academic self-concept associated with school success and achievement. While Black racial identification can influence girls' abilities to shun and disagree with external messages from the media and others about beauty, appearance, and sexuality (Duke 2000; Gordon 2008), the question of how girls develop their identities still remains.

Black girls' creative expression

The question of *how* Black girls are constructing their identities can be answered by scholars who have explored the various written, spoken, and performance-driven art forms used within supportive, youth communities (Green 2013; Muhammad 2012; Sears 2010; Winn 2010). These forms of creative expression emphasise collaborative spaces, critical pedagogy, and reflexivity, and allow Black girls an opportunity to let their voices flow and emerge. These spaces exist outside of conventional classrooms and represent communities of practice where Black girls can find themselves within and without the pressures of hegemonic societal forces.

An example of such a practice existed in the playwriting and performance programme for incarcerated girls, called Girl Time. In her study of African-American teenagers who participated in the programme as authors and actors for the productions, Winn (2010) uncovered the power of the creative practice that allowed the girls to escape low expectations, defy stereotypes, persevere, embrace positivity, and think critically about the carceral system they were prisoners within. With the freedom of self-expression and creativity that was encouraged and supported throughout the programme, the girls experienced an opportunity to share and rewrite their own stories.

With a focus on 'writing to define the self and build resiliency' (Muhammad 2012, 203), a five-week writing institute also focused on the stories of Black, adolescent girls and offered a space for them to record their experiences and negotiate internal tensions. As studies of mass media effects have shown, the tensions for Black girls can come from myriad sources and lead to serious outcomes (Gordon 2008; Patton 2006). Thus, Muhammad explained the institute as an opportunity for girls to explore their burgeoning identities through writing and challenge messages propagated through their formal education in schools. The individuals who led the Youth Voices programme also recognised the hidden agenda within formal school education and provided Black youth with a creative space to share their stories over the radio waves. Innovative practices such as these are the beginning of a growing trend to equip Black girls with the tools needed to engage in creative expression and identity development.

Self-talk: a conceptual link

Although racial identification and creative expression influence and exist in tandem with Black girls' identity formation, the internal voices of Black girls are also of great importance. Brown (1973) defined self-talk as intrapersonal speech or two-way communication within oneself. Brinthaupt, Hein, and Kramer (2009) also explained that such intrapersonal communication can also be viewed as 'the subjective experience of talking to oneself, including inner monologue or dialogue, auditory imagery, private speech, inner speech, self-talk, and self-statements' (82). Diller (1999) argued that 'self-talk both manifests and reinforces our beliefs about ourselves as ethical beings' (78). In other words, 'self-talk affects our actions, both directly and indirectly, because what we say to ourselves sets up expectation about our behavior patterns' (78).

Despite the labels and numerous measures of self-talk and applications of the concept in sport and clinical psychology (Brinthaupt, Hein, and Kramer 2009), self-reinforcing self-talk – as opposed to critical self-talk – has been linked to positive self-esteem, positive mood, self-regulatory functions, and neutralisation of negative life events. Though positive self-talk is powerful, Schwartz (1986) found that negative self-talk, or internal dialogue, is even more powerful and can outweigh the benefits of speaking positively to the self. Thus, he contended that concerns of negative self-talk must be addressed first before encouraging an individual to engage in positive inner dialogue. Such forms of dialogue that serve self-reinforcing and critical purposes are considered either private (i.e. aloud to oneself) or inner (within the self). Taken together, positive self-talk serves a powerful role in the lives of Black girls who may be discerning which messages to retain and which to relinquish from their cognitive schema.

In her conceptual article on the transformative ability of the inner voice, Chohan (2010) explained how students and teachers can 'delve deeper into the intricate aspects of their thought patterns and become increasingly conscious of their values, beliefs, and assumptions and how they in turn frame how they behave' (10). By cognitively organising and questioning assumptions and interpretations through regular conversations with the self, Chohan described how individuals can remove thoughts of irrationality, perfection, and judgement of others that damage classroom climates and teacher–student relationships. When applied to the context of Black curly girls, the influence of self-talk becomes more poignant because it provides a link to more fully understand the factors that influence identity development and self-perceptions regarding race, gender, and culture.

Black girls' self-talk in response to symbolic violence

In recent years, social media has offered a cyber space for girls to engage in self-talk while exploring racial identity, self-concept, and notions of beauty. Though traditional blogging served as a space for self-presentation on the web for young girls in the past (Bortree 2005; Stokes 2007), YouTube exists as a current medium for young girls to express themselves and engage in a community of practice. We argue that such a community has a positive influence on the identity development of Black girls engaged in the space and that this form of expression is similar to the counternarratives produced in programmes like Girl Talk, Youth Voices, and many others. Therefore, we investigate the narratives of Black girls who participate in YouTube as a medium to discuss their hair, a significant part of the self for many young, Black girls (Hesse-Biber et al. 2004). Drawing upon extant literature, we argue that YouTube vlogs are central sites where Black curly girls engage in self-love – the action taken to enhance or alter one's own or another's life (Hooks 2000) – to develop their emerging self-definitions. The research questions guiding this study were: how do Black curly girls use vlogs to engage in self-love; what is the subject matter of Black curly girls' online self-talk; and how is Black curly girls' online self-talk related to dominant discourses on natural hair?

Method

This study investigated the vlogs of Black curly girls that were uploaded to YouTube.com, a free, publicly accessible video sharing website where registered users can create personalised channels, post public comments, and send private messages to other users. For thousands of Black curly women – us, the authors, included – and increasingly Black curly girls of at least 13 years of age, YouTube.com is a forum to discuss a range of topics at the intersections of Black womanhood, Black girlhood, and Black hair. Our familiarity with the topic, the research setting, and the in vivo language often used in the setting enabled a tight research design and well-delineated constructs.

Procedure

The data described in this qualitative study were collected from December 2014 to March 2015. Using the YouTube.com search engine, we first employed a comprehensive sampling method to superficially examine 'every case, instance, or element in a given population' (Goetz and LeCompte 1984, 32). The phrase 'natural hair teen' cited approximately 1780 videos that we perused for a cursory understanding of the foci and structure of vlogs uploaded by Black curly girls, jotting notes as needed. Delimiting the study to Black curly girls whose primary purpose of uploading videos was to discuss hair required that we apply the website's filter to include only Black curly girls' personalised 'channels'. This step tapered the data set to include 15 channels, which were winnowed to 13 channels to exclude channels that featured or were co-constructed by adults as directors, producers, or discussants. The core sample included the channels of 13 Black curly girls, yielding a total of 95 vlogs to be extracted and analysed (Table 1).

Data extraction

Each of the 95 vlogs was recorded using NCapture and uploaded to NVivo to code, group, classify, and organise data. Because the girls' self-talk was both image-based and language-based, the videos were converted into analysable transcriptions that were double-checked against the recordings for accuracy of representation. To facilitate in-depth analysis, the channels of three Black curly girls ($n = 3$) were selected based upon

Table 1. Participant profiles.

Curly girl's channel title	Approximate age	No. of years natural	No. of vlogs
CurlZtotheMax	16–17	2	4
Vitamin Cee[a]	13–15	1	37
IamNaturallyMe[a]	15–17	<0	9
PhoenixSun	14–15	3	8
3A Curls	14–15	2	7
Free U.[a]	17	1	10
Veronica Stretch	13–15	1	4
Bossy_15	13–16	1	2
Currly Girl Thang	15	2	6
Good Hair Day	15	<0	1
The Fro Tho	13–15	1	1
SheDaBest12	13–15	1	1
BlondeBombShell11	13–15	2	5

[a]Indicates channels that were selected for in-depth sample.

the frequency of their online activity (e.g. the most talkative), yielding a total of 56 videos, 56 transcripts of the videos, along with descriptive notes and jottings about the videos.

Data analysis

Ethnographic content analysis (Altheide 1996) was conducted on the digital streams, transcripts, and notes. We first developed an indexing plan by combining provisional and dramaturgical coding schemes (Miles, Huberman, and Saldana 2014). Beginning with a provisional master code – SELF-TALK or TALK for short – we indicated the salient words and images that each girl projected, plus some sub-codes – TALK-OBJ (participant objectives), TALK-CON (participant conflicts), TALK-ATT (participant attitudes), TALK-EMO (participant emotions), TALK-SUB (video subject), and TALK-TEXT (video subtexts) – to delineate segments of data in each group of self-talk variables. Data for each of the three cases was indexed, clustered, and reduced to align with the three research questions. In general, statements and images that were indexed with any of the first four codes aligned with RQ1, data indexed with the fifth code aligned with RQ2, and data indexed with the sixth code aligned with RQ3. A content-analytic summary of themes is presented below, along with a more detailed description of each Black curly girl's self-talk.

Findings

In response to news reports of school-based bans and other forms of symbolic violence, which Black girls with naturally curly hair experience, this study investigated the ways in which Black curly girls – Vitamin Cee, IamNaturallyMe, and Free U. (pseudonyms) – interact with new media for self-love, what self-directed messages the girls share through new media, and the implications of such messages for dominant discourse about Black, curly hair (Table 2).

Vitamin Cee

'My immune system is attacking itself,' Vitamin Cee said as she began explaining to viewers her stress-induced bout with alopecia. She continues for four minutes more, while fluffing a fringe wig worn as a 'protective style' for the patches of curly hair underneath that she is nursing to good health. Having never chemically altered her natural curl pattern, Vitamin

Table 2. Content-analytic summary of themes.

Curly girl	How vlogs are used for self-love	Subject matter of vlogs	Relationship to dominant discourse
Vitamin Cee	Demonstrate self-care	Living with alopecia; achieving healthy curly hair	'I am not my hair'
IamNaturallyMe	Teach self-confidence	Experimenting with and styling curly hair	'I like it kinky'
Free U.	Preach self-acceptance	Affirming Black aesthetic; responding to symbolic violence	'I'm just happy to be nappy'

> Cee has been a curly girl all of her life, though her struggles with hair loss recently prompted her to document her experiences for others to see. This is Vitamin Cee's latest video; there are 36 older video logs uploaded to her YouTube channel, where she records her efforts to maintain naturally curly hair as a teenager with limited resources, some flak from peers, and an abundance of health issues.

Her third vlog, titled 'Teenage Natural Hair Story', is a seven-minute slideshow of pictures spanning 13 years, narrated by Vitamin Cee's voiceover and bold captions, with India Arie's popular song, 'I Am Not My Hair' playing in the background:

> [Chorus]
>
> I am not my hair
>
> I am not this skin
>
> I am not your expectations no, no
>
> I am not my hair
>
> I am not this skin
>
> I am a soul that lives within

The song is a celebration of inner beauty that the cheerful photographs and inspirational captions (e.g. 'No matter how much I have been through at a young age I keep smiling (:') suggest Vitamin Cee resonates with. Across her videos, Vitamin Cee discusses a variety of topics, including hair growth products, full coverage hairstyles and wigs, hair care routines, and her healthy hair journey.

IamNaturallyMe

IamNaturallyMe is the younger sister of BlackChicksRock (pseudonym), another YouTube vlogger whose natural hair channel has received more than 19 million views. Though IamNaturallyMe often references her adult sister in her videos, she started her own channel to address the unique needs of adolescent curly girls:

> When I went to school, I had a lot of compliments – especially from the girls – but I had a lot of stupid comments, like 'Are you getting dreads?' or 'Do you have a Jheri curl kit?' No I do not have a Jheri curl kit, but I just ignore it like I said in the other video. I ignore what people say … I'm not trying to please no one, as long as I like it, that's all that matters. Some of the girls say they can't do it. I have to tell them, 'Yes you can! You can do it if you want it. You can try it. I said the same thing. I thought I couldn't do it either. Just love your natural beauty.' That's all I say. Don't worry about what other people say … I wanted to go natural. I want to do my own thing … I like it. It's not for everybody. I like it. As long as you like it.

Free U.

Free U., a 17-year-old high school senior, opened her channel for the explicit purpose of reaching current and aspiring teen-aged curly girls. She approached the channel as an advice columnist, offering commentary at the juncture of hair, schooling, interpersonal relationships, and Black history. In her first vlog, she said to viewers:

> I know that transitioning into a natural hair state in high school while you're really young, you may be insecure about your hair texture but I'm just here to let you ... young women know that you are beautiful and that Black is beautiful, your hair is beautiful. ... I'm just here to serve as a shoulder to lean on, a shoulder to cry on, a shoulder to ask questions about.

In addition to explaining the purpose of her blog Free U. contextualised her vlogging in a historical perspective.

> Learning a lot about Blacks in America, Black people have been raped of their culture. We've been set up to fit this mode that we'll never fit. Black women are ashamed of their hair. We do everything that we can to straighten their hair out. I'm not knocking. That's a choice.

Free U. makes it very clear that the goal of her vlogging is to 'give advice, take advice, show you all my regimen, share with you products that I find amazing. My hair texture is 4A hair. All my friends are natural. I have one friend who is texlaxed'.

In her video titled 'Natural Hair Q & A HighSchool', which was requested by a specific user who asked,

> You should make a video on how you dealt with transitioning because I am now, but I am so scared to big chop because I know kids in my school will not react so smoothly and I am scared I won't feel as girly anymore and stuff. Oh, and how guys react to your natural hair. Were they nice about it?

Free U.'s response was complex and indicative of the self-talk strategies Black girls have used to combat negative self-perceptions about their hair and bodies.

> How I dealt with transitioning: I transitioned for 6 months, mostly during the summer time so she hid her new growth with roller sets (perm rods) and no one knew what she was up to. It can be difficult to have natural hair or short and natural hair while you're still in school with young-minded individuals, but I can tell you this: I'm not saying it shouldn't matter what they say about you, but you shouldn't let someone else take you away from something that you're doing that you know is something that is right. You shouldn't be ashamed at all of who you are, what you are, and what you have. What you have is beautiful. If someone tries to call you nappy-headed or whatever, that's there own ignorance. If you're not going to step up to the plate and educate them and try to tell them what's really good and what's right, then just ignore because they'll learn eventually. Or they will continue to be ignorant, but that's not your problem. So that's how I really deal with people at school. I'm older. I'm a senior. People warmed up to me. It's something that over time people have become more accepting of me. You will inspire girls and that's the beautiful thing to me. Inspiring people to do the same thing that I'm doing because I know what I'm doing is a beautiful thing.

Her vlog also addressed notions of femininity and how to feel 'girly' with natural hair:

> Having natural hair doesn't necessarily mean that you won't be able to be elegant ... braids to me are so pretty and so elegant. As you get more into this natural hair world, you'll learn so many hairstyles it will blow your mind ... Guys love my hair. Besides the ignorant guys who are like 'I like girls with long straight hair' – that's what they were raised around, that's what they

> see, that's all that they know – but guys love my hair. Guys love my hair, like it's crazy. Guys love big hair, they love big curly hair. No one wants to attract that kind of guy that's closed-minded, that has this bias against himself, you know that slave mentality, but with this head of hair I attract the most mind-blowing guys, like the smartest, most afrocentric, most down brothers. They come at me and it's crazy and I love it. Guys will be like I love that you can be beautiful just being you and you don't have to do all this extra stuff. I'm telling you. It's truly a beautiful thing. Were they nice about it? Yeah, the ones that you'd want to be nice about it. If you are really worried about what a boy would say about your hair, he's not the boy you wanna attract anyway. Why would you want to date someone who doesn't want you for you? Your natural hair is naturally you. It's you.

Use for vlogs

The in-depth sample of vlogs from Vitamin Cee, IamNaturallyMe, and Free U. represented a diverse range of uses. However, the various uses can be collapsed into four major categories, which include advice sharing, advice seeking, results sharing, and storytelling. These uses can be subsumed into the larger, overarching use of connecting with a community of people contemplating going natural, currently living a natural hair lifestyle, or on a natural hair journey. The use of connecting and interacting with a community was evident not only because of the existence of the channels on the YouTube platform, but each vlogger communicated with language frequently used within the community (e.g. big chop, transition, twa, etc.). Ruggerio (2000) explained the uses and gratifications of mass media like the Internet and argued that people use such media for four reasons: diversion (escape from daily routines), social utility (information acquisition), personal identity (reinforcement of beliefs, attitudes, and values), and surveillance (learning about a community, events, or other political affairs). The findings from the current study reflect the mass media theory.

First, the girls seemed to use their blogs as a platform to share advice with others. This was highly evident in the vlog entries from Free U. and less for Vitamin Cee who asked her audience to 'inbox' or post questions for them to answer. In addition to requesting audience questions, the girls also asked for advice. Specifically, in Vitamin Cee's first video, she posed a question about vitamins she could take to improve her hair health and growth. These requests for advice also emerged within vlogs when the girls engaged in tutorials, shared the outcomes of their latest hair ventures, and subsequently asked for advice from their audiences. Connected to advice seeking, the girls used their vlogs to share their hair care results. In a vlog from IamNaturallyMe, the results of her Havana twist style were the focus of the video. Lastly, and even more importantly, the girls seemed to subconsciously use their vlogs as a medium for storytelling. They told stories about their depression, about their experiences at school, and about how they achieved certain styles. These stories were part of the personal identity uses Ruggerio (2000) explained, which served to reinforce beliefs and values about natural hair and its beauty. While advice seeking, advice sharing, results sharing, and storytelling were the most apparent uses of the vlogs evident through the analysis, a critical perspective presents the vlogs as useful in countering the dominant discourse about natural, Black hair as undesirable.

Subject of vlogs

Tied to the uses of the vlogs, which served to support the girls as individuals and add to the virtual, natural hair community, the subject of the vlogs was also diverse. The vlogs centred on three major subjects that oftentimes overlapped – hair care, hair appreciation, and hair and life updates. In the category of hair care, the subject of the videos centred on the latest strategies the vlogger used to maintain her hair, which they communicated through tutorials or simply talking about their daily and weekly rituals. For example, Vitamin Cee explained her use and opinions about Hairfinity, a brand of vitamins for the promotion of healthy hair while IAmNaturallyMe discussed her process of using the tension method to blow dry her natural hair in preparation for installing a protective style. Further, the girls engaged in hair appreciation through positive talk about their natural hair. Although this subject was more apparent in the videos from Free U. because of her mission to answer questions and provide advice about natural hair, Iam-NaturallyMe and Vitamin Cee also spoke positively about their hair as beautiful and accepting their hair as part of themselves. Lastly, a general subject of the videos focused on hair and life updates in which the girls shared information about their school lives, recent hair experiences (i.e. going to the hair dresser, getting a hair cut, straightening, and colouring hair), and relationships with friends and boys.

Relationship to dominant discourse

Much like the young vloggers who communicated about their natural hair experiences, advice, and questions via YouTube with the hope of interacting within an online community of naturalistas, White (2005) also discovered the relationship between resistance and affirmation in her study of 14 African-American women who chose to wear their natural hair:

> It could be argued that for some African American women, the choice to wear one's hair natural is both an act of resistance and affirmation. Women who make the choice are resisting Eurocentric standards of beauty that, among other things, includes straight, long hair. The decision also affirms an Afrocentric standard of beauty where one's natural-born hair – free of chemicals or other straightening techniques – is valued. (White 2005, 296)

Thus, the behaviour of wearing one's hair in its natural state is not only symbolic of an internal struggle with the dominant discourse of a Eurocentric standard of beauty, but it also symbolises an external and visible action that challenges such a deeply reified notion of beauty.

As vlogger Free U. described in her video about her reasons for going natural, she characterised the experience as 'revolutionary'. Within the theoretical perspective of Black identity, Vandiver et al. (2001) explained nigresence theory and its stages within the expanded model which include pre-encounter (period of assimilation and self-hatred), encounter (event that catalyses introspection), immersion-emersion (intense Black involvement and anti-White attitudes), and internalisation (marked by high self-concept and activism). Although the theoretical model does not perfectly explain the ways individuals come to understand and act positively in relation to their racial identity, the idea of maturing into critical comprehension of identity was evident in the sample of vlogs within the study. For example, Free U., a 17-year-old senior in high school had much to say about her understanding of her natural hair, which explained a great deal about her self-concept with her racial identity. Her video, 'TheSimplyNaturalMe' was the best representation of this discourse, which comes in the form of a mini lecture in response to a set of questions: 'Your hair tells a story about who you are and where you come from. Intimidation, respect, [be] brave enough to love yourself for who you really are'. More than anyone else, she is clearly in tune with broader context of negativity surrounding naturals. This excerpt illustrates the powerful nature of the girls' vlogging that speaks against the symbolic violence against Black girls with natural hair.

Discussion: YouTube vlogs as 'homeplace' for black curly girls

Although the Black curly girls' in-depth sample of vloggers in this study sat alone in their bedrooms in front of cameras recording their videos to share with the world, we have found that the medium they chose to broadcast through works as a symbolic homeplace for Black curly girls. We argue that this homeplace, or 'the place of everyday existence within our homes and local community in which all human experience is grounded' (Gouthro 2005, 6) is a site of learning, self-love, and critical discourse where women and girls can come together to share their personal experiences, life events, and advice for others. Such a space is imperative for young Black girls who may be experiencing tensions with their identities because of problematic interactions at school, home, and in society in general.

It is important to note that not all Black curly girls have access to this kind of outlet; specifically, Black curly girls from poor and working class families who may not have the resources (e.g. technology, permission/support/quiet space/time/skills to record, edit, upload, and respond to inquiries about the videos) to engage in public discourse about Black hair in the ways that Vitamin Cee, IamNaturallyMe, and Free U. did. Future research should explore how class intersects with other identity markers as Black curly girls learn on their own terms to protect themselves from symbolic violence. Further exploration of the nature and implications of Black curly girls' self-talk is also necessary, as the words and imagery that we communicate to ourselves often 'resembles old internalized replays of other people's voices' (Diller 1999, 77). Educators, educational scholars, and anyone else who cares deeply about the social and academic worlds of Black adolescent girls ought to be concerned with how they make sense of and negotiate the totality of such chatter.

Disclosure statement

No potential conflict of interest was reported by the authors.

References

Altheide, D. L. 1996. *Qualitative Data Analysis*. Thousand Oaks, CA: Sage.

Bortree, D. S. 2005. "Presentation of Self on the Web: An Ethnographic Study of Teenage Girls' Weblogs." *Education, Communication & Information* 5: 25–39. doi:10.1080/14636310500061102.

Bourdieu, P. 1977. "Symbolic Power." In *Identity and Structure: Issues in the Sociology of Education*, edited by D. Gleeson, 112–119. Driffield: Studies in Education.

Brinthaupt, T. M., M. B. Hein, and T. E. Kramer. 2009. "The Self-talk Scale: Development, Factor Analysis, and Validation." *Journal of Personality Assessment* 91: 82–92. doi:10.1080/00223890802484498.

Brown, C. T. 1973. "The Pleasures of Self-talk." Paper presented at the annual meeting of the Central States Speech Association, Minneapolis, MN. http://files.eric.ed.gov/fulltext/ED077042.pdf.

Buckley, T. R., and R. T. Carter. 2005. "Black Adolescent Girls: Do Gender Role and Racial Identity: Impact Their Self-esteem?" *Sex Roles* 53: 647–661. doi:10.1007/s11199-005.

Byrd, A., and L. Tharps. 2002. *Hair Story: Untangling the Roots of Black Hair in America*. New York, NY: St. Martin's.

Chohan, S. K. 2010. "Whispering Selves and Reflective Transformations in the Internal Dialogue of Teachers and Students." *Journal of Invitational Theory and Practice* 16: 10–28. http://files.eric.ed.gov/fulltext/EJ942555.pdf.

Crenshaw, K. 1991. "Mapping the Margins: Intersectionality, Identity Politics, and Violence Against Women of Color." *Standard Law Review* 43: 1240–1299. http://www.jstor.org/stable/1229039?origin=JSTOR-pdf.

Davis, K. (Director). 2005. *A Girl Like Me* [documentary]. New York: Reel Works Teen Filmmaking.

DeCuir-Gunby, J. T. 2009. "A Review of the Racial Identity Development of African American Adolescents: The Role of Education." *Review of Educational Research* 79: 103–124. doi:10.3102/0034654308325897.

Diller, A. 1999. "The Ethical Education of Self-talk." In *Justice and Caring: The Search for Common Ground in Education*, edited by M. S. Katz, N. Noddings, and K. A. Strike, 74–92. New York: Teachers College Press.

Duke, L. 2000. "Black in a Blonde World: Race and Girls' Interpretations of the Feminine Ideal in Teen Magazines." *Journalism & Mass Communication Quarterly* 77: 367–392. doi:10.1177/107769900007700210.

Evans-Winters, V. 2011. *Teaching Black Girls: Resiliency in Urban Classrooms*. New York: Peter Lang.

Ferguson, A. A. 2001. *Bad Boys: Public Schools in the Making of Black Masculinity*. Ann Arbor: University of Michigan.

Goetz, J. P., and M. D. LeCompte. 1984. *Ethnography and Qualitative Design in Educational Research*. New York: Academic.

Gordon, M. K. 2008. "Media Contributions to African American Girls' Focus on Beauty and Appearance: Exploring the Consequences of Sexual Objectification." *Psychology of Women Quarterly* 32: 245–256. doi:10.1111/j.1471-6402.2008.00433.x.

Gouthro, P. A. 2005. "A Critical Feminist Analysis of the Homeplace as Learning Site: Expanding the Discourse of Lifelong Learning to Consider Adult Women Learners." *International Journal of Lifelong Education* 24: 5–19. doi:10.1080/026037042000317310.

Green, K. L. 2013. "The Way We Hear Ourselves is Different from the Way Others See us": Exploring the Literate Identities of a Black Radio Youth Collective." *Equity & Excellence in Education* 46: 315–326. doi:10.1080/10665684.2013.808506.

Hesse-Biber, S. N., S. A. Howling, P. Leavy, and M. Lovejoy. 2004. "Racial Identity and the Development of Body Image Issues Among African American Adolescent Girls." *The Qualitative Report* 9: 49–79. http://www.nova.edu/ssss/QR/QR9-1/howling.pdf.

Hooks, b. 1989. *Talking Back: Thinking Feminist, Thinking Black*. Boston, MA: South End.

Hooks, b. 2000. *All about Love: New Visions*. New York: Harper Perennial.

Jacob, I. 2002. *My Sisters' Voices: Teenage Girls of Color Speak Out*. New York, NY: Henry Holt.

Ladner, J. A. 1995. *Tomorrow's Tomorrow: The Black Woman*. Lincoln, NE: University of Nebraska. Identity development of urban girls. Looked at the experiences of Black girls in St. Louis.

Love, B. L. 2012. *Hip Hop's Li'l Sistas Speak*. New York, NY: Peter Lang. Identity development of urban girls.

Miles, M. B., A. M. Huberman, and J. Saldana. 2014. *Qualitative Data Analysis: A Methods Sourcebook*. 3rd ed. Thousand Oaks, CA: Sage.

Muhammad, G. E. 2012. "Creating Spaces for Black Adolescent Girls to 'Write it Out!'." *Journal of Adolescent & Adult Literacy* 56: 203–211. doi:10.1002/JAAL.00129.

Patton, T. O. 2006. "Hey Girl, am I More Than My Hair? African American Women and Their Struggles with Beauty, Body Image, and Hair." *NWSA Journal* 18: 24–51. http://www.jstor.org/stable/4317206.

Robinson, C. L. 2011. "Hair as Race: Why 'Good Hair' may be Bad for Black Females." *Howard Journal of Communications* 22: 358–376. doi:10.1080/10646175.2011.6177212.

Ruggerio, T. E. 2000. "Uses and Gratifications Theory in the 21st century." *Mass Communication and Society* 3: 3–37. doi:10.1207/S15327825MCS0301_02.

Schwartz, R. M. 1986. "The Internal Dialogue: On the Asymmetry Between Positive and Negative Coping Thoughts." *Cognitive Therapy and Research* 10: 591–605. http://www.cogdyn.com/documents/Schwartz.Asym.Pos_Neg.pdf

Sears, S. D. 2010. *Imagining Black Womanhood: The Negotiation of Power and Identity within the Girls Empowerment Project*. New York: Suny.

Stokes, C. E. 2007. "Representin' in Cyberspace: Sexual Scripts, Self-definition, and Hip Hop Culture in Black American Adolescent Girls' Home Pages." *Culture, Health, & Sexuality* 9: 169–184. doi:10.1080/13691050601017512.

Thomas, A. J., D. Hoxha, and J. D. Hacker. 2013. "Contextual Influences on Gendered Racial Identity Development of African American Young Women." *Journal of Black Psychology* 39: 88–101. doi:10.1177/0095798412454679.

Townsend, T. G., A. J. Thomas, T. B. Neilands, and T. R. Jackson. 2010. "I'm No Jezebel; I am Young, Gifted, and Black: Identity, Sexuality, and Black Girls." *Psychology of Women Quarterly* 34: 273–285. doi:10.1111/j.1471-6402.2010.01574.x.

Vandiver, B. V., P. E. Fhagen-Smith, K. O. Cokley, W. E. Cross, and F. C. Worrell. 2001. "Cross's Nigresence Model: From Theory to Scale to Theory." *Journal of Multicultural Counseling and Development* 29: 174–200. http://www.personal.psu.edu/faculty/b/j/bjv3/page2/assets/BJVetalJMCD01.pdf.

West, C. 2002. "A Genealogy of Modern Racism." In *Race Critical Theories*, edited by P. Essed and D. T. Goldberg, 90–112. Malden, MA: Blackwell.

White, S. B. 2005. "Releasing the Pursuit of Bouncin' and Behavin' Hair: Natural Hair as an Afrocentric Feminist Aesthetic for Beauty." *International Journal of Media and Cultural Politics* 1: 295–308. doi:10.1386/macp.1.3.295/1.

Winn, M. T. 2010. "'Betwixt and Between': Literacy, Liminality, and the Ceiling of Black Girls." *Race Ethnicity and Education* 13: 425–447. doi:10.1080/13613321003751601.

Super-Girl: strength and sadness in Black girlhood

Nia Michelle Nunn

ABSTRACT
This paper complicates notions of Black girlhood by examining the dual experiences of gendered racism that result in both strength and sadness in Black girls' educational experiences. I highlight the need for a curriculum of liberation to combat historical and current social conditions negatively impacting school-aged Black girls, such as harsh disciplinary practices, low academic expectations, and sexual objectification. The Super-Girl phenomenon serves as a metaphor illustrating the balance and imbalance of multiple social constructs. Utilising constructivist grounded theory [Charmaz, K. 2006. *Constructing Grounded Theory*. London: Sage], the key concepts in the research derived directly from the voices of 18 school-aged girls (8–13) as well as my observations, interpretations, and related experiences. Data collection utilising observation notes, interviews, written responses, and activity products provided from monthly sessions over the course of two years, offer critical insight into some of the complexities of Black girlhood. The most striking common themes abstracted from their voices were concepts related to 'strength' and 'sadness' in their lives. Thematic narratives were found to be most relevant to (1) negative teacher–student relationships, as well as, (2) policed bodies and sexual objectification. This work offers specific recommendations for future girl empowerment programming, curriculum, and evidence-based intervention development that can aide in liberating Black girls.

Introduction

Response to the call

An overwhelming number of negative images and stereotypical perceptions of Black girls and women plague today's society. Illustrating historical patterns of existing marginalisation and disenfranchisement imbedded in the general culture, these social realities are perpetuated in educational practices. In the article 'Other People's Daughters: Critical Race Feminism and Black Girls' Education,' scholars Venus E. Evans-Winters and Jennifer Esposito acknowledge a call and specific responsibility for Black female scholars to deconstruct, intervene, and present the common educational and social experiences of Black girls (Austin 1995; Evans-Winters and Esposito 2010). The National Women's Law Center and the NAACP Legal Defense and Educational Fund, Inc. provided an executive summary entitled, *Unlocking Opportunity for African American Girls: A Call to Action for Educational Equity* (2014), to highlight the

> … barriers that restrict and limit the educational opportunities of many Black girls, the impact of those barriers on the lives of African American girls and women, and the … available interventions that present opportunities to fundamentally improve life outcomes for young African American women … [encouraging] educators, school leaders, community leaders and members, advocates, policymakers, and philanthropic organizations to take action to advance the success of African American girls. (1)

This paper is an attempt to respond to the call for a critical analysis of Black girlhood. As a Black female scholar in education and psychology, I embrace the responsibility, personal passion, and a sense of urgency to recognise that Black girls must be given specific voice. There is a need for a curriculum of liberation to combat historical and current social conditions that negatively impact school-age Black girls, such as harsh disciplinary practices, low academic expectations, and sexual objectification. For more than 20 years, scholars have identified the ways in which Black girls are represented disproportionately in many markers of poor school achievement, leaving them behind in a range of academic measures related to college readiness. These markers of poor school achievement include, harsh school disciplinary consequences, such as suspension and expulsion (Aud, Fox, and Kewal-Ramani 2010), academic underachievement (Blake et al. 2011; Ford 1994, 2013; Noland, Arnold, and Clement 1980), implicit and/or explicit discrimination (Fordham 1993; Koonce 2012; Tonnesen 2013; Wilkins 2013), and strict dress codes with underlying sexually oppressive innuendos (Evans-Winters 2005; Price 2011; Roberts 1998). Although some of these disproportionate realities do not typically exceed that of Black boys, the educational outcomes for Black girls are gravely different and disproportionate when compared to their White male and White female counterparts (Asbury 1978; Wilkins 2013). Similar to their Black male counterparts, however, Black girls are also directly impacted by the school-to-prison pipeline when compared to their White female counterparts and the national average of all girls (Christian and Thomas 2009; Davis 2013; Hogg et al. 2008). For example, when deconstructing aggression and violence (primarily in school-aged Black girls), Waldron's profoundly highlights that the most common phrase from teachers, counselors, and administrators was that 'Girls are Worse' (2011).

The concept of *Super-Girl* provides a metaphor that illustrates the balance and imbalance of multiple social constructs. Guided by an intersectional approach (Collins 2000; Crenshaw 1991), critical race feminism (CRF), and Black feminist literature (hooks 1981), I shed light on gender and race simultaneously, to highlight often silenced social conditions that negatively impact school-age Black girls. In responding directly to the calls to action for educational equity (Evans-Winters and Esposito 2010), I also attempt to briefly address various links between historical and current social conditions impacting the common experiences of Black girls. By naming White privilege and patriarchal male privilege as part of this obfuscation of the needs of Black girls, this work can begin to dismantle faulty perceptions that Black girls and women carry inherent strength without substantial sadness.

I critique elements of previous literature to address how dangerous myths linking a non-feminine form of strength with an emasculated illustration of high self-esteem (Buckley and Carter 2005) can have a damaging impact on educational experiences in

Black girlhood. The *Super-Girl* model challenges non-feminine, emasculated illustrations, and other social designations of Black girlhood. The *'Super'* element describes multiple identities, as well as trials and tribulations relevant to the need to defend, protect, and save oneself and others, like that of a superhero. Followed by a hyphen, the capital *'G'* emphasises self-defined feminine power in Black girlhood. *Super-Girl* presents a new phenomenon about balancing both strength and sadness due to regular social battles. *Super-Girl's strength* describes a self-defined feminine power that fosters resilience and on-going decision-making in the face of gendered racism. *Super-Girl's sadness* defines historically rooted pain, sorrow, and sometimes debilitating current conditions and experiences as a result of gendered racism. The *Super-Girl* model illustrates the voices of Black girls through observations and interpretations of the gendered racism imbedded in the stories of Black girls' storytelling and processing of common school life realities.

The phenomenon of *Super-Girl* derived from narrative research focusing on 18 school-aged Black girls (8–13) who participate in a community-based girl empowerment programme. Guided by grounded theory research (Charmaz 2006; Strauss and Corbin 1998), the common experiences shared by participants' generated interest in redefining strength and acknowledging sadness in Black girlhood. Data collection and analysis utilising observation notes, interviews/focus group discussions, written responses, and activity products provided from monthly sessions over the course of two years, offer critical insight into some of the complexities of Black girlhood. Derived from data, *Super-Girl* presents a new phenomenon about balancing both strength and sadness due to regular social battles, decision-making, and on-going self-reflection. As a result of this process, specific recommendations are offered for future girl empowerment programming, curriculum, and evidence-based intervention development that can aide in liberating Black girls.

Conceptual framework

Intersectionality and CRF

The foundation of this work emphasises the critical need to focus on the intersection of race and gender, guided by the theoretical frameworks embodying *intersectionality* (Collins 2000; Crenshaw 1989, 1991) and *CRF* (Evans-Winters and Esposito 2010) to further understand school experiences in Black girlhood. The conclusion of this paper encourages parents, caregivers, educators, practitioners, mentors, and community leaders to begin or enhance girl empowerment programmes and interventions. It also brainstorms specific curriculum development suggestions for intervention strategies that serve or include Black pre-adolescent and adolescent girls in an effort to foster resilience and strengthen their sense of self while navigating their social realities.

Scholars Patricia Hill Collins and Kimberlé Williams Crenshaw originally presented the term *intersectionality* to describe the experiences of inequality for people of multiple social identities (Collins 2000; Crenshaw 1991). *Gendered racism* illustrates the immutable facets of the Black female human identity. As Perry, Pullen, and Oser (2012), describe gendered racism '... highlights her location at the intersection of gender and racial statuses, thus, previous research demonstrates that oppression cannot be reduced to a single experience of one of these identities, namely, sexism or racial discrimination' (335). The employment of *intersectionality* also helped to ignite the concept of *CRF*.

Evans-Winters and Esposito (2010) articulate that CRF derives from *Critical Race Theory* (CRT), which honours counter-narratives (stories that challenge the master narratives and majority perspective) to illustrate the multidimensionality of oppression faced by people of colour, recognising five primary tenets, presented by several scholars (Bell 1992; Crenshaw 1989; Delgado 1989; Delgado and Stefancic 2012),

> that have potential for informing educational research, curriculum, and policy formation: (1) race and racism are central, endemic, permanent and fundamental in defining and explaining how U.S. society functions, (2) challenges dominant ideologies, dominant narratives, and claims of race neutrality, objectivity, meritocracy, color-blindness, [normality] and equal opportunity, (3) is activist in nature and propagates a commitment to social justice, (4) centers the experiences and voices of the marginalized and oppressed, and (5) is necessarily interdisciplinary in scope of function (Delgado 2002; Delgado and Stefancic 2000; Solorzano and Yosso 2002; quoted from Evans-Winters and Esposito 2010, 15).

CRF offers all of the elements embedded in CRT in addition to the possibility for understanding and researching the specific educational experiences of school-aged Black girls.

Literature review

Why focus on Black girls?

> We are rarely recognized as a group separate and distinct from black men, or as a present part of the larger group 'women' in this culture. (hooks 1981, 7)

Presenting the complexities of race and gender, bell hooks (1981) emphasises that these identities cannot be divorced. Further, Black girls and women experience a dual impact of racist and sexist oppression (Collins 2000; Crenshaw 1991; hooks 1981). The present research encourages a targeted focus on Black girls, in an effort to ensure that these voices do not continue to fall through the cracks (Evans-Winters and Esposito 2010). In bell hooks', *Ain't I a Woman* (1981), she explains that, simultaneously serving as 'oppressor and oppressed', Black men conceptualise the anti-racist agenda and define the direction on combating racism with a patriarchal approach, and White women have defined a feminist agenda that honours White privilege. She further elucidates that,

> White women and Black men have it both ways. They can act as oppressor or be oppressed. Black men may be victimized by racism, but sexism allows them to act as exploiters and oppressors of women. White women may be victimized by sexism, but racism enables them to act as exploiters and oppressors of Black people. Both groups have led liberation movements that favor their interests and support continued oppression of other groups. Black male sexism has undermined struggles to eradicate racism just as white female racism undermines feminist struggle. (hooks 2000, 7)

Historically and presently, the word 'men' automatically refers to *White* men, the word 'Black' often refers to Black *men*, and the word 'women' refers almost always to *White* women. Current scholarship on Black children typically highlights the disproportionality and the oppressive experiences of Black boys (Kunjufu 1982, 2005; Landson-Billings 2011; Noguera 1997, 2008; Payne and Brown 2010). Similarly, the current research focused on 'girls' and girl empowerment, represents a predominantly White population and cultural approach (Lindergren et al. 2011). Throughout the literature, separate distinctions are made between 'Black children' (primarily focused on Black boys) and 'girls' (explicitly referring to White girls) (Clark 1982; Payne and Brown 2010; Wade 1996). This work is not designed to detract from research and movements that alter the conditions and strengthen the lives of Black boys and men, nor is it designed to emphasise a 'battle of the oppressed' between all girls, rather it is designed to encourage a more in depth analysis of a socially constructed population. Having the ability to target and transform the negative experiences of socially constructed populations, such as Black girls, benefits all populations.

The schooling experiences of many Black girls

The calls to action are necessary because on-going experiences of Black girls in our nation's schools are rarely considered or discussed. Research on the self-esteem of school-age girls consistently reports high markers among Black females compared to their White female counterparts (Adams 2010; Buckley and Carter 2005; Jaffee and Mahle Lutter 1995; Milikie 1999; Nicolas et al. 2008; Wade 1996). Understanding social stressors relevant to racism and sexism, as well as Black girls' strength, perseverance, and independence linked to healthy self-esteem should lead to a positive perception of them. However, Buckley and Carter (2005) identify Black girls' high self-esteem to be based on masculine and androgynous (both feminine and masculine) gender role characteristics. The masculinisation of Black girls and women has historical roots in the USA, interlocking racism and sexism (hooks 1981). Genderless work expectations during slavery meant that White slave masters forced a Black woman to do the work of a Black man, further challenging her femininity and identity as a woman. In schools today, disciplinary responses to various behaviours displayed by Black girls are increasingly similar to the pattern of criminalising disciplinary responses experienced by Black boys (Davis 2013). Recognising that some teachers', counsellors', and administrators' perceptions are that 'girls are worse' (Waldron 2011), one might fear that the school-to-prison pipeline for Black girls will get even worse.

Research has suggested that the current behaviours and identities that Black girls exercise in schools are to their detriment (Fordham 1993, 1996). Often categorised by stereotypically 'Black' characteristics such as, loud, aggressive, and masculine, Fordham (1993, 1996) suggests that it would be better for the success of Black girls' education if they would choose to implement more of a 'race-less persona'. Fordham defines a 'race-less persona' as the absence of behavioural and attitudinal characteristics related to a particular race. Contradictory to Fordham's suggestion, O'Connor (1997) summarises positive findings regarding characteristics of school resilience in Black girls, 'the families who not only taught them about race, class, and gender oppression, but also participated in family conversations that explained to them how to combat racist, classist, and sexist forces' (quoted from Evans-Winters and Esposito 2010, 13). These characteristics serve as major tools for developing protective coping factors and transformative action against the ways in which racism, sexism, and classism manifest in school classrooms.

Although salient social class elements of intersectionality are very important and not articulated in this paper, it is critical to note that social class and economic resources yield unique experiences in Black girlhood. In it's calls to action, the executive report presented by National Women's Law Center and the NAACP Legal Defense and Educational

Fund, Inc. illustrates 'systemic educational barriers and challenges produce life-long economic obstacles, such as limited job opportunities, lower earnings, and disproportionate representation among those in poverty. As a result Black girls are uniquely vulnerable to a *school-to-poverty pathway*' (1). Given the status of Black girls as lagging behind on a range of academic measures related to college readiness, Evans-Winters and Esposito (2010) articulate that 'because of racism, sexism, and class oppression in the US, African-American girls are in multiple jeopardy of race, class, and gender exclusion in mainstream educational institutions.'

With limited investment in the specific future of Black girls and inadequate representations in the general school curriculum, Black girls are also disproportionately represented in empowering school activities (e.g. athletics, clubs, and other extracurricular activities). Despite this very point in their lives when they are most in need of attention, support, and encouragement – Black girls are often trapped in environments that do not fully support their personal and academic development. For this reason, there is an urgent need for on-going empowering experiences and curriculum that fosters the resilience to combat gendered racism for Black girls.

An example of curriculum invested in Black girlhood includes the work of Ruth Nicole Brown in her book *Hear Our Truths: The Creative Potential of Black Girlhood* (2013). Brown (2013) presents Saving Our Lives Hear Our Truths, or SOLHOT, a radical youth intervention, provides a space for the creative performance and expression of Black girlhood and how this creativity informs other realisations about Black girlhood and womanhood. Founded in 2006 and co-organised by the author, SOLHOT is an intergenerational collective organising effort that celebrates and recognises Black girls as producers of culture and knowledge (Brown 2013). Processing through a CRF lens, empowering curriculum work designed to liberate Black girls can offer activities, tools, and perspectives – that welcome storytelling, creativity, decision-making processing, and critical thinking about personal, school, and general social realities.

Research questions and purpose – inquiring about Black girlhood

Research questions that guided this study include,

(1) How did the girls contribute to an evolving empowerment curriculum?
(2) How did they respond to activities relevant to identity development and self-understanding?
(3) How did they utilise 'Sister Circles' (focus group discussions) to share and process their schooling experiences?
(4) How can the results from on-going data collection and analysis be used to develop girl empowerment curriculum and evidence-based interventions?

The *first purpose* was to examine stories of educational experiences from the perspective of a group of Black girls. The *second purpose* was to engage in an on-going processing of historical and present social factors (issues/dynamics) relevant to redefining *strength* and deconstructing *sadness* in Black girlhood in an effort to help the girls share (breathe through) their experiences and develop coping strategies and/or action plans-especially in school. The *third purpose* was to utilise the voices of Black girls to bring awareness to, and, to support educators, practitioners, and researchers in developing, implementing, and evaluating girl empowerment curriculum and evidence-based interventions relevant to (or involving) Black girls.

Researcher background and relationship – identity memo #1

A primary method for answering the research questions and honouring the study's goals was to capitalise on the experiential data process. As the primary researcher and a professor in education in the college town where I was born and raised – my access, activism, and commitment to the community encourages me to incorporate personal experience and understanding as a valued part of the inquiry process. For many years, prior to working in higher education, I served as a school psychologist at the elementary school where I attended as a child and all of the participants in this study attended. I have an existing rapport with all of the participants, as the oldest (13 years old) was a first grader when I began my career. I also participated in general school, extracurricular, enrichment, and/or empowering programmes with some of their caregivers as a child. Therefore, this experiential data technique has roots that value technical knowledge and research background, but also personal experience as both the facilitator and researcher of this girl empowerment work.

Wearing many head wraps in the community, as I like to call it, my extensive relationship with the girls and their families has allowed me to facilitate and study this girl empowerment academy (GEA) programme in the community – where I also participated in girl empowerment work like GEA as a young girl. I could not be more grateful to have fabulous college students and other local community members, as we work together to offer the girls various opportunities for girl empowerment (e.g. lunch groups, afterschool 10-week programmes, monthly Saturday programmes, and summer workshops). As a youth, it was always exciting when college students mentored and participated in enrichment activities with us, so I had the privilege to create an opportunity to supervise and mentor two Black college women, during this two-year project (student researcher/facilitators). I can remember it being particularly powerful to have college students of colour and especially Black women college students in my life. It provided an incredibly positive self-image and love for learning that I valued as a little girl.

Overview of methods and analysis

This work values grounded theory research methodologies (Charmaz 2006; Strauss and Corbin 1998), 'a qualitative research design in which the inquirer generates a general explanation (a theory) of experiences shaped by the views of participants' (Creswell 2013, 83). The methods explore how this community-based *curriculum of place* provides '... a cultural space from which it might be possible to wage a counter movement ... ' (Perry, Pullen, and Oser 2012, 2) compared to what they typically experience in learning spaces, such as school.

Grounded theory from a constructivist and interpretivist perspective, as presented by Charmaz (2006) was selected for this study because a theory is not yet available to explain or understand girl empowerment processes and narratives of Black girlhood. In this method of grounded theory, a theoretical phenomenon is developed during a study and in constant interaction with the data, providing flexibility to constantly process explanations and understandings developed by the researcher and participants throughout the study. Constructivist grounded theory (Charmaz 2006) is an interpretive approach to qualitative research that has flexible guidelines in developing a theory that depends on the researcher and participants views, values, beliefs, feelings, assumptions, and ideologies of individuals and common experiences between people rather than on the methods of research. It provides an opportunity to reveal hidden networks, situations, and relationships that make visible hierarchies of power, communication, and opportunity through rich data, such as observation notes, quotes, written samples, and researcher memoing.

Maxwell (2005) presents an engaging and brief reflective writing exercise he calls a *researcher identity memo* that helps researchers examine how one's beliefs and emotions connect to the work being done. Similar to the empowering work and curriculum development for the girls, the *researcher identity memo* exercises allowed me to (1) reflect on my prior connections to the topic, people, setting, (2) to acknowledge the nature of my assumptions, and (3) to examine what I wanted to accomplish, learn, and offer by doing this study. In addition to *research identity memos*, multiple sources of data were included in the research, such as (1) observation field notes and reflections, (2) recorded field notes from focus group interviews and discussions, and (3) products from interventions and activities. Incorporating adapted pieces from existing girl empowerment curricula and informal exchanges with the girls, Maxwell (2005) suggests that these structured and unstructured sources of data can reduce the risk that our conclusions would reflect only the systematic biases or limitations of a specific source or method.

Several strategies for dealing with any potential validity threats were considered utilising a checklist for validity testing presented by Maxwell (2005). Prior to presenting the checklist, he encourages a process of ruling out validity threats and increasing credibility of conclusions by acknowledging potential researcher bias and reactivity. I recognise that my values and expectations influence the conduct and conclusions of the study and for this reason I implemented practices to avoid negative consequences by engaging in regular written reflection memo exercises. By the very nature of the project and primary data collection system of observation field notes and reflection memos, the grounded theory process honours reflexive practice in my efforts to strengthen the development, implementation, and evaluation of this GEA curriculum. As the primary researcher, I also identify as part of the cultural sharing group I am studying – so instead of working to avoid influence on the outcomes, I sought to understand how I am identifying and/or influencing the outcomes. Several strategies were considered from Maxwell (2005) that helped to protect the study from invalidity:

- *Intensive, long-term involvement.* Prolonged researcher engagement with 'repeated observation and interviews, as well as the sustained presence of the researcher in the setting studied, can help to rule out spurious associations and premature theories' (Maxwell 2005, 110). My familiarity with the girls and consistent connection describes complete participation and full engagement as the facilitators and researchers of the programme.
- *Intervention.* The intervention here speaks to our role and presence as qualitative researchers who are conscious and willing to examine how our biases, values, and experiences influence the development, implementation, and evaluation of the

curriculum and study. Maxwell (2005) explains that 'in field research, the researchers presence is always an intervention in some ways ... and the effects of this presence can be used to develop or test ideas about the group or topic studied' (111).

- As discussed, both structured and unstructured methods of data collection help to give credibility to a study. For example, after completing the survey we (researchers and participants) had a discussion about the experience and in later sessions reflected on the overall results of the survey. These discussions gave so much more insight in to the already statistically significant elements of the survey.
- *Respondent validation.* Maxwell presents respondent validation as 'systematically soliciting feedback about your data and conclusions from the people you are studying' (111). We (researchers and facilitators) actively engaged the girls in the highlights, main ideas, and even interesting quotes displayed on chart paper during *Sister Circles* (focus group discussions).
- *Searching for discrepant evidence and negative cases.* The research team (student research team members and myself) reviewed the data regularly. I also had access to a critical friends group, which consisted of a small group of colleagues who provided feedback on our interpretations of the data. These regular structures of receiving feedback were valuable strategy for checking biases, assumptions, and flaws in the logic or methods.
- *'Rich' data.* In this study, I attempt to present the voices, feelings, actions, and meanings heard from the girls, including verbatim quotes and notes on observations from focus group discussions and other activities included in the curriculum.

Research participants

GEA research participants consisted of 18 girls ages 8–13, in grades 4th (5), 5th (4), 6th (3), 7th (2), 8th (4), who identify as both 'Black' and 'girl'. The girls for GEA were recruited because of an existing trusted relationship and prior work with them and their families. Periodically with the help of Black college women and community activists, my independent study mentees (student researchers) and I facilitated GEA monthly meetings, activities, and events – primarily at a historic African-American community centre. Serving as convenience sampling – because of the existing nature of the programme and relationships, the 18 girls were purposefully selected to participate in this study. Human research subjects approval, parental permission, and participant consent were granted for all 18 girls over the course of two years (2013–2015).

Procedures and curricular activities

Year 1

Who I am! Poetry activity. Each girl selected adjectives from a list of 50 words (i.e. friendly, powerful, attractive, smart, vivacious, etc.) on a personal characteristics inventory. They highlighted words to describe characteristics they identify with (actual self) and characteristics that they want to identify with (ideal self). The words were then utilised to write a 'Who I am!' poem as an icebreaker activity. Adjective selections served as a helpful source of data regarding the girls' perceptions of themselves and notes were taken from the girls' discussion on the activity.

Mini-personal attributes survey. Early in the study each girl completed the Mini-Personal Attributes Survey (MPAS). MPAS is a 20-item survey that was read aloud while participants independently selected a response. The MPAS gathered information about the girls' self-esteem (e.g. 'I know my strengths'), sense of optimism (e.g. 'I feel comfortable with myself'), locus of control (e.g. 'I believe that some people are born lucky'), and physical attractiveness (e.g. 'I dislike looking at my body'). The girls indicate their personal attributes on a 4-point Likert scale from 'strongly disagree' to 'strongly agree'. The MPAS was adapted in to a 'mini' version of the International Personality Item Pool (Goldberg 1999) where items were previously tested for validity and reliability (http://ipip.ori.org).

Phenomenal women discussion and pottery. This open-ended discussion on girlhood and phenomenal women was guided by a series of questions: *What does it mean to be a girl? What are the pros and cons of being a girl?* After reading Maya Angelou's Phenomenal Woman poem (Angelou 1978), we asked: *What does it mean to be a phenomenal woman? Who are some phenomenal girls and women that you admire? Why?* Discussing strength and creativity while using pottery clay to make bowls, heart shapes, plates, and abstract objects, we allowed the girls to navigate the discussion. After pottery, we passed out copies of Lupita Nyongo's speech on *Dark Beauty* (*Essence Magazine*, May 2014) and asked the girls to take turns reading segments aloud while underlining parts of the speech that stood out to them.

Positive self-concept activities. The first activity focuses on developing a positive self-concept. As part of the activity each girl has an opportunity to say a positive statement about herself (personality, abilities, and looks) and something positive about her neighbour or another girl in the group. In the second activity, designed to strengthen self-concept, each girl selected an affirmation from a list to recite daily. The affirmations selected were recorded for each participant and discussed at the following GEA sessions. Finally, the girls were asked to write an inspiring letter to themselves utilising the language from the affirmations selected.

Participant enrolment packets. As part of the data analysis, GEA participant enrolment packets were reviewed. Some of the questions included in the enrolment packets inquired about each girls' interests/hobbies, future career aspiration, favourite/least favourite school subjects, and the activities they desired for girl empowerment work.

Year 2

Sister Circles. In an effort to implement more of a participant directed programme, the girls were asked to brainstorm activities and hot topics that they wanted to address in sessions. The extensive discussions and walls taped with notes filling chart paper turned into regular monthly focus group discussions, we called *Sister Circles* as part of each GEA session. Most of the *Sister Circles* began with facilitators asking generally broad questions, such as, how have you been? What's been going on in your world lately? Sometimes the older girls asked to meet and talk in separate sessions from the younger girls and other times everyone met together. The culture of *Sister Circles* was that the girls told their stories or asked questions while we took notes on displayed chart paper to help bullet or summarise what we were hearing. Eventually, some of the girls participated in taking notes on chart paper during the *Sister Circle* discussions. Although, the discussions were primarily guided by the girls, as researchers and facilitators there were times when we led with a few specific focus group questions, often about school, friendship dynamics, problem solving, and other issues that we knew were current and directly relevant to their lives.

Results

The first year represents data from more structured activities and led to basic numeric findings, as well as field notes from observation activities that resulted in coded concepts and ideas. The most striking common theme abstracted from the data in the first year were the concepts of '*strength*' and '*sadness*' in their lives, as a result of our assessment of their personal characteristics, self-esteem, sense of optimism, locus of control, physical appearance, and self-understanding. Consistent references or connections to the idea of *strength* and *sadness* in their lives resurfaced throughout the first year.

Year 1

Strength and sadness emerges. The preliminary findings derived from the MPAS and revealed strong relationships. As a result of the study, the girls indicated that they have the ability to (1) identify their strengths while they also tend to dislike themselves in general and (2) they acknowledge their strengths and are able to self-regulate their mood. We also found that the same participants who (3) know their strengths tend to be more satisfied with their physical appearance. Conversely, girls who identified that they (4) dislike looking at their bodies expressed often feeling sad. In addition, the same girls who (5) expressed feelings of sadness tend to see difficulties everywhere and are less likely to take responsibility for their decision-making. Finally, the results indicated that this (6) sense of sadness creates a struggle to cope with some of their daily experiences. Inline with the MPAS findings, we highlighted how their conversations and engagement in the girl empowerment activities illustrated strength and sadness oriented data.

Strength oriented data. The poetry lines that the girls most commonly wrote and discussed to describe their 'actual-selves' included … 'I am … *strong,* I am … *thoughtful,* I am … *intelligent,* and I am … *attractive*'. The enrolment papers for all of the girls also provided an illustration of their strengths and confidence in their academic functioning ('I am good at math') and social functioning ('I have a lot of friends'), as well as future career aspirations, such as a 'doctor', 'artist', 'police officer', 'lawyer', and 'chef'. Similar to the data illustrated from the MPAS, the girls did not seem to struggle with identifying their strengths.

Additional conversations of strength in girlhood and womanhood were highlighted from the phenomenal women activity. With fingers deep in clay, the girls recited generic ideas about the significance of being a girl, 'girls are strong', 'girls are unique', and 'girls are smart'. When brainstorming a list of positive self-images and role models whom everyone in the room admired, we developed an extensive list of people and names of phenomenal women that included but are not limited to their mothers, sisters, aunts, grandmother, mentors, as well as Dr Dorothy Cotton, Angela Davis, Maya Angelou, bell hooks, Michelle Obama, Kiki Palmer, Beyonce, and others.

Afterward, the girls took turns reading a speech by Lupita Nyongo at the 2014 Essence Festival on *Dark Beauty*. As they read, we asked them to underline parts of the speech that they liked or stood out most to them. While Lupita introduced the power of positive self-imagery in the media, multiple girls underlined parts of the speech that we categorised as a quote relevant to strength. In one of the most common underlined quotes, Lupita says 'I am surrounded by people who have inspired me, women in particular whose presence on-screen made me feel a little more seen and heard and understood.' The girls also underlined and talked about the segment where Lupita later descried how ' … a flower of confidence couldn't help but bloom inside [her]. When [she saw a model with dark complexion, she] inadvertently saw a reflection of [herself] that [she] couldn't deny.' We rewrote the most commonly underlined quotes on chart paper to deconstruct the messages together. As a result, the girls concluded that they too respond well to positive self-images. Without facilitator/researcher guidance, one of the girls pointed to the extensive list of phenomenal women and said, 'These women represent our flowers of confidence.'

Sadness oriented data. The sadness communicated by the girls first derived from their commonly selected words to describe their 'ideal-self', as some of their poetry read, 'I wish I were more … *confident*,' 'I wish I were more … *mature*,' 'I wish I were more … *powerful*,' & 'I wish I were more … *courageous*.' However, the presence of sadness was made most evident through the girls' body language while completing the MPAS. When presented with statements like 'I often feel sad,' 'I am often in a bad mood,' and 'I dislike looking at my body,' we noted that the energy of the room completely shifted, as the girls looked away with eyes of discomfort, slouched into the seat of their chairs, and hovered over their surveys as if to ensure that no one around them could see their responses of 'agree' or 'strongly agree.'

Lupita's speech had segments of sadness that resonated with the girls, as they underlined, 'I remember a time when I too, felt unbeautiful' and ' … when I was a teenager my self-hate grew worse.' Following the discussions after Lupita's speech, the girls were focused on the concept of feeling 'unbeautiful' and to combat the fear of this feeling growing 'worse,' we engaged in a variety of activities to focus on building a positive self-concept. In one activity called 'Happy To Be Me!' some of the girls struggled to answer questions asking them to identify something they like about their personality or something positive about the way they look. Eventually the exercise asked the girls to acknowledge something unique and positive about another girl in the group. This was a much easier task and interestingly enough, out of 20 affirmations, there were 4 most commonly selected and processed for several empowerment sessions following the deconstruction of Lupita's speech:

- 'I am a well-loved and well respected person.'
- 'It matters little what others say. What matters is how I react and what I believe.'
- 'I release the need to prove myself to anyone as I am my own self and I love it that way.'
- 'I love and respect myself unconditionally.'

Over the course of several sessions, we continued to discuss the affirmations and many girls found them to be useful to read and think about when they experienced, disappointment and self-doubt, particularly in classroom settings. Overall, the girls indicated that with regular exposure (i.e. statements posted on their mirrors, school planners) and practice saying the affirmations, it helped them to remove or cope with their sadness.

Year 2

The second year represents data from more unstructured engagement that led to more depth on their strength and sadness as well as a more explicit focus on experiences relevant to race and gender. In reflecting on the data from the first year, when the evidence spoke to the girls' sadness, we realised that our response was always an activity or discussion that emphasised positivity to help them fix or cope with their pain. We rarely let them be sad, angry, or frustrated without a structured response or activity to intervene and essentially turn it off. In the second year, we aimed for more open conversation and a participant directed curriculum. We started the year gathering for what we called, *Sister Circles*. During *Sister Circles* we sat together in a circle, the girls were engaged in many focus group styled planning sessions to brainstorm girl empowerment hot topics, skills, strategies, and activities. When we allowed them this freedom in guiding the conversations, the most common themes and topics highlighted in the data reveal the ways in which many of the girls experience a dual impact of racist and sexist oppression. These gatherings generated conversations about the desire to deal mostly with social frustrations at school and the issues primarily relevant to race and gender. Data characterises the voices, laughter, silliness and pain through quotes and conversations captured in field notes and sometimes displayed on chart paper. Thematic narratives derived from quotes recorded in field notes and discussions that followed were found to be most relevant to (1) negative teacher–student relationships and (2) policed bodies and sexual objectification.

Racism and teacher–student relationships. One of the most striking conversations and a repeated hot topic at *Sister Circles* was that of the girls' stories about and perceptions of their White teachers.

> Straight up ... White teachers are racist! (8th grader)

> There is something about the way they [White teachers] always 'ook at us [Black students]. I can't explain it ... it's like they expect us to fail. (6th grader)

> I get extra time on tests and this one teacher seemed annoyed and she kind of gave me a look ... a look like she was implying that I wouldn't do well (6th grader)

One girl breaks a silence by asking 'Why do White people think they can just touch my hair without asking?' (5th grader) ... she grabbed her long extension braids, sucking her teeth and smiling while everyone laughed. Another girl adds 'I'm crackin' up because I had a teacher who always used to touch my hair until I was finally like, excuse me .... Uh, this is not a petting zoo' (8th grader). Their stories were followed by so much laughter the girls were rolling all over the rug.

The girls continued to share stories and express various emotions about these interactions with teachers and started discussing the injustices imbedded in disciplinary practices:

> When we're in groups of 2 or 3 or don't let it be 6 of us … we get in trouble. They say we're too loud, but it's just the sight of us (7th grader).
>
> Racism has so much to do with how things go down … consequences at school are different if you're Black … You can always witness White kids breaking the rules … it's ignored (8th graders).

Policed bodies and sexual objectification.

> And if you're Black AND a girl, the dress code is different for you too … even though our bodies are not all the same … right? … it still feels like a dress code for Black girl bodies (8th grader).
>
> It's always the girl's fault. We fight each other … jealous over stupid stuff like whose gotta bigger booty [everyone laughed] … we turn into entertainment for boys (7th grader).
>
> The other day at school this boy called me a THOT! [that hoe over there] (4th grader).

Sister Circle time offered the girls an opportunity to elaborate on the feelings associated with these statements and experiences. They were encouraged to analyze their responses and sometimes brainstorm different responses as a group. They also seemed very interested in learning about the history or potential explanations for these experiences, as we defined stereotypes, racism (individual and institutional), discussed White privilege, perceptions of Blackness, historical conditions of Blackness, as well as, sexism and sexual objectification reinforced in social media. Every conversation was unfortunately cut short, as the girls were eager to continue sharing their stories, ask questions, and brainstorm future responses to similar circumstances in their lives.

***My Black girlhood* – identity memo #2**

Growing up in a predominantly White neighbourhood, I remember being no more than five years old when a little White girl asked me if I could wash my skin colour off and suggested that I try. While taking a bath, I told my parents about it and asked why I would ever want to wash off the colour of my skin. To support my curiosity and to help prevent it from turning into sadness, anger, or self-hatred, my parents responded by plastering my room walls with some of the most beautiful, intelligent, talented, and transformative Black women from history and the present. Despite my constant exposure to White girlhood as the standard of beauty and intellect, I grew up with Black Cabbage Patch dolls, reciting 'The Wiz' instead of 'The Wizard of Oz', and other positive self-images that helped to normalise Blackness and girlhood. In my experiences, with the power of White supremacy and patriarchal dominance embedded in structures (e.g. curriculum) and existing in some of the mildest daily interactions, it sometimes takes emotional effort to choose my battles – to decide when to correct or educate someone, to argue, or to simply walk away. Rooted in sadness, I think anger and rage develops when we do not have or use effective strategies for coping or addressing dehumanising experiences. Given the vulnerability in Black girlhood, I think my parents put an extra effort into processing and exposing me to the struggles and greatness of Black girlhood. They wanted to ensure that as part of my identity development and overall humanness, my collective identity as a Black girl was something to be proud of.

For me, Black girlhood does not have one meaning or illustrate one specific experience. With so many differences and similarities to celebrate and understand about Black girls and women throughout the world, we represent multiple experiences of privilege and disadvantages relevant to access and resources, such as economic and educational capital. The concept of intersectionality teaches that various elements of our identity (class, sexuality, ability, and faith) are simultaneously operating and help to explain our experiences and perceptions of the world as human beings. However, when addressing on sight and immediate encounters with the outside world, we are immediately 'Black' and 'female'. The combined identity can represent both cultural links of joy and shared stories of inequity relevant to our Black girlhood and womanhood. Too often, negative perceptions, stereotypes, and structurally reinforced conditions for Black girls and women calls for a targeted focus and a united understanding towards liberating Black girls from a commonly inequitable existence.

In an effort to combat negative images or perceptions of Black girlhood, the foundation of my girl empowerment experience started in a predominantly Black Girl Scout troupe at a local community centre, led by my mother and a number of other Black mothers with their daughters. My mother and several of, what I like to call, my community mothers raised us with high expectations and gave us exposure to girl empowerment work, civic responsibility, college and career mentors, and cultural capital. Additional local programmes and activities throughout my childhood provided opportunities to have pride in my identity. Similar to what my home represented for me, I now understand how girl empowerment curricula and opportunities were healing and healthy spaces for processing many experiences including those relevant to race and gender at school or, in other areas of our lives.

My personal and professional passion involves the creating of curriculum and spaces that offer authentic decision-making, problem solving, and even healing. With all of the ambition and energy in my early years as a school psychologist and as one of the only staff members of colour, I was often coined as the one to deal with the 'problem' children, who were mostly Black, and because I was the one with the 'relationship' with the children and their families (code for I wasn't in fear of the parents), I could handle it. Often one of few willing to take the time to genuinely get to know families, I found myself dealing with many disciplinary issues relevant to power struggles between adults and children, commonly White teachers and Black students. Issues that consumed my practice were teachers common concerns across elementary, middle, and high school about the behaviour of Black girls. More specifically, teachers were reporting behaviours of 'defiance', 'disrespect', or 'insubordination' with notes typically relevant to the student having an 'attitude' and 'defying authority'. Many girls would be sent to my office at school or would be their by choice to process school dynamics with me after school. I would give them a loving lecture about respectful communication with people and bla bla bla … while they respectfully restrained themselves from rolling their eyes and then they would often repeat, 'But … You should have HEARD the way she TALKED to me!!!' We would then brainstorm responses to this form of communication or ways to prevent it.

I understood what they were talking about, but my level of empathy for them dramatically increased last fall when I personally experienced the harsh communication that the girls often complained about receiving from their teachers. I was walking down the middle school hallway after dropping off a house key to my son at lunch. The fire alarm went off.

Children scurried in military lines while teachers frantically galloped down the halls assuring everyone that it was a drill, but encouraging them to take it seriously. As I walked out of the building to my car, I passed a line of middle school children. A short, heavy-set White woman with long grey hair and glasses rushed up behind my head and screamed in a disgustingly angry tone … 'WHAT are you DOING!' My body clenched and then I slowly turned around with the look that I give my children that says 'Have you lost your mind?' She looked back at me and said, 'Oh, you're a parent' and walked away with no apology. I was beyond irritated. My son was humiliated … and all I can clearly remember as I processed the situation with others was me repeating, 'But … You should have HEARD the way she TALKED to me!!!' I experienced (over the course of doing this study) the exact harsh treatment that the girls often describe. This teacher thought I was a 13-year old Black girl and hollered at me with such disrespect, aggression, and ultimately with a dehumanising tone. It was violent. It was gross. With this striking verbal attack, my immediate reaction was to protect my body. It was not a safe or pleasant feeling by any means.

When I think about this idea of the Super-Girl, I think that she is constantly navigating her response to regularly demeaning social experiences that permeate many of her days. I too, engage in an on-going processing of my responses to the strength and sadness in my life as a Black woman. I too, am Super-Girl. This early exploration of the Super-Girl is a metaphorical tool for combatting experiences relevant to racist and sexist oppression in an effort to develop a curriculum of liberation. I consider it a responsibility and honour to continue learning, brainstorming, accessing resources, and offering opportunities that benefit Black girls in developing healthy identities while navigating their social realities.

Implications and recommendations for liberating Black girls

This paper encourages and recognises the urgency to conduct research that highlights the daily experiences of Black girls and how they can better be supported through girl empowerment work. Girl empowerment programmes and interventions can provide evidence-based strategies to improve social support, self-efficacy, self-esteem, locus of control, optimism, and body image. In reflecting on the need to target and liberate Black females, a major theme in Malcolm X's 1960's speeches taught that a Black woman is the most disrespected, neglected, and least protected person in America. In order to not embody a negative identity or see oneself as a constant, powerless social victim, a healing process and opportunity to liberate Black girls through girl empowerment curricula can begin to serve as a solution.

Recommended girl empowerment work elements/activities:

(1) Engage in activities that help girls identify/name personal characteristics, how they see themselves, how they want to see themselves, and examine how much derived from internal or external forces.
(2) Encourage girls to discuss what it means to be a girl and where their ideas and perceptions come from. Begin to provide safe spaces and activities to help girls examine body image coupled with activities to help reconstruct existing negative images.
(3) Teach critical thinking and consumption of media and popular culture (e.g. analysing messages from the news, music videos, movie roles, advertisements, social media, etc.). The girls should be encouraged to ask questions and examine ideas.

(4) Provide a history lesson on intersectionality, introducing Anna Julia Cooper and other trailblazers (such as Sojourner Truth, Mary Church Terrell, and Amanda Berry) who broke the silent suffering of Black girls and women. Teach how their efforts and strategies addressed the oppression and need for liberation relevant to race, gender, class, and various intersecting socially constructed realities.
(5) Offer positive self-images of women (e.g. guest speakers, video clips, readings). Expose girls to opportunities provided in college and potential careers to help ignite their passion for learning and making a healthy contribution to society.
(6) Teach social justice and activism. Strengthen the girl's social and political awareness that incorporates an anti-racist, feminist perspective. Teach concepts that help them understand power, privilege, and oppression in society.
(7) Teach and brainstorm problem-solving processes that aide in effective decision-making, while establishing safe spaces to name sadness and frustration in their lives, but particularly at school.
(8) Provide a strong sense of social support through bonding and sisterhood activities that help to strengthen their communal connection and responsibility to one another.

Honouring intersectionality and attending to the complexities of being a Black girl, this work supports scholars' suggestions for a healing and empowering source of intervention (Austin 1995; Evans-Winters and Esposito 2010; Perry, Pullen, and Oser 2012). To address strength and sadness in a liberating manner, girl empowerment work can provide healthy identity development and self-understanding in Black girlhood.

Conclusions

Despite the research highlighting elevated levels of self-esteem for Black girls (Buckley and Carter 2005), we illustrate a phenomenon of the *Super-Girl*, to describe an on-going balance and imbalance of strength and sadness. With the guidance of grounded theory, this study highlights the need to recognise strength and sadness as structural constants and individual experiences. The results inform future girl empowerment curricula aimed to foster resilience and enhance personal/social transformation, including: strategies for coping, decision-making/problem solving, mood regulation, positive body image, and personal strength identification and execution. Though high self-esteem is a critical quality of development, it cannot stand alone when encountering individual and institutional gendered racism. The results also suggest a need to incorporate lessons on power, privilege and oppression to help explain the historical and present nature of their self-understanding and experiences. This study encourages girl empowerment curricular designs and research that provide Black girls with tools and strategies as they navigate their school and social realities.

Disclosure statement

No potential conflict of interest was reported by the author.

References

Adams, P. E. 2010. "Understanding the Different Realities, Experience, and use of Self-Esteem Between Black and White Adolescent Girls." *Journal of Black Psychology* 36 (3): 255–276.

Angelou, M. 1978. *And Still I Rise*. New York: Random House.

Asbury, C. A. 1978. "Cognitive Factors Related to Discrepant Arithmetic Achievement of White and Black First Graders." *Journal of Negro Education* 47 (4): 337–342.

Aud, S., M. Fox, and A. Kewal-Ramani. (2010). "Status and Trends in the Education of Racial and Ethnic Groups (NCES 2010–2015)." U.S. Department of Education, National Center for Education Statistics. Washington, DC: U.S. Government Printing Office.

Austin, R. 1995. "Sapphire Bound!" In *Critical Race Theory: The Key Writings that Formed the Movement*, edited by K. Crenshaw, N. Gotanda, G. Peller, and K. Thomas, 426–437. New York: The New Press.

Bell, D. 1992. "Racial Realism." *Connecticut Law Review* 24: 363–379.

Blake, J., B. Butler, C. Lewis, and A. Darensbourg. 2011. "Unmasking the Inequitable Discipline Experiences of Urban Black Girls: Implications for Urban Educational Stakeholders." *Urban Review* 43 (1): 90–106.

Brown, R. N. 2013. *Hear our Truths: The Creative Potential of Black Girlhood*. Urbana: University of Illinois Press.

Buckley, T. R., and R. T. Carter. 2005. "Black Adolescent Girls: Do Gender Role and Racial Identity: Impact Their Self-Esteem?" *Sex Roles* 53 (9–10): 647–661.

Charmaz, K. 2006. *Constructing Grounded Theory*. London: Sage.

Christian, J., and S. S. Thomas. 2009. "Examining the Intersection of Race, Gender, and Mass Imprisonment." *Journal of Ethnicity in Criminal Justice* 7 (1): 69–84.

Clark, M. L. 1982. "Racial Group Concept and Self-Esteem in Black Children." *Journal of Black Psychology* 8 (2): 75–88.

Collins, P. H. 2000. *Black Feminist thought: Knowledge, Consciousness, and the Politics of Empowerment*. 2nd ed. New York, NY: Routledge.

Crenshaw, K. 1989. *Demarginalizing the Intersection of Race and Sex: A Black Feminist Critique of Antidiscrimination Doctrine, Feminist Theory and Antiracist Politics*. 139–167. Chicago, IL: University of Chicago Legal Forum.

Crenshaw, K. W. 1991. "Mapping the Margins: Intersectionality, Identity Politics, and Violence Against Women of Color." In *Critical Race Theory: The Key Writings that Formed the Movement*, edited by K. Crenshaw, N. Gotanda, G. Peller, and K. Thomas, 357–384. New York: The New Press.

Creswell, J. W. 2013. *Qualitative Inquiry and Research Design: Choosing among Five Approaches*. 3rd ed. Los Angeles, CA: Sage.

Davis, J. 2013. "Disproportionate Juvenile Minority Confinement: A State-Level Assessment of Racial Threat." *Youth Violence and Juvenile Justice* 11 (4): 296–312.

Delgado, R. 1989. "Storytelling for Oppositionists and Others: A Plea for Narrative." *Michigan Law Review* 87: 2411–2441.

Delgado, Bernal D. 2002. "Critical Race Theory, Latino Critical Theory, and Critical Race-Gendered Epistemologies: Recognizing Students of Color as Holders and Creators of Knowledge." *Qualitative Inquiry* 8 (1): 105–126.

Delgado R., and J. Stefancic. 2000. Introduction. In *Critical Race Theory: The Cutting Edge*, edited by R. Delgado and J. Stefancic, 2nd ed., xv–xix. Philadelphia: Temple University Press.

Delgado, R., and J. Stefancic. 2012. *Critical Race Theory: An Introduction*. 2nd ed. New York: New York University Press.

Evans-Winters, V. 2005. *Teaching Black Girls: Resiliency in Urban Classrooms*. New York: Peter Lang.

Evans-Winters, V. E., and J. Esposito. 2010. "Other People's Daughters: Critical Race Feminism and Black Girls' Education." *Educational Foundations* 24 (1): 11–24.

Ford, D. Y. 1994. "Underachievement Among Gifted and Non-Gifted Black Females: A Study of Perceptions." *Journal of Secondary Girted Education* 6 (2): 165–175.

Ford, M. 2013. "The Impact of School Board Governance on Academic Achievement in Diverse States." Theses and diss., University of Wisconsin Milwaukee.

Fordham, S. 1993. "Those Loud Black Girls: (Black) Women, Silence, and Passing in the Academy." *Anthropology and Education Quarterly* 30 (3): 272–293.

Fordham, S. 1996. *Blacked Out: Dilemmas of Race, Identity, and Success at Capital High*. Chicago: University of Chicago Press.

Goldberg, L. R. 1999. "A Broad-Bandwidth, Public Domain, Personality Inventory Measuring the Lower-Level Facets of Several Five-Factor Models." In *Personality Psychology in Europe*, edited by I. Mervielde, I. Deary, F. De Fruyt, and F. Ostendorf, Vol. 7, 7–28. Tilburg: Tilburg University Press.

Hogg, R. S., E. F. Druyts, S. Burris, E. Drucker, and S. A. Strathdee. 2008. "Years of Life Lost to Prison: Racial and Gender Gradients in the United States of America." *Harm Reduction Journal* 5 (4): 1–4.

hooks, b. 1981. *Ain't I a Woman: Black Women and Feminism*. Cambridge, MA: South End Press.

hooks, b. [1984] 2000. *Feminist Theory: From Margin to Center*. Cambridge, MA: South End Press.

Jaffee, L., and J. Mahle Lutter. 1995. " Adolescent Girls: Factors Influencing low and High Body Image." *Melpomene Journal* 14 (2): 14–22.

Koonce, J. B. 2012. "'Oh, Those Loud Black Girls!': A Phenomenological Study of Black Girls Talking with an Attitude." *Journal of Language and Literacy Education* 8 (2): 26–46.

Kunjufu, J. 1982. *Countering the Conspiracy to Destroy Black Boys*. Chicago, IL: African American Images.

Kunjufu, J. 2005. *Keeping Black Boys out of Special Education*. Chicago, IL: African American Images.

Landson-Billings, G. 2011. "Boyz to Men? Teaching to Restore Black Boys' Childhood." *Race, Ethnicity and Education* 14 (1): 7–15.

Lindergren, E. C., A. Baigi, E. Apitzch, and H. Bergh. 2011. "Impact of a Six-Month Empowerment-Based Exercise Intervention Program in Non-Physically Active Adolescent Swedish Girls." *Health Education Journal* 70 (1): 9–20.

Maxwell, J. A. 2005. *Qualitative Research Design: An Interactive Approach*. 2nd ed. Thousand Oaks, CA: Sage.

Milkie, M. A. 1999. "Social Comparisons, Reflected Appraisals, and Mass Media: The Impact of Pervasive Beauty Images on Black and White Girls' Self-Concepts." *Social Psychology Quarterly* 62 (2): 190–210.

Nicolas, G., J. E. Helms, M. M. Jernigan, T. Sass, A. Skrzypek, and A. M. DeSilva. 2008. "A Conceptual Framework for Understanding the Strengths of Black Youths." *Journal of Black Psychology* 34 (3): 261–280.

Noguera, P. 1997. "Reconsidering the Crisis Confronting California Black Male Youth: Providing Support Without Further Marginalization." *Journal of Negro Education* 65: 219–236.

Noguera, P. 2008. *The Trouble with Black Boys: … And Other Reflections on Race, Equity, and the Future of Public Education*. San Francisco, CA: Jossey-Bass Press.

Noland, S. A., J. Arnold, and P. Clement. 1980. "Self-Reinforcement by Under-Achieving, Under-Controlled Girls." *Psychological Reports* 47: 671–678.

Nyongo, L. 2014. "The Speech that Has Everyone Talking." *Essence Magazine*, May, p. 93.

O'Connor, C. 1997. "Dispositions Toward (Collective) Struggle and Educational Resilience in the Inner City: A Case Analysis of Six African American High School Students." *American Educational Research Journal* 34: 593–629.

Payne, Y. A., and T. Brown. 2010. "The Educational Experiences of Street-Life-Oriented Black Boys: How Black Boys Use Street Life as a Site of Resilience in High School." *Journal of Contemporary Criminal Justice* 26 (3): 316–338.

Perry, B. L., E. L. Pullen, and C. B. Oser. 2012. "Too Much of a Good Thing? Psychosocial Resources, Gendered Racism, and Suicidal Ideation Among Low Socioeconomic Status African American Women." *Social Psychology Quarterly* 75 (4): 334–359.

Price, A. J. 2011. "Power, Culture, and Dress Codes: Schooling and the Regulation of the Black Male Body." Paper presented at the annual meeting of the 35th Annual National Council for Black Studies, Cincinnati, OH.

Roberts, D. 1998. *Killing the Black Body: Race, Reproduction and the Meaning of Liberty*. New York: Vintage Books.

Solorzano, D., and T. Yosso. 2002. "Critical Race Methodology: Counterstorytelling as an Analytical Framework for Education Research." *Qualitative Inquiry* 8 (1): 23–44.

Strauss, A., and J. Corbin. 1998. *Basics of Qualitative Research: Techniques and Procedures for Developing Grounded Theory*. 2nd ed. Thousand Oaks, CA: Sage.

Tonnesen, S. C. 2013. "'Hit It and Quit It': Responses to Black Girls', Victimization in School." *Berkeley Journal of Gender, Law & Justice* 28 (1): 1–28.

Unlocking Opportunity for African American Girls: A Call to Action for Educational Equity. 2014. "Report presented by National Women's Law Center and the NAACP Legal Defense and Educational Fund, Inc." September 19, Obtained online. http://www.naacpldf.org/files/publications/Unlocking%20Opportunity%20for%20African%20American%20Girls%20-Executive%20Summary_0.pdf.

Wade, T. J. 1996. "The Relationships Between Skin Color and Self-Perceived Global, Physical, and Sexual Attractiveness, and Self-Esteem for African Americans." *Journal of Black Psychology* 22 (3): 358–373.

Waldron, L. M. 2011. "'Girls Are Worse': Drama Queens, Ghetto Girls, Tomboys, and the Meaning of Girl Fights." *Youth & Society* 43 (4): 1298–1334.

Wilkins, A. C. 2013. "Review of Learning the Hard Way: Masculinity, Place, and the Gender Gap in Education." *Gender & Society* 27 (6): 939–940.

Reparative readings: re-claiming black feminised bodies as sites of somatic pleasures and possibilities

Esther O. Ohito and Shenila Khoja-Moolji

ABSTRACT

Black girls and women in the west reside at the nexus of racism and sexism, pinned down by a vitriolic hate for the black feminised body that is wedded to legacies of slavery. Dominant discourses configure these bodies as animalistic and other (than human), thus informing a range of (educational) policies, practices, and programmes. These narratives shape teachers' curricular and pedagogical practices in ways that potentially objectify and wound black girls. In this paper, we use Andrea Lee's *Sarah Phillips* [Lee, Andrea. 1984. *Sarah Phillips*. Boston, MA: Northeastern University Press] and Danzy Senna's *Caucasia* [Senna, Danzy. 1999. *Caucasia*. New York: Riverhead] to trouble said dominant discourses by engaging in 'reparative readings' [Sedgwick, Eve. 2003. *Touching Feeling: Affect, Pedagogy, Performativity*. Durham: Duke University Press Books] of the texts' black female protagonists. We re-read these main characters' bodies as sites of pleasure and possibility, not singularly or solely harm. In doing so, we show how curriculum theorising can be mobilised for repair, and can function to humanise othered and marginalised bodies.

Yonder they do not love your flesh. They despise it
You got to love it, you!
[L]ove it, love it … For this is the prize.

– Baby Suggs (Morrison [1987] 2004, 101)

A melee is unfolding at a fast-food restaurant in Brooklyn, a borough in New York City. It is a violent altercation among a group of black teenagers, all believed to be students at a nearby high school, which is located in this bustling metropolis of the United States. The crowd watches from the perimeter of the imaginary ring, filling the thin spring air with cheers and jeers as several black girls led by 16-year-old Aniah Ferguson hurl blows and kicks that dent 15-year-old Ariana Taylor's flesh (Quad8 2015). Fists and feet fly furiously and unceasingly until Ariana lies still, knocked unconscious. An inquisitive onlooker captures video footage of the incident. Soon thereafter, this footage goes viral, flooding first social

---

This article was originally published with errors. This version has been corrected. Please see Corrigendum (http://dx.doi.org/10.1080/09540253.2016.1264686)

media avenues, then formal news channels. Reports from these mainstream outlets are as disconcerting and disheartening as the incident itself. Descriptions of the black girls as 'savage' (Edwards 2015) and 'brute' (Badia et al. 2015) are uttered. These weighted labels – long anchored to and associated with black bodies – are demonstrative of 'misogynoir' (Bailey 2010), the unique amalgamation of anti-blackness, racism, and sexism that is directed at black women in the western world. These words are seeds in the grounds in which the dominant discourse about black girls and women that reduces this population to barbaric, grotesque, and uncouth are planted, and then fertilised by a peculiarly vitriolic brand of hate. A noteworthy feature of the reporting on this squabble is the attention paid to Aniah's body, which is left semi-clothed because a ripped shirt leaves her chest exposed and covered only by a bra. In fact, one commentator notes that perhaps this video receives widespread attention precisely due to the visibility of her body and the bareness of her flesh.

The reasons for the fracas described are less significant to us than the media's portrayal of the black girls that are trapped within its borders. This is because the black girl's body has historically been articulated as an aberration, thus informing a range of current educational policies, practices, and programmes. These include curricular choices and pedagogies that configure the black girl as object, thus making her susceptible to racial violence in classrooms and schools (Boston and Baxley 2007; Pinder 2008). In this article, we attend to how the black feminised body as produced through discourse impinges upon this body as lived-in. Using feminist perspectives on corporeality alongside Sedgwick's (2003) notion of reparative reading as our theoretical foundation, we focus on the racialised body inhabited by the black girl in its fleshy presence and *re*-read this body as a site of pleasures and possibilities. By foregrounding the interaction of race and gender in corporeal formation, we respond to feminist scholars such as Spelman (1982) who argues that, 'bodies are always *particular* bodies … We cannot seriously attend to the social significance attached to embodiment without recognizing this' [emphasis added] (128). We *re*-view – or look at and look again at – the scorn underlying the discourses for *particular* bodies that are raced as black and gendered as girl or woman (Hill Collins [1997] 2007; Morrison [1987] 2004; Spelman 1982) by taking up two novels: Andrea Lee's *Sarah Phillips* (1984) and Danzy Senna's *Caucasia* (1999).

We centre the flesh when re-viewing *Sarah Phillips* (Lee 1984) and *Caucasia* (Senna 1999) to excavate potentials and knowledges about black, female bodies that are often bypassed or made invisible in and through dominant discourses. Our posture then explicitly aims to resist persistent productions of black girls' bodies as abject and animalistic. Our analysis acknowledges and resists the troubling normative narratives about black feminised bodies pervasive in western discourses broadly, and in schools especially. We focus on how feminist attentiveness to these bodies as texts (Baszile 2008) – and their imbrication with other bodies – may initiate openness toward seeing and knowing the multifariousness of black girls and women. Moreover, we motion towards a re-visioning of these raced and gendered bodies that may re-shape curricular and pedagogical practices. This, we contend, may expand possibilities for who Aniah, Ariana, and other black girls like them might become in classrooms and schools – and how they might somatically experience and, indeed, *love* their bodies in pedagogical spaces – as well as how they might be seen and experienced beyond the limits of discourses that reduce their richly nuanced and expansive selves to singularly 'savage.'

We theorise black bodies as 'weeping, living, hurting' (Bakare-Yusuf 1999, 313), thus allowing us to pay attention to scenes of encounters within *Sarah Phillips* (Lee 1984) and *Caucasia* (Senna 1999) steeped in the characters' experiences of the flesh, and to highlight the implications of the embroilment of race and gender that attention to black feminised bodies illuminates. In other words, instead of seeing black feminised bodies as *already* distinct and determined by defined and static boundaries, we show how they are always *becoming* – how their surfaces are repeatedly re-constituted upon contact with other bodies (Ahmed 2000, 2004; Weiss 1999), how they are (re)made in and through this contact, and how their intimate connections to other bodies produce dynamic subjectivities. Our readings offer theoretical and pedagogical apparatus for educators to utilise when endeavouring to re-read the black feminised body and to re-claim it from its constitution as repugnant and 'other' (than human) in pedagogical settings.

Summarising the texts under analysis

Our two text selections are contemporary additions to curricula investigations into the complex role of corporeal visibility in the development of racial identity. With regard to blackness, this relationship between who one 'is' and who one is perceived to be based on the racially marked body is captured most explicitly in the notion of 'passing' (Hobbs 2014; Rummel 2007). In literature, this aged inquiry has been undertaken by (black) writers in canonical works such as *The Autobiography of an Ex-Colored Man* (Johnson [1912] 1995), *Cane* (Toomer [1923] 2011), and *Passing* (Larsen [1929] 2007), which are staples in middle and high schools across the United States as part of English Language Arts curricula. In this section, we offer an overview of *Sarah Phillips* (Lee 1984) and *Caucasia* (Senna 1999) in order to foreshadow our examination of scenes of interest, and to establish rationale for the theoretical approach and methods of inquiry used in our forthcoming analyses.

Set in the 1970s, *Sarah Phillips* (Lee 1984) traces instances in the life of the eponymously named protagonist, who describes herself as 'tall and lanky and light-skinned, quite pretty' (4). The reader accompanies Sarah as she grows up in a middle-class neighbourhood in Philadelphia, Pennsylvania, graduates from Harvard University, an elite institution in the United States, and then sets out to experience life as an expatriate in Europe. *Caucasia* (Senna 1999), which is also set in the 1970s, is written from the perspective of Birdie Lee, the teenaged girl-child of a black, male professor and a white woman. Birdie's parents are involved in the Civil Rights Movement but in different ways: her father writes about it, while her mother occupies a more traditionally activist stance. Birdie is Cole's younger sister. Cole is easily ascribed blackness because of her dark skin, which contrasts Birdie's light-coloured skin. This difference in complexion becomes especially significant when Birdie's mother lands in legal trouble and her parents elect to split the family. Birdie, as the bearer of skin that gives her bodily access to whiteness, joins her white mother on the lam, and Cole attaches to her black father. Birdie masks her identity by assuming that of a white, Jewish girl. She adopts new moniker, Jesse, along with new stories about family, school, and life events. Readers learn about Birdie's tenuous transformation into Jesse, and witness her grappling with the tension between a stable inner black 'self' and the volatile outward appearance of a body that others mostly mark as visibly white.

Sarah Phillips (Lee 1984) and *Caucasia* (Senna 1999) appeal to us because they depart from the ways in which we expect to find black women and girls portrayed in novels – that is, as victims of the violence of racism and sexism, and/or as disempowered receptacles, unable to address, redress, and resist such and other forms of harm. In other words, the novels *surprise* us in their depiction of black girls and women. As such, these texts give us fodder with which to challenge entrenched curricular representations of black girls and women as deficient and lacking (power).

Curricula representations of black feminised bodies

Generally, there are few frames in and through which black feminised bodies become sensible vis-à-vis racial and gender identity in both fiction and nonfiction curricula texts. Literature, for example, offers endless examples of black women and girls as lascivious, licentious objects – reincarnations of Mammy or Aunt Jemima, the sexless, passive nurturer; Jezebel, the harlot; and Sapphire, the aggressor (Hill Collins 1999; Jewell 1993; West [2008] 2012). Hill Collins (1999) argues that, 'Portraying African American women as stereotypical mammies, matriarch, welfare recipients, and hot mommas has been essential to the political economy of domination fostering Black women's oppression' (142). It has also been integral to the birth of the 'politics of respectability' (Gross 1997) in black (American) culture. As Gross (1997) explains, 'Claiming respectability through manners and morality furnished an avenue for African Americans to assert the will and agency to redefine themselves outside the prevailing racist discourses' (para. 3). However, the 'ideological nature [of the politics of respectability] constituted a deliberate concession to mainstream societal values.' In other words, the 'politics of respectability' rely upon whiteness as the measuring stick for digestible forms of black woman-ness, and therefore contribute to the 'political economy of domination fostering Black women's oppression.' These politics inform many contemporary texts, wherein the prototypical black woman – as represented by Mammy – is reborn. In these curricula worlds, only this black woman is recognisable as valorous; that is, only she heralds the passivity and piousness that is constitutive of acceptable black womanhood. As such, these 'politics of respectability' institute standards for black womanhood that sort black girls and women, legitimising some – often those who are middle and upper class – and delegitimising others, often those who are poor and working class (Pickens 2014; White 2001).

In addition to Mammy, Jezebel, and Sapphire, the 'tragic mulatto' is a trope common in novels about racial identity in relationship to black feminised bodies. Although she is the offspring of one black and one white parent, the colour of her skin allows her to be read as white. She can 'pass,' and therefore rattle seemingly fixed racial categories. Yet she also suffers internal conflicts – as well as the trauma of rejection and even the ultimate fate of death – which spin from her insatiable longing for an unattainable 'pure' whiteness (Caspary 1929). In other words, she, too – like Mammy, Jezebel, and Sapphire – is a sorry figure.

In the context of education post 1970s, curricula texts commonly arouse the pitying of black girls by featuring this group as dejectedly poor or working class, unwed and pregnant, uneducated, addicted to drugs, and/or stricken with disease resulting from promiscuity (Pinder 2008). This is the stark backdrop against which hooks (1992) advocates for the consumption of said curricula texts through an 'oppositional gaze,' or one that resists locking black girls and women into a fractional humanity. Woyshner (2006) offers a similar recommendation, suggesting that pedagogues might engage critically with these already-circulating images. Woyshner encourages teachers to deconstruct existing popular representations of women with attention to which dimensions of identity are included and excluded, and with a goal of enhancing students' visual literacies. The dearth of diverse images of black girlhood and womanhood in books that are found in schools is pointed to by Boston and Baxley (2007). Boston and Baxley note that there is a need for such diversity given research linking black girls' development of positive self-conceptions to exposure to positive textual representations of black femininity. We echo Boston and Baxley's (2007) call for increased multidimensional portrayals of black girls and women; however, in line with hooks and Woyshner, we find promise and (em) power(ment) in performing different readings of Lee's (1984) Sarah and Senna's (1999) Birdie, fictional personifications that contrast the dominant incarnations of black feminised bodies that are currently floating freely in and through curriculum.

Theoretical overview

Reading the body

The Cartesian mind/body dualism has been a sturdy philosophical and conceptual assumption in much western writing (Spelman 1982). Here, the mind, which is representative of rationality/reason, is privileged when compared to the body, which reflects affect/ emotion. This binary is raced and gendered, as are those in the margins who have historically been assumed to be made of and driven by 'primitive' bodily desires and emotions (Oyěwùmí 1997; Spelman 1982). As Oyěwùmí (1997) explains, the 'other' then, occupies a *particular* body. Broadly, scholarship on the body approaches the corpus either as exclusively biological or as absolutely socially constructed. These conceptualisations of the body matter for how it is studied. The latter view – body as a social configuration – often leads researchers to overlook the material body and emphasise the contexts of its production and operation; whereas the former – body as natural – limits researchers to exploring the biology of the body (Bordo 1993). The postmodern turn has meant the ascendancy of the perception of the body as socially constructed, which has therefore entailed homogenising its experiences. However, scholars from various feminist traditions have called for more nuanced attention to the body. Some have focused distinctly on the corporeal dimensions that frame individuals' experiences of the world within a particular point of view. This has required attending to experiences of bodies as raced, gendered, classed, religioned, ethnicised, and otherwise identified. These bodies are, of course, felt and lived along the edges of longer histories. We situate ourselves within this lineage of scholarship that seeks to accentuate resources – for joy, love, and, ultimately, healing and repair – from and for the black feminised body. Our mode of inquiry is anchored by Hill Collins' ([1997] 2007) consideration of race and gender inequities as linked by a common 'disdain for the body' (398). Therefore, our engagement with bodies in these literary texts intentionally works against dominant (mis)readings by illustrating the capacities, as opposed to deficits, of black feminised bodies for our protagonists and for us, as both readers and researchers.

In addition to Hill Collins' ([1997] 2007) perspective on the body as the corporeal connection of racial and gender oppressions, we hinge our analyses on Spillers' (1987) distinction between the flesh and body in order to embrace the somatic tenor of lived experience. Spillers (1987) argues that 'before the "body" there is the "flesh," that zero degree of social conceptualization that does not escape concealment under the brush of discourse, or the reflexes of iconography' (67). For Spillers, this distinction is vital to recognising the wounding of black flesh during the era of slavery – enacted through the searing of the skin with every lash of the whip, the altering of human tissues, and the rupturing of veins. The separation between human and non-human occurred here. Ergo, enslaved Africans were only flesh, not bodies and, therefore, not humans. The ramifications of this distinction are present in contemporary times. One such implication includes the fact that how the flesh is articulated in and through discourse then translates into how specific raced and gendered bodies are interpreted within frames that place restrictions on who is eligible to be human. To explore how flesh moves into and out of these gendered and raced significations, we rely upon Hall's (1997) theorisation of race as a 'floating signifier.' Hall notes that race does not denote anything permanent or static; instead, it is an always-moving, fluid target that has multiple meanings – meanings that are often determined, again and again, through discursive practices. Our readings of *Sarah Phillips* (Lee 1984) and *Caucasia* (Senna 1999) take up this metaphor to delineate the processes and moments when bodies slip into and out of their racial markings, and capture the effects and feelings that follow. At the same time, we highlight the moments and scenes when racial markings are made into an experiential or observational phenomenon as an effect of specific political and social configurations, including the orientation of the readers as meaning-makers. This hints at the various ways in which flesh is transformed into bodies, and how those bodies are then experienced and interpeted. Our reading resists the association of blackness with 'particular bodies' as always-already-present and shows the contours of its permeability. Most significantly, however, prioritising the fleshiness of bodies gives us the space to explore possibilities of being and becoming (human) that may be freeing for the characters in the texts, for our readers, and for us, as curriculum scholars.

Reparative reading

Our attempt to make ascertainable black feminised raced and gendered bodies as robust producers of pleasures and possibilities is informed by Sedgwick's (2003) advice on reparative reading. A reparative reading directs readers to extract 'sustenance from the objects of a culture – even of a culture whose avowed desire has often been not to sustain them' (Sedgwick 2003, 150). Sedgwick notes that a reader may have many relationships with her object of study, each with different consequences for belief and action. She contrasts paranoid readings, which direct us to critique and expose the operation of power, with reparative readings, which attend to the textures and affects that are mobilised by objects of study. A reparative reading gestures towards possibilities in and through its performativity of knowledge. This approach, as Britzman (2002) notes, is Sedgwick's contribution to the new 'work of theory,' which is indistinguishable from 'the work of love' (123). For our purposes here, we are interested in re-visiting and re-claiming black women's bodies as sites of multiplicity so as to allow for the possibility of deepened understandings of the tie between race and gender as inscribed on bodies. Through the lens that Sedgwick proposes, we embark on an exploration of the embodiment and performance of race in the two texts under consideration, as well as an interrogation of resonant corporeal encounters that are present in the novels.

Reparatively reading black feminised bodies in curricula texts

Utilising these theoretical perspectives in our examination of *Sarah Phillips* (Lee 1984) and *Caucasia* (Senna 1999) draws our focus to scenes of encounters within the novels that take on the main characters' experiences of the flesh. Next, we extend beyond black feminism's response to the aforementioned dominant discourses, which has resulted in a preoccupation with the representation and interpretation of the black feminised body through the 'twin logics of injury and recovery' (Nash 2014, 25). We expand upon this thinking to show how the interembodiment or 'intercorporeality' (Weiss 1999) inherent in these corporeal entanglements provides spaces for black feminised bodies to serve as sites of pleasures and sources of possibilities.

Feminist methods of inquiry

To undertake the work of re-claiming the black feminised body in a western, and therefore, white male-dominated context inevitably entails going against the grain of hegemony. We find two feminist methods – reflexivity and writing – ideal for our aim.

Reading reflexively

Reflexivity, or the act of 'self-critical sympathetic introspection and the self conscious *analytical* scrutiny of the self as researcher' [emphasis in original] (England 1994, 82) is indispensable to us, given our rejection of positivistic notions of objectivity the rationale for which is well-supported in literature on feminist projects such as this. Reflexivity 'induces self-discovery and can lead to insights and new hypotheses about the research questions.' We approach reflexivity as a method (Fook 1999) and utilise it as an instrument with which to investigate fragments of our histories in order to unveil the nature of the investments that we bring to this article. We do so with the recognition that our analyses are inherently partial and unavoidably incomplete. Both of us are 'women of color' who reside in bodies that have been marked as sub-/non-human historically and in the present. That is one reason for our collaboration. In our marginalised positions, we have found room for both subversion and sustenance by pursuing an alliance that has taken form in this joint writing process/project. The significance of this joyous collaboration in the setting of a hostile academy cannot be overstated. It is, therefore, especially pertinent for us as women of colour scholars to centre our raced bodies as we read the novels and struggle to produce meanings from the protagonists' fictional worlds, which are quite contrary to our own embodied realities in our worlds.

Writing reflexively

As alluded to earlier, our selection of *Sarah Phillips* (Lee 1984) and *Caucasia* (Senna 1999) is influenced by our fascination with the authors' portrayals of black women, which feeds our intrigue and curiosities about the novels. We untangled the threads of this attraction by responding to reflexive writing prompts (Luttrell 2010) during the research process, and elaborating on our personal attachments to these texts. We then used our answers to those prompts to inform our writing of stories – that is, our penning of 'narratives that situate one's own writing in other parts of one's … research interests, familial ties, and personal history' (Richardson and St. Pierre 2005, 965). In doing so, we relied upon writing as a method of inquiry (Richardson 2000) in order to link our feminist commitments to a mechanism that allows us to make explicit our belief in the subjectivity of knowledge. Our 'writing voices' (Richardson and St. Pierre 2005, 960) can be heard in the vignettes that follow.

Esther's black be(com)ing

There are a few half- and full-length mirrors in my home. Each is strategically placed in a location that forces my eyes to rest upon it as I scurry, often hurriedly, from one room to the next, typically preoccupied with one thing or the next. Each mirror demands that I pause, often mid-step, and pay complete attention to my reflection. When I do so, my eyes are met by the image of a head of thick, black, rebelliously interwoven hair strands perched atop a buxom body – complete with a rotund posterior – that is clothed in skin the colour of an overly ripe plum. My love for this hair and this body and this skin is actively and continuously cultivated. It is purposeful, and in sharp contrast to the contemptuousness that I amassed for my reflection during the four years that I attended high school in the leafy suburb of a Midwestern city in the United States, when this hair and this body and this skin were juxtaposed against the thin, obedient, often blonde hairs of my white, generally slender-bodied Scandinavian classmates. I felt, paradoxically, hyper- and in-visible in that setting – at once totally exposed and tremendously unknown. However, despite this hair and this body and this skin, I was rather indifferent to blackness as I understood it in my teenaged mind. As a Kenyan immigrant, I treasured the strong cultural connections that I maintained to my specific tribal group – the Luo people – and my country of origin. This was of no consequence to those outside my immediate transnational family and community, who most readily identified me as a black girl/woman, assigning me membership in a racial category to which I had no intrinsic affiliation, and neither a willingness nor a yearning to join. Nevertheless, I *became* black in the United States, and was inextricably bound to this category by how others read what was visible on my corpus. There was no bodily escape. Now, as an adult, blackness is more of a political position than a racial identity – a construct that I opt into and foreground instead of – and sometimes to the detriment to – my Luo-ness, my Kenyan-ness, and my conflicted sense of (African-) American-ness. In the United States, it is also a corporeal certainty that is latched onto this hair and this body and this skin. It is this fascination with the somatic timbre of the gap between how one sees oneself racially and how one is perceived by others that led me to *Sarah Phillips* (Lee 1984) and *Caucasia* (Senna 1999). A range of emotions percolated as I read these texts, and most prominent was the unshakable feeling of envy tinged with awe. I consumed details of the protagonists' winding escapades, page by page, and thought of how incredibly liberating it must be to *love* one's racial body and racial self with such unwavering confidence. Sarah and Birdie present me with visions – albeit complicated ones – of what it may be to 'live free in this black body' (Coates 2015, 8). I am yet to catch that glimpse in my myriad of mirrors, yet still, I look. I look and hope. I am hopeful.

Shenila's embodied marginality

As a brown, immigrant, muslim woman, my body is always-already assumed to be threatened by the violence of muslim men, my religion, my culture, and/or country of origin,

Pakistan. Over time I have tried different ways to become 'visible' in a predominantly white academy which reproduces Eurocentric knowledges – including by aligning myself with scholars who write about Islam, muslims, and the postcolonial condition, perhaps assuming that the contagious effect will enhance my body as it connects with these broader networks, as well as choosing to explicitly write about border concerns often in and through disciplines and lines of inquiry such as feminisms, Islam/muslim cultures, and politics of education that are already-marginalised within the normative field of education. Hence, in addition to my embodied marginality, my writing also creates additional forms of marginality – the latter being an affect of my own political and intellectual investments. Reading the two novels produced a sense of anxiety in me as I tried to grapple with the protagonists' ambivalent relationships to their bodies. Sarah Phillips in particular emerged as a figure that somehow could momentarily transcend the histories of subjugation that became visible in her black body, quite unlike what I have ever been able to do. Her character made me aware of how aware I usually am about the brown-ness of my body, and her nonchalant attitude became an object of desire for me. I, too, want to *embody* a body that does not have to constantly be reminded of its colour. At the same time, the acute consciousness of being raced and moving about the world as a visibly coloured body across the screen of blank, drab, whiteness is an effect of histories of subjugation that bodies like mine seem to have internalised, concretised even. Reading the two novels then illustrated for me what it might look and feel like to have – even fleetingly – a *translucent* body unencumbered by its corporeality.

Finding pleasures and possibilities in black feminised bodies

In line with our theoretical framework and methods, we elucidate episodes in *Sarah Phillips* (Lee 1984) and *Caucasia* (Senna 1999) that fuel open-ended and celebratory readings of black feminised bodies. Gail Weiss' conceptualisation of Merleau-Ponty's notion of 'intercorporeality' is integral to our objective. Weiss (1999) argues that 'the construction of the body and the production of body knowledge is not created within a single, autonomous subject (body) but rather that body knowledge and bodies are created in the intermingling and encounters between bodies' (5), both human and not so. This idea is useful as we highlight specific scenes that signal the malleability of the black raced and gendered body. Hence, we ask: What do black feminised bodies *do* in these novels? What do their entanglements with other bodies make realisable? We briefly introduce select moments in each text before zeroing in on a pivotal scene. In doing so, we name and then elaborate on key findings that surface from our reparative readings: black feminised bodies as sites of pleasures, and locations for possibilities.

Feeling embodied pleasures

In *Sarah Phillips* (Lee 1984), it is Mrs Jeller, an old woman 'brown skinned, with a handsome square face,' (82), who reminds the main character of the consequences of the visibility and materiality of her body. This occurs when Sarah spends a long afternoon visiting Mrs Jeller, swimming in the vivid details of the aged woman's life. After this, Sarah muses as follows: 'I felt very aware of my body under my clothes. For the first time, I was sensing the complicated possibilities of my own flesh – possibilities of corruption, confused pleasure, even death' (85). What becomes apparent is that it is through this interaction with Mrs Jeller that Sarah gains an awareness of how her options for a 'viable life' (Butler 2004) are locked into her body, and its racialised and gendered inscriptions. This awareness percolates years later when Sarah becomes the feature of her white, French boyfriend's arguably cruel story, which tears into her racial self. Henri and his friends deny her entry into the realm of the fully human precisely because they read her body as black, and impose upon it the racial identity that she has spent years alternately ignoring and attempting to transcend. Sarah reports that, 'his silly tale … illuminated for me with blinding clarity the hopeless presumption of trying to discard my portion of America' (Lee 1984, 12). Yet, at the same time, there are moments when Sarah pushes upon the constraints and historical meanings of bodies like hers for the purpose of entertainment. Both Sarah and Henri enjoy 'nigger jokes' (12), and in one instance, she giggles when Roger, Henri's friend, calls her a 'pasteurized Negress' (13). Furthermore, Sarah is quite comfortable with her body. She shows this by playing with its potential as a source of corporeal pleasure and joy. She seems to revel in the knowledge that her body is desired by Henri and his two friends, and casually has sexual escapades with all three men. In this polyamorous situation, Sarah is the architect of her own sensual pleasure, exhibiting sexual freedom typically viewed as out of reach for the proper black woman, whose primary concern is expected to be pious chastity, as demanded by the 'politics of respectability' through which her actions are filtered.

A core scene in this novel signals Sarah's controlled deployment of her flesh for the purpose of her own and others' somatic ecstasy. Sarah explains that sometimes when she and the three men would return home late 'bored and dreamy,' (6) they would play a game they called Galatea. When reminiscing about her participation in this game, Sarah remembers that: 'I stood naked on a wooden box and turned slowly to have my body appraised and criticized', (6–7). Sarah's words conjure up accounts of the trading of black bodies during the Atlantic slave trade, where enslaved Africans were displayed in public squares, serving as walking advertisements for purchase by buyers who could abuse – that is, poke, prod, pull, push, slice, or strike – their skin and flesh with abandon. Additionally, this scene makes an intertextual reference to French artist Louis François Charon's rendering of another Sarah: Sarah 'Saartjie' Baartman (Figure 1). Completed in 1815, the drawing shows three white men, one white woman, and a dog staring with what we read as a mixture of curiosity and anthropological fascination at Saartjie's body, which – like Sarah's during the game of Galatea – is elevated by a wooden box (britishmuseum.org).

Born circa 1789 in what is present-day South Africa, Saartjie was transported to Europe by British doctor Alexander Dunlop (Holmes 2007, 5). There, she became a staple – a sensation – in freak shows around London then Paris (Holmes 2007; Willis 2010). For more than five years, her bodily features were placed in contrast to – and used to normalise – the anatomy of the average white woman. Gilman (1985) emphasises that Saartjie was displayed so that European audiences could gawk at 'the steatopygia, or protruding buttocks, the other physical characteristic of the Hottentot female which captured the eye of European travelers … The figure of Sarah Baartman was reduced to her sexual parts' (223). For a price, visitors to the various circus-like productions in which she was exhibited under the stage name 'The Hottentot Venus' were allowed to ogle at her buttocks, which were often portrayed in drawings as exaggerated and pronounced, and ponder her body. For an extra fee, audience members

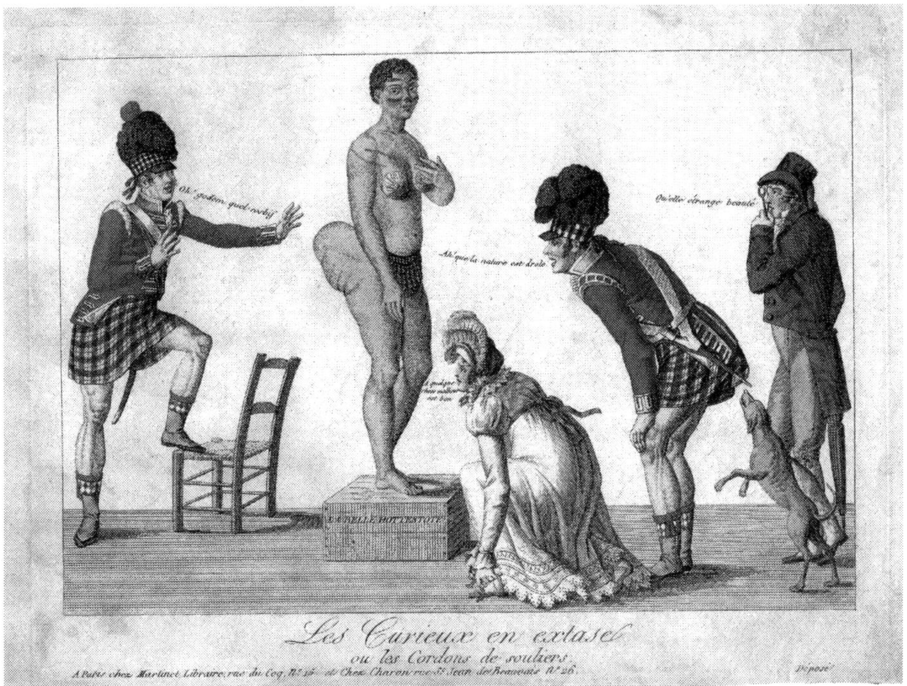

Figure 1. Les Curieux en extase, ou les cordons de souliers. Source: Wikimedia Commons.

could poke her with a stick to satisfy their desire to know if she was, indeed, real. For slightly more money, men could view her labia, which was often described as elongated as if to confirm her bodily deviance. Public interest in Saartjie as a specimen of corporeal abnormality eventually waned, as did the paltry income that she earned from her 'performances.' At the tail end of her short life, it is alleged that Saartjie turned to prostitution for survival and alcohol for comfort. She died destitute – and reportedly of severe sickness – in 1815, the same year that Charon completed his visual rendering of her. Yet the objectification of her body continued, as did capitalistic, patriarchal profiteering from it: Saartjie's remains were used in scientific experiments and – specifically her brain, skeleton, and genitalia – remained available for public viewing at a Paris museum until 1974 (Holmes 2007; Willis 2010).

Saartjie's story is a historical example of misogynoir manifested. We must wonder if by naming the novel's protagonist Sarah, Lee is employing a tactic of subversion and concertedly re-claiming Saartjie's voice, sexuality, and body. Charon's illustrative depiction of a specific episode in Saartjie's life – although likely an imagined or inferred one – shares striking similarities with Lee's portrayal of Sarah during the game of Galatea insofar as both women's bodies appear as flesh to be (de)valued then consumed by white audiences. What is at play in both instances is the exoticising and eroticising of the black woman's body. Sarah's situation, however, does not mirror Saartjie's relegation to an object whose thoughts and feelings can only be guessed. In fact, it appears that Lee travels great lengths to remix the original scene/sin by positioning Sarah agentically and asserting that she gleefully directs the action. Sarah's use of first person pronouns here is important. It confirms her consent to and *enjoyment* of the eroticism of the encounter with her white male companions. Sarah assumes her position on the wooden platform willingly. Whereas Charon's representation of Saartjie confines her to a denigrated, victimised, sexualised, 'savage,' Lee's crafting of this particular scene re-presents Sarah as a sensual, desired, and desiring woman who is consciously mobilising her raced fleshiness to extract corporeal pleasure. Through this episode, Lee rejects misogynoiristic articulations of black feminised bodies while adding texture to the intertwining of race, gender, bodies, and power as lived by black women.

It is crucial to note that this episode may incite visceral reactions in some readers. After all, images of black women's naked bodies variously degraded are common sights in the repertoire of curricula (and cultural) texts in the United States. These visuals are often leveraged to elicit shame and disgust at our collective and prior – or so we desperately want to believe – racist or prejudiced selves. Such images of harm are intended to offend the postmodern, western, feminist reader's sensibilities, and thereby propel this reader into racial and social justice-oriented action. Lee, however, does not give readers the option of digesting this component of the narrative quite so easily and linearly. She creates a scene laden with powerful traces of historical wounding, as well as (Sarah's) ambivalence and insouciance towards that wounding. Lee's positioning of Sarah on the wooden box seems to aspire to evoke both our rational repulsion and our corporeal titillation by simultaneously recalling the traumas of enslavement, and interrupting our expected or settled interpretation of that past and of the black feminised body as solely injured by that history.

Beyond that specific scene, Sarah is amused and aroused by her male partners' behaviours at many points of interaction. For example, she once observes with delight that 'the three boys were funny and horny and only occasionally tiresome; they told me I was beautiful and showed me off to their friends at cafes and discos and at the two drugstores' (Lee 1984, 7). In other words, by centring the sexual gratification that she derives from being wanted and lusted after, Sarah deflects the glare of the 'white gaze' (Morrison 1992) that flattens Saartjie to a thing boxed into a corpus that is a lewd and lascivious object, and orchestrates a re-viewing of the black feminised body as a site that composes and traffics in desire and pleasure. This text, therefore, can be reparatively read as 'an effort to divert the critical gaze from the racial object to the racial subject' (Morrison 1992, 90).

We are carefully avoiding placing major events from Sarah's life as expressed in the novel along a continuum of liberation and agency on one end (that is, Sarah as always free to do as she pleases with her body) versus disempowerment and pathology on the other (that is, Sarah's body as a perpetual object of perverted male use). This would obscure Lee's point in this text where there is ownership of flesh, which is constrained by histories, *and* there is a re-writing of that history, which is bound to and distorted by the flesh. Lee does not restrict the reader's response to black feminised bodies to feelings of sadness, despair, and hopelessness that are rooted in pain. In her writing of the game of Galatea, Lee re-imagines the dehumanising trading of enslaved Africans – a historical occurrence dripping with embodied affective intensities of pain – as an event that sources for Sarah a carnal pleasure that was reserved for those deemed human, and therefore considered out of the reach for the black woman. Here, Lee re-positions the black feminised body as capable of producing and embracing a broader scope of emotion than is expected. What is suggested is that doggedly retaining the capacity to *feel* in and through the flesh – in spite of past and present misogynoir that reminds black girls and women that our bodies are not wholly our own – is an enactment of resistance and self-love.

Locating possibilities

Senna's *Caucasia* (1999) – and specifically, the protagonist's experiences as captured in the text – centre on the relationship between the performance of race and the materiality of the body. Readers are made privy to the unsettled and unsettling relationship that exists between the novel's main character, Birdie, and her body. For Birdie, her body is a familiar and trustworthy haven in which she finds solace when she and her mother, whilst on the run from the law, 'disappeared into America … [d]ropped off without a name, without a record' (Senna 1999, 1). As Birdie says, when she and her mother become fugitives, 'our bodies disguised us' (139). This is possible only because Birdie's body is so visibly pliable in terms of race that she considers it 'as a toy' that she can use to 'disappear into the world' (65). Yet the fissure between Birdie's exterior – which is often read as white – and her interior, which she insists is black, has utility. She says, 'I would look at my own body the way I looked at another's' (190), noting that, 'my real self – Birdie Lee – was safely hidden beneath my beige flesh … [W]hen the right moment came, I would reveal her.' Unlike her classmate Samantha, whose 'blackness was visible' (223) on the exterior, Birdie assumes blackness as a racial identity that exists inside her. What is noteworthy here is that Birdie's body allows her racial mobility that disturbs the established white/black dichotomy. It shakes the grid upon which this binary rests, highlighting the interstices between the two points. Yet Birdie eschews whiteness, and seems wholly disinterested in the privilege that her light-coloured flesh affords her. However, in interactions with others, what she presents as this seemingly innate and static black identity becomes precarious and contestable precisely because of her body. Her body is a Judas in that it betrays her when it comes into contact with other bodies. It marks her invisible to her father, Deck, who seems to have a stronger affinity for Cole, Birdie's sister, whose bodily features – 'the burst of mischievous curls … the full pouting lips' (56) – can be more readily recognised as black. It marks her as suspicious to Carmen, Deck's girlfriend, who scornfully asserts that Birdie is 'Cole's little sister, even if she doesn't look like a sister' (93). When Birdie and Cole encounter a gaggle of Irish girls at a department store, it is Cole who endures racist taunts labelling her 'darkie' (Senna 1999, 40). In short, Birdie's body renders her unknowable as a black subject to those who see her. For Birdie, the chasm between the exterior and the interior as highlighted in interactions with others results in a disembodying dissonance. A reparative reading, however, posits that what this very chasm also does is allow her to re-make herself in each new encounter and to indulge multiple possibilities of who and what she may be. We argue that the chasm – borne of intercorporeal encounters with others – actually offers Birdie possibilities for a range of subjectivities. As significant as the kind of freedom linked to these possibilities is Birdie's continued choice of blackness as a racial identity. That she chooses blackness allows us to read her as not simply a modern-day tragic mulatto.

In the scene that is central to our analysis, the reader is ushered into Birdie's contemplations on losing her virginity. At this juncture in the story, Birdie, as a fugitive has assumed a public persona as Jesse, a white girl. Her performance is so convincing that, as she says, 'it was as if my mother believed … I was white, believed I was Jesse' (Senna 1999, 275). Birdie, however, clings to her private identity as a black girl. This shapes her considerations of a sexual mate: 'Maybe I would never be able to go all the way with a white boy' she remarks, explaining that

> sex was the only time, outside the body, when a person became one with another, when two people really melted into one body. Allowing a white boy inside of me would make my transformation complete, something I wasn't ready for.

Like *Caucasia's* (Senna 1999) Sarah, Birdie seems to be cognizant that in a sexual encounter, perhaps the densest form of intercorporeal entanglement, 'identity itself become[s] instituted' (Ahmed 2000, 7) – that is, confirmed, questioned, and/or un/made. Birdie's realisation only deepens her allegiance to an inner self that she feels is racialised as black.[1] This episode illuminates how the slipperiness of race as a concept creates a multitude of possibilities for how this identity may take form in each intercorporeal entwinement. Yet these options are neither unending nor a matter of simple cognitive choice; the body, as marked, constrains the very possibilities that it creates. For Birdie, one possibility that is created in intermingling with others is the potential of becoming white. In this specific scene, we see Birdie acknowledging then refusing that possibility, and choosing blackness as an identity. For her, there is belonging in blackness, not self-loathing, as is characteristic of the tragic mulatto figure. Being black enables her to maintain a connection to her father and her sister, both of whom she loves deeply. That she craves blackness is especially relevant given that she exists in a society within which whiteness sits at the zenith and blackness at the nadir of what is worth wanting. Moreover, she opts for blackness despite the fact that her body allows her the freedom to 'pass' as white. This choosing of a black racial identity is an activation of her agency, as it is in contrast to an earlier segment in the narrative when she passively resigns herself to whiteness: 'I would become white – white as my skin, hair, bones allowed. My body would fill in the blanks, tell me who I should become, and I would let it speak for me' (Senna 1999, 1).

Birdie offers us several insights into the black feminised body's multiplicity. Primarily, she challenges fixed categories and knowledges about race, and emphasises the notion that knowledges of the self and others as raced are both fluid – that is, always in-the-making – and constricted. Moreover, she proves that our subjectivities are simultaneously emergent and contingent upon our interactions with others. She also shows us that the corporeal body is both noun and a verb in that it is a thing and it does things: it is captor and captured, actress and acting. Race, therefore, is not (re)made either abstractly or in isolation – the body, as identifiable through other markers such as gender, and in relationship to other bodies, is implicated in its (re)configuration. Through Birdie, we see how bodies are intimately connected with other bodies, how their surfaces are (re)constituted within each interembodied or intercorporeal encounter, and how they are experienced racially in and through this very contact. Lastly, through her, we also see that the black feminised body is not a singular, unified construction. Birdie shows us that bodies *become* black, and that this blackness is both unstable and plural. In other words, Birdie demands that we expand our ideas of what this black feminised body may look like, may be, and may do. Her experiences in the text highlight the relationship between the conceptual category of race, its performance, and the lived-ness or materiality of the body. They teach us that bodies are at once ours and not, instantly private and public. Birdie also assures us that bodies are unavoidably relational and integral to the production and nexus of race and subjectivities, or racial subjectivities.

Making sense of black fleshiness

When paired, *Sarah Phillips* (Lee 1984) and *Caucasia* (Senna 1999) highlight the imbrication of race, gender, and bodies, the manner in which the function of each impinges upon that of the others, and the unique set of implications this has for the black feminised bodies that are caught in the crosshairs. The texts illuminate the inseparability of visible, embodied social constructs like race and gender from lived experiences of the skin and flesh. The novels also challenge the western belief in self-contained and self-sustaining autonomy by showing that these skin and flesh covered bodies are woven into intricate networks, and become sensible only in relation to other bodies in those webs.

Sarah and Birdie's efforts to make sense of their corporeal fleshiness seem to heed the advice conveyed through Baby Suggs, a central figure in Toni Morrison's *Beloved* ([1987] 2004). In a monologue, the black woman commandingly says, 'Yonder they do not love your flesh.' This revelation, she adds emphatically, means that, 'You got to love it, you!' (104). Sarah loves her black flesh, and fishes it out of a deep river of historical wounding and trauma. Birdie has a more complicated relationship with her flesh because of its racial marking and how that is read by others, but loves her blackness, despite the fact that is indiscernible on her body. Her encounters with others who reify its illegibility as black only deepen her possessive investment this racial identity. Again and again, she chooses to be black, rejecting the seduction and allure whiteness, electing, instead, for the kind of deepened attachment to two of her family members that blackness provides her with access to, and the possibilities for belonging that creates. Sarah shows the black feminised body as coveting and coveted, and Birdie shows us that this body can personify multidimensional identities in ways that are covetable. Together, these two texts toil in tandem to unravel the threads that hold together normative readings that cast black girls and women as already and always lamentably other(ed).

Toward reparative curriculum and pedagogy

How might our deliberations of *Sarah Phillips* (Lee 1984) and *Caucasia* (Senna 1999) be situated in the context of education and translated through teachers' curricular and pedagogical choices? We explore this question here with a focus on what implications such action may have for black feminised bodies, and how educators may take up notions of such bodies as sites of pleasures and possibilities in classrooms and schools.

As numerous scholars have indicated, classrooms are microcosms of society at large; therefore, they are intricately woven into the hegemonic structures and forces that frame life for educators and students both inside and outside of them. Social differences are, as we know, both produced anew and reproduced in classroom settings. The National Council of Teachers of English (NCTE), arguably the most influential professional organisation for all teachers of English in the United States, has responded to that knowledge by releasing guidelines for 'a gender balanced curriculum,' explaining that as educators:

> We must all search for texts that will initiate conversations and questions about gender roles and the perceptions of appropriate behavior and activities. Through these conversations and questions, teachers can be instrumental in helping students reflect on gendered expectations. Teachers can challenge those expectations by showing options and alternatives so readers seek to confront the inequities they find in their own lives (2008, 'Guidelines,' para. 4).

NCTE's guidelines aim to make lucid the ways in which educators' curricular responses to gender differences contribute to either expanding or contracting students' world views and views of themselves in the world. However, while applauding the intention, we must cautiously observe that responses such as these – that is, those unanchored to understandings of how our *readings* of texts, and the characters within, them are as vitally harmful or healing as our very selection of texts – risk sanctioning the use of curriculum and pedagogical practices that merely re-articulate sedimented discourses that maintain the status quo. What we are insisting is that the task of expanding complex understandings of gender in classrooms and schools must pivot upon educators equipping learners to engage in readings that take seriously corporeality. This may increase knowledge of how 'particular bodies' are made with and against other bodies, thus deepening attention to the singularity of the experiences of those bodies as related to what is written into their flesh and skin. Such readings would have to foreground the racial axes along which bodies are made and experienced in relation to each other, thus serving as pedagogical interventions that move towards repair, and away from further wounding and harm for black bodies. We suggest, then, that educators also take up the materiality of embodiment and interembodiment when working to 'initiate conversations and questions about gender.' This would foreground the racialised, sexualised, and otherwise marked ridges along which bodies are made and experienced. We imagine that the resulting dialogues would point to alternate – perhaps less injurious – ways in which black feminised bodies, especially, might be seen and experienced in classroom spaces and schools, with consequences for how these bodies are seen and experienced – and perhaps even loved – in private and public spheres outside classroom spaces and schools.

Toward a counter-hegemonic love for black feminised bodies

We conclude by attuning ourselves to Aniah, Ariah, and the clique of black girls at the fast-food restaurant in Brooklyn, New York. Situating these black girls in a broader and historical and socio-political context is integral to understanding why they are named 'savage' and hailed as 'brute' by the media. Black bodies, as Spillers (1987) urges us to remember, continue to be configured in dominant discourse about race and gender in ways that are permanently wedded to the legacies of slavery. However, if bodies are texts, then they are open to varied interpretations and primed for re-readings. It is through such re-readings that possibilities for multiple ways of feeling and being both black and girl or woman may become available to those in these bodies. Therefore, the knowledges about black feminised corpuses that we have invoked and produced in this article lead us toward reparative and healing readings of the black teenagers' bodies. It is through this process of reparative reading that we re-claim their raced and gendered bodies and affirm their right to simultaneously be in those bodies fully and be fully human in the world. Thus, it is through this process that we demonstrate our love for their black feminised bodies, and ultimately, for their very humanity. Such is the labour of the counter-hegemonic work in which we are engaged as curriculum scholars. It is, necessarily, about doing 'the work of love' – in theory and in the flesh.

Note

1. A discussion of the questions regarding the existence of an idealized, unified, and/or essential self that are raised by this scene can be found in Butler's (1990) *Gender Trouble*.

Acknowledgements

The first author wishes to express deep thanks to Dr Candice M. Jenkins for substantive feedback on initial thoughts about the texts under study, and early iterations of this article that subsequently emerged from those seed ideas. The second author wishes to thank Dr Nancy Lesko for introducing her to the curriculum of the body.

Disclosure statement

No potential conflict of interest was reported by the authors.

References

Ahmed, Sara. 2000. *Strange Encounters: Embodied Others in Post-coloniality*. New York: Routledge.
Ahmed, Sara. 2004. *The Cultural Politics of Emotion*. New York: Routledge.
Badia, Erik, Barry Paddock, Tracy Tracy, and Rich Shapiro. 2015. "Brute Arrested in McDonald's Beating has Long Rap Sheet." *NY Daily News*, March 13. http://www.nydailynews.com/new-york/nyc-crime/brute-shown-stomping-victim-mcdonald-beating-arrested-article-1.2146819.
Bailey, M. 2010. "They aren't Talking about Me." Crunk Feminist Collective. http://www.crunkfeministcollective.com/2010/03/14/they-arent-talking-about-me/.
Bakare-Yusuf, B. 1999. "The Economy of Violence: Black Bodies and the Unspeakable Terror." In *Feminist Theory and the Body: A Reader*, edited by J. Price, and M. Shildrick, 311–324. New York: Routledge.
Baszile, D. T. 2008. "Beyond All Reason Indeed: The Pedagogical Promise of Critical Race Testimony." *Race Ethnicity and Education* 11 (3): 251–265.
Bordo, Susan. 1993. *Unbearable Weight*. Berkeley, CA: University of California Press.
Boston, G. H., and T. Baxley. 2007. "Living the Literature." *Urban Education* 42 (6): 560–581.
Britzman, D. 2002. "Theory Kindergarten." In *Regarding Sedgwick: Essays on Queer Culture and Critical Theory*, edited by S. M. Barber, and D. L. Clark, 121–142. New York: Routledge.
Butler, Judith. 1990. *Gender Trouble*. New York: Routledge.
Butler, Judith. 2004. *Undoing Gender*. New York: Routledge.
Caspary, Vera. 1929. *The White Girl*. New York: J. H. Sears & Co.
Coates, Ta-Nehisi. 2015. *Between the World and Me*. New York: Spiegel & Grau.
Edwards, Ashley. 2015. "Teen Beaten by Gang of Girls in Brooklyn McDonald's Brags about Internet Fame." Pix11.com. http://pix11.com/2015/03/12/teen-beaten-by-gang-of-girls-in-brooklyn-mcdonalds-brags-about-internet-fame/.
England, K. V. L. 1994. "Getting Personal: Reflexivity, Positionality, and Feminist Research." *The Professional Geographer* 46 (1): 80–89.
Fook, J. 1999. "Reflexivity as Method." *Annual Review of Health Social Sciences* 9: 11–20.
Gilman, S. L. 1985. "Black Bodies, White Bodies: Toward an Iconography of Female Sexuality in Late Nineteenth-Century Art, Medicine, and Literature." In *'Race,' Writing, and Difference*, edited by H. Louis Gates, Jr., and K. A. Appiah, 223–261. Chicago, IL: University of Chicago Press.
Gross, K. N. 1997. "Examining the Politics of Respectability in African American Studies." *Almanac* 43 (28). http://www.upenn.edu/almanac/v43/n28/benchmrk.html.
Hall, S. 1997. "The Spectacle of the 'Other'." In *Representations: Cultural Representations and Signifying Practices*, edited by S. Hall, 223–279. London: Sage.

Hill Collins, P. [1997] 2007. "Pornography and Black Women's Bodies." In *Gender Violence: Interdisciplinary Perspectives*, edited by L. L. O'Toole, J. R. Schiffman, and M. L. K. Edwards, 395–403. New York: New York University Press.

Hill Collins, P. 1999. "Mammies, Matriarchs, and Other Controlling Images." In *Feminist Philosophies*, edited by J. Kournay, J. Sterba, and R. Tong, 142–152. Upper Saddle River: Prentice Hall.

Hobbs, Allyson. 2014. *A Chosen Exile: A History of Racial Passing in American life*. Cambridge: Harvard University Press.

Holmes, Rachel. 2007. *African Queen: The Real Life of the Hottentot Venus*. New York: Random House.

hooks, bell. 1992. *Black Looks: Race and Representation*. Boston: South End Press.

Jewell, K. Sue. 1993. *From Mammy to Miss America and Beyond. Cultural Images and the Shaping of US Social Policy*. New York: Routledge.

Johnson, James W. [1912] 1995. *The Autobiography of an Ex-colored Man*. Mineola: Dover.

Larsen, Nella. [1929] 2007. *Passing*. New York: W. W Norton.

Lee, Andrea. 1984. *Sarah Phillips*. Boston, MA: Northeastern University Press.

Luttrell, W. 2010. "Reflexive Writing Exercises." In *Qualitative Educational Research: Readings in Reflexive Methodology and Transformative Practice*, edited by W. Luttrell, 469–480. New York: Routledge.

Morrison, Toni. 1992. *Playing in the Dark: Whiteness and the Literary Imagination*. Cambridge: Harvard University Press.

Morrison, Toni. [1987] 2004. *Beloved*. New York: Vintage.

Nash, Jennifer C. 2014. *The Black Body in Ecstasy: Reading Race, Reading Pornography*. Durham: Duke University Press.

NCTE (National Council of Teachers of English). 2008. "Guidelines for a Gender-balanced Curriculum in English Grades 7–12." http://www.ncte.org/positions/statements/genderbalanced712.

Oyěwùmí, Oyèrónkẹ́. 1997. *The Invention of Women: Making an African Sense of Western Gender Discourses*. Minneapolis: University of Minnesota Press.

Pickens, T. A. 2014. "Shoving Aside the Politics of Respectability: Black Women, Reality TV, and the Ratchet Performance." *Women & Performance: A Journal of Feminist Theory* 24 (2): 1–18.

Pinder, P. J. 2008. "The 'Black Girl Turn' in Research on Gender, Race, and Science Education: Toward Exploring and Understanding the Early Experiences of Black Females in Science, a Literature Review." *Journal of African American Studies* 18 (1): 63–71.

Quad8 [screenname]. 2015. "Teenage brawl at NY McDonald's!" Youtube.com. https://youtu.be/IFdl7EmeNog.

Richardson, L. 2000. "Writing: A Method of Inquiry." In *Handbook of Qualitative Research*. 2nd ed., edited by N. K. Denzin, and Y. S. Lincoln, 923–948. Thousand Oaks, CA: Sage.

Richardson, L., and St. Pierre, E. A. 2005. "Writing: A Method of Inquiry." In *Handbook of Qualitative Research*. 3rd ed., edited by N. K. Denzin, and Y. S. Lincoln, 959–978. Thousand Oaks, CA: Sage.

Rummel, K. 2007. "Rewriting the Passing Novel: Danzy Senna's *Caucasia*." *The Griot* 26 (2): 1–13.

Sedgwick, Eve. 2003. *Touching Feeling: Affect, Pedagogy, Performativity*. Durham: Duke University Press Books.

Senna, Danzy. 1999. *Caucasia*. New York: Riverhead.

Spelman, E. 1982. "Woman as Body: Ancient and Contemporary Views." *Feminist Studies* 8 (1): 109–131.

Spillers, H. 1987. "Mama's Baby, Papa's Maybe: An American Grammar Book." *Diactrics* 17 (2): 65–81.

Toomer, Jean. [1923] 2011. *Cane*. New York: Liveright.

Weiss, Gail. 1999. *Body Images: Embodiment as Intercorporeality*. New York: Routledge.

West, C. [2008] 2012. "Mammy, Jezebel, Sapphire, and Their Homegirls: Developing an 'Oppositional Gaze' Toward the Images of Black Women." In *Lectures on the Psychology of Women*, edited by J. C. Chrisler, C. Golden, and P. Rozee, 286–299. Long Grove: Waveland Press.

White, E. Frances. 2001. *Dark Continent of Our Bodies: Black Feminism and the Politics of Respectability*. Philadelphia: Temple University Press.

Willis, D. 2010. *Black Venus 2010: They Called Her 'Hottentot'*. Philadelphia: Temple University Press.

Woyshner, C. 2006. "Picturing Women: Gender, Images, and Representation in Social Studies." *Social Education* 70 (6): 358–362.

Mapping the margins and searching for higher ground: examining the marginalisation of black female graduate students at PWIs

Dari Green, Tifanie Pulley, Melinda Jackson, Lori Latrice Martin and Kenneth J. Fasching-Varner

ABSTRACT
The number of Black females enrolled in colleges and universities has grown in recent years, particularly at predominately white institutions (PWIs). Currently, research on the rise of Black females at PWIs is limited and fails to adequately address the emotional, social, and mental well-being of these students. Recent studies also largely ignore the critical roles that natural and formal Black female faculty play in serving as a buffer between Black female graduate students (BFGS) and PWIs more broadly. From a critical perspective using counter-narrative, we address the limitations of the scholarly literature on BFGS and other challenges faced by BFGS. We come to the disappointing – albeit unsurprising – conclusion that PWIs should do more to make the academy a welcoming place for BFGS, however, the ways in which PWIs function make support for BFGS unlikely. We conclude with a discussion about the implications of continued marginalisation of BFGS at PWIs for individuals, families, communities, disciplines, and for PWIs across the nation.

Education is a social institution filled with contradictions, false expectations, and hidden discrimination (Brown v. Board, 1954; Margolis and Romero 1998; Fasching-Varner et al. 2014). Academic women of colour, particularly Black women, are often most affected by such behaviours and the challenges that accompany them (Hill-Collins 1986; Williams et al. 2005; Patton 2009). Racism and sexism have plagued the lives of Black women in the United States from the country's conception and these inequalities continue to shape the experiences Black women today (Collins 1989; Bell 1993).

We examine the experiences of Black female graduate students (BFGS) at predominately white institutions (PWIs) by mapping the margins (Crenshaw 1991, 1995) within higher education. We propose Black Feminist Realism (BFR), as a new conceptual by-product of Bell's racial realism (1992) and Collin's *Black Feminist Thought* (2000). BFR extends existing critical race and feminist work accounting for both race and gender without excluding the whole of oneself in the reality in which Black female life exists. Choosing race loyalty versus gender solidarity invisibilises the permanence of not only racism but patriarchy as well (Guy-Sheftall and Cole 2003). We utilise an intersectional approach (Crenshaw 1991, 1995) to draw upon counter-narratives and stock stories, shifting the lived experiences of BFGS at PWIs from the margins to the centre of analysis.

Universities in America may provide opportunities for upward mobility while also perpetuating social inequality (Hurtado 1994; Ellis 2001; Smith, Hung, and Franklin 2011). Some offer that academia reifies racial hierarchies and gender-biases, with both covert and overt racism, despite laws and policies aimed to combat them (Johnson-Bailey 1999; Wallace and Bell 1999; Smith, Hung, and Franklin 2011). While diversity quotas are 'met' at institutions across the nation, universities often present contradictory actions, marginalising some groups and privileging others (Wallace and Bell 1999; Steele 2003; Williams et al. 2005). Black women stand at a focal point between two influential and dominant systems of oppression: their race and their gender. Traditional dominant approaches to sites of difference when examined through categorical isolation (hooks 1990; Tower and Chair 2002; Wilkins 2012), pigeonhole progress for marginalised communities. Scholarship is given voice from the margin when identities crosscut multiple axes of oppression and/or domination (Collins 1989).

Black Feminist Thought frames our research, followed by an examination of the higher education landscape that sets the stage for mapping the margins (Crenshaw 1991, 1995). Derrick Bell's racial realism (1992) permeates this project in that we identify the fluidity of race as a fixed category, notwithstanding its social constructionist nature. Given the use of what we term BFR we will also present and highlight what we believe to be its three major tenets:

1 Survival and sustainability of the Eurocentric interests at the individual and institutional level will continue to dominate and replicate due to its critical mass;
2 A segregated knowledge, not subjugated amongst stakeholders of the academy persists. All actors within the structure occupy the same space yet the production of knowledge has limits; and
3 There is 'no exodus'. The institution was not designed with the knowledge production of Black female scholarship in mind. It replicates the demands of mainstream society as it was designed to do.

Black Feminist Thought

To understand the unique experiences of an individual, it is important to examine the intersection of an individual's race, class, and gender (Crenshaw 1991, 1995; Hill-Collins 2000). A traditional misunderstanding assumes that those identity markers simply cross paths, however, for our purposes, intersectionality means the way in which they each inform, influence, and interact with each other (hooks 1990; Crenshaw 1991, 1995; Tokarcyzk and Fay 1993; Hill-Collins 2000; Pollard and Welch 2006; Mills 2011). In other words we recognise that as a principle of intersectionality, race is classed and gendered, that gender is raced and classed, and the class is raced and gendered (Collins 1989; Crenshaw 1991, 1995; Roberts 1998; Ellis 2001; Pollard and Welch 2006; Fasching-Varner et al. 2014). The interaction is not linear but instead rhizomatic and atomic in nature. Black feminist thought, which encompasses both feminist and critical theories, consequently allows the particularly distinctive experiences of Black women as a site of knowledge creation to be understood intersectionally (Collins 1989). Feminist theories traditionally emphasise the oppressive conditions of women, challenging traditionally male dominated spaces; critical theories, similarly, challenge mainstream perspectives, emphasising the experiential knowledge of minorities (Lorde 1984a, 1984b; Johnson-Bailey 1999; Hill-Collins 2000; Scheurich 2002). When exploring the dissatisfaction and isolation reported among BFGS, we suggest that it is imperative to examine the longstanding problem of racism in America while considering the permanence of race and racism structurally embedded in PWIs (Bell 1992; Fasching-Varner et al. 2014)

Given that society functions on the free-market neoliberal demands that are satisfied with continuous stratification by identity, the goal should not centre on finding a 'solution' to a problem as there really is no 'problem', per say (Bell 1992; Crenshaw 1995; Fasching-Varner et al. 2014). Rather our goal might be to explain the historical context that has led to the point at which we find ourselves and to examine potential implications for future BFGS (Jones-Johnson 1988; Hurtado 1994; Johnson-Bailey 1999; Ellis 2001). By portraying African-American women as self-defined, self-reliant individuals confronting race, gender, and class oppression, we counter invisibility and produce scholarship that adds value to both our individual and collective self-identity (Jones-Johnson 1988; Hill-Collins 2000; Howard-Hamilton 2003; Pollard and Welch 2006; Wilkins 2012) This approach also fosters a fundamental paradigmatic shift in how scholars within systems of oppression might exist while re-conceptualising the social relations of dominance and resistance (Hill-Collins 1986, 2000; Feagin 2006; Martinez 2014).

Ideologically, Black female identities in the United States were constructed hierarchically from a socio-historical perspective in a way that positions Black women as inferior to every group from Black men, through white women, to white men (Roberts 1998; Wallace and Bell 1999; Evans 2007a, 2007b; Stovall 2013). Black women are multiply burdened from both historical and contemporary perspectives that have thrived on the application of dichotomous pairings within our parlance of 'Black', 'female', and 'poor' identities (each with their dichotomous privileged counterpart), positioning these women in inferior positions as compared to white, male, and elite counterparts within a free-market system (Hill-Collins 1986; Crenshaw 1991, 1995; Delgado 1995; Mabokela and Green 2001; Oliver and Shapiro 2006). Consider Walker's (1990) *The Color Purple*. White men, white women, and Black males sought to position Black women at the bottom of the hierarchy.

The search for higher ground

Tenure and full professorship have been structured as the ultimate accolades in the academy, but must be met with a stark skepticism, given that the so-called architects of knowledge who established these protections and achievements come from those most privileged in society. Consider the following excerpt from Tower and Chair (2002) in *The Questions of Tenure*,

> The basic document that undergirds academic employment, the 'Statement of Tenure and Academic Freedom' published by the American Association of University Professors, dates to 1940 – a time when women and minorities were even less prevalent in the academy and when the respective roles of men and women in society were more narrowly defined. (37)

Promotion and tenure documents demonstrate most visibly the structural inequality perpetuated within the academy directly connected to an antiquated view of categories of race, class, and gender. Issues relating to difference are almost always excluded from the language, culture, and customs of the academy, including the documents that govern the ultimate protections provided academics. The success of most graduate students hinges upon how well we navigate the academic space (Mabokela and Green 2001; Pollard and Welch 2006; Shavers, James, and Moore 2014; McGee and Kazembe 2015). BFGS who complete their programmes fall behind the curve in the outcomes of high-ranking positions and salaries, and have most often not been provided with adequate mentorship or empowerment to navigate the expectations within the racist, patriarchal, classist landscape they enter as faculty (U.S. National Center for Education Statistics 2012).

We consider that access to education was a closed system for minorities and women (Hill-Collins 2000; Guy-Sheftall and Cole 2003; Feagin 2006; Evans 2007a, 2007b). Black female graduate students earning advanced degrees at PWIs might be considered symbolic progress. Neoliberals, neoconservatives, and incrementalists have hijacked the idea that through education Black women are somewhat less excluded from the promise of social mobility in the 'new post-racial America'. The legacy of institutionalised slavery and Jim Crow that permeates access to and experience in higher education (see Feagin 2006; Alexander 2012). When the intersections of the broad categories of race, class, and gender are problematised as part of the navigation process within academic settings, sites of difference can be seen as operating as points of reference for interaction.

Research suggests that it is psychologically taxing and emotionally isolating for BFGS, given that they are the most isolated group to attend PWIs (Ellis 2001; Steele 2003; Shavers, James, and Moore 2014). As of 2013, white females composed 35% of all full-time faculty and 26% of professors in post-secondary institutions, while Black women composed only 6% of full-time faculty and 4% of full-time professor positions in the same institutions (U.S. Department of Education 2012; Journal of Blacks in Higher Education 2014); BFGS may have difficulty in developing relationships with mentors of similar backgrounds, and to the extent such mentors exist they are often overburdened and overtaxed (Evans 2007a, 2007b; Dowdy 2008; Patton 2009; Journal of Blacks in Higher Education 2014); consequently these students are offered upward mobility within a space that perpetuates structural inequality (Feagin 2006; Oliver and Shapiro 2006).

Mapping margins

Aimed at making BFR more salient, we examine three constructs that exist within academic institutions, which propagate inequities. The first construct is a *lack of representation* of people of colour, particularly Blacks in the academy. Though the number of graduate degrees earned by BFGS attending post-secondary institutions has increased by about 9% since the 1999–2000 academic year, Blacks are underrepresented when compared to whites on PWI campuses, even accounting for demographic distributions (U.S. Department of Education 2012; Journal of Blacks in Higher Education 2014). The stakes of success within these institutions are often heavily influenced by the relationships established between faculty and students (Fashing-Varner 2009; Hill-Collins, 1986; Hurtado 1994; Wallace and Bell 1999). Faculty members can be selective about whom they will mentor, seeking only students who will most likely continue their intellectual legacy (D'Augelli and Hershberger 1993; Hurtado 1994; Johnson-Bailey 1999; Mabokela and Green 2001; Fashing-Varner 2009).

> Tenet 1: Survival and sustainability of the Eurocentric interests at the individual and institutional level will continue to dominate and replicate due to the critical mass represented by those interests. The disproportionate representation of scholarship across categories of race, class, and gender remains contested as difference is characterized dichotomously within a structural hierarchy.

Central to the relationship between lack of representation and tenet 1 is white supremacy. If we consider how intellectual legacy is accomplished through homogeneity in a broad racial framing of production of knowledge, then this construct demonstrates that Eurocentric interests are inevitable where there is no racial or gendered parity across categories of race, class, and gender.

The second construct is the *prevalent misconception of what constitutes scholarshi*p and Black female's consequent *need to create 'new knowledge'* (Collins 1989). Whiteness is privileged in part due to its critical mass, with the majority of knowledge disseminators being white. Scholarship dominating the academy is predominately Eurocentric contributing to the dehumanisation of Black bodies (Roberts 1998; Hill-Collins 2000; Feagin 2006). Black womanhood, furthermore, is oft complex, as race is perceived and framed as more salient (Bell 1992). BFGS face a 'double jeopardy' given their race and sex (Brown and Keith 2003). BFGS must either succumb to mainstream conceptual bias(es) underpinning theory and research, or have their work viewed as atypical, less rigorous, exotic, superfluous, etc. (Collins 1989; hooks, 1989; Wallace and Bell 1999; Howard-Hamilton 2003; Wilkins 2012). If we understand scholarship as a formal production, identification, and organisation of what is considered knowledge and we recognise that this process is political at best and discriminatory and eugenicist at worst, the consequence of the choices Black females must make in the academy is daunting (Crenshaw 1991, 1995; Roberts 1998).

> Tenet 2: An unsubjugated, segregated knowledge persists amongst stakeholders of the academy. All actors within the structure occupy the same space yet the production of knowledge has limits.

There is nothing subtle or ambiguous about invisibility and silence. Key to a subjugated knowledge is the dichotomous relationship of superiority and inferiority. The most important problem to consider here is how the discourses legitimise a relegated status when terms like 'subjugated' are germane to the discipline. Furthermore, we consider segregated akin to 'separate but equal', identifying epistemological and ontological differences only.

The third construct for consideration in mapping the margins is that of *identity crisis* and the academic persistence of Black females, despite what they experience with respect to their overall well-being. While access to higher education for Black women is not easy, it is with those very degrees that Black women are positioned to combat social inequality (Collins 1989; Mabokela and Green 2001; Dowdy 2008).[1] Students of colour experience physiological, psychological, and behavioural stresses, known as racial battle fatigue, from micro-aggressions that are experienced in hostile campus climates (Ellis 2001; Smith, Hung, and Franklin 2011; Franklin, Smith, and Hung 2014). BFGS have reported that their time in graduate school was characterised as both racialised and gendered contradictions (Collins 1989).

> Tenet 3: There is 'no exodus'. The institution was not designed with the knowledge production of Black female scholarship in mind. It replicates the demands of mainstream society as it was designed to do.

While some Black women scholars are accepted into the mainstream canons, such scholarship does not mitigate 'racial stereotypes and images both explicitly and implicitly that mock and signal the inferiority of people of color' (Feagin 2006, 12). For Black female students who make it through the admissions process, their arrival to PWI campuses presents gendered racism, a lack of opportunities, a lack of community, and a lack of institutional support beyond the glib and superficial articulations that go something like 'we are so glad you're here' as the faculty turn their backs on these students and spend the rest of their time avoiding the students (Wallace and Bell 1999; Franklin, Smith, and Hung 2014). While BFGS seek higher education to obtain upward mobility, many find in the academy a microcosmic replication of the larger post-racial, fully-racial society where inequities related to race, gender, and power relations are extended (Jones-Johnson 1988; hooks 1989; Oliver and Shapiro 2006; Feagin 2006). This disturbing landscape is most evident when we see how little has changed in terms of the tenure ratio between white males and women and their minority counterparts over the past 30 years. White males are five times more likely to hold a tenure track position than are minorities and/or women (Tower and Chair 2002).

Each of these constructs helps map the margins of higher education, including a lack of representation, the prevalent misconception of scholarship, and identity crisis experienced by women of colour to characterise the margins as contestable space in which BFGS at white institutions find themselves.

Counter-narrative

Counter-story is a powerful tool used to contribute to an 'othered' perspective of a dominant ideology (Hill-Collins, 1986; Martinez 2014). Counter-stories seek to reveal the absurdity that lies within dominant narratives, drawing upon and valuing the experiential knowledge base of marginalised people as authoritative sources of data. Delgado (1995) described counter-story as a 'counter-reality that is experienced by subordinate groups, as opposed to those experiences of those in power' (194). Those in power do not participate in the 'out-group' experience; instead they experience the naturalisation of a superior position (Delgado 1995; Collins 1989). Martinez (2014) uses the 'stock story versus counter-story' method to offer two dialogues side-by-side to explain a single event. The audience is able to understand one situation from the view of the status quo, and then from the perspective of a minority.

We present both a stock story as well as a counter-story, intended to represent an amalgamated set of experiences narrated into single stories which exemplify institutionalised racism in the academy (Delgado 1995). The narratives centre on a young woman by the name of Hope, a BFGS at Research I flagship State University. Hope recalls her experiences being accepted into graduate school, meeting her advisor for the first time, and her realisation that only her white colleagues received full funding.

Stock story

Setting

Admissions committee meets to discuss the applicants for admission during the fall semester. In this programme, a decision is generally made only after one's official documents are received and the Graduate Admissions Committee conducts a final evaluation. If a student meets the general requirements for admission and the department or programme recommends admission, the student is admitted. Applicants who meet the minimum requirements are not guaranteed admission, because some graduate programmes set higher standards and many have limited space and facilities.

Blanco: Good afternoon gentlemen, and Miss Susan. Thank you for attending this meeting today. We have to finalize the list of students to be admitted in the fall and the slots are limited. There has been an increase, as you know, in the number of students being permitted into the program due to the recent decline in completion rate in the program. Today I have before you eight applicants.

Johnson: Eight? Certainly we cannot accept all eight? How will we fund eight students?

Blanco: We will get there, Johnson, hold tight… Of these applicants, half are minorities with a social science background. The other half are not minorities and have an educational background indirectly related to the field.

Rice: [coughs].

Blanco: [Makes eye contact with Rice and smirks]. Each of the students has met the minimum requirements for acceptance and I believe that accepting all of the students would be beneficial to boost diversity not only within the department, but also the University.

Johnson: You still have not stated whose grant will fund all of these students. With all of the cuts to higher education there is no way that we can host this many students.

Blanco: Now about that question, Johnson, I have decided that we will allow the students to choose whether or not this is the place for them. I suggest that we offer acceptance to the students and allow the minority students a fee waiver and minority scholarship so that they don't have to pay tuition. There are reasons those funds exist. The other half of the students, though their backgrounds are not specifically related to our departmental studies, have come from an interdisciplinary department of some sort, and all but one has done relevant research.

Rice: I definitely could use an extra hand with crunching some numbers.

Susan: I could use help transcribing, as well!

Blanco: So, then, there we have it. That wasn't so hard now was it? Meeting adjourned.

The director of graduate studies, Blanco, prepares acceptance letters to be emailed to the students. All of the students, but one, gladly accept their invitation.

Counter-story

Setting

It is the first day of the fall semester. All of the students gather in the seminar room. Their emotions range from angst to excitement. The professor walks in and introduces himself.

He soon turns it over to the students all of whom give an introduction, although a biography had been provided by each of them a week earlier.

Student 1:	My name is Harry. I have a background in engineering, but now I am interested in crime. I am working closely with Dr. Johnson, as I was appointed as his graduate assistant.
Student 2:	My name it Frank. I am a local minister who is interested in community.
Student 3:	My name is Elizabeth. I am interested in STEM research. I will be working with Dr. Susan on qualitative studies.
Student 4:	He was a no show, but his biographical information indicated he was from the local area and had been teaching in the local public school system.
Student 5:	My name is Hope. I am interested inequality and race.
Student 6:	My name is Keisha. I am interested in race, gender, crime, community, and family.
Student 7:	My name is Destiny. It's my first time in this state. I came from an HBCU. I am interested in qualitative studies.

After the students complete their formal introductions, class continues. Three hours later, when the lecture ends, Hope turns to Keisha and asks: 'So now it's official; every white person I've met in this department says they are funded. Are you funded?'

Keisha replies:	Yeah, all that I've spoken with have said the same thing. I am not funded but I received a tuition waiver.'

The other minority students confirm that they, too, came into the programme without funding, but agreed to accept their lot, as they conceded that at least they had the opportunity to further their education, despite having been the guinea pigs of the new standardised test for admission.

Later:	The end of the fall semester. Hope phones her mother to vent about the experiences that she has had within the department.
Hope's mother:	Hey, Baby (in her thickest Southern accent).
Hope:	(unexcitedly) Hey, Ma.
Hope's mother:	What's wrong Hope? Seems like every time I hear from you, you're sad. Is something going on in your marriage?
Hope:	Ma, why is that always your first thought? My marriage is perfectly fine. Hope's mother interjects with apologies.
Hope continues:	It's these racist folks who are doing the very things that they want to teach about. It's ridiculous. I mean, since day one when I found out they didn't give one Black person funding, I should have known. To not have one Black faculty member, I should have run away. I just don't know what to do. I just get more and more bitter.
Hope's mom:	Now, Hope, we've already had this conversation. You can't let anyone steal your joy. Your education is not for them folks ... What happened this time?
Hope:	Well, you know I was glad that they finally granted me funding after they found out I was 'well-rounded', but after I walk in to talk to the guy I'm supposed to be working for, he looks at me like I am not even there. Then he has the nerve to tell me, 'You know you're only funded because Student 4 didn't show?' I mean, they just don't care what they tell you around here. Not to mention that they offered it to Frank in front of my face, but he refused it. When I mentioned that I was pregnant you know what he told me, Ma? You know what he said?
Hope's mother:	What'd he say, Hope?

Hope: He said, 'Is this what you wanted, Hope?' When I explained it wasn't necessarily planned, he insinuated that I should terminate my pregnancy! Black lives matter, Ma! Not to mention the men in the department get pats on the back when they are expecting; we get hints at abortion! [Hope cries hysterically]

Hope's mom: Hope, calm down. Go there and do what you got to do. You don't have nothing to prove. You know you're intelligent. We are organic intellectuals. Teach them some theories of your own, Child. I know it's hard but your grandparents wish they could have even seen the day that they'd be walking in your shoes. You have so many generations relying on you.

Hope interrupts: But, Ma, they talk down to me. They will take insight from folks that don't even have a background in this field. They either try to talk over, above, or around you. I walked in Johnson's class and you know what he said?

Hope's mom: What's that, Hope?

Hope: He said, 'You know what I've realized after all these years? I have always worked with Africans, never African-Americans.' I told him I'm Black and he looked at me crazy. How can they be so educated and lack so much common sense, Ma? How can they just treat people like that and get away with it?

Hope's mom: Honey, your day will come and you will speak to nations. Don't you worry, Honey, you have greatness within you. Don't let it make you bitter; instead become better, and take their money and buy you something nice.

Hope: You're right. As long as I keep publishing, they may keep giving me these *necessary* pennies.

They laugh and the call ends. The following day Hope decides to survey women around the department about their experiences. Hope speaks to three students from a range of cohorts, socioeconomic, and racial backgrounds. She first speaks with Britney. Britney describes the racial and cultural climate at the PWI she attends. In describing the climate, she emphasises how racism is prevalent and social identities intersect as a deciding factor for professors when deciding to work with students. She states:

> Racism definitely exists in higher education, unquestionably within my department. Coming from one mid-sized close-knit department, to a much larger university that wasn't so supportive, I immediately felt culture shock and quickly noticed the different experiences and treatment amongst professors and students. Although the department tries to make discrimination indistinguishable, it is clear that certain professors work with certain students based on their race and gender.

Evan, another student in the same department and university, states:

> I do believe that racism exists in higher education. I also believe that it exists in my department. I believe these things because the data shows that racism in the United States is systemic and I do not believe that higher education is exempt from the equation and I have seen it [covertly] play out in my department.

Kate, a white woman, also notices and acknowledges the differential treatment amongst students in this graduate programme. She states:

> I have witnessed it first-hand. I started the program with x number of Black students. It was noticeable that they were treated differently than the white students. The professors (of course not all of them but it still has been palpable among many) often seemed to criticize them more, were often displeased with the topics they chose to research, and there seemed to be disdain of some of their ways of talking. Also, they seemed to be neglected and isolated in terms of funding and assistance.

Surprisingly, Hope finds that she is not alone in her beliefs or experiences. The faculty and University displays a pattern of behaviour common to those found across the nation. People of colour, more specifically Black women, suffer at the hand of marginalisation.

Black Feminist Realism

In his piece *Faces at the Bottom the Well: the Permanence of Realism*, Bell explained racial realism as follows: 'For over three centuries, this country has promised democracy and delivered discrimination and delusions. Racial realism insists on both justice and truth' (99). The application of realism to specific sectors of society is not only important, but the methods by which it can be applied seem to be endless. The lives of BFGS within the academy are not categorically isolated, as it appears in the discourse and rhetoric within the literature (Crenshaw 1991, 1995; Hill-Collins 2000; Pollard and Welch 2006; Mills 2011; Shavers, James, and Moore 2014). We introduce here the term *BFR* (Collins 1989; Bell 1992), extending the social justice components of both racial realism and black feminist thought.

Bell (1992) suggested:

> Black people will never gain full equality in this country. Even those herculean efforts we hail as successful will produce no more than temporary 'peaks of progress,' short-lived victories that slide into irrelevance as racial patterns adapt in ways that maintain white dominance. This is a hard-to accept fact that all history verifies. (373)

Combining elements of these two canons in the field, we propose BFR. In doing so, we expand upon our three tenets through further analysis given the counter-stories we presented. At its core, BFR 'explicitly' defines the whole of the Black female as agent. In this context, there is no *duality of urgency* that forces Black women to choose either race or gender, since such positionality is problematised due to social stratification. BFR articulates three tenets:

> Survival and sustainability of the Eurocentric interests at the individual and institutional level will continue to dominate and replicate due to its critical mass. The disproportionate representation of scholarship across categories of race, class, and gender remains contested as difference is characterized dichotomously within a structural hierarchy.

Like any other entity of the free market, the academy must have ultimate winners, relative winners, relative losers, and ultimate losers (Fasching-Varner et al. 2014). School systems, the academy not exempt, are key institutions in regulating who has access to wealth and prestige and how much should be allotted them. In a situation such as the exchange between the admissions committee members determining acceptance to the university, we capture the rationale of dominant interests for acceptance disguised in color-coded rhetoric. The use of the terms 'diversity' and 'minority' is not explicit and multiply disadvantage in this social setting. As BFGS, we must acknowledge the fact that there are indeed a limited amount of resources to be shared amongst us. Race and gender are determinant factors in who is chosen to be among the losers. We must acknowledge the contribution that we make to the system that we oppose. The transmission of knowledge respectively in PWIs is protected within the walls of whiteness. Tenet 2 encompasses one important barrier that limits how scholarship from the margins are framed:

> A segregated knowledge, not subjugated amongst stakeholders of the academy persists. All actors within the structure occupy the same space yet the production of knowledge has limits.

As race, class, and gender interact in white space, Black women are placed in a unique position in terms of structural inequality. Hope's positionality encompasses the interplay of race, class, and gender that alone function to produce ontological and epistemological difference. Through Hope's conversation with her mother, we establish her multiply burdened identity as she reflects upon the impact this space has on her material, social, and mental life. Albeit through the use of language deflection or superior rationale (Feagin 2006), we consider, too, that the nature of critical thinking allows for abstract ideas to reason away discriminatory practices in the academy that reinforce white superiority in terms of intellectual property (Grant 2012). Tenet 3 impacts representativeness when it comes to beliefs about white–black differentials in the academy:

> There is 'no exodus'. The institution was not designed with the knowledge production of Black female scholarship in mind. It replicates the demands of mainstream society as it was designed to do.

In the context of social practices the accumulation of negative experiences can cause sociocultural and psychological stress, and thus create a barrier to being successful in graduate school. The academy will never represent, serve, or address the interests of the most marginalised and underrepresented of society, but they will do so for those from dominant and over-represented factions of society (Fasching-Varner et al. 2014). Universities are doing their jobs and take measures to maintain balance in the stratified system. As such we must not allow an exodus of BFGS to take place as a result of this.

BFR acknowledges that race and gender are real, including in their consequences (i.e. gendered racism, pay-wage gaps) (Collins 1989; Crenshaw 1991, 1995; Bell 1992). Despite claims that there are negotiations that can be made within these categories, such fluidity does not exist; these are fixed areas of life. If one contends that these areas are indeed fluid, we suggest that they are fluid and fixed simultaneously. If we consider wealth inequality, the academic achievement, gender, and wage gaps, or the prison–industrial complex, each is a manifestation of social inequality in America (Collins 1989; Roberts 1998; Scheurich 2002; Guy-Sheftall and Cole 2003; Oliver and Shapiro 2006; Fasching-Varner et al. 2014).

If any form of negotiations were to exist in these areas there would only be two options: (1) to conform to one's exploitation or (2) to be a non-conformist to one's exploitation (Crenshaw 1991, 1995; Bell 1992; Beeghley 2005; Feagin 2006). These are the same two options many BFGS face today. While Black Feminist Thought suggests the resistance of hegemonic tools, this may cater more to the 'knowing' of the Black woman than the actual 'being' (Hill-Collins 2000). BFR brings the whole, non-fragmented person to bear where she is neither an 'other' nor a subordinate, due to the 'realist' understanding of her positionality in society. The Black female is able to lose the hopelessness that accompanies the myths that derive their power from her belief in them (Bell 1992; Steele 2003; Shavers, James, and Moore 2014). At the nexus of BFR is a framework that allows for a non-bifurcated Black female identity.

Conclusion

This article seeks to understand the regime of white supremacy, the subordination of BFGS, and to examine the relationship between the social structure of the academy and its professed ideals. We move toward a theoretical extension of realism that can account for both race and gender, BFR. The stock and counter-narratives presented explore the experiences of BFGS. These serve to illuminate a well-known, but less publicly discussed phenomenon that many BFGS experience every day in the hallowed halls of the academy: the reification of a racialised and gendered hierarchy. These narratives illustrate the stories of countless numbers of Black women across the nation and are intended to serve as experiential knowledge and therefore data, to counter other narratives, which decentralise race in society (Lorde 1984a, 1984b; Hill-Collins 1986; hooks 1989; Pollard and Welch 2006). The stories are intended to collectively represent more than a single instance. The narratives feature characters who represent university faculty, graduate students who identify as Black women, and the families of underrepresented students.

> We move toward a contemporary theory of BFR, which no longer requires a 'duality of urgency', causing Black women to choose between their race and gender. BFR unmutes the Black woman's identities as Black women are liberated from being either solely Black or solely woman, but whole, through understanding the system in which we exist. In other words, this construct upends abstract notions of a bifurcated self by recognizing categories of race, class, and gender as real (active) agents with real outcomes, which expands upon concepts of gendered-racism. Recognizing the intersectionality of these agents as real, speaks more powerfully to the systemic practices that shape the way we understand the conflation of race/ gender, and race/class. We offer three working tenets of BFR to combat the lack of representation, the prevalent misconception of scholarship, and identity crisis experienced by Black women, which characterize the margins that Black female graduate students at white institutions experience. To be successful, Black women need the appropriate assistance, moral support, resources, mentors, advisors, and best tools to progress in any doctoral program. The ultimate tool of success for Black women who find themselves in this situation is to not be disillusioned by the American ethos of meritocracy, however, as it is merely a façade both in the academy and in broader social spaces.
>
> The reality is that a disproportionate amount of Black women are the most dissatisfied students at PWIs. Though academia is often portrayed as a field that combats inequities, many Black women find it as the field that actually reifies 'racial hierarchies' and gender-biases by marginalizing some groups and privileging others. Women of color, particularly Black women, stand at the focal point where two influential and dominant systems of oppression meet: their race and gender-BFR.

Graduate programmes of all kinds need a system in place that makes all BFGS feel welcome. For change to be perpetual, graduate programmes cannot solely focus on racial inequality but must understand that race and sex are mutually exclusive categories that affect women of colour. The fact that Black women have to frequently wonder whether identity privileges or disadvantages them by their identity is a significant issue in society and academia. Many women of colour acknowledged that gender and racial discrimination in higher education thrives; professors who are more willing to work with students of other genders and/or ethnicities are evidence of this. When Black women were asked to share experiences that they perceived to be racist and/or sexist, a significant number reported incidents that they deemed to be racist, not only at their university, but also within their current departments. The large number of women who acknowledged that racism was existent meant that, while many were aware that theoretically race and gender were social constructions, the consequences were real. Given this reality, the authors of this piece wish not only to further problematise this social issue, but to move from theory to praxis by leading the next generation of scholars to understanding and resolving to end the hierarchical formations within the academic and social world (Stovall 2013).

Note

1. We acknowledge that there are many pathways in the fight for equity and social justice and that many have fought the battles of this war without the benefit of tertiary education. We are merely suggesting that through higher education degrees Black women have some semblance of access that facilitates the fight for equity.

Disclosure statement

No potential conflict of interest was reported by the authors.

References

Alexander, M. 2012. *The New Jim Crow*. New York: The New Press.

Beeghley, L. 2005. *The Structure of Social Stratification in the United States*. Boston, MA: Allyn & Bacon.

Bell, D. 1993. *Faces at the Bottom of the Well: The Permanence of Racism*. New York: Basic Books.

Bell, D. 1992. "Racial Realism." *Connecticut Law Review* 24: 363–379.

Brown, D., and V. Keith. 2003. "(Dis)Respected and (Dis)Regarded: Experiences of Racism and Psychological Distress." In *In and Out of Our Right Minds: The Mental Health of African American Women*, edited by D. Brown, 178–203. New York: Columbia University Press.

Brown v. Board of Education of Topeka, 347 (U.S. Supreme Court May 17, 1954).

Collins, P. H. 1989. "The Social Construction of Black Feminist Thought." *Signs* 14 (4): 745–773.

Crenshaw, K. 1991. "Mapping the Margins: Intersectionality, Identity Politics, and Violence against Women of Color." *Stanford Law Review* 43 (6): 1241–1299.

Crenshaw, K. 1995. "Critical Race Theory: The Key Writings That Formed the Movement." In *Mapping the Margins: Intersectionality, Identity Politics, and Violence against Women of Color*, edited by K. Crenshaw, N. Gotanda, G. Peller, and K. Thomas, 357–383. New York: New Press.

D'Augelli, A. R., and S. L. Hershberger. 1993. "African American Undergraduates on a Predominantly White Campus: Academic Factors, Social Networks, and Campus Climate." *The Journal of Negro Education* 62 (1): 67–81.

Delgado, R. 1995. *The Rodrigo Chronicles: Conversations about America and Race*. New York: New York UP.

Dowdy, J. 2008. *Ph.D. Stories: Conversations with my Sisters*. New York, NY: Hampton Press.

Ellis, E. M. 2001. "e Impact of Race and Gender on Graduate School Socialization, Satisfaction with Doctoral Study, and Commitment to Degree Completion." *Western Journal of Black Studies* 25 (1): 30–45.

Evans, S. 2007a. *Black Women in the Ivory Tower*. Gainesville: University of Florida Press.

Evans, S. 2007b. "Women of Color in American Higher Education." *The NEA Higher Education Journal* 15 (1): 131–138.

Fashing-Varner, K. 2009. "No! The Team Ain't Alright! The Institutional and Individual Problematics of Race." *Social Identities* 15 (6): 811–829.

Fasching-Varner, K., R. Mitchell, L. Martin, and K. Bennett-Haron. 2014. "Beyond School-to-Prison Pipeline and Toward an Educational and Penal Realism." *Equity and Excellence in Education* 47 (4): 410–229.

Feagin, J. 2006. *Systemic Racism: A Theory of Oppression*. New York: Routledge.
Franklin, J., W. Smith, and M. Hung. 2014. "Racial Battle Fatigue for Latina/o Students: A Quantitative Perspective." *Journal of Hispanic Higher Education* 13 (4): 303–322.
Grant, C. 2012. "Advancing Our Legacy: A Black Feminist Perspective on the Significance of Mentoring for African-American Women in Educational Leadership." *International Journal of Qualitative Studies in Education (QSE)* 25: 101–117.
Guy-Sheftall, B., and J. Cole. 2003. *Gender Talk*. New York: The Ballantine Publishing Group.
Hill-Collins, P. 1986. "Learning form the Outsider Within: The Sociological Significance of Black Feminist Thought." *Social Problems* 33 (6): 514–532.
Hill-Collins, P. 2000. *Black Feminist Thought: Knowledge, Consciousness and the Politics of Empowerment*. New York: Routledge.
hooks, B. 1989. *Talking Back: Thinking Feminist, Thinking Black*. Boston, MA: South End Press.
hooks, B. 1990. *Yearning: Race, Gender, and Cultural Politics*. Brooklyn: South End Press.
Howard-Hamilton, M. 2003. "Theoretical Frameworks for African American Women." *New Directions for Student Services* 2003: 19–27.
Hurtado, S. 1994. "Graduate School Racial Climates and Academic Self- Concept among Minority Graduate Students in the 1970s." *American Journal of Education* 102: 330–351.
Johnson-Bailey, J. 1999. "The Ties That Bind and the Shackles That Separate: Race, Gender, Class, and Color in a Research Process." *Qualitative Studies in Education* 12: 659–670.
Jones-Johnson, G. 1988. "The Victim-Bind Dilemma of Female Black Sociologists in Academe." *American Sociologist* 19: 312–322.
Journal of Blacks in Higher Education. 2014, October 17. *Journal of Blacks in Higher Education*. Retrieved July 23, 2015, from Black Faculty in Higher Education: Still Only a Drop in the Bucket. http://www.jbhe.com/features/55_blackfaculty.html
Lorde, A. 1984a. "The Master's Tools Will Never Dismantle the Master's House." In *Sister Outsider: Essays and Speeches*, edited by A. Lorde, 110–114. Berkeley, CA: Crossing Press.
Lorde, A. 1984b. *The Master's Tools Will Never Dismantle the Master's House*. Berkley, CA: Crossing Press.
Mabokela, R., and A. Green. 2001. *Sisters of the Academy: Emergent Black Women Scholars in Higher Education*. Sterling: Stylus.
Margolis, E., and M. Romero. 1998. "'The Department is Very Male, Very White, Very Old, and Very Conservative': The Functioning of the Hidden Curriculum in Graduate Sociology Departments." *Harvard Educational Review* 68: 1–33.
Martinez, A. 2014. "A Plea for Critical Race Theory Counterstory: Stock Story versus Counterstory Dialogues Concerning Alejandra's 'Fit' in the Academy." *Composition Studies* 42 (2): 33–55.
McGee, E., and L. Kazembe. 2015. "Entertainers or Education Researchers? The Challenges Associated with Presenting While Black." *Race Ethnicity and Education* 19 (1): 1–25.
Mills, C. 2011. "Body Politic, Bodies Impolitic." *Social Research* 78 (2): 583–606.
Oliver, M., and T. Shapiro. 2006. *Black Wealth / White Wealth: A New Perspective on Racial Inequality*. 2nd ed. New York: Routledge.
Patton, L. 2009. "My Sister's Keeper: A Qualitative Examination of Mentoring Experiences Among African American Women in Graduate and Professional Schools." *Journal of Higher Education*, 80 (5): 510–537.
Pollard, D., and O. Welch. 2006. *From Center to Margins: The Importance of Self-Definition in Research*. Albany: State University of New York Press.
Roberts, D. 1998. *Killing the Black Body: Race, Reproduction, and the Meaning of Liberty*. New York: Vintage.
Scheurich, J. 2002. *Anti-Racist Scholarship: An Advocacy*. New York: University of New York Press.
Shavers, M., L. James, and I. Moore. 2014. "The Double Edged Sword: Coping and Resiliency Strategies of African American Women Enrolled in Doctoral Programs at Predominately White Institutions." *Frontiers: A Journal of Women Studies* 35 (3): 15–38.
Smith, W., M. Hung, and J. Franklin. 2011. "Racial Battle Fatigue and the Miseducation of Black Men: Racial Microaggressions, Societal Problems, and Environmental Stress." *Journal of Negro Education* 76 (4): 63–82.

Steele, C. 2003. "Stereotype threat and African American student achievement." In *Young Gifted and Black: Promoting High Achievement Among African American Students*, edited by T. Perry, C. Steele, and A. Hilliard, 109–130. Boston: Beacon Press.

Stovall, D. 2013. "14 Souls, 19 Days and 1600 Dreams: Engaging Critical Race Praxis While Living on the 'Edge' of Race." *Discourse: Studies in the Cultural Politics of Education* 34 (4): 562–578.

Tokarcyzk, M., and E. Fay. 1993. *Working-Class Women in the Academy: Laborers in the Knowledge Factory*. Boston: University of Massachusetts Press.

Tower, C., and R. Chair. 2002. "Faculty Diversity: Too Little, Too Late." *Harvard Magazine* 104 (4): 33–37. http://www.harvard-magazine.com/on-line/030218.html.

U.S. Department of Education. 2012. "National Center for Education Statistics." The Condition of Education 2012.

Walker, A. 1990. *The Color Purple*. New York: Pocket Books.

Wallace, D., and A. Bell. 1999. "Being Black at a Predominantly White Institution." *College English* 61 (3): 307–327.

Wilkins, A. 2012. "Becoming Black Women: Intimate Stories and Intersectional Identities." *Social Psychology Quarterly* 75: 173–196.

Williams, M., D. Brewley, R. Reed, D. White, and R. Davis-Haley. 2005. "Learning To Read Each Other: Black Female Graduate Students Share Their Experiences at a White Research I Institution." *The Urban Review* 37: 181–199.

Revealing a hidden curriculum of Black women's erasure in sexual violence prevention policy

Sara Carrigan Wooten

ABSTRACT

This article aims to challenge the framework by which rape and sexual assault prevention in higher education are being constituted by centring Black women's experiences of sexual violence within a prevention and response policy framework. Numerous research studies exist in the literature regarding the specific experience of sexual violence for Black women within a national context that remains deeply committed to White supremacy [Buchanan, N. T., and A. J. Ormerod. 2002. "Racialized Sexual Harassment in the Lives of African American Women." *Women & Therapy* 25 (3/4): 107–124; Crenshaw, K. 1989. "Demarginalizing the Intersection of Race and Sex: A Black Feminist Critique of Antidiscrimination Doctrine, Feminist Theory and Antiracist Politics." *University of Chicago Legal Forum* 140: 139–167; Donovan, R., and M. Williams. 2002. "Living at the Intersection: The Effects of Racism and Sexism on Black Rape Survivors." *Women & Therapy* 25 (3/4): 95–105; McNair, L. D., and H. A. Neville. 1996. "African American Women Survivors of Sexual Assault: The Intersection of Race and Class." *Women & Therapy* 18 (3/4): 107–118; Omolade, B. 1989. "Black Women, Black men, and Tawana Brawley – The Shared Condition." *Harvard Women's Law Journal* 12: 11–23; West, C. 2002. "Battered, Black, and Blue: An Overview of Violence in the Lives of Black Women." *Women & Therapy* 25 (3/4): 5–27]. Using the critical pedagogy principle of 'hidden curriculum' or how what is directly communicated through educational processes also conveys unstated values, judgments, and regulatory norms, the author analyses the first report of the White House Task Force to Protect Students from Sexual Assault [2014. Not Alone: The First Report of the White House Task Force to Protect Students from Sexual Assault] for race-neutral language that contributes to the silencing of the sexual violence that Black college women experience. The necessity of race-conscious sexual assault policy is discussed.

It is without doubt that women are at high risk of an attempted or completed rape while in college (Baum and Klaus 2005; Fisher, Cullen, and Turner 2000; Karjane, Fisher, and Cullen 2002; Koss, Gidycz, and Wisniewski 1987; U.S. Department of Justice 2002). While prevention programmes and response resources have been implemented over the past two and a half decades, the effectiveness of these measures in reducing the actual rate of sexual violence occurring in higher education remains uncertain. The recently renewed federal focus on this reality of higher education should signal significant changes in approaches to sexual violence prevention, but the conversation that has arisen remains entrenched in the same understandings of sexual violence that have been guiding prevention and response work for decades. Specifically, the framework being deployed remains deeply committed to a race-neutral approach to policy and programming development, where 'victims' and 'survivors' are never contextualised regarding salient legal and sociocultural histories between different racial groups of women within the USA.

While women are the broad target audience for rape and sexual assault prevention education, the discourse on sexual violence lacks cultural distinctions and historical specificity. Rape and sexual assault are often discussed in terms of universal definition and framed as a personal, individual trauma. As the national conversation about sexual violence in higher education demonstrates, the racial and ethnic identities of survivors are rarely points of significant analysis, particularly in terms of distinct cultural understandings of sexual violence and the resulting impact of those distinctions on the willingness to report. Instead, the rape survivor and the perpetrator of rape function as ahistoric, acultural figures. All that matters are the violent acts themselves and proving whether or not they occurred. Rape in this sense is forced to be a neat and tidy experience, a series of acts that fit into a number of acceptable boxes, generally modelled off of what has been written into law through consensus regarding definitions of violent conduct. Prevention and response policy has thus followed a similar trajectory of instituting a number of measures or check boxes that, if met, render the institution as having fulfilled the extent of its obligations.

This paper aims to challenge the framework by which rape and sexual assault prevention in higher education are being constituted by centring Black women's experiences of sexual violence within a prevention and response policy framework. I will engage with numerous research studies, narratives, and theoretical arguments regarding the specific experience of sexual violence for Black women within a national context that remains deeply committed to White supremacy (Buchanan and Ormerod 2002; Crenshaw 1989; Donovan and Williams 2002; McNair and Neville 1996; Omolade 1989; West 2002).

Using the critical pedagogy principle of 'hidden curriculum' or how what is directly communicated through educational processes also conveys unstated values, judgments, and regulatory norms, this paper attends to a hidden curriculum of Black women's erasure from campus sexual violence policy and programming through race-neutral language.

Race-neutrality in policy is a manifestation of a colour-blind social ethos in the USA, where to identify race is to be racist (Bonilla-Silva 1997, 2002). Thus, racism persists through discursive means while disguised as racial sensitivity. Colour-blind or race-neutral policy privileges and normalises Whiteness while masquerading as the equalisation of all races. By not accounting for racial difference, sexual violence policy has often promoted the sociocultural values and understandings of such violence from the perspective of White women.

While the importance of examining and accounting for race has been a predominant focus of other forms of inquiry into education, including K-12 educational achievement, the school to prison pipeline, and leadership initiatives and mentoring programmes for students of colour in college, the intersections of race and gender are conspicuously absent from most conversations about campus sexual violence. This is particularly troubling, given the scholarship produced by Angela Davis, the Combahee River Collective, Mary Ann Weathers, the Third World Women's Alliance, Audre Lorde, bell hooks, and countless others on sexual violence perpetrated against Black women. Thus, this paper will provide examples of the dehistoricisation of our current discourse of sexual violence in higher education in order to attend to the need for a raced, as well as gendered, policy lens.

Theoretical frameworks

Black feminist theory and Critical Race Feminism are the guiding theoretical frameworks for this paper. Black feminist theory identifies Black women's experiences of oppression as intersectional, rather than 'occurring along a single categorical axis' (Crenshaw 1989, 140). Black feminist theory provides a unique lens through which to understanding dominant frameworks embedded in our discourses about sexual violence as well as our prevention and response policy. Where White feminist theorising has named sexual violence against women as a manifestation of male power and domination over female sexuality and desire, Black feminist theorizing critiques this discourse for its erasure of the racial sexual terror that White men have historically exerted over Black women.

Critical Race Feminism is a framework within legal academia that has grown out of Critical Race Theory to address the gendered aspects of structural injustices, particularly within the law. To this point and perhaps most salient for this article, Wing identified that 'existing legal paradigms have permitted women of color to fall between the cracks, so that they become, literally and figuratively, voice-less and invisible under so-called neutral law or solely race-based or gender-based analysis' (2003, 2). By utilising an intersectional lens:

> Critical race feminists focus on the intersection of race and gender, emphasizing the anti-essentialist premise that women of color are not simply white women with the added factor of race or men or color with the added factor of gender. They call for a deeper understanding of the lives of women of color based upon their multiple identities. (Wing and Willis 1999, 3)

Given the extensive interaction between higher education sexual violence policy and the law, CRF offers a nuanced theoretical framework through which to identify the implications of race-neutrality.

This paper also utilises Giroux's theorisation of 'hidden curriculum' to explore the socio-political motivations for race-neutral campus sexual violence policy (Giroux 1983; Giroux and Penna 1979). Trading the schooling identified in Giroux's (1983, 285) three tenets regarding the relationship between schools and broader society for higher education policy, the tenets of the relationship between said policy and broader society for this paper could be defined as: (1) Higher education policy cannot be understood as removed from the socio-political context in which it is situated; (2) Higher education policy functions as sites of the construction and promotion of discourse, meaning, and subjectivities; and, (3) the common-sense values and beliefs that guide and structure higher education policy are not a priori universals, but social constructions based on specific normative and political assumptions. Thus, one of the guiding theoretical arguments of this paper is that race-neutrality within higher education policy serves to obfuscate the significance of race in all areas of campus sexual assault prevention and response and reflects the socio-political norms of what critical race theory identifies as the White supremacist patriarchy that characterises the USA. Race-neutrality functions within policy to buttress that normative values of Whiteness and subvert the racialised contexts of campus sexual violence. Thus, a hidden curriculum of Whiteness is embedded within sexual assault policy in higher education.

Black women and sexual violence

One in five Black[1] women in the USA has experienced a rape at some point during the course of their lives (Black et al. 2011, 2). Breiding, Chen, and Black found that four in ten Black women have 'been a victim of rape, physical violence, or stalking by an intimate partner in their lifetime,' (2014, 27). While the lifetime prevalence of sexual violence for Black women has been studied to some extent within the literature, the same cannot be said for research on campus sexual assault and rape. One of the few studies that specifically examined college women's lifetime experiences of sexual violence across different racial groups found that 10% of Black college women had experienced an attempted or completed rape since the age of 14 (Koss, Gidycz, and Wisniewski 1987, 166). However, the racial demographic data were not further disaggregated for incidence rates specifically during the college years. Carmody and Washington found that 37.6% of Black college women in their study had experienced a rape (2001, 427). Again, however, the researchers did not isolate incidents of rape within the study to the college years. Additionally, the campus sexual violence research that has been done has not adequately surveyed Historically Black Colleges and Universities (HBCUs), which graduate almost 20% of African-American college students (Krebs, Lindquist, and Barrick 2010; Provasnik and Shafer 2004). In their study of sexual violence against college women attending HBCUs, Krebs, Lindquist, and Barrick (2010) found a 14.2% incidence rate for attempted or completed rape since entering college for all women surveyed. The rate of completed rape for Black women specifically since entering an HBCU was 9.6% (Krebs et al. 2011, 3653).

The lack of inquiry into Black college women's experiences of sexual violence in higher education may be in part due to their lack of status as 'ideal victims'. Capers locates this lack of legitimate status as victims of rape in colonial misogyny, asserting 'In short, Black women were marked as naturally promiscuous, having less need or desire for foreplay than white women, and generally less discriminating in their choice of sexual partners' (2013, 865). These powerful and pervasive ideas of Black female promiscuity and by contrast White female purity ultimately 'reinforce existing structures of power in our society' (De Welde 2003, 85). Ultimately, Black women are the antithesis of the ideal rape victim due to centuries of racist and sexist ideology aimed at protecting White supremacy.

Policy presently renders the victim of sexual violence a neutral figure, but we are never neutral actors. Our histories are written onto our bodies, and our encounters with one another draw upon those histories. Thus, it is not surprising that the ideal victim of rape has been constructed to be an attractive (but not too attractive) White, heterosexual, gender normative, virginal woman. This construction is what Black women who have survived a rape are measured against. Given this, the question is how to reach Black women, who live outside of that image, and how to understand sexual violence as a community or historical trauma (Oetzel and Duran 2004; Whitbeck et al. 2004; Yuan et al. 2006), rather than a race-neutral and exclusively individual one.

In academic research, policy development, and prevention programming design, language is of paramount importance. Feminist poststructuralists have illuminated the gendered nature of language, but language is also highly racialised. 'Sexual violence' is not just a list of specific violent acts, but rather refers to and produces numerous simultaneous meanings that are historically situated and shift across contexts. The term 'rape' itself has had shifting meanings throughout US history, indicating that our constructions of what constitute sexual violence have never been static (Freedman 2013). Brownmiller referenced the power of language in relation to sexual violence in her groundbreaking work on the sociocultural origins of rape:

> Women are trained to be rape victims. To simply learn the word 'rape' is to take instruction in the power relationship between males and females. To talk about rape, even with nervous laughter, is to acknowledge a woman's special victim status. We hear the whispers when we are children: girls get raped. Not boys. The message becomes clear. (1975, 309)

But beyond this understanding of the fear that is arguably instilled in all girls and women regardless of race, sexual violence is imbued with cultural specificity and historical context for different communities. Such histories shape the way that different racial and ethnic communities of women and men move through the world, shape public response to incidents of rape and sexual assault, and impact what resources are made available and to whom. The present historical and cultural racial silences within campus sexual assault policy are juxtaposed to the urgent federal call to increase reporting by survivors on college campuses. By not accounting for the extremely complex histories of sexual abuse perpetrated against Black women in the USA, and the raced and gendered dynamics of higher education institutions, effective sexual violence prevention and response resources for Black college women within higher education will remain elusive.

Literature review

The sexual violence that Black women have historically been subjected to has been well explored in the literature, as well as the racist and sexist stereotypes that have endured against Black women since slavery. Black women were subjected to rampant sexual abuse at the hands of White men as a form of control from slavery through segregation (Buchanan and Ormerod 2002; Crenshaw 1989; Omolade 1989; Wriggins 2015). One result of this has been the persistent silencing of Black women's experiences of sexual violence committed by White men (Omolade 1989). As Crenshaw notes, the legal system has never been designed to protect Black women from rape by White men:

> When Black women were raped by white males, they were being raped not as women generally, but as Black women specifically: Their femaleness made them sexually vulnerable to racist domination, while their Blackness effectively denied them any protection. This white male power was reinforced by a judicial system in which the successful conviction of a white man for raping a Black woman was virtually unthinkable. (1989, 158–159)

Wriggins echoes the historical lack of legal recourse for Black women, where 'the rape of Black women by white or Black men, on the other hand, was legal; indictments were sometimes dismissed for failing to allege that the victim was white' (2015, 424). The persistent legacies of slavery have also resulted in silencing Black women's rape by Black men, for fear of buttressing the racist caricatures of Black men's sexuality (Omolade 1989). Rather than appearing to encourage such characterisations, and be seen as betraying one's community, Black women have chosen silence (Omolade 1989). Such silences make race-neutral policy and programming for sexual violence in higher education all the more problematic. Rather than explicitly examining the distinct experiences of sexual violence for Black women versus White women, all women are lumped together in a homogenous group, where disparate concerns and needs are inconsequential. If policy and programming pay no mind to the reality that Black college women may feel pressure to be silent about their assaults, then Black women will never be adequately reached for support.

Black women are more likely to be blamed and less likely to report their assaults as a result of the racist and sexist treatment of their sexuality (Donovan and Williams 2002). The historical characterisation of Black women as lascivious has rendered them inherently 'rapable' and thus lacking substantive avenues of recourse (Donovan and Williams 2002; West 2002). Such characterisations of Black women are not isolated to those who commit acts of violence against Black women. While Donovan and Williams (2002) focused on the risk of '[internalized] oppressive images' held by therapists treating Black women rape survivors, the same internalisations can be expected to exist within the walls of higher education by administrators and sexual assault adjudicators tasked with responding to survivors. McNair and Neville observe that:

> One of the few differences [in behavior after a sexual assault] is that African American women are less likely than White women to disclose the incident to significant others and report the assault to public-service agencies (e.g., police, rape crisis center; Feldman-Summers and Ashworth 1981; Kidd and Chayet 1984; Wyatt 1992). (1996, 110)

The internalisation of stereotypes about Black women by Black women themselves (i.e. that Black women are strong and must be strong at all times), apprehension about being accused of having caused their assault due to the perceptions that they are always sexually available, fear of a racist backlash that may result from reporting a White assailant, and fear of contributing to racist stereotypes about Black men when reporting a Black assailant are all distinct and specific points of concern for Black women survivors of sexual violence. It is reasonable to conclude that such concerns would be held by Black college women as well and may be even more heightened for those attending Predominantly White Institutions. These critical points of concern for Black women substantiate why race-neutral sexual violence and response in higher education is worthy of interrogation.

Critical Discourse Analysis as a methodological framework for exposing race-neutrality

Van Dijk describes Critical Discourse Analysis (CDA) as an analytical framework 'primarily interested and motivated by pressing social issues, which it hopes to better understand through discourse analysis' (1993, 252). Those who utilise CDA in their research seek to make 'a political critique of those responsible for [the perversion of discourse] in the reproduction of dominance and inequality' (253). Luke, citing Rattansi (1992), describes the 'discursive deracialization' of minoritised groups in education, including women and racial minorities, that manifests itself as the 'exclusion and silencing of issues of difference under the auspices of a color-blind, gender-blind, homogenous approach to curriculum and instruction' (1995, 38). Luke argues that CDA allows an unveiling of such deracialisation within education specifically. By treating policy as a form of social curriculum, CDA provides a methodological lens through which to reveal dominant discourses through 'neutral' linguistic biases.

Applying CDA to policy requires Fairclough's (1989, 1995) model of 'three interrelated processes of analysis, which are tied to three interrelated dimensions of discourse' (Janks 1997, 329). Fairclough's analytic processes of CDA are: text analysis or description; processing analysis or interpretation; and social analysis or explanation (Janks 1997, 329–330). Thus, in my analysis of federal recommendations for higher education approaches to both sexual assault prevention and response practices, I will move through these interrelated analytical processes to connect race-neutral language with larger social patterns and histories of silencing Black women's experiences.

Federal policy and a hidden curriculum of Black women's erasure

In 2014, The White House Task Force to Protect Students from Sexual Assault released its first report titled *Not Alone*. President Obama created the Task Force as part of a broader initiative to address widespread inadequate institutional response to student survivors of campus sexual violence. I selected this report due to it being the first comprehensive publication released by the Obama administration in the wake of the 2011 Dear Colleague Letter, which revised mandates for campus sexual assault response and adjudication under Title IX. While the report itself is targeted to campus administrators, its title is meant to provide reassurance to student survivors of sexual violence that the administration is concerned about the support they receive in the aftermath of an assault or rape. *Not Alone* is divided into four chapters: guidelines on campus climate surveys; guidelines for preventing sexual assault on campus; how to respond effectively to students who have been assaulted; and improving federal enforcement and transparency.

My analysis of *Not Alone* centred on several documents linked to in the electronic version of the report. The links are available in the hard copy of the report as well. These documents were chosen due to their best practices focus for prevention and response policies – they provide insight into the kinds of recommendations the Obama administration is focused on. The components of *Not Alone* analysed for this article are: Office for Victim Assistance (OVA) climate survey guidelines (2014, 8), a report examining sexual assault prevention programming effectiveness (2014, 9), a bystander intervention fact sheet (2014, 10), sample language for higher education institutions to use when describing reporting and confidential disclosure of sexual violence (2014, 12), a checklist for campus sexual misconduct policies (2014, 12), and guidelines for crisis intervention and response resources (2014, 15). An example of a provided link in the report that was not analysed for this article is the link for the administration's Public Service Announcement, which featured President Obama, Vice President Joe Biden, and several male celebrities encouraging men to obtain consent from women before engaging in sexual activity (10).

For a preliminary text analysis, I examined these documents for eight terms that would indicate racial identity as a guideline or policy priority: colour, race/racial, ethnic/ethnicity, culture/cultural, and minority. At the conclusion of this review, only one document explicitly mentioned race/ethnicity. A second document could be interpreted as implicitly discussing race/ethnicity, but could also be interpreted differently depending on the standpoint of the reader.

The only document to explicitly discuss race/ethnicity was the OVA climate survey guidelines. In suggesting a number of factors to include in such surveys, the OVA included race/ethnicity as a demographic characteristic. Additionally, the OVA cautioned administrators to consider the racial make-up of the student body, stating,

> While data on race/ethnicity is important, on some campuses it may unintentionally identify individual students. Therefore, schools should have a clear plan for who will have access to the data, where data will be stored, and how data will be analyzed and reported. (11)

An example of this might be the unintentional identification of an American Indian or Native American student attending a Predominantly White Institution, where American Indian or Native American student representation has been historically minute.

A potential reference to race/ethnicity was found in the CDC report for the Task Force regarding the effectiveness of various prevention programmes. A meta-analysis of available sexual assault prevention programming was conducted to identify what works and what does not for long-term incidence reduction. Within this report, the researchers asserted 'prevention programs and strategies should be culturally relevant and appropriate, in content and approach, to the individuals and/or groups served' (DeGue et al. 2014, 34). As there was no further context to what was meant by 'culturally relevant and appropriate', it is unclear if this was meant to highlight the need for race/ethnicity to be a factor in prevention programming, or if the researchers were suggesting that prevention programming should take into account the current trends, interests, and life stage of college students in its design.

For the remaining documents, there is no mention of race or ethnicity, students of colour, distinct cultural concerns and needs, or minority students. In the document on key components of sexual assault resources, the terms 'survivors' and 'victims' are used throughout with no racial or ethnic distinction. Campus officials are urged to 'engage in practices that are effective so that survivors get the help they need, and campuses are not wasting vital resources on services which don't accomplish this goal' (1). Furthermore, the document includes an urging that 'services need to be flexible, varied and provided by well-trained people to address the variability in what survivors want and need', and one suggestion made to address this is the necessity of protecting survivors against victim blaming by sexual assault response professionals (2). By using victim blaming as a general concept, an opportunity to identify different types of victim blaming was missed. While all women may generally fall victim to misogynistic constructions aimed at absolving men from responsibility for perpetrating rape, as the literature has demonstrated, those constructions can be acutely racist in nature as well. When policy does not recognise racist victim blaming, it fails to account for non-White women on campus.

In their suggested guidelines for confidentiality and reporting of sexual violence, the Task Force identifies that confidential reporting mechanisms must be provided for students. This includes identifying those within an institution who will be trained to respond to survivors in a supportive manner and who survivors can be assured will take them seriously, which should in turn have the effect of increasing reporting. Such policy 'is intended to make students aware of the various reporting and confidential disclosure options available to them – so they can make informed choices about where to turn should they become a victim of sexual violence', (2). But, such suggestions limit a survivor's concern only to that of being believed about their assault. For Black women survivors on a college campus, their concern about reporting may extend well beyond just being believed to a fear of microaggressions or overt racism from those they are seeking help from. When race is not a factor in how sexual assault policy is written, there are few assurances to non-White students that they will interact with officials trained in anti-racist response practices in addition to anti-sexist ones.

The recommendation document for bystander intervention practices on campuses is another point of the privileging of White women's behaviour on campus over Black women's. The document contends 'bystanders (also referred to as witnesses, defenders, or upstanders) are a key piece of prevention work', (1). Bystander intervention is premised on the notion that all people attending a party or social gathering can and should be vigilant for sexual assault-prone behaviour. A prominent scenario used in bystander training is that of attending a party with a female friend who has been drinking heavily and disappears into a room with an unknown man. Bystander intervention has become a key pillar of sexual assault prevention in recent years, in part due to the substantial amount of research conducted on fraternity rape as well as party culture and alcohol abuse in relation to rape in higher education. However, bystander intervention prioritises White college student behaviour. Research has demonstrated that Black college students are less likely to engage in party culture on campus, particularly as it relates to binge drinking when attending both Predominantly White Institutions (PWIs) and Historically Black Colleges and Universities (HBCUs) (Meilman, Presley, and Cashin 1995; Meilman, Presley, and Lyerla 1994; Zapolski et al. 2014). The result is that campuses have failed to develop and push prevention mechanisms that address the contexts within which Black women report being assaulted.

Conclusion

As demonstrated in this paper, Black college women have been grouped into one general collective of 'women' in higher education policy, which serves to undermine their particular histories, needs, and concerns while simultaneously privileging White frameworks and understandings of sexual violence. I have described several places within the federal documents analysed where race, and the concerns of Black women specifically, could be instructive for administrators using these guidelines. As Omolade (1989) suggested, if a Black woman is raped by a White man on campus, she may have serious concerns regarding the effect of her reporting on perceptions of her race, as well as her gender. If she is raped by a Black man, she may have misgivings about reporting to law enforcement, for fear of reinforcing pervasive racist stereotypes about Black male sexuality. By not openly discussing race as a factor within campus sexual assault prevention and response, Black women on campus are not being assured that their particular experiences will be understood and supported by administrators who may be trained on how to respond to incidents of sexual violence generally, but have no understanding of how race may influence those incidents. Such misgivings may also impact how Black women utilise resources in the aftermath of an assault. As Weist et al. (2014) found, Black women and White women may have different 'postassault helpseeking behaviors', including differences in the use of crisis centres, mental health services, and hotlines. The researchers specifically found that Black women utilise these resources at a lower rate than White women. Such resources are typically part of a comprehensive campus sexual assault response effort, making information regarding the frequency of their use by Black women versus other socio-demographic groups on campus of particular importance for campuses when implementing those services.

Additionally, when race-neutral prevention programming is in place, Black women may feel silenced. Just as the scenarios above may affect reporting, they also may impact Black women's experiences of prevention programming. If Black women do not feel safe in articulating their experiences or their concerns due to the fear of being perceived as promiscuous, 'angry Black women', racist against Whites, or betraying their community, those women do not have a solid outlet within which to express themselves. Bringing race into prevention programming conversations would open up representational spaces that have consistently been foreclosed, not only for Black women, but for other students of colour as well.

Policy-makers as well as university administrators, particularly those working with PWIs, would benefit greatly from the application of Black intersectional feminist and critical race feminist theories to campus sexual assault prevention and response. These frameworks would offer a sociocultural as well as a structural lens through which to assess the unique features of campus sexual violence itself in addition to strategic solutions. Simultaneous to this, more research is needed on how Black women who have survived sexual violence during college rationalised their decision-making in the aftermath of their assaults as well as their interactions with campus officials, law enforcement, and healthcare providers. By rejecting homogenised constructions of sexual violence, we are better equipped to resist the neo-liberal call for one-size-fits-all educational policies currently reflected in federal initiatives about sexual violence prevention while centring Black women's needs, perspectives, and voices within higher education.

Note

1. While the research cited in this paper largely analyses the historical legacies of slavery and rape on African-American women in the USA, I will use Black instead of African-American throughout to reference Black women's experiences of sexual violence in higher education. This is due to the assumptions made about Black women by both African-American and non-Black people in the USA regarding their ancestry. For example, a Haitian woman with an American accent may be mistaken for an African-American woman because of basic judgements regarding her skin colour, present location, and accent. Thus, non-African-American Black women are often still presumed to be African-American and thus are subject to the myriad racist notions about African-American women's sexuality that makes them vulnerable to sexual violence.

Disclosure statement

No potential conflict of interest was reported by the authors.

References

Baum, K., and P. Klaus. 2005. "Violent Victimization of College Students, 1995–2002." National Crime Victimization Survey. http://www.ocpa-oh.org/Campus%20Safety/Violent%20Victimization%20of%20College%20Students.pdf.

Black, M. C., K. C. Basile, M. J. Breiding, S. G. Smith, M. L. Walters, M. T. Merrick, J. Chen, and M. R. Stevens. 2011. *The National Intimate Partner and Sexual Violence Survey (NISVS): 2010 Summary Report*. Atlanta, GA: National Center for Injury Prevention and Control, Centers for Disease Control and Prevention.

Bonilla-Silva, Eduardo. 1997. "Rethinking Racism: Toward a Structural Interpretation." *American Sociological Review* 62: 465–480.

Bonilla-Silva, Eduardo. 2002. "The Linguistics of Color Blind Racism: How to Talk Nasty about Blacks Without Sounding 'Racist'." *Critical Sociology* 28 (1–2): 41–64.

Breiding, M. J., J. Chen, and M. C. Black. 2014. *Intimate Partner Violence in the United States – 2010*. Atlanta, GA: National Center for Injury Prevention and Control, Centers for Disease Control and Prevention.

Brownmiller, Susan. 1975. *Against Our Will: Men, Women, and Rape*. New York: Ballantine Books.

Buchanan, N. T., and A. J. Ormerod. 2002. "Racialized Sexual Harassment in the Lives of African American Women." *Women & Therapy* 25 (3/4): 107–124.

Bystander-Focused Prevention of Sexual Violence. 2014. https://www.notalone.gov/assets/bystander-summary.pdf.

Capers, I. Bennett. 2013. "Real Women, Real Rape." *UCLA Law Review* 60: 826–882.

Carmody, D. C., and L. M. Washington. 2001. "Rape Myth Acceptance among College Women: The Impact of Race and Prior Victimization." *Journal of Interpersonal Violence* 16 (5): 424–436.

Checklist for Campus Sexual Misconduct Policies. 2014. https://www.notalone.gov/assets/checklist-for-campus-sexual-misconduct-policies.pdf.

Climate Surveys: Useful Tools to Help Colleges and Universities in Their Efforts to Reduce and Prevent Sexual Assault. 2014. https://www.notalone.gov/assets/ovw-climate-survey.pdf.

Crenshaw, K. 1989. "Demarginalizing the Intersection of Race and Sex: A Black Feminist Critique of Antidiscrimination Doctrine, Feminist Theory and Antiracist Politics." *University of Chicago Legal Forum* 140: 139–167.

DeGue, S., L. A. Valle, M. K. Holt, G. M. Massetti, J. L. Matjasko, and A. T. Tharp. 2014. "A Systematic Review of Primary Prevention Strategies for Sexual Violence Perpetration." *Aggression and Violent Behavior* 19 (4): 346–362.

De Welde, K. 2003. "White Women Beware!: Whiteness, Fear of Crime, and Self-Defense." *Race, Gender & Class* 10 (4): 75–91.

Donovan, R., and M. Williams. 2002. "Living at the Intersection: The Effects of Racism and Sexism on Black Rape Survivors." *Women & Therapy* 25 (3/4): 95–105.

Fairclough, N. L. 1989. *Language and Power*. London: Longman.

Fairclough, N. L. 1995. *Critical Discourse Analysis*. London: Longman.

Fisher, B. S., F. T. Cullen, and M. G. Turner. 2000. *The Sexual Victimization of College Women*. (NCJ 182369). Washington, DC: U.S. Department of Justice, Office of Justice Programs.

Freedman, E. B. 2013. "Redefining Rape: Sexual Violence in the Era of Suffrage and Segregation." *The American Historical Review* 119 (4): 1213–1215.

Giroux, H. A. 1983. "Theories of Reproduction and Resistance in the New Sociology of Education: A Critical Analysis." *Harvard Educational Review* 53 (3): 257–293.

Giroux, H. A., and A. N. Penna. 1979. "Social Education in the Classroom: The Dynamics of the Hidden Curriculum." *Theory & Research in Social Education* 7 (1): 21–42.

Janks, Hilary. 1997. "Critical Discourse Analysis as a Research Tool." *Discourse: Studies in the Cultural Politics of Education* 18 (3): 329–342.

Karjane, H. M., B. S. Fisher, and F. T. Cullen. 2002. *Campus Sexual Assault: How America's Institutions of Higher Education Respond*. Final report, NIJ Grant # 1999-WA-VX-0008. Newton, MA: Education Development Center.

Key Components of Sexual Assault Crisis Intervention/Victim Service Resources. 2014. https://www.notalone.gov/assets/intervention-resources.pdf.

Koss, M. P., C. A. Gidycz, and N. Wisniewski. 1987. "The Scope of Rape: Incidence and Prevalence of Sexual Aggression and Victimization in a National Sample of Higher Education Students." *Journal of Consulting and Clinical Psychology* 55 (2): 162–170.

Krebs, C. P., K. Barrick, C. H. Lindquist, C. M. Crosby, C. Boyd, and Y. Bogan. 2011. "The Sexual Assault of Undergraduate Women at Historically Black Colleges and Universities (HBCUs)." *Journal of Interpersonal Violence* 26 (18): 3640–3666.

Krebs, C. P., C. H. Lindquist, and K. Barrick. 2010. *The Historically Black College and University Campus Sexual Assault (HBCU-CSA) Study*. Final Report, NIJ Grant # 2007-WG-BX-0021. Research Triangle Park, NC: RTI International.

Luke, Allan. 1995. "Text and Discourse in Education: An Introduction to Critical Discourse Analysis." *Review of Research in Education* 21 (1995–1996): 3–48.

McNair, L. D., and H. A. Neville. 1996. "African American Women Survivors of Sexual Assault: The Intersection of Race and Class." *Women & Therapy* 18 (3/4): 107–118.

Meilman, P. W., C. A. Presley, and J. R. Cashin. 1995. "The Sober Social Life at Historically Black Colleges." *The Journal of Blacks in Higher Education Autumn* 9: 98–100.

Meilman, P. W., C. A. Presley, and R. Lyerla. 1994. "Black College Students and Binge Drinking." *The Journal of Blacks in Higher Education* 1994 (4): 70–71.

Oetzel, J., and B. Duran. 2004. "Intimate Partner Violence in American Indian and/or Alaska Native Communities: A Social Ecological Framework of Determinants and Interventions." *The Journal of the National Center* 11 (3): 49–68.

Omolade, B. 1989. "Black Women, Black men, and Tawana Brawley – The Shared Condition." *Harvard Women's Law Journal* 12: 11–23.

Preventing Sexual Violence on College Campuses: Lessons from Research and Practice. 2014. https://www.notalone.gov/assets/evidence-based-strategies-for-the-prevention-of-sv-perpetration.pdf.

Provasnik, S., and L. L. Shafer. 2004. *Historically Black Colleges and Universities, 1976 to 2001*. (NCES Publication No. 2004-062). Washington, DC: U.S. Government Printing Office.

Sample Language for Reporting and Confidentially Disclosing Sexual Violence. 2014. https://www.notalone.gov/assets/reporting-confidentiality-policy.pdf.

U.S. Department of Justice. 2002. "Bureau of Justice Statistics." *National Crime Victimization Survey*. [Record-Type Files]. ICPSR22902-v2. Ann Arbor, MI: Inter-university Consortium for Political and Social Research [distributor], 2008-12-10. doi:10.3886/ICPSR22902.v2.

Van Dijk, Teun A. 1993. "Principles of Critical Discourse Analysis." *Discourse & Society* 4 (2): 249–283.

Weist, M. D., L. Kinney, L. K. Taylor, J. Pollitt-Hill, Y. Bryant, L. Anthony, and J. Wilkerson. 2014. "African American and White Women's Experience of Sexual Assault and Services for Sexual Assault." *Journal of Aggression, Maltreatment, and Trauma* 23 (9): 901–916.

West, C. 2002. "Battered, Black, and Blue: An Overview of Violence in the Lives of Black Women." *Women & Therapy* 25 (3/4): 5–27.

Whitbeck, L. B., G. W. Adams, D. R. Hoyt, and X. Chen. 2004. "Conceptualizing and Measuring Historical Trauma among American Indian People." *American Journal of Community Psychology* 33 (3–4): 119–130.

White House Task Force to Protect Students from Sexual Assault. 2014. Not Alone: The First Report of the White House Task Force to Protect Students from Sexual Assault. https://www.notalone.gov/assets/ovw-climate-survey.pdf.

Wing, Adrien K. 2003. "Introduction." In *Critical Race Feminism: A Reader*, edited by Adrien K. Wing, 2nd ed., 1–15. New York: New York University Press.

Wing, Adrien K., and Christine A. Willis. 1999. "From Theory to Praxis: Black Women, Gangs, and Critical Race Feminism." *Berkeley Journal of African-American Law and Policy* 11 (1): 1–15.

Wriggins, Jennifer. 2015. "Rape, Racism, and the Law." In *Race, Class, & Gender: An Anthology*, edited by Margaret L. Anderson and Patricia Hill Collins, 9th ed., 424–431. Boston, MA: Wadsworth Publishing.

Wyatt, G. E. 1992. "The Sociocultural Context of African American and White American Women's Rape." *Journal of Social Issues* 48 (1): 77–91.

Yuan, N. P., M. P. Koss, M. Polacca, and D. Goldman. 2006. "Risk Factors for Physical Assault and Rape among Six Native American Tribes." *Journal of Interpersonal Violence* 21 (12): 1566–1590.

Zapolski, T. C., S. L. Pedersen, D. M. McCarthy, and G. T. Smith. 2014. "Less Drinking, Yet More Problems: Understanding African American Drinking and Related Problems." *Psychological Bulletin* 140 (1): 188–223.

Curriculum as colour and curves: a synthesis of Black theory, design and creativity realised as critical curriculum writing

Lucinda McKnight

ABSTRACT

This article looks to three inspirational Black women, bell hooks, Stacey McBride-Irby and Patricia Williams, in the pursuit of radical curriculum. While today curriculum is critiqued as racialised, gendered, sexualised and classed, the formats of curriculum documents such as text books, units of work and lesson plans have changed little. These documents are often conceived as linear sequences of steps leading to outcomes, and their voices are distanced and 'neutral'. Drawing on a doctoral study of curriculum design in Australia, this article embraces a different approach by opening up a unit of work on girls' popular culture to hooks' invocations to teach to transgress, so that curriculum might be experienced as colour and curves, rather than a monochrome route to a pre-determined end point. Through this, along with hooks, I invite teachers to live pedagogy, rather than to deliver it.

Introduction: one shade of grey

Currently, in Australia, curriculum is grey and not in a good way. In schools we have a culture of 'rampant standardisation' (Comber 2011, 722) that seeks primarily and unreflexively to promote human capital for ever-expanding national and global economies (Reid 2010). Instead of curriculum as 'complicated conversation' (Pinar 2011), we have curriculum as 'the defined and mandated set of knowledge and skills that schools are required to teach and assess' (Victorian Curriculum and Assessment Authority 2012). In the Australian National Curriculum, gender equality is absent as a priority, and racial inequality is addressed by a reductive, tick-box approach. New pressures on teachers result in the performance of phallicism (McRobbie 2009), interpreted here as a hegemonic licensing of masculinist curriculum tools (Grumet 1988) predicated on compliance; teachers are advised, for example, to look out for a text that 'ticks off both the Asian and Indigenous requirements' (Sykes 2012, 24). In this neoliberal imaginary, education is 'a defined progression towards an end product' (Grumet 1988, 24): no curves in sight, on this journey through a monochrome landscape of ostensible personal and professional neutrality (Apple 2004, 10).

In a doctoral study completed in 2014 I sought to think more colourfully and creatively about curriculum, designing a unit of work with a group of teachers in a private coeducational secondary school outside Melbourne. I read of curriculum as story that reconstitutes the past and imagines the future (Connelly and Clandinin 1988), as redolent with autobiography and the performance of identity (Greene 1992), as "tentative and provisional, a temporary and negotiated settlement between the lives we are capable of living and the ones we have" (Grumet 1988, xiii). While these ideas helped shade in a fuller picture, works created by three Black women pedagogues emerged for me as particularly meaningful: academic bell hooks' *Teaching to Transgress* (1994), Patricia Williams' *The Alchemy of Race and Rights: Diary of a Law Professor* (1991) and doll designer Stacey McBride-Irby's reflections on praxis (Barbie Collectors 2009a, 2009b). These three women, as they colour in, go beyond the lines, transgressing, changing and complicating as they speak, write and act. In this paper, I discuss my engagement with their thinking, in a search for an engaged pedagogy of curriculum design, and offer examples, as provocations, of what this might look like; these examples take the form of critical curriculum writing, in both written and visual media, though incorporated images from a visual diary and writing from a research journal.

The approach taken in my doctoral project was to collect materials and stories from my everyday life, as I designed curriculum; I aimed to represent a standpoint (Smith 1987, 2005) outside of mandated curriculum policy, linking curriculum to broader personal and social contexts. The images collected are not merely illustrations, but contribute to a layering of image and story, suggesting the struggles, denials and ambivalences from which our pedagogical choices emerge. As an artist, I have spent time re-imagining, merging and working with these images in order to be able to publish them, giving readers a sense of the contents of the visual diary, and in this instance, the ways women of colour are included there. With my teacher collaborators, I produced a unit of work promoting skills in multimodal analysis of online play spaces. Individually, I wrote a thesis discussing the denigration of girls' media in culture and education. Yet the visual diary and my research journal tell other stories, too, particularly in relation to colour.

Reading and watching

This paper therefore also does work of redress. The formal thesis document, stored in my university's online repository, does not foreground these thinkers as key influences. An early White, male academic adviser did not encourage me when I said I loved their ideas, and I became hegemonically complicit in turning away from them, to read and cite Barthes, Derrida, Foucault and Bakhtin. Students and early career researchers on contracts may be particularly swayed to the ways Black women can be delegitimised in the academy (hooks 1994).

In the context of this recognised elision, the ways I encountered hooks, Williams and McBride-Irby are worth noting. I came to hooks (Figure 1) first, via a conference presentation given by a young White male teacher, on Education Theory in the English Classroom. Williams (2012) showed us a YouTube video of hooks speaking on why we should teach popular culture, and spoke of her influence in making his practice both radical and critical. This message seemed particularly timely, as the newly introduced Australian National Curriculum had demoted the study of the more democratic 'text' in favour of 'Literature' as one of three organising strands. This narrowing of text, the

Figure 1. Author/artist's impression of bell hooks, inspired by images in visual diary.

removal of a rationale for studying popular culture, hooks' 'medium for understanding the politics of difference' (Media Studies Association 2009) symbolised for me a re-entrenchment of conservative canonicity. One of the (White male professor) architects of the new curriculum had been quoted in a national newspaper announcing that critical literacy-style readings of texts, alert to racism and sexism, were 'nonsensical' ((Ferrari 2008, 1).

In this climate, in which being politically correct requires being apolitical, hooks' recognition of teaching popular culture as a form of resistance resonated, even as it might have 20 years previously, when *Teaching to Transgress* was first published. She recognises popular culture as pedagogical in itself, not only as a text around which classroom pedagogy might be enacted; this validated my study, as I sought to use girls' media around which to design curriculum. Hooks' feminist perspective on Freire's description of a banking model (1994, 52) of educational inputs and outputs also seemed recursively timely, as transactional curriculum was colonising Australian schools, in the form of the Ralph Tyler (1949) style backwards design approach (Wiggins and McTighe 2005) defining teaching as 'a means to an end' (2005, 19). This curriculum rubric was also in marked contrast to other reading I was doing, around reflexive and critiqued curriculum, by writers such as Elizabeth Ellsworth.

Ellsworth led me to Williams (Figure 2), although hooks refers to her as well (1994, 74). Reading Ellsworth's *Difference, Pedagogy and the Power of Address* (1997), I came across her description of Williams' writing and attempts to colour in legal discourse by employing different literary devices, including those of parable, parody and poetry, ultimately aiming to close the gap between discourse and lived experience. I had heard the exhortations of writers including Pinar (2011) to think differently about curriculum, yet had not been readily able to find creative and purposeful examples; in the margin of my notebook, I wrote 'Could I do this?' I immediately read Williams and wondered if she might inspire me to close the gap between curricular discourse and experience. She is 'interested in the way legal language flattens and confines in absolutes the complexity of meaning inherent in

Figure 2. Author/artist's impression of Patricia Williams, inspired by images in visual diary.

any given problem' (2009, 6). What would it mean to think like this with mandated curriculum?

Yet when I talked about this with my adviser, he was unfamiliar with Williams' work and keen for me to use Walter Benjamin as a frame for writing personal vignettes about curriculum design, and Dorothy Smith to theorise gaps between professional and personal discourses; he mentioned the pursuit of 'rigour' and I was not confident enough to counter this with hooks' argument that rigour can emerge from playfulness (1994). Benjamin and Smith proved useful. Yet there is another unwritten Ph.D. thesis there, one that could have performed de-centring work with an explicit conceptual 'framework' provided by hooks and Williams. This imagined work exists within a vast negative (in the photographic sense) space of possibility, a contrast to what is allowed and produced in a White dominated academy. This is work that can now be called into the positive, free of doctoral supervision, with all its entanglements.

Reading hooks and Williams, I began to think about race as a pedagogical imperative. Yet it was not until I encountered the work of McBride-Irby (Figure 3) that these ideas synthesised for me into a commitment to running a parallel study not shared in meetings with my supervisor. I had been researching, in an autoethnographic sense, Mattel's pinkly pastel Barbie website for some 18 months, watching my daughter playing on it and exploring it myself to find appropriate activities both for my child and for the secondary classroom., when I clicked on a hotspot, a book with the letters So in Style (SIS) on the cover. Suddenly I was on a page where all the dolls were Black, as if I had gone down a rabbit hole, like Alice, to find myself in a world recognisable yet different. I wrote in my journal: 'Never seen this! Why is blackness so hidden? Have to drill down into site to find Black dolls? Shocking!' Looking back, this response itself is racialised. I am slow to understand that 'white women do not notice that Barbie is white' (Rogers 1999, 57). Nevertheless, despite a vague story about one of the Black dolls being a friend of Barbie's, the Black and White dolls do not hang out together, and the SIS site is several clicks away from the home page, buried in the site's architecture.

Figure 3. Author/artist's impression of Stacey McBride-Irby, inspired by images in visual diary.

I began reading about Stacey McBride-Irby, the designer of these dolls, and found that she had been prepared to share, via social media, her thinking in creating a whole range of African American dolls for Mattel. Through her generous oral elucidation of design rhetoric (Kress 2010), McBride-Irby demonstrates the pedagogical intent in doll craft, as a non-traditional space for the imagining of future subjectivities. Her YouTube videos (2009) depict design as deeply personal, alive with memory, dream and ambition, invoking generational interplay and closely tied to a curriculum of community. She tells us, of the genesis of the SIS dolls:

> Grandma wasn't too fond of me [wanting to be] a designer. She worked as a seamstress for the fashion district and she didn't see too many African American designers, so she was kind of protecting me. She didn't want my dream to be crushed. I am creating a line of dolls that I feel my grandmother would be proud of. (Barbie Collectors 2009b)

This access to design rhetoric is unusual in a world where products of the culture industries are apparently made by anonymous (White) designers, and courageous when in the employment of a corporation as aggressively litigious and controlling as Mattel (Strangelove 2005, 138). McBride-Irby provides tangible and heartfelt evidence that design (whether of dolls or curriculum) is political, that pedagogy is not neutral; she models reflexivity about the situatedness of curriculum in story, where lesson, life and activism come together as play. She performs for us the 'engaged voice' (hooks 1994, 11) of the pedagogue speaking to us from her unique standpoint of lived experience, a perspective located, but never fixed (Smith 1987, 2005).

Despite providing the freedom McBride-Irby speaks of, to design her own range of dolls, Mattel clearly does not go far enough: by 2011, she has moved on to start her own company to fill a niche that has 'largely gone unsupported by the three major toy manufacturers' (2011). Like Williams, McBride-Irby is interested in filling gaps, both in the market sense of the corporate world whose language she co-opts, and in bringing into life her own racially motivated vision for the futures of young girls through doll design:

> I know little girls love to play out art, love to play out drill team or cheerleading, play out music, but I wanted to make sure they had an aspirational theme also, that moms will hone in on and let little girls know that you can play music but you also need to enjoy math too or science, or journalism. Writing: it's great! I just wanted to make sure I was answering my community's needs with the different skin tones, the hairstyles, the fashion. I wanted to make sure it was what we see in the outside world, I wanted to put [that] into these dolls. (Barbie Collectors 2009a)

Moving ahead and staying still

As the study progressed, my journal and visual diary began to represent my own preoccupation with race. I read about the dangers of buying into Black Barbie (Ducille 2003), the pedagogical disappointment attendant on strategically introducing a Black doll to the classroom (Paley 1994) and Black Barbie's power to transcend, to transform self and image (Raynor 2009). I collected pictures of Black Barbies and White Barbies. The teachers, a group of five women with Anglo and Mexican Australian backgrounds, with whom I was collaborating were not so interested in race, though. I showed them the SIS website and they were duly shocked too, even challenging me:

> Kids construct their own meaning for what they revisit and by what they stress. Like it took you 18 months to get past blonde Barbie. What does that say about you? That you weren't seeking out ... 'Anybody? Is there somebody I can identify with? Is it here, is it here, is it here ... ?'

Yet the drivers for the activities we write are our desires for students to be aware of how their gender identities are manipulated by corporations, and Mattel's global dominance – race is subsumed by middle class White feminism for White students, even though Zoe, who has dark skin, says to us early on that:

> I've never had a Barbie. Couple of reasons. Number one. Grew up really poor and we never had toys, so, that's fine with me, because I didn't want one as well, much like you, I was actually quite a critical child and this [holds up doll with flourish, facing others] is something I'll never look like. I knew that these proportions were ridiculous, and I'd never have the blonde hair and the blue eyes and that's fine, I didn't want to, that was fine, and until Barbie came out in a tanned Mexican looking version, I was not going to get one and I'm kind of opposed to them all.

Also reading Bakhtin (1981, 1984), I related his heteroglossia to what was taking place, with the centripetal forces of supervision and collaboration shaping and confining my study, when increasingly, in my journal, it blew out and began to be populated by more colourful and coloured images, like those I have represented earlier, in the figures of hooks, Williams and McBride-Irby. In a last ditch attempt to be an outlaw, inspired by hooks, I mocked up another unit, with a dark skinned Muslim girl on the cover and wrote the title 'Who's that girl?' on the front. I left the multiple pages inside blank, representing our inability to articulate as curriculum what we discussed looking at the Black and Muslim dolls. This is the dimension of the study most powerfully informed by hooks, Williams and McBride-Irby, yet absent from the thesis. In another version of negative space, I sent it along with the official unit, but no one mentioned it, and I felt as if insisting on discussing it would be to force my interests on the teachers; I am aware of the power relationships between academic and teacher co-researchers, and also critiques of liberatory pedagogy (Ellsworth

1992; Villaverde 2008) – I know some of the younger teachers in the group already read my feminism as authoritative discourse.

How do I portray myself here? I am constructing this paper as a White woman seeking a confessional space, admitting that just like Mattel, I have to hide Black women deep in my notes, providing excuses for this. I might also appear as a White woman fascinated by the exotic other, performing Stuart Hall's disavowal as 'the strategy by which a powerful fascination or desire is both indulged and at the same time denied' (1997, 267). I am, as Hall describes, simultaneously embracing two contradictory beliefs, one official and one secret. Yet this might also be read as an epiphanical narrative, in which I perform the engaged and reflexive voice of pedagogy – an engaged pedagogy as advocated by hooks, as a place where teachers can grow too (1994, 21). During my study, I start to look back over what I have done, and realise that all the dolls I have taken into school as a stimulus for discussion are White. Almost all the slides in my presentation for teachers show White dolls. I begin to critique my readings in different ways, and to write about race in the vignettes I am creating to link work and life, vignettes that might be justified by reference to Walter Benjamin, or Patricia Williams.

Power and colour

As I write this, I wonder also about what kind of position of power I might hold, even as a junior researcher, as a White woman, and remember hooks' observation that calls to sisterhood, or awakening, cannot be romanticised (1994, 102). How might I reproduce the servant/served relationship in scholarship, as hooks asks? This question challenges me: as a White Australian, my history of race relations is about attempted elimination (Wolfe 2006, 402), more than servitude. Indigenous Australians might ask, 'What right have you got to write about us?' and question whether I write just to make myself (and other Whites) feel better (Wheatley in Heiss 2003, 14). Have I collected images in my visual diary to 'master' them? Why should my voice be included in this issue? How do I expect Black readers to feel? Grateful? To dwell in this thinking too long, however, is to feel paralysed, to miss an opportunity to participate in constructive dialogue and reconciliation. As I write in my thesis, in the single paragraph in which I do reflect on our elision of race (I had other similar paragraphs in that document, but deleted them, sensing an undertow of significance dragging me away from my neatly defined and approved research question about how we design curriculum around girls' texts):

> What does it say about us that we did not use these texts [images of culturally diverse dolls] in the unit, despite experiencing perhaps our own most powerful learning around them? I should acknowledge here that this is not the learning verbally acknowledged by the teachers, who later thank me for professional learning in multimodal literacies. This is based on my own interpretations of heightened interactions and responses in the meetings, and subsequent comments and actions. What does it say about our performative pedagogical imaginations that despite being shocked at the limited representations of Black dolls on the Barbie website, and intrigued by the apparent freedoms of the hijab-wearing Fulla [Muslim doll], we cannot see ourselves using them in the classroom? I can only assume that, as in my story [the vignette Colour], we felt out of our depth with this material, and we would need to be much more 'literate' – a word Elinor [teacher] uses in relation to multiliteracies – to feel comfortable with it, or perhaps to perceive it as being of much more importance to our students.

I note here the word 'using'. This is also the verb we often choose in relation to theorists: how are we 'using' them? Yet in this context, it may be invidious, especially in light of what hooks says about appropriation, and exploitation by White academics (1994). She calls for reciprocity and dialogue, and invites input from all her students, of all colours. White voices might attempt to acknowledge the myriad assumptions that White people have, and seek to respectfully and ethically do work in dialogue with Black women, acknowledging rather than appropriating, and moving towards the 'literacy' that might enrich teaching.

Thinking with hooks, Williams and McBride-Irby, we might move towards reflexive writing around our assumptions in curriculum, as research methodology and classroom tool. This could involve the incorporation of image, text, anecdote and fable to complicate instructions. This might mean writing curriculum in colour, acknowledging that we write using Blackness or Whiteness as means of understanding ourselves and our worlds (Williams 1991), that in doing so we call into play the potential for colour blindness, for slipping easily into essentialised positions.

What are our aims in this work – not the aims of curriculum outcomes as skills for the 2030 workforce. McBride-Irby says, 'I want little girls to say, "I had an African American Barbie that I loved"' (2009). My dream would be for my daughter to click on Barbie.com and see Black and White dolls there, friends playing together, and for us to think nothing of it, for that to be normalised in the products of the culture industries and in our lives. Yet perhaps this is the kind of happy ending that exposes my own inability to grasp the 'profound and unrelenting misery and sorrow' of race relations (1994, 75) – hooks uses these words about male domination, but they may also be relevant here. My vision, therefore, might be a 'lie of harmonious multiculturalism' (hooks 1994, 31) that ignores past injustice. Just as Williams muses on newspaper headlines, legal lectures and everyday happenings, I am aware that in the months in which I have been writing this article, Aboriginal Australian footballer Adam Goodes has been publically vilified; Serena Williams, as 2015 Wimbledon champion, has been subjected to extraordinary racist and sexist abuse; at least two terrible, racially motived acts of terrorism have taken place in the United States and a child in my own family has told me, out of the blue, that, 'if the Queen had a dinner party, she wouldn't want to invite Black people'. At work, our online lecturer evaluation system is used as a vehicle for the racist and misogynist abuse of a Black member of staff.

Contemplating the above, the bland selection of a tick-box Indigenous text to address racism, seems entirely inadequate. Instead, we might accompany the familiar curriculum design work of lesson planning with eclectic practices of writing, collection and assemblage, of both 'real' and fictive elements, to alchemise the connection between practice and life that hooks also advocates. This might be realised as a kind of critical curriculum writing for teacher reflection, the thinking that McBride-Irby performs on YouTube, with childhood photographs and videos linking personal history to the design process. I have attempted this within this article as well, incorporating images from my visual diary, transcribed for legal reasons through further work of visual ethnography (Pink 2007), work of merging, knowing, doing and making (Pinar in Leavy 2009, 3). In sketching, I consciously create further representations and spend time with these images, again in the spirit of redress, making amends, drawing lines that are curved, not pixelated, lines that might speak of both melancholy and tenderness, in Judith Butler's recognition of emotion in renunciation (2007). This is, again, work of complicating, of deliberation and reflection, countering reductive readings of Black women's bodies as text. These drawings are not for sale, for advertising or ogling, but for elucidation, and recognition, they foreground the impressionistic nature of interpretation; they resist clarity of line and make curriculum in colour, as pedagogic texts themselves performing Black presence in this article.

As race is less invisible to me now, I might walk into a classroom and present a doll to children as White Barbie, such a small and seismic shift. Or I might walk in with an African American Barbie to talk about Barbie. This has been an important decentring for me, emerging from working with hooks, Williams and McBride-Irby. This is not a change that could have come from working with Benjamin. Although the synergistic thinking of these three women is relevant to much broader curriculum inquiry, and any area benefiting from explicit and reflexive articulation of the rhetoric of design and the desire to transgress rather than to deliver or deposit knowledge, they have coloured in my skin for me. Do I just perform what I critique: the confinement of Black female academics to race? I am wary of contributing to how dominant groups might appear to be inclusive and affirming, yet at the same time partition these theorists into particular academic preoccupations. 'Race' might therefore be similarly addressed and nullified, much as it is on the Barbie website, where the Black dolls are buried in a darker and culturally tweaked palette, both present and absent, special (subject) and different (other), but never starring on the home page, at least when I was looking.

Williams alludes to this problem when she describes how her publisher has to fight to have the US Library of Congress categorise her work as anything other than 'Afro Americans- Civil Rights', when she herself thinks 'Autobiography' or 'Gender Studies' would be more appropriate (Williams 1991); fundamentally, she sees her work as not being about race, but about 'boundary' (1991, 256). In Australia it may be said that White academics have 'recuperated indigeneity to emphasise difference' (Wolfe 2006, 389): the very process of recognition as racism.

As educators we need to be alert to these risks, in designing curriculum and seeking to transgress, to test boundaries. To see curriculum in colour and curves, we might begin, even, as Williams advocates, to critique the monolithic constructions of Black and White (1991, 256), writing about how we all take with us to the classroom the discursive properties of our colour. Williams' work could be on mainstream curriculum studies text lists, so that pre-service teachers can think with her about the 'governing narratives or presiding fictions by which [they] am constantly reconfiguring [themselves] in the world' (1991, 256), in all senses, not just in relation to race. In curriculum planning, we could think not only about what we include, but how we include it (1991, 83), using other kinds of writing, not units of work, to explore this. If we need templates, we could create them with hooks' voice in our minds, so that any classroom activity is open to spontaneity and flexibility (1994), incorporates the narratives of students and allows for teacher interest in student subjects, and for teacher narrative as well, as described by Baszile (2008). This suggestion feels oxymoronic, heteroglossic, both exciting and uncomfortable. Instead of ticking outcome boxes, we might ask, prompted by this template:

- Where are the places I might depart from the script?
- Where can I negotiate something different with students?
- How do my curricular choices demonstrate my respect and care for my students?

- How is my lesson different from others, in order to cater for the particular needs of students in my class?
- How do I resist a fixed teacher stance?
- How do I enable rigour to emerge from playfulness?
- How do I open myself up to critique from my students?

With such a template foregrounding this kind of thinking, it may become a natural part of praxis. With McBride-Irby, we might reflect on curriculum to see how it performs our dreams and desires, locating these in our histories and broader cultural contexts, and by articulating all these things, open them to critique. We might explicitly seek to create future subjects who are more than efficient workers, reignite the firepower of teachers (McBride-Irby speaks of girls' firepower created by the affirmative power of popular culture) damped down by multiple processes of de-professionalisation (Forde and McPhee 2006).

Critical curriculum writing: three examples

What might these other kinds of writing around curriculum look like? How do these influences I have described play out in practice? My own work in this area is very much in progress, but the following examples provide ways in to thinking about this. I offer three pieces of writing from my doctoral notes as attempts and provocations, which might encourage others to link narrative and curriculum theorising, as Williams does, and to interrupt the stark imperatives of instruction with asides and questions, with an awareness of the addressivity of curriculum: we write it as someone, we address it to someone. The first two examples are vignettes, written in a reflective and anecdotal fashion, yet centred on teaching practice and literature, seeking to alchemise the personal and professional, and to situate these within broader culture, performing my own colouring in of the politics of my curriculum praxis in relation to race. The third example is an extract from the unit of work we designed, and might be an introduction and way in to any unit of work, in any subject, targeting reflexivity in general, not necessarily in regard to race. This third piece contrasts with the grey language of the Australian National Curriculum's descriptors, which tell teachers that students will, for example:

> Understand and explain how the text structures and language features of texts become more complex in informative and persuasive texts and identify underlying structures such as taxonomies, cause and effect, and extended metaphors (ACELA1531). (Australian Curriculum and Assessment Authority 2010)

The examples that follow are writing to inquire (Richardson and St Pierre 2007) not writing as data, so no discourse analysis follows; rather, they resonate with and against the more academic writing that has preceded them and anticipate the writing that others may do in response.

Example one: coloured (Vignette written in 2013, remembering childhood and teaching in London in 1994)

Colour really begins for me, as a child, with a full set of seventy two Derwent pencils. They have names like Rose Madder Lake and Oriental Blue – names I will never forget, nor that first lesson in the use of the specific to enchant the reader. That red might not be red after all, but something else entirely. Or that black might be Ivory Black, or that Gunmetal might be one of many greys. I play with these pencils in a neat brick house in a former orchard suburb of Melbourne, Australia. They are much nicer than the pencils at school and I take great care never to drop them and break their leads.

Later I use colour with my students, handing out perfumed roneoed sheets of words in Imperial Purple, essays and reflections on colour, inculcating my classes into a particular sensibility, a romance with imaginative colour. What is your favourite colour? What does that say about you? Use colour to tell your story. I teach a metalanguage of colour, a broader palette, a precious aesthetic. *Write an essay about green.* I am pleased with the results: vivid vocabulary, effective imagery and reflection on the nature of the true self. *Which colour are you?*

Colour comes with me overseas to an imagined green and pleasant land. As a supply teacher I walk into a grimy girls' comprehensive class in south London to find a sheaf of photocopies awaiting me. *The Highwayman* by Alfred Noyes. I glance through the first verse:

THE wind was a torrent of darkness among the gusty trees,
The moon was a ghostly galleon tossed upon cloudy seas,
The road was a ribbon of moonlight over the purple moor,
And the highwayman came riding—
Riding—riding—
The highwayman came riding, up to the old inn-door.

The students stare at me dully, before I even start to read. I am just another supply from the agency. It is February and the day will be dark outside, before school even ends. I do not know the poem but the paradigm is familiar – the narrative poem or ballad at Year 8. Repetition, a rollicking rhythm and romance. Irresistible hooks to draw them in, to overcome the inevitable student resistance to poetry. I decide to read the poem aloud to play up these hooks and, pleased with my performance, move on to questions. *What is the atmosphere of this poem?* No one stirs. I envisage the next hour as tooth-pulling torture. *What does the darkness make you think of?* Several hands go up.

I am delighted and choose a girl in the far right corner. *Yes? Why do the baddies always have to be black? Why is darkness always frightening? We always study stuff where black is bad. How do you think that feels for us?* She goes on, and on, and on. I am floored, flabbergasted. Can we be talking about the same poem? This is not in my script. I have never even taught Black students before. I didn't even choose the poem. Look, I was even trying to do the right thing by choosing a Black student to answer. *I* am not the villain. I struggle to collect myself and pick up the pieces of the lesson, but for long moments I cannot. I have been jolted from my standpoint to hers, and colour will never be the same. *Which colour are you?* Only a white person could ask that and not even think about skin. Galloping through my mind is the thought: *she is right, she is right, she is right.* And I have never even considered this before.

At the same time I feel a kind of impatience. *Oh no, not now. This is too big for here.* Why does she have to disrupt my lesson with this? WHAT DO YOU EXPECT ME TO DO ABOUT IT? Vaguely, I recognise her: she is Prissy in *Gone with the Wind*; David Gulpilil in *Walkabout*; Eve Fesl, the guest speaker, who called the Year 9's ancestors rapists and murderers.

Disobedient. Dangerous. Unpredictable. Unruly. She is unruly. Not Ivory Black. Unruly Black. Everyone is talking. The lesson has bolted and I must seize the reigns. So I close it all down, employ the obfuscatory modality of teacher talk. *Yes, you could be right, that seems a very interesting observation, that might be a very good avenue for some further research, perhaps you could include some thoughts on this in your written response to the poem. Moving right along now …*

Almost twenty years later, in 2012, I watch *Redfern Now*, a fictional television series about Aboriginal people in Sydney. A young Black boy receives an Indigenous scholarship to a private school, where he is required to stand and sing the Australian national anthem at assembly. He knows his father refuses to sing it at the football and he stays seated and silent. He is eventually expelled. I google the full version of *Advance Australia Fair*.

I don't think I can sing this anthem again myself. Even the sanitised version. I think about the student in London. I try to imagine the location of the pure text, the version of *The Highwayman* that was set without malice, the version of the national anthem that won the competition in 1974 to public acclaim. I cannot find them. In bed, my husband says he is ashamed that our children have to sing the anthem at school. I lie beside him silently. I know we won't do anything about it.

*Some weeks later at a conference, studying a publisher's display, I pick up a book titled *100+ Ideas for English*. On page 75, as Idea 62, under the heading *Telling More Stories* I read: *The Highwayman is a tale of passion and tragedy that has some very effective visual imagery.*

Example two: curriculum in capitals (vignette written in 2012)

Sometimes in research epiphanical moments result from random coincidences. I am writing this late in the study when my focus is zooming in and out alarmingly. One moment I'm deep in, designing an activity, and the next I'm the researcher, stepping back and making broad statements. Plus there's this metalanguage breaking through, as if I can't keep it out. All these voices must be held in tension, if you can bear it.

I am reading Ellsworth at the kitchen table, amidst filthy breakfast dishes, toast crumbs and unopened mail. I am thinking, in Ellsworth's words, about teaching positions, about teachers addressing students, about the way there is no mode of address in teaching, that much is erased or denied. She tells me to read Patricia Williams, who finds gaps, fragments, montages, dissolves time and space, positions the reader as a subject in motion. Could I do this? I am writing and writing and writing. I am pretty much writing out this whole book. My hand needs a break. I open some mail.

The first item is the latest Victorian Association for the Teaching of English journal, *Idiom*. The title this time is *Anything but Mockingbird: What Texts to Study in Years 7–10*. The cover shows a mockingbird upside down, still clinging to a branch and singing. I open to the first page and begin to read … suddenly I am upside down and inside out and back to front. What has happened? What change has been wrought here? Is this what they mean when they say a Ph.D. changes you? Here are teachers addressing teachers in a professional journal.

NOT ONE OF THESE ARTICLES COUNTENANCES THE TEACHER BEING RACIST.

I am writing again, scribbling, scrawling, in diagonal lines down a page to fit it all in, now in capitals, now underlining, stabbing dashes, slipping commas in like scythes …

> The teacher is outside the text, beyond it – this performs teacher identity as distant, immune, this is a FICTION – teacher holds all the insights, teacher and text as static, with the student to be acted upon, THIS is the subject position offered to us by English teacher discourses, the alignment of authoritative discourses, cultural heritage, national curriculum – it's a masquerade, it's dishonest, how are we holding this together?

I read on only to see that …

NOT ONE ARTICLE EVEN MENTIONS RACISM IN AUSTRALIA IN RELATION TO THE NOVEL.

To Kill a Mockingbird is said to be *a gripping portrait of prejudice and racism in the 1930s*. Students are given *an introduction to the attitudes prevalent in the south of the USA at the time* (hell, I've heard people call Aboriginal people … well … terrible things, in 2012). The book *opens their eyes*: students' eyes. First these writers address saintly non racist teachers who are implicitly WHITE, and now I realise all the students they address are WHITE too.

THESE ARTICLES ADDRESS WHITE TEACHERS AND IMAGINE WHITE STUDENTS IN A COUNTRY WHERE RACISM DOES NOT EXIST.

There is no possibility of a Black student opening a White teacher's eyes to racism. What if a student knew more about racism than the teacher? Can a class of Aboriginal kids, or Somali refugees, or Muslim kids have their eyes opened by a benevolent, wise white teacher, to racism? Well, yes, I suppose we can all learn to walk more in each other's shoes. BUT in the journal's scenarios, the teacher never learns anything. The text is closed to her. It is sealed, watertight, to be handed over. *To Kill a Mockingbird* is great for teaching plotting, use of humour, rhetoric, narrative voice and allusion and so on. WHAT? What about *To Kill a Mockingbird* as a profoundly racist text?

ALL THE TEXTS DESCRIBED HERE ARE TO BE TRANSMITTED TO STUDENTS.

If you are lucky a text ticks off both the Asian and Indigenous work requirements, one article suggests. How is teaching being constructed here? Ticking boxes? These articles are telling me what texts are about. *Let me explain*, says one writer, and proceeds to tell me the meaning of Hamlet. No one suggests the study of *To Kill a Mockingbird* might be a space for thinking, in dialogue with students, about what this text might mean in the contexts of each person present, TEACHER INCLUDED, in the context of the school, the community, the nation. Instead, in this journal, the teacher knows what the text means (if she has read enough crib notes) and the students will know sooner or later too.

I am reminded of my experiences in a London school and fill another page with notes. It's likely that none of what I have written above in capitals would seem novel to me if I were Black. That's how this works, this glitterbomb metaphor, one fragment reflecting and creating further effects. But where do I go with this epiphany? Some of the people who have written the articles in the journal are friends. I've gone all haywire in my own professional community. How will I keep belonging? What is the point of stabbing with my pen at the kitchen table? Who can I talk to about this? I do the dishes and go to collect the kids from school, where I can't talk about this with anyone.

Extract from 'Play On': introduction to the unit, addressed to the teachers with whom I am working

Creating curriculum

I'm writing this to you as a proposition, from one teacher to another, from researcher to co-researcher. It's a story in questions arising from our conversation about how we might teach, a fiction that comes to life as you read and contemplate how you might enact these words. I use the pronouns 'I', 'you' and 'we' deliberately, in contrast to the language of learning outcomes, in which these pronouns are absent, and the interests of the writers and agency of the teacher are effaced by performing student subjects – 'they'.

I address this to you, rather than to students, to move away from the textbook as well as the public document. This is not to deny the agency of the student, but to reclaim a place for the teacher, and for the dialogic creation of curriculum within, rather than outside of our profession. I address this to you because I hope to recognise you as a professional artist initiating and creating unique experiences with your students, rather than as a facilitator for, or foil to the performing student.

I deliberately avoid describing this as a unit, with all the clear-cut borders that implies. It slips through into what comes before and what comes after, one node of a theme that underlies our work: the legitimacy of a range of voices, interests and perspectives enacted through listening to each other in physical and virtual spaces. If our purpose (certainly mine, and possibly yours) is to open us up to the possibility of living different lives, we would like teachers and students to *question* and we would embrace questioning as as both critical and creative, interpretive and productive.

Further beliefs that underpin this include:

- That we create versions of knowledge with our interactions with each other and students. 'What can we learn from our students about this?' and 'What assumptions do we bring to this?' are key questions.
- That teaching and learning are embodied practices, involving emotions and feelings, to which we bring our own narratives. We explore these narratives through communication, with the possible aim of coming to know, trust, respect and even to love each other, although this is not necessarily the case.
- That collaborative and interdisciplinary ways of working help us meeting the challenges of new demands in subject English.
- That curriculum (incorporating pedagogy, rather than informing it) might be conceived of as a 'complicated conversation', and the suggestions made here are further ways of initiating conversations with students. This is not 'the way' to study this text, just *a* way, and I invite you to speak back to it.
- That the voice with which I write this is itself a fiction; curriculum has a narrator and is performed anew with each interpretation. This reflexivity keeps the story alive and you might ask of these suggestions not 'what does this mean?', but 'what can I make this mean this time?'
- That we don't really know what we teach or what is learnt. Assignments and assessments are other fictions. We can only know some of our intentions and surmise some of their effects.

Getting started (the italic bits are my asides)

Aims

Thinking about what we would like students to know/do *(as Elinor suggested)*:

- We would like kids to be able to think critically about online play spaces, especially in relation to the way they might contribute to constructing gender, and also to normalising and increasing consumption.
- We would like kids to recognise online worlds as deliberately constructed, rather than 'natural' spaces. *Remembering that classrooms are constructed spaces as well.*
- We would like kids to identify and experiment with multimodal forms of communication to create different play spaces. *Recognising our own biases in valuing some types of play spaces over others.*

Thinking about what we would like to know/do:

- We would like to find out about kids' own experiences of interaction with brands, particularly through online play sites. *Remembering our own childhood play experiences.*
- We would like to be able to develop confidence in interpreting multimodal texts and modelling this in the classroom.

Anything more to add here?

Conclusion

When Anne, one of the teachers with whom I was working, read this introduction to our unit (Example 3, above), she said:

> I tell you what I did like, Lucinda, I liked the language that you were using, because if you think about the way that, yeah, we look at the language of the national curriculum, it is very alienating, I have to say. When I did the audit of the Year 7 course, you're pretty well trying to make things, the good stuff of what you do, you're trying to make it fit. [forceful voice] Like, it doesn't really inform what you teach, it's not enough of a springboard. It's ... it's like you try to tick it off. I find it a very unhelpful document, just as a practising teacher. But I liked this, the language of this, I found this really engaging to read. So, I felt like I was being ca ... carried along with it ... it was good. It was practical. It was good fun ... It felt meaningful ... and safe.

This response suggests how as a designer of curriculum, I might write to transgress, finding an engaged voice of curriculum writing that exists 'in dialogue with a world beyond itself' (hooks 1994, 11), yet not in an authoritative way. This article serves as a call to work (a rif on the unit of work) to others to similarly seek engaged pedagogy, reflexive analysis of locations of authority in the classroom, sensitivity to voice and explicit discussion of race and colour, in the academy as well as at school. As a White woman, informed by hooks, Williams and McBride-Irby, I seek innovative ways of writing and representing that avoid appropriation, acknowledge conflict and recognise how traditional discursive practices of curriculum design allow for the assertion of dominant paradigms, for example, by failing to acknowledge that the teacher herself might be racist. I also seek to celebrate the ways hooks and Williams, in the academy, and McBride-Irby, in the cultural industries, show us that people, and things, *can* be different.

In achieving this, I try to avoid reductive readings of Black women's theories as being only relevant to race and resist the insertion of new knowledge into existing life-worlds, without challenging them (Baszile 2008). Through the performative act of curriculum design, we are potentially part of 'the creation of oppositional analytic and cultural spaces' (Mohanty in hooks 1994, 22). In looking to achieve this, I have synthesised the work of these three Black women pedagogues into critical curriculum writing, recognising each of their contributions to making teaching transformative, and the classroom still potentially 'the most radical space of possibility' (hooks 1994, 12) in the school or academy. I welcome correspondence and dialogue with other teachers and scholars who may be interested in expanding this concept of critical curriculum writing to further colour in this space and perceive how curriculum does not reside in documents, but shimmers across our lives.

Disclosure statement

No potential conflict of interest was reported by the authors.

References

ACARA (Australian Curriculum and Assessment Reporting Authority). 2010. *English*. ACARA. Accessed August 29. http://www.australiancurriculum.edu.au/english/curriculum/f-10?layout=1#level7.

Apple, M. W., and Taylor & Francis. 2004. *Ideology and Curriculum*. 3rd ed. New York: RoutledgeFalmer.

Bakhtin, M. 1981. *The Dialogic Imagination: Four Essays*. Austin: University of Texas Press.

Bakhtin, M. 1984. *Rabelais and his World*. Translated by H. Iswolsky. Bloomington: Indiana University Press.

Barbie Collectors. 2009a. "So in Style Dolls Friends of Barbie Meet the Designer Part One." Accessed 30 August. http://www.youtube.com/watch?v=rgGvEJ5DW7U.

Barbie Collectors. 2009b. "So in Style Dolls Friends of Barbie Meet the Designer Part Two." Accessed 33 August. http://www.youtube.com/watch?v=FEQXqSQLKVo.

Baszile, D. T. 2008. "Beyond All Reason: The Pedagogical Promise of Critical Race Testimony." *Race, Ethnicity and Education* 11 (3): 251–265.

Butler, J. 2007. *Gender Trouble*. 4th ed. New York: Routledge.

Comber, B. 2011. "Changing Literacies, Changing Populations, Changing Places: English Teachers Work in an Age of Rampant Standardisation." *English Teaching Practice and Critique* 10 (4): 5–22.

Connelly, F. M., and D. J. Clandinin. 1988. *Teachers as Curriculum Planners: Narratives of Experience*. New York: Teachers' College Columbia University.

Ducille, A. 2003. "Black Barbie and the Deep Play of Difference." In *The Feminism and Visual Culture Reader*, edited by A. Jones, 337–348. London: Routledge.

Ellsworth, E. 1992. "Why Doesn't This Feel Empowering? Working through Repressive Myths of Critical Pedagogy." In *Feminisms and Critical Pedagogy*, edited by C. Luke, and J. Gore, 90–119. New York: Routledge.

Ellsworth, E. 1997. *Teaching Positions: Difference, Pedagogy and the Power of Address*. New York: Teachers' College Press.

Ferrari, J. 2008, . "Curriculum Must Clarify How to Teach Reading- Spelling Out What's Best." *The Australian*.

Forde, C., and A. McPhee. 2006. *Professional Development, Reflection and Enquiry*. London: Paul Chapman.

Greene, M. 1992. "Foreword." In *Feminisms and Critical Pedagogy*, edited by C. Luke, and J. Gore, ix–xi. New York: Routledge.

Grumet, M. R. 1988. *Bitter Milk*. Amherst: University of Massachussets Press.

Hall, S. 1997. "The Spectacle of the Other." In *Representation: Cultural Representations and Signifying Practices*, edited by S. Hall, 223–290. London: Sage/The Open University.

Heiss, A. 2003. *Dhuuluu-Yala To Talk Straight: Publishing Indigenous Literature*. Canberra: Aboriginal Studies Press.

hooks, b. 1994. *Teaching to Transgress*. New York: Routledge.

Kress, G. 2010. *Multimodality: A Social Semiotic Approach to Contemporary Communication*. London: Routledge.

Leavy, P. 2009. *Method Meets Art: Arts-based Research Practice*. New York: The Guilford Press.

McRobbie, A. 2009. *The Aftermath of Feminism: Gender, Culture and Social Change*. London: SAGE.

Media Studies Association. 2009. "On Cultural Criticism: Why Study Popular Culture?" *Cultural Criticism and Transformation*. Accessed 29 August. https://www.youtube.com/watch?v=KLMVqnyTo_0.

Paley, V. G. 1994. "Princess Annabella and the Black Girls." In *The Need for Story: Cultural Diversity in Classroom and Community*, edited by A. H. Dyson, and C. Genishi, 145–154. Urbana, IL: National Council of Teachers of English.

Pinar, W. F. 2011. *What is Curriculum Theory?* New York: Routledge.

Pink, S. 2007. *Doing Visual Ethnography: Images, Media and Representation in Research*. 2nd ed. London: Sage.

Raynor, S. 2009. "My First Barbie: Transforming the Image." *Cultural Studies Critical Methodologies* 9: 179–185.

Reid, A. 2010. *Accountability and the Public Purposes of Education*. Australian Education Union. Accessed 22 August 2016. http://www.aeufederal.org.au/Publications/2010/NS/AReid.pdf.

Rogers, M. F. 1999. *Barbie Culture*. London: Sage.

Smith, D. 1987. *The Everyday World as Problematic*. Boston: Northeastern University Press.

Smith, D. 2005. *Institutional Ethnography: A Sociology for People*. Walnut Creek, CA: AltaMira Press.

Strangelove, M. 2005. *The Empire of Mind: Digital Piracy and the Anti-capitalist Movement*. Toronto: University of Toronto Press.

Sykes, H. 2012. "Choosing Literary Texts for the Australian Curriculum." *Idiom* 48 (2): 23–25.

Tyler, R. W. 1949. *Basic Principles of Curriculum and Instruction*. Chicago: University of Chicago Press.

Victorian Curriculum and Assessment Authority. 2012. *Implementing the Australian Curriculum: Explicit Teaching and Engaged Learning of Subjects and Capabilities*. Victorian Curriculum and Assessment Authority. Accessed 29 June 2014. www.vcaa.vic.edu.au.

Villaverde, L. E. 2008. *Feminist Theories and Education Primer*. New York: Peter Lang.

Wiggins, G., and J. McTighe. 2005. *Understanding by Design*. 2nd ed. Association for Supervision and Curriculum Development.

Williams, P. J. 1991. *The Alchemy of Race and Rights: Diary of a Law Professor*. Cambridge: Harvard Univesity Press.

Williams, J. 2012. "Education Theory in the English Classroom: A Guide to Critical Thinking Workshop presented 3 October 2012." Australian Association for the Teaching of English National Conference. Sydney: Australian Association for the Teaching of English.

Wolfe, P. 2006. "Settler Colonialism and the Elimination of the Native." *Journal of Genocide Research* 8 (4): 387–409.

Black women's bodies, ideology, and the public curriculum of the pro- and anti-choice movements in the US

Maria del Guadalupe Davidson

ABSTRACT

This paper explores how opposite sides of the abortion debate employ a discourse of endangerment to mobilise political support for their ideologies about black women's bodies. I examine the role of black women within that rhetorical strategy through various rhetorical artefacts. To analyse these artefacts, I employ the theoretical framework of ideological or ideographic criticism. This framework helps us see how the artefacts used by both pro and anti-choice movements 'condition' the audience not merely to adopt a set of 'beliefs and behavior, but a vocabulary of concepts that function as guides, warrants, reasons, or excuses for behavior and belief'. Though the two sides of the abortion debate differ in their overt political views, they turn out to share an implicit ideology about black women. This ideology prevents the voices of black women from being heard and valued in a debate that is nonetheless focused on black women's bodies.

Introduction: a history of control

Wombs have always been contested political sites. For example, Tina Campt analyses how the German nation state and its self-conceptualisation was challenged when many white, German women bore mixed raced children fathered by African colonial troops during the occupation of Germany after the First World War. Since 'racial mixture is the ultimate test of racial difference' (Campt 2005, 32) and a perceived threat to the purity of German identity, many children born of these interracial sexual transgressions were later sterilised – which by the way was illegal under 'existing laws' (Campt 2005, 64). Through Campt's analysis, we can see how the vulnerability of German identity turned out to be 'apparent through the [white] female body as a vehicle, conduit, or site of entry for potential pollution/contamination' (Campt 2005, 41). It is no wonder that white women's wombs became one focal point of state control during the Third Reich.

I begin with this example of the Third Reich's effort to control white, German women's reproductive capacities for a couple of reasons. First, from a historical point of view, corrosive and patriarchal Nazi ideology and the history of eugenics intersect in significant ways with the politics of black women's reproduction in the US. During enslavement, the wombs of black women were seen as bearers for the plantation – the valued machine creating generation after generation of bonded labour – and thus subject to control by the state. After enslavement, black women's reproductive capacity came under the control of the state in a different way, however; it came to be regarded primarily as a threat to American identity and arguably continues to be regarded as such to this day. To use Campt's language, black wombs post-enslavement are recast as 'a vehicle, conduit, or site of entry for potential pollution/contamination' of the white nation state. Secondly, the Third Reich is a common example of a rigid system of social control. Campt argues that when you 'combine' an 'essentialist' understanding of race together with 'a discourse of racial endangerment', you have 'a powerful tool [for] political mobilization, with often unpredictable results' (Campt 2005, 38).

This paper explores how the dangerous combination of essentialism and a discourse of endangerment plays itself out in the rhetoric of both the pro- and anti-choice movements in the US; and subsequently, how those of us who design black feminist curriculum can use ideological criticism to make sense of the way in which the black womb is framed in discourses related to abortion and choice as well as ways to resist such framing. To pursue this issue, I investigate how opposite sides of the abortion debate employ a discourse of endangerment – whether it concerns the endangerment of reproductive freedom, racial endangerment, community endangerment, or the endangerment of life – to mobilise political support for their ideologies. I am interested in the role of black women within this rhetorical strategy through various rhetorical artefacts from both the pro and anti-choice movements, such as billboards, websites, documentaries, public demonstrations, etc. To analyse these artefacts, I employ the theoretical framework of ideological or ideographic criticism, because as Foss writes: 'when rhetorical critics are interested in rhetoric primarily for what it suggests about beliefs and values, their focus is on the ideology manifest in an artifact' (Foss 1996, 291). This framework helps expose how the artefacts used by both pro and anti-choice movements attempt to 'condition' the audience not merely to adopt a set of 'beliefs and behavior, but a vocabulary of concepts that function as guides, warrants, reasons, or excuses for behavior and belief' (Foss 1996, 294). Though the two sides of the abortion debate differ in their overt political views, they turn out to share an *implicit* ideology about black women and black wombs. This ideology prevents the voices of black women from being heard and valued in a debate that is nonetheless *focused* on black women's bodies.

One result of these 'struggles -social and political- [that] take place over which meanings and ideologies will predominate' (Foss 1996, 294) is that black women can experience, for lack of better terminology, an *existential hysterectomy*. That is to say that even though their wombs are capable of reproduction, they are rendered womb-less through a hegemonic rhetoric of control that erases *their* own voices about *their* bodies and *their* reproduction. Hortense Spillers identifies a similar phenomenon when she describes the enslaved mother as both 'mother' and 'mother-dispossessed' (Li 2006, 14). The slave is a mother, yet she is denied the right to her offspring. Likewise, in the rhetoric espoused by the pro and anti-choice movements, the wombs of black women become contested sites – and black women become dispossessed of their reproductive rights as well as their reproductive capacity.

Teaching about black women's reproduction in the US

When students are taught about the history of black enslavement in America, they may encounter narratives that frame enslavement as a 'trade' (an exchange of black men, women, and children for money, goods, or services). Or, they may be taught that enslavement was a *peculiar* institution in which good, but complicated, patriots like Thomas Jefferson and George Washington participated because *that's how things were back then*. Some students may be shown the darker aspects of enslavement – whippings, dissolution of families, dehumanisation of people based on the specious idea of race. More problematic interpretations of enslavement occur when teachers/professors uncritically present enslavement as a narrative of patriarchy denied, where black men are unable to participate in patriarchal power, thus leading to a continued struggle for black men to be seen as 'men' in a society that has emasculated them. What if one approach to teaching students about slavery pivoted from each of these issues to focus on the reproductive control exerted by white society over black women's lives? To do so, broadens the dialogue, centres black women's experiences, and makes evident how Black women living in the US have historically and continually experienced controls and restrictions not only on their physical labour but also on their reproductive labour.

We see this clearly during enslavement when black women were reduced to their productive capabilities: first as workers producing goods that fuelled the slavocracy, and second as producers of the labourers who safeguarded the system of enslavement. Even before enslavement was widespread, various laws established the black female body as exploitable. Paula Giddings provides the following example:

> In 1629, Virginia administrators had designated 'tithable persons' as all those that 'worke in the ground of what qualitie or condition soever.' In 1643, however, tithable persons included all adult men and in addition *Black* women. (Gidding 1984, 36)

The last sentence in Gidding's quote is crucial because it shows the moral degradation as well as the physical masculinisation of black women. In her work, bell hooks challenges the notion that enslavement is a narrative of *emasculation* (Hooks 1981, 20). What she argues is often missed or simply ignored is how black women became *de facto* men in terms of their physical production capacity, that is, 'tithable persons' – being forced to work 'in the fields alongside black men' (Hooks 1981, 22) – and the way they were treated – whippings and other kinds of physical punishment the likes of which white women simply did not have to endure.

The masculinisation and denigration of the black female body has an air of calculation and deliberation about it. We see this, again, in the establishment of laws designed not only to create a racial hierarchy but also a gender hierarchy that kept black women doubly subjugated. To pivot slightly from this to a related issue for a moment, perhaps one of the destructive laws passed by the state of Virginia having to do with black women's status and reproductive capacities is Act XII which states:

> Children got by an Englishman upon a Negro woman shall be bond or free according to the condition of the mother, and if any Christian shall commit fornication with a Negro man or woman, he shall pay double the fines of the former act. (Gidding 1984, 37)

Setting aside the issues of fines a white man or woman had to pay if he/she had sexual intercourse (forget about consent) with a person of African descent, what is important about this law is that a child followed the condition of the mother *regardless* of the status of the father. Even if a white woman gave birth to a black man's child, her child would not be subject to enslavement based on this law because she was not subject to enslavement. Virginia's Act XII *ensured* that black women's children – past, present, and future – would be enslaved because as a black woman during that time she would probably be enslaved. This is not to say that a white woman who gave birth to an interracial child would not face stigma and social repute. Though to be sure such a condition would be challenging, it is hard to say that such difficulty compares to a life time of bondage not just for you but your children and your children's children. Putting a finer point on this matter, Giddings states, 'The circle of denigration was virtually complete with this law, which managed to combine racism, sexism, greed, and piety within its tenets' (Gidding 1984, 37).

Black women's wombs post-enslavement

Although more needs to be written about black women's reproductive capacity in the years following emancipation, it would be short sighted to assume that a society fixated on black women's wombs for nearly 200 years would all of a sudden lose interest in them once black women are no longer legal chattel. Indeed, black women's reproductive capacities continued to be a site where both discipline and control was exercised. Post-emancipation, black women's wombs were no longer a productive resource to be exploited but instead came to be viewed as a threat to white, Anglo-Saxon society.

To analyse this claim we must take a step back to the formation of the idea of *race* in America. In his seminal text *Race: The History of an Idea in America*, Thomas F. Gossett does a remarkable job of tracing the formation of the difficult concept of race and racial formation in the US and England. He writes, 'When the English colonists first landed in this country, they immediately encountered one race "problem" in the Indians. In a few years they imported another when, in 1619, the first boat-load of Negro slaves arrived' (Gossett 1997, 3). Race has been a 'problem' – primarily because of the hierarchy and ideology it imposes – in American society ever since Europeans came to these shores, and it did not cease to be so after blacks were freed from bondage. When it was no longer *legal* to exploit black women's reproductive capacity post-emancipation, there was a fear that black [problem] women (as well as other non-white or not quite white[1] women) might one day out produce white Anglo Saxon women. Roberts provides us with an example of this fear writing that in texts like:

> *Racial Hygiene* ... Thurman B. Rice [for example] warned that 'the colored races are pressing the white race most urgently and this pressure may be expressed to increase.' The twentieth-century eugenicists were not content to rely on evolutionary forces to eliminate biological inferiors, they proposed instead government programs that would reduce Black birthrate. (Roberts 1999, 57)

This fear of being 'pressed' prompted a discourse of racial endangerment that led to new measures to control black women and their reproductive capacity. Two ways that we can analyse this new imagining of the black womb rooted in the *fear* of overproduction are through Patricia Hill Collins controlling images and the rise of the eugenics and birth control movements, as cited by Roberts, in the mid ninetieth century.[2]

In *Black Feminist Thought*, Patricia Hill Collins articulates four categories or controlling images that post-enslavement functions didactically in white society instructing whites how to treat the black female body, they are the mammy, the jezebel, the matriarch, and the welfare mother. In brief, the mammy figure functioned in the white imagination as 'the faithful, obedient domestic servant' (Hill Collins 1999, 71). The matriarch 'symbolizes the "bad" black mothers'. Matriarchs are 'overly aggressive, unfeminine women' who 'emasculate their lovers and husbands' (Hill Collins 1999, 74). The breeder woman image which developed 'during slavery … portrayed Black women as more suitable for having children than white women' (Hill Collins 1999, 76). Post-enslavement, the breeder image changed into the third controlling image – the welfare mother or (queen) whose fertility is seen as 'unnecessary and even dangerous to the values of the country … ' (Hill Collins 1999, 76). The final controlling image is that of the jezebel (or hoochie) who is typically seen as 'sexually aggressive … Jezebel's function was to regulate all Black women to the category of sexually aggressive women, thus providing a powerful rationale for the widespread sexual assault by white men typically reported by Black slave women' (Hill Collins 1999, 77).

Of these four controlling images articulated by Hill Collins, the welfare mother is the most pertinent to our discussion about black women and reproduction since, again, she represents the updated version of the 'breeder image' from slavery (Hill Collins 1999, 76). This image is used to justify society's imposition 'into black women's decisions about fertility' (Hill Collins 1999, 78). Whereas the breeder woman was valuable through her reproductive labour, the welfare mother is a drain on society's resources. She is typically described as idly sitting around, waiting for her welfare check, and 'passing on her bad values to her offspring' (Hill Collins 1999, 79). This is clearly what rancher and self-proclaimed patriot Cliven Bundy[3] referred to when he told a reporter 'one more thing that he knows about the Negro':

> They didn't have nothing for their young girls to do. And because they were basically on government subsidy, so now what do they do … they abort their young children, they put their young men in jail, because they never learned how to pick cotton. And I've often wondered, are they better off as slaves, picking cotton and having a family life and doing things, or are they better off under government subsidy? They didn't get no more freedom … They got less freedom.

Bundy's statement contains a complicated confluence of the issue of freedom and fertility. Young black women who have 'nothing' to do, get three things according to Bundy – they get pregnant, they get government assistance, and they get abortions. In Bundy's reasoning, the black female body post-enslavement has lost its sense of purpose. While enslaved, the black female body had clear direction and was directed – it was a body that laboured in the field and laboured bearing children. But after enslavement, the black female body has lost its use to society and has become a burden.

Although Cliven Bundy's remarks are a convergence of racism, anti-choice, Antebellum apologia, sexism, and victim shaming it may come as a surprise to find that a similar image of the breeder woman appears in the founding of the birth control movement in this country, a movement dedicated to freeing (mainly white) women from the confines of childbirth. The birth control movement, likewise, represents black women's reproduction as harmful to society.

A vital service for whom?

Margaret Sanger, founder of the American Birth Control League which later became the Planned Parenthood Federation of America, is rightfully celebrated by the pro-choice movement for her efforts to bring birth control and choice to 'women'. She is also justly praised by some women because her 'early activism' – in a way – was 'pro-woman' and because she was 'vehemently feminist' (Roberts 1999, 57). Sanger, to her credit, believed that unwanted pregnancy could potentially hurt women by leading to unsafe abortions. Women would be more fulfilled, she argued, if they were able to choose to become or not to become pregnant thereby 'liberating women's sexual pleasure from the confines of maternity, marriage, and Victorian morality' (Roberts 1999, 57). For Sanger, birth control was about agency and freedom, she states: 'No woman can call herself free who does not own and control her own body. No woman can call herself free until she can choose consciously whether she will or will not be a mother' (Roberts 1999, 57).

Nevertheless, Dorothy Roberts argues that what was described as an option – birth control – for white women of means became a 'method of sound social policy' to control the fertility for poor women (Roberts 1999, 58). Through Sanger's example, we can see how 'birth control can be used to achieve coercive reproductive policies as well as liberation' for some women (Roberts 1999, 58). Whereas white women of means were liberated by birth control, poor women and black and brown women were sterilised by the thousands in this country, simply because their wombs were seen as destructive to society because they could not produce good stock. As stated by David Starr Jordan (a former president of Stanford University): 'Poverty, dirt, and crime ... are due to poor human material ... it is not the strength of the strong but the weakness of the weak which engenders exploitation and tyranny' (Roberts 1999, 159). It was the desire to protect good American stock (i.e. puritan descended) which fuelled the eugenics ideology of the pro-choice movement.

After the First World War, Dorothy Roberts argues that Sanger shifted her argument away from reproductive choice to eugenics and mass sterilisation. In Sanger's reasoning, birth control became a way of stopping procreation and as such could 'serve the national interest' (Roberts 1999, 72) because 'the multiplication of the unfit posed a threat to the political stability of the nation as well'. After all, Sanger exclaims that 'these people can vote'! (Roberts 1999, 73) Sanger's beliefs, like several other key thinkers in the eugenics movement (Dalton, Starr, etc.), hinged upon concerns about birthrate. Those in the movement argued that smart, well-off people have too few children while the unintelligent poor have too many. Sanger goes on to say, in words that are full of patriotism and Christian piety, that 'On its negative side it shows us that we are paying for and even submitting to the dictates of an ever-increasing, unceasingly spawning class of human beings who never should have been born at all' (Roberts 1999, 74). The diseased black, brown, and/or poor woman is a precursor to the welfare mother who breeds children who should have never been born.

To address the birthrate 'problem' in the 1990s, government officials eventually encouraged many black, brown, and poor women to use Norplant (a birth control device implanted in a woman's arm). Although Norplant was very effective at controlling fertility (Roberts 1999, 105), it also has terrible side-effects one of which is 'excessive bleeding' (Roberts 1999, 122). Despite the severe discomfort many women experienced, policy-makers saw Norplant as a means of effective 'domestic population control' (Roberts 1999, 104). While the US federal government 'slashed' programmes designed to help the poor during the 1990s, it increased Medicaid funding for Norplant. Roberts writes that 'By 1994, states had already spent 34 million on Norplant related benefits'

(Roberts 1999, 108) and at least half of those using Norplant were on Medicaid (Roberts 1999, 108). Not only did local governments make Norplant more easily available, 13 states turned directly to 'measures to implant poor women with Norplant' (Roberts 1999, 109), many of these measures involved offering women some financial incentive or required Norplant 'as a condition of receiving benefits' (Roberts 1999, 109).

Here we have identified three distinct stages in the history of black women's reproduction in the US: (1) the commodified black womb under enslavement; (2) the diseased black womb that should be sterilised during the early twentieth century; (3) the welfare womb that must be controlled through contraception in the latter half of the twentieth century. One aspect that unites all three of these eras is a language of liberation combined with a tactic of coercion. Through an ideological analysis of the pro- and anti-choice movements, we can see that the *theme* of liberation informs the implicit and explicit messaging of these movements. Coercion underlies the rhetoric about black women's wombs yesterday, today, and probably tomorrow.

The twenty-first century's rhetoric of black endangerment

2010 was a jarring year for black women's wombs. To the horror of many black activists and scholars, the anti-choice group, Heroic Media, installed billboards in Austin, Texas with the message: 'The Most Dangerous Place for Black People is in the Womb.' Since then, similar billboards have found their way to major cities across the country funded by organisations like toomanyaborted.com and MissouriLife.org with messages that read 'Black Children Are An Endangered Species'. Though the billboards and other digital content associated with them are certainly meant to shock viewers, something far more insidious is also occurring. On the milder side ('milder' here is used ironically), such billboards engage in shaming black women for exercising the fundamental right to privacy, articulated by Roe. On the more extreme side, the billboards liken the black female body to a death chamber and mark (by its wording) all black girls and women as actual or potential murderers of black children. Literally, to be inside the space of a black womb is depicted as being more dangerous than the South Side of Chicago during a shoot out, *or* inside of a super max prison, *or* fighting in Afghanistan, *or* ghettoised in poor public schools, *or* walking in Sanford, FL with a hoodie, *or* walking in the middle of the street in Ferguson, *or* asking for help-while black- after you've been in a car accident.

Picking up on the mantra of black death, the organisation LEARN – which stands for Life Education and Resource Network – operates the website 'Black Genocide'. Its goal is to bring more African-Americans into the anti-choice movement and to inform the black community that Planned Parenthood engages in 'eugenics and genocide' *specifically* against black people. They write:

> Planned Parenthood is the largest abortion provider in America. 78% of their clinics are in minority communities. Blacks make up 12% of the population, but 35% of the abortions in America. Are we being targeted? Isn't that genocide? We are the only minority in America that is on the decline in population. If the current trend continues, by 2038 the black vote will be insignificant. Did you know that the founder of Planned Parenthood, Margaret Sanger, was a devout racist who created the Negro Project designed to sterilize unknowing black women and others she deemed as undesirables of society? The founder of Planned

> Parenthood said, 'Colored people are like human weeds and are to be exterminated.' Is her vision being fulfilled today?[4]

Although this quote is attributed to Sanger, its source is unverifiable. It seems to be misquoted or completely fabricated by LEARN and others in the anti-choice movement. The group goes on to state:

> … that since 1973 Black women have had about 16 million abortions … Since the number of current living Blacks (in the U.S.) is 36 million, the missing 16 million represents an enormous loss, for without abortion, America's Black community would now number 52 million persons. It would be 36 percent larger than it is. Abortion has swept through the Black community like a scythe, cutting down every fourth member.[5]

Unlike Heroic Media, LEARN's rhetoric plays on the fear of racial endangerment at the hands of a segment of white society that is bent on limiting the black population. Yet, like Heroic Media, LEARN not only attacks Planned Parenthood they also name black women as *accomplices* in the *genocide* of black people. Black women are ultimately responsible for the loss, they claim, of 16 million black lives. By some estimates, these numbers may be close to the number of black lives lost in route to the Americas during the so-called Transatlantic Slave Trade. What a heavy, unethical, and corrosive burden to lie on black women!

In addition to Heroic Media and LEARN, the group Priests for Life organises 'Pro-Life Freedom Ride' to mirror the freedom rides that helped end segregation in the South. During one of the rides in 2011, the group planned a stop at the grave of Martin Luther King Jr., where they held a rally and carried signs that read: 'Abortion' – not heart disease or illness related to poor health care or anything else – 'Abortion is the #1 killer of Blacks in America.' Priests for Life and their supporters believe that the struggle to end abortion, not mass incarceration, income inequality, or marriage equality (which has finally been won) – is the great civil rights struggle of our time. Perhaps one of the most inflammatory comments made by Alveda King – head of African-American outreach and a niece of Dr. Martin Luther King Jr. – is:

> Today, the little baby in the womb appears to his or her mother very much like a little slave. He or she cannot decide whether he or she will live or die, but the mother, sometimes the parents, the medical providers (though I say that cautiously because it is not a medical procedure to kill a person) … those decisions are made without the baby having a lawyer to defend his or her human life. He or she is just like a slave at mercy of slave owners.[6]

The pro-choice response

In an effort to counter these attacks, in February 2012 Planned Parenthood began showing Carol McDonalds' documentary *A Vital Service: African American Stories of Reproductive Health Care.* Based on narratives from black women, it portrays Planned Parenthood as a friend and supporter of the black community by showing women who have received reproductive services through Planned Parenthood. The documentary is set up as a series of narratives where mostly black women tell stories about their positive interactions with the organisation. Like LEARN and Priest for Life, Planned Parenthood also relies on statistics and information designed to educate the black community on issues related specifically to black women's reproduction. So, for example, Planned Parenthood wants black people to know that they provide breast exams, which are:

> … especially important for African-American women for whom the disease presents a particular challenge. Among women diagnosed with breast cancer, African-American women are most likely to die from the disease – they are 40 percent more likely to die of breast cancer than white women[7]

Additionally, Planned Parenthood wants the black community to know that:

> Planned Parenthood health centers have provided health care in the United States for almost 100 years and know that a disproportionate number of African-American women face multiple barriers to accessing quality, affordable health care, which leads to higher rates of both unintended pregnancy and abortion. For nearly a century, Planned Parenthood has worked to address racial and economic bias in access to health care. More than anyone else, we work to prevent abortions by providing women with important information about sexual health, including helping them select the appropriate form of contraception, if that is a choice they would like to make. Improved access to reproductive health services as well as addressing overall economic challenges, go a long way to combating disparities in the African American community.[8]

On its surface, we may see Planned Parenthood's claims as supportive of black women, their overall health, and their reproductive choices. Nevertheless, Planned Parenthood's language is paternalistic. Rather than using a language of partnership working with black women, they talk about how they work *for* the black community. And, they do not discuss the ways that black women and black people have been crusaders for their own health care. Finally, Planned Parenthood does a very poor job of acknowledging its connection to the eugenics movement. By not acknowledging its paternalistic language and problematic history, is Planned Parenthood following a pattern of coercive action that is not entirely dissimilar from that of the anti-choice movement? In any case, there are strong ideological claims on both sides, and these claims are rooted in a hegemonic belief about black women's reproductive capacity.

The ideological battle over black wombs

Although ideological criticism has origins in structuralism, semiotics, Cultural Studies, and Marxism, Sandra Foss notes all of these movements are 'rooted in some basic notions about ideologies and how they function' (Foss 1996, 294). What is noteworthy here is that the 'notion that multiple ideologies – multiple patterns of belief – exist in any culture and have the potential to be manifest in rhetorical artifacts' (Foss 1996, 294). Although there is space for a multiplicity of belief within any given culture, what typically happens is that one ideology gets 'privileged over others in [our] culture' (Foss 1996, 294). Though they stand on opposite sides, I would argue that the pro- and anti-choice movements share a similar ideology about black wombs. That ideology is predicated on a historical and socially dominant belief that black women and their wombs need to be controlled because ultimately black women are not capable of making rational decisions about their reproduction. Foss perfectly explains how one ideology can emerge from groups seemingly on different sides of the political spectrum, writing that: '… a particular ideology becomes hegemonic as a result of a process in which a variety of groups forge an accord with one another or tacitly give their consent that perspective will be allowed to dominate' (Foss 1996, 294). Due to the predominance of the shared ideology that supports the pro- and anti-choice movements, black women's voices and perspectives are repressed or simply ignored. This hegemonic bind 'constitutes a kind of social control, a means of symbolic coercion or a form of domination of the more powerful groups over the ideologies of those with less power' (Foss 1996, 294).

Thus, when engaging in a black feminist critique of the harmful ideology of a white and patriarchal society, the question is not 'how do we resist?' because black women have always resisted, but rather 'how do we make the other listen?'. So for example, soon after the offensive billboards appeared in 2010, Sistersong and Trust Black Women released a joint statement responding directly to the Heroic Media and other organisations over the billboards:

> Yesterday, racist billboards went up in Soho attacking black women and our human rights by claiming 'the most dangerous place for an African American child is in the womb.' SisterSong, a coalition of 80 women of color and Indigenous women's organizations, denounces this cynical attempt to use race during Black History Month as an excuse to assault women's rights. Black women are not the pawns of these white people who erect such billboards. We find them offensive, racist, sexist and – most of all – disrespectful of our decision making, our 400-year history of raising and caring for black children, and our human right to make health care choices for ourselves.[9]

The group goes on to provide 'talking points' that black women may use to refute the allegations of black genocide. In spite of the efforts of both groups to push back, the assaults continue. Putting a finer point on the issue Foss writes: 'When an ideology becomes hegemonic through a process of accord and consent, it accumulates "the symbolic power to map or classify the world for others"' (Foss 1996, 295).

This short but sobering analysis of the power of an ideology that has negatively framed black wombs for over 200 years should remind us that there is no magic bullet, no single thing that will prevent the continued misreading of black women's bodies simply because the ideology that posits black wombs as destructive and in need of control (in one form or another) is sown into the very tapestry of the American psyche. Nevertheless, resistance is possible. Bringing the discussion back to the connection between black women and curriculum one way that scholars of reproductive history (black and white) are challenging curriculum related to reproductive technologies and the ideologies that support them is by making visible the brutality that accompanied the creation of fields like gynecology. Terri Kapsalis is one such scholar. In her essay 'Mastering the Female Pelvis: Race and the Tools of Reproduction', Kapsalis argues that the medical community (past and present) pays homage to Dr J. Marion Sims for his efforts to cure 'vesico-vaginal fistulas' which are 'small tears that form between the vagina and urinary tract or bladder that cause urine to leak uncontrollably' (Kapsalis 2002, 263). Valorised by the medical community Dr J. Marion Sims is 'remembered as the Father of American Gynecology, Father of Modern Gynecology, and Architect of the Vagina' (Kapsalis 2002, 263). Complicating Sims' legacy, Kapsalis's essays explains that although Sims was certainly a thoughtful and gifted physician, he never would have been as successful if he did not have unfettered access to black enslaved women's bodies to experiment on. Such access allowed Dr Sims to work on and perfect his technique to cure vesico-vaginal fistulas. Like other whites of the time, Dr Sims held beliefs about black women's bodies that were harmful and reductive seeing them as 'inherently more durable than white women' (Kapsalis 2002, 273). Even more disturbing, Sims operated on enslaved black women in full view of audiences who attended the surgeries literally in his 'backyard hospital' (Kapsalis 2002, 269). Access also meant doing vaginal surgery on the women without anaesthesia. Writing about an enslaved woman called 'Lucy' Kapsalis notes: 'And as if the pain of unanesthetized vaginal surgery were not traumatic enough, after this first operation, Lucy nearly died from infection due to a sponge Sims had left I her urethra and bladder' (Kapsalis 2002, 273).

Based on the work of Kapsalis's and others, black (and white) women scholars are challenging how medical history is – and continues to be – de-historicised and de-racialised in the US. What such challenges ostensibly look like is either re-writing medical texts so that they reflect the abuse of black women's bodies and gives voice to women like 'Lucy' by acknowledging their suffering; *or* by presenting counter curriculum in the form of essays, articles, and books like those written by Roberts (1999) and Khiara M. Bridges[10] that takes up such issues related to race and reproduction. Black women designing curriculum that pushes back against the decontextualised history of men like J. Marion Sims is a part of black women's justice work. Such a curriculum re-narrates the history of gynecology, re-humanises the enslaved black women who had not choice in whether they would participate in the gynecological experiments of men like Sims, and most importantly presents a counter ideology to the prevailing toxic medical ideology that posits black women as exploitable other and continues to impact black women's reproductive freedom today.

This discuss of curriculum, black women's bodies, and reproductive technologies suggests that black women scholars and activist should be more attuned to the role of ideology in justifying our oppression and how, for example, the pro- and anti-choice movements and their rhetorics of control 'maintain a position of dominance' by positing black women as incapable of controlling their bodies. Ultimately the billboards posted by Heroic Media and videos made by Planned Parenthood are simply 'one of thousands of everyday activities' that these and other groups have used to 'express, construct, and reinforce [their] ideologies' about black women's bodies for centuries.

To conclude – and again I realise that a longer and more detailed discussion must be had – black women must continue to think strategically about how to develop a rhetoric of resistance as a counter to the ideology propagated by both the pro- and anti-choice movements – even if they are not listening. A rhetoric of resistance, in this case, is rooted in the belief that black women are agents capable of making their own decisions. In the end, black women's wombs are not spaces to be fought over by others, sites of social control, or places where any group can freely ejaculate their ideologies of endangerment. Black women's wombs belong to black women and only black women can and should decide what is right for them.

Notes

1. I take the phrase 'not quite white' from Wray's book (2006).
2. We should, by the way, also closely consider the historical significance of the creation of eugenics as a social scientific movement with the publication of Francis Galton's *Hereditary Genius* (1869) and the full emancipation of all black people in America (1865). Here I am referring to 19 June 1865 (also known as Juneteenth). This is the date that slaves in Texas were notified of their freedom some two years after the Emancipation Proclamation.

3. Cliven Bundy was hailed a hero by some for defying the Bureau of Land Management in 2014. For more information, see Nagourney's (2014).
4. 'Planned Parenthood', date accessed August 27, 2015. http://www.blackgenocide.org/planned.html
5. 'Approximate Number of African American Deaths Since 1973' date accessed August 27, 2015.
6. 'Pro-Life Freedom Rides Inspired by Historic US Civil Rights Events', date accessed August 27, 2015.
7. 'Our Issues', date accessed August 27, 2015. http://www.priestsforlife.org/africanamerican/blog/index.php/pro-life-freedom-rides-inspired-by-historic-us-civil-rights-eventshttp://www.plannedparenthoodaction.org/get-involved/pp-black-community/our-issues/
8. 'Our Issues', date accessed August 27, 2015. http://www.plannedparenthoodaction.org/get-involved/pp-black-community/our-issues/
9. 'New Racist Anti-Choice Billboards Show Up in NYC', date accessed August 27, 2015. http://feministing.com/2011/02/24/new-racist-anti-choice-billboards-show-up-in-nyc/
10. See Bridges (2011).

Disclosure statement

No potential conflict of interest was reported by the author.

References

Bridges, Khiara M. 2011. *Reproducing Race: An Ethnography of Pregnancy as a Site of Racialization*. Berkeley: University of California Press.

Campt, Tina M. 2005. *Other Germans: Black Germans and the Politics of Race, Gender, and Memory in the Third Reich*. Ann Arbor: University of Michigan Press.

Foss, Sonja K. 1996. *Rhetorical Criticism: Exploration and Practice*. Prospects Heights, IL: Waveland Press.

Gidding, Paula J. 1984. *When and Where I Enter: The Impact of Black Women on Race and Sex in America*. New York: Bantam Books.

Gossett, Thomas G. 1997. *Race: The History of an Idea in America*. New York: Oxford University Press.

Hill Collins, Patricia. 1999. *Black Feminist Thought: Knowledge, Consciousness, and the Politics of Empowerment*. New York: Routledge Press.

Hooks, bell. 1981. *Aint I a Woman: Black Women and Feminism*. Boston: South End Press.

Kapsalis, Terri. 2002. "Mastering the Female Pelvis: Race and the Tools of Reproduction." In *Skin Deep, Spirit Strong: The Black Female Body in American Culture*, edited by Kimberley Wallace-Sanders, 263–300. Ann Arbor: University of Michigan Press.

Li, Stephanie. 2006. "Motherhood as Resistance in Harriet Jacob's Incident in the Life of a Slave Girl." *Legacy* 23: 14–29.

Nagourney, Adam. 2014. "A Defiant Rancher Savors the Audience That Rallied to His Side." *The New York Times,* April 23.

Roberts, Dorothy. 1999. *Killing the Black Body: Race, Reproduction, and the Meaning of Liberty*. New York: Vintage Press.

Wray, Matt. 2006. *Not Quite White: White Trash and the Boundaries of Whiteness*. Durham: Duke University Press.

Index